DESIRING
ITALY

BY SUSAN CAHILL

ANTHOLOGIES

Wise Women:
Two Thousand Years of Spiritual Writing by Women

Writing Women's Lives:
Autobiographical Narratives by
Twentieth-Century American Women Writers

Growing Up Female:
Stories by Women Writers from the American Mosaic

Among Sisters:
Short Stories of the Sibling Bond

Mothers:
Memories, Dreams, and Reflections by Literary Daughters

Women and Fiction

Women and Fiction II

New Women and New Fiction:
Contemporary Short Stories

Motherhood:
A Reader for Men and Women

Big City Stories
(with Thomas Cahill)

The Urban Reader

Desiring Italy

FICTION
Earth Angels

NONFICTION
A Literary Guide to Ireland
(with Thomas Cahill)

DESIRING ITALY

EDITED AND WITH AN
INTRODUCTION BY

SUSAN CAHILL

FAWCETT COLUMBINE

NEW YORK

A Fawcett Columbine Book
Published by Ballantine Books

Copyright © 1997 by Susan Cahill

http://www.randomhouse.com

Library of Congress Cataloging-in-Publication Data
Desiring Italy / edited and with an introduction by Susan Cahill.—1st ed.
p.   cm.
ISBN 0-449-91080-6
1. Italy—Description and travel.   2. Visitors, Foreign—Italy.
3. Women travelers—Italy.   I. Cahill, Susan Neunzig.
DG426.D45   1997
914.504'929—dc21   97-3973

Cover design by Ruth Ross
Cover photo © Tony Stone Images
Interior design by Ann Gold

Manufactured in the United States of America

First Edition: April 1997

10   9   8

For Kristin Maria

Daughter and traveling companion, molto simpatica . . .
Remembering Assisi at dawn,
And, always, the sun and deep shadows of Naples.

Contents

Introduction

Italy pleasures more visitors than any other country in Europe. Enchanted travelers, male and female, come home to report her blisses, yearning only to return. They seduce their listeners with the particularities of the beloved's sensuality: Tuscany, Titian, Café Sant'Eustachio, *paglia e fieno deliciosa*. As memories flow, new journeys are conceived.

Writers have been declaring their love of Italian cities, art, and people for centuries—Goethe, Stendhal, Byron, Shelley, Dickens, Robert Browning, Ruskin, Henry James, and D. H. Lawrence are the best known. But still to be heard are the stories of women's passions for Italy. As writers of travel essays, memoirs, and fiction, as exiles, pilgrims, and pioneers of one sort or another, they have, from multiple points of view in widely varying tones, had their say. *Desiring Italy* gathers together their best testimonies—beautiful mixtures of affection, intelligence, and wit. Few write simply as tourists, as one-trip reporters. Each woman has found there a world of art or love, of personal meaning—an encounter of such profound interest she must tell it.

If there is a unifying theme, it may be an intuition and embrace of the wholeness of life in Italy. Instead of the divorce between body and spirit, the secular and the sacred that alienates the more Protestant ethos of northern countries (and climates), in Italy physical and spiritual experience feels like one vibrant continuum. Perhaps it is the liberating humor of this acceptance of complexities and contradictions that intrigues and pleases women. Perhaps it is the pleasure that quickens the daily ordinary: the eating, the caring for children, the *passeggiata*. Sexual experience, masculine

and feminine, seems like an embodied fact of life—a mixed, mysterious blessing—rather than polarized modes of discourse or problems to be solved. No wonder the many women who've come to
Italy and chosen to stay for good.

How have women writers remembered the joy of their times in
Italy? Why are travelers so often happy here? Can the lover explain
the mystery of the beloved?

The writer guides in this book reveal the resonant subtleties of
real places and imperfect people. In fiction and nonfiction, they
describe coming to understand something significant about a
place. For some (Mary McCarthy in Florence, Edith Wharton in
Milan), it is Italy's prominence in the world of architecture; for
others (Patricia Hampl in Assisi, Florence Nightingale in Rome), it
is Italy as the setting of a passionate religious experience. One
woman defines her decision to stay in Italy, to work here and not
return to America, as "a renunciation of rigidity." A few others,
charmed by her sheer physicality and sociability, write stories of
erotic love as memory (Edith Wharton's "Roman Fever"), as aesthetic possibility (Elizabeth Spencer's "The White Azalea" and
Francine Prose's "Cauliflower Heads"), or as romantic dream
(Elizabeth von Arnim's *The Enchanted April*, in which sunny
Portofino on the Italian Riviera represents the fertile core of love
and its paradisial transformations). As William Zinsser said in *They
Went: The Art and Craft of Travel Writing*, "Some of the best travel
writing turns up in novels and short stories."

Collectively, all the pieces serve a double purpose: first, as a brilliant literary companion for readers; and second, as a guide for
travelers to the particular places described within each selection.
Following each selection is a commentary to help the traveler connect as fully as possible with the individual writer's sense of a particular place. I have visited the places named and evoked in all the
writings. Following Mary McCarthy through Brunelleschi's Florence and walking George Eliot's and Elizabeth Bowen's Rome and
Mary Shelley's Venice, to mention only a few examples, gave me an
unforgettable portion of their delight. My travels also enabled me
to see for myself, with map in hand, how closely their descriptions
and references match the places and settings as they are today.

That became the focus of each commentary—helping the traveling reader situate herself along the writers' routes and within their personal context.

I've also elaborated on aspects of places that especially concern the cultural history of women. For example, Muriel Spark's travel essay on Venice praises Titian's painting of the Assumption in the *Frari*; my comments address the significance of the feast of the Assumption of Mary within contemporary feminist spirituality. Mary Taylor Simeti's excursion to Enna in Sicily has as its background the myth of Persephone and Demeter and the importance of the Goddess to contemporary women, subjects which I discuss. Women's resistance to fascism during World War II is relevant to the selections from the autobiographical narratives by Iris Origo.

Not only the cultural focus of many writings suggests a woman's perspective or special interest. The women writers who love Italy also take a different tone from what we hear in the travel notebooks of Dickens, Hawthorne, or Henry James. The women's narratives come across with a down-to-earth concreteness. They're irreverent, critical, and anecdotal, but they are never brittle, mean-spirited, or smug at the Italians' expense. Italian religion is never (or almost never) dismissed as superstition or the Italians' warmth as crudeness. No narrator observes safely from a cool, all-knowing, aesthetic distance. Rather, their affection for the place and people moves the current of their prose.

The snobbery heard from many travel writers and travelers on the subject of the *Mezzogiorno*, as Southern Italy is called, does not trouble the women writers who love the South. (That's not to say you don't have to watch whatever's snatchable, as everyone must in any poor place.) But despite the petty crime, seeing the South through the eyes of unpuritanical writers (Shirley Hazzard, Rose Macaulay, Ann Cornelisen, Barbara Grizzuti Harrison, and Mary Taylor Simeti), as I have done on my most recent visit, is a revelation: Italy's Southern face, her most hidden, varied, and ancient expression—Greek, Roman, Byzantine, Arabic, African, Norman, Spanish—is astonishingly beautiful and handsome, a disturbing and haunting memory.

Often, though, the writer/traveler finds, not the exotic, but the

common and ordinary to be the richest and most fascinating territory. Eleanor Clark's attention is on the communal spaces of Rome:
she leads us around Roman fountains and their piazzas. Muriel
Spark's and Marcella Hazan's Venice presents the pleasures of
walking the canals and *campos*—the neighborhood hangouts of
local people—and of cooking, marketing, and snacking at a *bacaro*.
Theirs is a different take from the hallucinatory effect of Byron's
Venice or that of the phobic William Dean Howells, America's
Venetian ambassador in the nineteenth century. Whereas James
Boswell dismissed Siena as a boring, "tedious" act, Kate Simon,
who is no wide-eyed cheerleader among travel writers, walks us
through a hill city of surprises, foolishness, and luminous Sienese
beauty. Even her interest in the signs of Tuscany's Etruscan past
comes across as more easy-going than D. H. Lawrence's furious
(but wonderful) *Etruscan Places*.

This love for the spaces of community (markets, piazzas, churches)
over more individualistic pursuits has its consequence: an acceptance—at times, delighted—of human imperfection, a fact of Italian
life and character. With their capacious spirits and the courage of
their contradictions, the writers in this book look directly but never
censoriously at the excesses and omissions of Italian ways. Accordingly, the names of these writers belong to the finest tradition of
American and British women's nonfiction and fiction: George Eliot,
Mary Shelley, Edith Wharton, Elizabeth Bowen, Mary McCarthy,
Francine Prose.

The travel sections of bookstores are well stocked with the
regularly reprinted editions of travel essays by Goethe, Lawrence,
and William Dean Howells. A literary companion to Italy from
the points of view of first-rate women writers/travelers serves to
particularize our sense of the country. Women writers have something different to tell us or they tell their stories in a different key.
For a number of women, both historical and fictional, represented in this book, Italy is the destination and the journey itself,
a familiar metaphor for the life-long pilgrimage toward the self's
interior. The place and the process act together as a sort of
double catalyst; a change of heart is a strong motif of the Italian
experience. The autobiographical slant of such travel writing is

clear. And when Elizabeth Bowen in *A Time in Rome* names as one of the desires of her journey "a liberation from the thicket of the self," there is no contradiction between the traveler's search for and invention of self and her exhilirating sense of freedom from its constrictions. Both are dimensions of the self's story that Italy lets play. In a few cases, the women's writings are forgotten (Francesca Alexander's *Roadside Songs of Tuscany*) or hard to find (Iris Origo's extraordinary war diary, *War in Val D'Orcia*). Once discovered, however (and followed on foot, by car, and on the train), the well-known and unfamiliar writers of *Desiring Italy* amply reward the curious and the adventurous, resonating as deeply with present-day lovers of Italy as the widely quoted opinions of, say, John Ruskin. Having their impressions of Europe's ancient heart and soul in one volume serves all traveling readers who desire the company of uncommon witnesses.

On the map of my personal history Italy is a major benevolent presence, which is how it figures in the lives of the women who write about it in this book. My first taste was the first golden summer of my marriage. Part of it we spent in Rome (as hot and crowded as we'd been warned) with my best friend, a woman who spoke Italian, and her lover. At night they took us to Trastevere. Later on, we spent anniversaries in Tuscany, in Venice, then, with our children, the feast of Epiphany (and Befana) in Piazza Navona, then more seasons in Rome. This spring, my daughter and I went south to Naples through Basilicata (or Lucania) and finally to Sicily. (Trapped in a train by a mud slide that cut all electrical and telephone lines, I thought with some anxiety as afternoon turned into night and then past midnight and as the many engineers became more ineffectual and the stranded passengers more resigned, that, like Mary Taylor Simeti, we might wind up staying on Persephone's island forever. My daughter, a younger, freer spirit, remembers the country of that train ride as a place where "it is easy to imagine that myths come dancing out of the hills.")

At some point—in Tuscany in 1991—I read *Italian Days* by Barbara Grizzuti Harrison. It's a thrilling book, a woman's memoir that shows how erotic and spiritual good travel writing—and travel—truly are: the discovery of ecstatic spaces, the breaking free, the unexpected recognitions, both personal and cultural, the craving for beauty—all these come together. (Jan Morris has said that earthiness and spirituality are the twin vernaculars of Italy.) *Desiring Italy* is the product of my determination to find and follow more such writers to the places they celebrate. So these pages represent my chosen assembly of warmhearted, amusing, and learned cicerones narrating the turns and plots of the Italian worlds they love. Visiting their places and tracing their routes and backgrounds has meant for me more happy journeys. One vivid image of these literary pilgrimages is of walking, or rather, of ascending domes, hill towns, the heights of Genoa, San Miniato, and Posillipo. At the summits come the peaks of the Apennines, the turquoise sea, the light—the smile—of Rome at sunset. Love of life, renewed, seducing, is the theme. The writers in this book have given it the names you see in the table of contents.

I have not tried to represent every region or every well-known city and town within this book's three main geographical divisions of the North, Rome, and the South. The point of the collection is not to serve as a comprehensive travel/literary guide to the entire peninsula nor is it to function as a practical guide (to hotels and restaurants), though it does specify directions, bus routes, walks, and restaurants (in the case of Marcella Hazen in Venice) that concern a writer's territory. My main interest has been to gather lively and insightful writings by women about Italian places and people that, as a traveler, I, too, have found compelling and often glorious.

—*Susan Cahill*
New York City, 1997

Overtures

KNOLE

18 MARCH 1912

Suddenly, I have decided to go to Italy. Telegrams are flying to people who might possibly take me. Of course I should love to throw a toothbrush into a bag, and just go, quite vaguely, without any plans or even a real destination. It is the Wanderlust. And then I want the sun so badly, and to get away too, right away. Wouldn't you like to, in green Archie, from one little town with red roofs perched on a hill to another, and never minding the fleas, and making friends with the dirty children, and taking them all for drives in green Archie? And if it was not warm enough in the North, you would drive Archie onto a railway truck and go away down to Sicily. Isn't that much more than travelling luxuriously with wagons-lits, and couriers, and rooms kept for one in the best hotels in all the big towns? Mother can't understand why I would *rather* go without a maid.

—Vita Sackville-West, from *Letters*

Appropriating the cultural skills of Greece and sending them forth with the Roman legions, Italy spread civilization through Europe. After the fall of Rome and the spread of Christendom, which soon sank into the long, unproductive Dark Ages, it was again Italian artists and craftsmen, architects and scientists who carried the Renaissance across the continent from Blois in western France to Warsaw. Even the walls of the Kremlin and some buildings inside were the work of Italians. Yet with all their extraordinary creative vigor, the fantasy and joy in life of the mixture of peoples who inhabit the sunny peninsula, the Italians could not manage to produce an organization of society worthy of their talents. Some Italians celebrate the ideal of indolence, of *dolce far niente*, as a superior philosophy to glum striving. Affectionately, but with a tinge of apology, Luigi Barzini, author of *The Italians*, extolled the stubborn dedication to habit, to self-delusion, to keeping order at a minimum. The prize-winning Milan journalist Indro Montanelli calls it the "Italian disease" and believes it stems from the Counter-Reformation, which "cut off Italy and made it impermeable to that Protestant spirit in which the great industrial revolution of the West found its motive force and moral standards.". . .

—Flora Lewis, from *Europe: A Tapestry of Nations*

The pace of an authentically Italian meal is distinctly musical. The first movement, the pasta or soup, is a *presto agitato*, fast and eager. The meat is cut, lifted and chewed in a calmer *allegro*, while the fruit introduces a stately *adagio* of slow, careful selection, aristocratic discarding, exquisite peeling with knife and fork, the deliberate, slow jaws returned to serenity. We have now reached the interminable *lento*. Although your bread, wine and first course were brought with the speed that accompanies emergencies—a hungry man is a man in serious trouble—the waiter, having fed you, turns to more urgent matters, rather like the physician who no longer finds you interesting after the acute ailment disappears. It may be that, like other Schweitzers, he scorns thanks and money. Whatever, getting your check will take time and more time. And no one but your wife and the Americans at the next table will understand your impatience. Why should you be annoyed when you've been so quickly and fully fed while others, *poveretti*, are tearing their bread in agony?

One learns, in time, to sit out the waiter's evaluation of the state of his patients and begins to realize that the passion for Italian food is less a need for veal in six styles or chicken in three than a yearning for Italianness. So, even if your diet forbids you *penne*, *agnellotti*, fettuccine and spaghetti with a hundred names, you will eat pasta because you see it eaten with a total joy, a concentration of pleasure, as if it were a rare Lucullan dish rather than the habitual staple served at least once a day. You will plunge and wallow in the manipulating, slurping, moistly shining, sexy happiness, not so much to eat as to share the buoyant Italian greed for experiencing deeply, everything, from roaring in a winner at the races to the wash of peach juice in the mouth.

—Kate Simon, from "The Subject Is Eating,"
in *Italy: The Places in Between*

Whenever I go anywhere but Italy for a vacation, I always feel as if I have made a mistake. All too often I have changed my plans and left—from a ski resort in the French Alps, a mountain town in Switzerland, a country house in Provence—to get to Italy as soon as possible. Once across the border I can breathe again. Why bother to go anywhere, I think in those first ecstatic moments of reentry, but Italy?

What do we find in Italy that can be found nowhere else? I believe it is a certain permission to be human that other countries lost long ago. Not only is Italy one of the few places left where fantasy runs unfettered as Luigi Barzini said in *The Italians*, "even instruments of precision like speedometers and clocks are made to lie in Italy for your happiness"; it is also one of the few places that tolerate human nature with all its faults. Italy is the past, but it is also the future. It is pagan, but it is also Christian and Jewish. It is grand and tawdry, imperishable and decayed. Italy has seen marauding armies, Fascists and Communists, fashions and fripperies come and go. And it is still, for all its layers of musty history, a place that enhances existence, burnishes the moment. . . .

—Erica Jong, from "My Italy"

THE NORTH

The British fell in love with Florence and Tuscany before any other part of Italy. We were the first to discover, as tourists, her splendid cities and churches, her art and her countryside and our appreciation of her cooking has something to do with this long-standing love affair. Tuscan dishes evoke the tender climate and brilliant light, the gentle harmony of contrasting hills and valleys, vineyard and rock, squat silver olives and slender dark cypresses and the pastel hill towns we see in the background of paintings by artists like Masaccio, Uccello, Fra' Angelico, Fra' Filippo Lippi and Piero della Francesca.

Milan and the north of Italy also got to know Tuscan cooking early, when they were inundated with *trattorie toscane* offering fresh, light dishes quite different from their own rich, heavy foods. The greatest of Tuscan cooking is an idea deep in Italian minds, bound up with the reverence they feel for the region that produced so many of their geniuses, that generated so many of their ideas about art, literature, science, politics, individual liberty and love, and whose vernacular became their standard language.

—Claudia Roden, from *The Food of Italy*

Today we saw the most beautiful of views and the melancholy man. The view was like a line of poetry that makes itself; the shaped hill, all flushed with reds and greens; the elongated lines, cultivated every inch; old, wild, perfectly said, once and for all: and I walked up to a group and said "What is that village? It called itself [*]"; and the woman with the blue eyes said, "Won't you come to my house and drink?" She was famished for talk. Four or five of them buzzed round us and I made a Ciceronian

* Left blank in her diary.

speech about the beauty of the country. But I have no money to travel with, she said, wringing her hands. We would not go to her house—a cottage on the side of the hill: and shook hands: hers were dusty; she wanted to keep them from me; but we all shook hands and I wished we had gone to her house, in the loveliest of all landscapes. Then, lunching by the river, among the ants, we met the melancholy man. He had five or six little fish in his hands, which he had caught in his hands. We said it was very beautiful country; and he said no, he preferred the town. He had been to Florence: no, he did not like the country. He wanted to travel, but had no money: worked at some village: no, he did not like the country, he repeated, with his gentle cultivated voice: no theatres, no pictures, only perfect beauty. I gave him 2 cigarettes; at first he refused, then offered us his six or seven little fish. We could not cook them at Siena, we said. No, he agreed, and so we parted.

It is all very well, saying one will write notes, but writing is a very difficult art. That is one has always to select: and I am too sleepy and hence merely run sand through my fingers. Writing is not in the least an easy art. Thinking what to write, it seems easy; but the thought evaporates, runs hither and thither. Here we are in the noise of Siena—the vast tunnelled arched stone town, swarmed over by chattering shrieking children.

—Virginia Woolf, from *A Writer's Diary*

LOMBARDY

MILAN

Edith Wharton

A self-described "incorrigible life-lover" who, "drunk with seeing and learning," craved travel, Edith Wharton named Italy her first European love and her annual visit the happiest time of the year. Best known as a writer of fiction, she comes across as one of "the most accomplished practitioners [of travel writing] in American literary history" in her two books about the architecture and art of Italy, Italian Villas and Their Gardens *(1904) and* Italian Backgrounds *(1905), according to biographer R. W. B. Lewis. Her approach to Milan is that of a woman possessed of her own taste who is not to be bullied into appreciation or censoriousness by Ruskin—with whom, she says, she "had been saturated."*

FROM *ITALIAN BACKGROUNDS*

PICTURESQUE MILAN

It is hard to say whether the stock phrase of the stock tourist—"there is so little to see in Milan"—redounds most to the derision of the speaker or to the glory of Italy. That such a judgment should be possible, even to the least instructed traveller, implies a surfeit of impressions procurable in no other land; since, to the hastiest observation, Milan could hardly seem lacking in interest when compared to any but Italian cities. From comparison with the latter, even, it suffers only on a superficial estimate, for it is rich in all that makes the indigenous beauty of Italy, as opposed to the pseudo-Gothicisms, the trans-Alpine points and pinnacles, which Ruskin taught a submissive generation of art critics to regard as the typical expression of the Italian spirit. The guidebooks, long accustomed to draw their Liebig's extract of art from the pages of this school of critics, have kept the tradition alive by dwelling only on the monuments which conform to perpendicular ideals, and by apologetic allusions to the "monotony" and "regularity" of Milan—as though endeavouring in advance to placate the traveller for its not looking like Florence or Siena! ...

But, it may be asked, though Milan will seem more interesting to the emancipated judgment, will it appear more picturesque? Picturesqueness is, after all, what the Italian pilgrim chiefly seeks; and the current notion of the picturesque is a purely Germanic one, connoting Gothic steeples, pepper-pot turrets, and the huddled steepness of the northern burgh.

Italy offers little, and Milan least of all, to satisfy these requirements. The Latin ideal demanded space, order, and nobility of composition. But does it follow that picturesqueness is incompatible with these? ...

There is another, a more typically Italian picturesqueness, gay rather than sinister in its suggestions, made up of lights rather than of shadows, of colour rather than of outline, and this is the picturesqueness of Milan. The city abounds in vivid effects, in suggestive juxtapositions of different centuries and styles—in all those incidental contrasts and surprises which linger in the mind after the catalogued "sights" have faded. Leaving behind the wide modern streets—which have the merit of having been modernized under Eugène Beauharnais rather than under King Humbert—one enters at once upon some narrow byway overhung by the grated windows of a seventeenth-century palace, or by the delicate terra-cotta apse of a *cinque-cento* church. Everywhere the forms of expression are purely Italian, with the smallest possible admixture of that Gothic element which marks the old free cities of Central Italy. The rocca Sforzesca (the old Sforza castle) and the houses about the Piazza de' Mercanti are the chief secular buildings recalling the pointed architecture of the north; and the older churches are so old that they antedate Gothic influences, and lead one back to the round-arched basilican type. But in the line of national descent what exquisite varieties the Milanese streets present! Here, for instance, is the Corinthian colonnade of San Lorenzo, the only considerable fragment of

ancient Mediolanum,* its last shaft abutting on a Gothic archway
against which clings a flower-decked shrine. Close by, one comes
on the ancient octagonal church of San Lorenzo, while a few minutes' drive leads to where the Borromeo palace looks across a
quiet grassy square at the rococo front of the old family church,
flanked by a fine bronze statue of the great saint and cardinal.

The Palazzo Borromeo is itself a notable factor in the picturesqueness of Milan. The entrance leads to a court-yard enclosed
in an ogive arcade surmounted by pointed windows in terra-cotta
mouldings. The walls of this court are still frescoed with the Borromean crown, and the *Humilitas* of the haughty race; and a
doorway leads into the muniment-room, where the archives of the
house are still stored, and where, on the damp stone walls, Miche-
lino da Milano has depicted the scenes of a fifteenth-century villeg-
giatura. Here the noble ladies of the house, in high fluted turbans
and fantastic fur-trimmed gowns, may be seen treading the mea-
sures of a mediæval dance with young gallants in parti-coloured
hose, or playing at various games—the *jeu de tarots,* and a kind of
cricket played with a long wooden bat; while in the background
rise the mountains about Lake Maggiore. . . .

Not far from the Borromean palace, another doorway leads to a
different scene: the great cloister of the Ospedale Maggiore [Gen-
eral Hospital], one of the most glorious monuments that man ever
erected to his fellows. The old hospitals of Italy were famous not
only for their architectural beauty and great extent, but for their
cleanliness and order and the enlightened care which their inmates
received. Northern travellers have recorded their wondering admiration of these lazarets, which seemed as stately as palaces in
comparison with the miserable pest-houses north of the Alps.
What must have been the astonishment of such a traveller, whether
German or English, on setting foot in the principal court of the
Milanese hospital, enclosed in its vast cloister enriched with trac-
eries and medallions of terra-cotta, and surmounted by the
arches of an open loggia whence the patients could look down on

*The Roman town of Mediolanum became known as Milan.

a peaceful expanse of grass and flowers! Even now, one wonders whether this poetizing of philanthropy, this clothing of charity in the garb of beauty, may not have had its healing uses: whether the ugliness of the modern hospital may not make it, in another sense, as unhygienic as the more picturesque buildings it has superseded? It is at least pleasant to think of the poor sick people sunning themselves in the beautiful loggia of the Ospedale Maggiore, or sitting under the magnolia-trees in the garden, while their blue-gowned and black-veiled nurses move quietly through the cloisters at the summons of the chapel-bell. . . .

But nothing in Milan approaches in beauty the colour-scheme of the Portinari chapel behind the choir of Sant' Eustorgio. In Italy, even, there is nothing else exactly comparable to this masterpiece of collaboration between architect and painter. At Ravenna, the tomb of Galla Placidia and the apse of San Vitale glow with richer hues, and the lower church of Assisi is unmatched in its shifting mystery of chiar'-oscuro; but for pure light, for a clear shadowless scale of iridescent tints, what can approach the Portinari chapel? Its most striking feature is the harmony of form and colour which makes the decorative design of Michelozzo flow into and seem a part of the exquisite frescoes of Vincenzo Foppa. This harmony is not the result of any voluntary feint, any such trickery of the brush as the later decorative painters delighted in. In the Portinari chapel, architecture and painting are kept distinct in treatment, and the fusion between them is effected by unity of line and colour, and still more, perhaps, by an identity of sentiment, which keeps the whole chapel in the same mood of blitheness,—a mood which makes it difficult to remember that the chapel is the mausoleum of a martyred saint. But Saint Peter Martyr's marble sarcophagus, rich and splendid as it is, somehow fails to distract the attention from its setting. There are so many mediæval monuments like it in Italy—and there is but one Portinari chapel. From the cupola, with its scales of pale red and blue, overlapping each other like the breast-plumage of a pigeon, and terminating in a terra-cotta frieze of dancing angels, who swing between them great bells of fruit and flowers, the eye is led by insensible gradations of tint to Foppa's frescoes in the spandrils—iridescent saints and angels in a setting of pale classical architecture—and thence to another frieze of terra-cotta seraphs with rosy-red wings against a background of turquoise-green; this lower frieze resting in turn on pilasters of pale green adorned with white stucco *rilievi* of little bell-ringing angels. It is only as a part of this colour-scheme that the central sarcophagus really affects one—the ivory tint of its old marble forming a central point for the play of light, and allying itself with the sumptuous hues of Portinari's dress, in the fresco which represents the donator of the chapel kneeling before his patron saint. . . .

The reader who has followed these desultory wanderings through Milan has but touched the hem of her garment. In the Brera, the Ambrosiana, the Poldi-Pezzoli gallery, and the magnificent new Archæological Museum, now fittingly housed in the old castle of the Sforzas, are treasures second only to those of Rome and Florence. But these are among the catalogued riches of the city. The guide-books point to them, they lie in the beaten track of sight-seeing, and it is rather in the intervals between such systematized study of the past, in the parentheses of travel, that one obtains those more intimate glimpses which help to compose the image of each city, to preserve its personality in the traveller's mind.

For the Literary Traveler

Wharton's Milan, as she exclaims in these pages, is a matter of "vivid effects," "suggestive juxtapositions," and "exquisite variety."

A selective walking tour of the city she loved (she was an indefatigable traveler and no doubt would have climbed to the top of the Duomo for the vistas of the Italian Alps—the stairs begin outside the north transept) would include the ex–OSPEDALE MAGGIORE or CA' GRANDE (since 1958 the University of Milan); CASTELLO SFORZESCO (Bellini's superb *Madonna of the Pomegranate* is in the tower room of the PINACOTECA); the lovely PIAZZA DE' MERCANTI with the LOGGIA DEGLI OSII nearby. A few minutes further west (beyond the PINACOTECA AMBROSIANA and PALAZZO BORROMEO and past the Catholic University with its cloisters by Bramante) is the ancient basilica of SANT'AMBROGIO (379–86), the most impressive church in the city, where Augustine listened to St. Ambrose, the Bishop of Milan, preach. (Wharton quotes *The Confessions* in her novel *The Gods Arrive:* "I heard Thy voice crying to me; 'I am the Food of the full-grown. Become a man and thou shalt feed on me.'") The basilica's splendid Romanesque pulpit, the fifth-century mosaics in the chapels, the ninth-century ciborium and altar casing, the Byzantine-style baldacchino—all these qualify as the "vivid" and "exquisite" effects Wharton found throughout the city. Augustine's conversion and baptism in Milan, especially his explanatory "*Credo quia absurdum*"—"I believe because it is absurd"—would have captivated Wharton, whose fiction has the mystery of the heart and the workings of the spirit at its core.

But nothing, in her estimation, surpasses the PORTINARI CHAPEL (under restoration in 1996) in the Church of Sant'Eustorgio at Porta Ticinese. She considered it Milan's crown jewel.

Francine Prose

Born in Brooklyn, Francine Prose is the author of many highly acclaimed novels and several volumes of short stories. The novel Household Saints, *set in New York's Little Italy, dramatizes the operatic quality of Italian culture (and religion). At home in this world of extremes, she catches the sweet and harsh, the mystical and loony. She has traveled widely, publishing her fiction and impressions of places in the* New York Times, *the* New Yorker, *and the* Atlantic Monthly.*

Her choice of Milan as the setting of "Cauliflower Heads," a story of a honeymoon from hell, is significant for travelers to Italy. It's easy to miss the special character of Milan. The ideologue husband doesn't even look for it. The city is beyond his self-absorbed imagination, deadened as it is with the stereotypes and preconceptions he brought with him. The power of the city— like marriage—reveals itself only if attention is paid. Finding the beauty of Milan, the bride comes to her senses.

CAULIFLOWER HEADS

Europe was crawling with adulterous couples. Mostly, for some reason, one saw them at ruins, respectfully tripping over the archaeological rubble. Just like regular tourists they seemed to be under some terrible strain, but unlike regular tourists they hardly looked at anything, so that when, say, a lizard streaked across their path they'd jump and fall into each other with apologetic smiles, more like awkward teenagers than adults risking the forbidden.

In the ruins of Herculaneum, Susanna saw the quintessential adulterous couple leaving one of the underground rooms just as she and Jerry were entering. The couple started as if they'd been caught embracing, as if they often met in the cave-like room and were shocked to see anyone else. They looked vaguely Eastern European— raincoats in the summer heat and frumpy business suits. The woman was pretty, in a frizzy way, with oddly colorless eyes and hair. She carried a leather briefcase and wore sensible, mannish shoes. The man was tall and also had colorless hair combed to cover a bald spot.

Later, when Susanna and Jerry stopped at a trattoria down the road, the couple were eating lunch there, or rather chain-smoking through it. A haze hovered over the plates of food they ordered and didn't touch. Once, when the woman lit up a smoke, her lover pushed back her sleeve and pressed his cheek to the inside of her forearm.

Watching, Susanna felt something inside her chest go soggy and expansive, like that trick when you pleat a drinking-straw wrapper and then drip water on it. Across the table Jerry was happily tucking away his penne al'amatriciana. Jerry and Susanna had only been married three weeks. Susanna wondered: Wasn't one's honeymoon cruelly early to be envying the adulterous?

Of course she couldn't ask Jerry. *That* would have been cruel, and even if he managed not to take it personally, he'd think she was silly for worrying about this when the planet was dying.

When Jerry saw a lizard in the ruins he took a picture of it. He was very aware of how many species were disappearing. If he and Susanna ever had children, he wanted to show them animals that by then might no longer exist. Susanna couldn't picture the children she and Jerry might have, and certainly not a cozy scene around the lamplit kitchen table: Jerry showing the children photos of vanished animal life.

And yet Jerry's hobby—elegiac nature photography—had deeply moved Susanna when they first fell in love. They'd met when Jerry came to speak at Susanna's college; Jerry lived near the college and was brought in at the last minute after the scheduled speaker, a former cabinet member, tried to get off a plane in mid-flight when the movie ended.

Jerry was a consultant on radioactive waste disposal. When your town dump glowed in the dark, your mayor called Jerry. Jerry gave Susanna's class the global bad news with such deep personal grief that she was overcome with longing to protect him from what he knew. He told them to look to the right, then the left, and imagine the people on both sides with giant green cauliflower heads. Then he said they were kidding themselves, because this would never happen; they would not evolve into toxic creatures capable of thriving on environmental poisons. They would die and the earth would die and turn into a radioactive desert glowing in the sunless sky. Then the college students were filled with shame for having imagined that they could be saved.

Jerry had said, "It's up to your generation to make sure it doesn't happen." And Susanna had thought: Well, obviously. Jerry would show her how.

Perhaps this was the reason their courtship was so intense: it was as if the bomb had dropped and they had fifteen minutes to live. All through Susanna's last semester they met in a dark bar near campus where married professors met girl students, though Jerry was single and didn't teach, so really there was no need.

Susanna had forgotten to think about her future beyond graduation, which made it easier, when school ended, to move from the dorm to Jerry's house. On summer evenings they frequented the same dark bar near campus. The girls had gone off to glamorous internships, the professors home to their families and the books they'd been meaning to write. Leaning so close their heads touched, Jerry told Susanna stories: twice his office had been burglarized and strategic files stolen. In July he heard some hopeful news and gripped her hand till it hurt: some PCB-eating macrophage had looked good in the lab.

But after they'd lived together that winter he seemed to forget about her saving the world, and even that she was in it, so that often he seemed surprised and pleased to find her in his house. Susanna tried to see this as a positive sign. Perhaps if he over-estimated the chance of her vanishing from his life he might also be mistaken about the ozone layer. She herself was worried about the future of the planet and so felt petty and ashamed when the subject began to seem like an annoying tic of Jerry's. If you took pleasure in a sunny day, he brought up global warming. Several times she'd caught herself on the edge of saying that she would rather the world end than have to think about it all the time.

But anyone could see that Jerry was right. That spring a toxic dump site turned up in their back yard; well, not actually their back yard—two or three miles down the road. Susanna and Jerry stood on a bluff overlooking the devastation. Acres of muddy bull-dozer tracks, glittery patches of broken glass, strips of bloody gauze unfurled like a vampire fraternity prank.

Jerry cleared his throat and said, "Probably we should get married."

It bothered Susanna a little—proposed to at a dump site!—but she told herself it was perfect: the marriage of the future. At once dedicated and resigned, she had told Jerry yes.

So they had come to Italy, combining their honeymoon with the world ecology conference in Milan, to which Jerry had been invited to give a brief address. They landed in Rome and rented a car and drove south to Pompeii and Herculaneum, where, as Susanna watched the adulterous couple cannibalizing each other at the next table, Jerry washed down his pasta with wine and said, "What amazes me is how people can go to these ruins and not take it per-sonally. I mean, no one who died here or at Pompeii thought the big one was going to hit. It was just business as usual, reading the paper, baking bread ... bingo. You're history. These tourists trip through, acting like it's someone else's problem, and it never crosses their mind that they're looking at Main Street a hundred years from now."

Susanna said, "Jerry, give them a break. They're tourists on vacation." Sometimes she felt it was mean of him to want people to think like he did.

But why was the adulterous couple so tense and distracted and silent? Susanna wondered what they had left behind and how much time they had. She thought of the lovers of Pompeii, killed in each other's arms. The lovers of Pompeii were charred to ash, the Herculaneans covered with mud.

"Vacation!" Jerry snorted. "They should see what *I* see." He meant the statistics that crossed his desk: wildly alarming health reports and grim projections into the future. Susanna thought of paintings of St. Jerome with a human skull on his desk; most likely the saints of the future would have printouts instead of skulls. But would there be saints in the future, and who would paint their portraits to hang in the museums when there were no people left to go to museums and see them?

The farther north they traveled, the better Susanna liked it. She was glad when they left the South, where the dust and heat made everything shimmer ambiguously, like in spaghetti Westerns that don't care if you follow the plot. She was happiest in Umbria and the spookier parts of Tuscany, where you felt the romance these people craved was not the romance of love but the romance of poisoning each other with undetectable toxins. She particularly liked Gubbio: so stony, so unforgiving. You could wait out the apocalypse in one of its thick-walled palaces; there your life would be hard and clean with no disturbing soft spots.

At first Jerry trailed Susanna up the steep cobbled streets, panting and making coronary jokes. But soon he was talking about how life here whipped you into shape: no wonder the old ladies had such terrific calves. Sometimes Susanna hung back and let him pull her uphill, but at the church doors she broke away and hurried in ahead. She didn't like to watch him paging through his Michelin Guide, entering the churches with his head in a book. He approached each cathedral like a research problem; once she saw him peering into an empty confessional.

In Florence, at San Lorenzo, before an altar painting of saints, a British child was asking her parents how the different martyrs died.

"That's all she wants to know," her father said to Susanna. "What happened to the poor blokes."

Jerry pointed to the tray of eyeballs that St. Lucy was carrying. "Know what those are?" he asked the girl. "Marbles," he answered for her, and the adults giggled nervously.

Jerry had no patience with martyrs; he said they were deluded and psychotically self-indulgent. He said, "Life is short enough without asking someone to shorten it for you." His favorite frescoes were of people engaged in ordinary tasks, oblivious to the big moment: fishermen angling peacefully in the Red Sea while Pharaoh's soldiers are drowning; gamblers dicing in the shadow of the Crucifixion. For Jerry, these had the relevance of the latest news—just transpose the sailors in the sea to the otters in the oil spill. And in fact, like so much of the news, these paintings made Susanna feel guilty.

She was starting to feel guilty a lot—guilty for being a tourist. How she envied the travelers who fought for their sightseeing pleasure against the fear of missing something and some greater unnamed dread. She even envied the retirees who knew they deserved a vacation. Was that more or less pathetic than envying the adulterous? Jerry said the best cure for guilt was taking positive action, but it was hard, in foreign towns, knowing what action to take. And really, had she ever? She'd known to go up and ask Jerry for a copy of his speech, but she was no longer sure that seducing him was a step toward saving the world.

There was a new thing Jerry liked in bed: pinning her hands above her head. It made her feel like St. Sebastian waiting for the arrows. Jerry was polite about it. Before he did it he stopped and smiled, embarrassed, asking permission. He didn't take criticism well, he got quite pouty and sulky, so Susanna didn't mention that it wasn't her favorite thing. She just went passive, thinking, I'm the Gandhi of the bedroom, and feeling guilty for thinking of Gandhi in this debasing context. Gandhi was her hero; she and Jerry had that in common.

Her parents had feared that her worshipping Gandhi might be a warning sign of anorexia, though it should have been obvious how much she liked food. Jerry worried the opposite; sometimes he dissuaded her from a second helping of pasta. He encouraged her to wear clothes that showed off her skinny body, miniskirts and halters in which she looked about twelve. He especially approved of her dressing like that for his colleagues. She knew she was a trophy to him and felt guilty for liking that, too.

She also liked it and also felt guilty when they got to Milan and checked into the hotel where the conference was being held, and at the first night's dinner-dance Jerry steered her through the room, and she felt her blond hair and tiny white dress dazzling the famous ecologists. On the street, with Italian girls around, she didn't feel so dazzling—but most of the ecologists were middle-aged men, even older than Jerry. For them she was all youth and sex rolled up in one female body. This reassured her in a way she'd missed since she and Jerry met. She knew it was unliberated if what you were doing for the planet was making ecologists happy with fleeting moments of fantasy sex. But wasn't even that better than doing nothing at all?

It was easy to feel pretty in the hotel dining room, amid the black enamel and chrome and pots of swollen white lilies. She and Jerry sat down and couldn't very well get up when they found themselves sharing a table with three Politburo members. In fact, they were Bulgarian, or so their name cards said. They nodded at Jerry and Susanna and then stared grimly ahead. Sometimes they whispered to each other. Susanna thought of the couple at Herculaneum. Had she mistaken Eastern European social style for some special intensity?

All the waiters looked like male models with designer white jackets. Serving, they brushed suspiciously close to Susanna's bare arms, and the space around her felt charged, a pleasing distraction from the strain of dining with Bulgarians. The dance band, five Malaysian kids, played a kind of modified swing. Susanna pulled Jerry out on the floor, where she pressed herself against him and spread her legs and bent her knees so her skirt rode up on her hips. Jerry jitterbugged well enough, and as he twirled her around, she threw back her head and closed her eyes and felt the eyes of the ecologists warming her arms and legs.

*   *

Outside the conference room they picked up earphones for simultaneous translation. The first speaker was a professor from the University of Milan, who welcomed the participants and expressed his hope that together they could solve their common problems and that this year, unlike last, the discourse would not bog down in petty nationalist grievances. The current crisis was everyone's fault, no one country's more than the rest.

One by one the ecologists made their way to the podium. Each spoke for ten minutes and took questions from the floor. Everyone chain-smoked feverishly in the audience and on stage; after every few speeches they took a coffee break and chain-smoked in the hall. Several of the speakers reported on particular rivers or mountains or forests. Meditating on the depletion of the earth's resources had lined their faces and made them look brooding, unacademic, and Yves Montandish. The Europeans talked slowly and out of the sides of their mouths. The Americans were stiffer, more boyish, and, like Jerry, more nervous.

Jerry's speech was too close to lunch and did not go well. It was very different from what he'd told Susanna's class. Perhaps he should have asked them to look to both sides and imagine their colleagues with cauliflower heads. Instead, he dimmed the lights and projected a map his office had compiled showing nuclear dump sites across the U.S.: tiny death's-heads speckled the screen like fly spots on a napkin. He said these sites would be uninhabitable for a million years. There were many death's-heads, and the audience got silent. As Jerry ran through the statistics on radioactive sludge, Susanna fiddled with the headset and listened to him in French and Italian female voices.

When the house lights came back on, the ecologists blinked grumpily and lit up. "Questions?" said Jerry and someone called out, "What action is being taken?" But Jerry could only stammer and hedge like a White House press corps frontman, like someone who'd work for nuclear dumpers instead of struggling against them. "It's difficult," he said. "Mostly our work so far has been to identify sites, inform local residents, and begin to put pressure on the government. Otherwise, it's hard to know just what action to take . . ." He smiled the same silly smile with which he asked Susanna if he could pin her hands behind her head.

A palpable dissatisfaction rose from the audience, mingling with the smoke from their French cigarettes. Susanna wished Jerry had told the stories he'd told in the college bar, the break-ins at his office, the hard disks mysteriously crashed, the secret reports sent through the mail that somehow never got there. That would convince the ecologists that he was already risking all, that what he did was critical and not just academic. And who were these professors to fault him for not doing more? Didn't they know that what to do was the central question of Jerry's life?

A professor from Madrid got up and said, "I'm sorry. You must forgive us if we find this . . . hesitance . . . hard to believe. Here in Europe we all grew up watching John Wayne, expecting this from America: instant cowboy justice."

Everyone laughed and Jerry said, "That's the difference right there. We all grew up thinking that John Wayne was a right-wing fascist. You know," he went on, "I used to feel hesitant talking politics to Europeans, I thought you'd had so much sad history, what could I possibly know? But now in terms of suffering I think we're pulling way out ahead of you guys."

After that there was a silence. A lunch break was announced.

In the lobby the morning's speakers were being congratulated and invited to repeat their presentations in glamorous-sounding cities. Susanna and Jerry stood all alone in a circle of dread. No one would make eye contact with them, people went out of their way to avoid them, so that when at last someone approached, Jerry and Susanna turned away and had to turn back awkwardly when the person started talking.

The tall young man before them was someone Susanna had noticed; it would have been hard not to, he stood out from the crowd. He was dressed in a leather jacket and jeans, with greasy shoulder-length blond hair and an earring; he looked like a movie villain's psycho right-hand man. Perhaps he was an ecoterrorist—there had to be some of them here—and Susanna braced herself for his righteous attack on Jerry.

Instead, in a heavy accent he said, "I think you are very brave man. We all know your Pentagon and C.I.A. are vicious crazy killers. I am Gabor Szekaly. Greenpeace. From Hungaria. Forgive my English is not good."

"Your English is great," said Susanna. "I mean, compared to our Hungarian."

"You speak Hungarian?" said Gabor.

"No," said Susanna. "I just meant—"

"I don't know about *brave*," Jerry said. "But from time to time it does get hairy. My office gets broken into more often than Zsa Zsa Gabor's hotel room."

"Gabor?" said Gabor.

"An actress," Jerry explained. "With lots of heavily insured diamond jewelry that keeps getting ripped off in Las Vegas."

"Hungarian?" said Gabor.

"Originally," said Susanna. "But no one you'd want to know."

Gabor smiled and lowered his head and kissed Susanna's hand. She noticed that his earring was a tiny Coptic cross, and felt guilty for finding his kiss so pleasurable and disturbing.

"Welcome to the conference," Gabor said. "We will be seeing each other, okay?" He turned on his heel and headed across the lobby, a funny walk with elements of a swagger and a scurry.

"Great," said Jerry. "Terrific. Wouldn't you know Count Dracula would be the one guy who liked my speech?"

The conference became like the mother ship, feeding and sustaining them. After one day Susanna and Jerry stopped leaving the hotel. The ecologists warmed up to Jerry and flirted with Susanna. There were lots of internal politics which Susanna didn't get but which lent the panels a buzz of tension; you felt you might be missing something if you didn't go.

Susanna was acutely aware of where Gabor sat in the room. Already he seemed to have bonded with many conference members with whom he talked volubly, pounding their shoulders and arms. He'd brought a girl who appeared only at meals and sat with him, alone in a corner, always in total silence. The girl wore jeans and a denim jacket and smoked like a chimney. She was tragic and spectacular-looking with a mop of black curly hair, but she stayed on the edge of things and didn't flash it, like Susanna.

Three days into the conference Gabor's turn came to speak, and he ran up to the microphone like a boxer jogging into the ring. Susanna half expected him to vault the seminar table. Angrily he seized the mike and began shouting in Hungarian, rattling off the difficult sounds at the speed of Spanish. All the translation channels went dead; you could almost hear the translators wondering how to proceed—wondering did they have to shout to convey Gabor's meaning? At last they fell back on their calm, expressionless translatorese.

"We are in a time of terrible crisis," Susanna heard on the English channel, "a time that calls for immediate action." Gabor pounded his fist on the table. "Terrible violence is being done to us and we must retaliate, lash ourselves to the back of the whales and wait for the terrible Japanese whalers; we must tie ourselves to the tracks of the terrible nuclear trains. Or better yet we must disable the trains and sink the terrible ships."

Gabor went on for a long while, yelling and beating the table. Finally he finished and rushed out into the hall. After a round of wild applause the audience followed him out. While the others stopped at the coffee cart, Susanna and Jerry found Gabor, who was sweating profusely and making snuffling noises.

"I loved your speech," said Susanna. "I mean I really loved it. It's so important to remind people that we haven't got time, that we must stop talking and act—" She stopped in mid-sentence because her face felt hot and also because her tone—and for all she knew, her actual words—were horrifyingly familiar. It was what she'd said to Jerry after his speech at her college. She thought, I am the lowest of the low. I am an ecology groupie. She glanced at Jerry to see how he was reacting. He was shaking Gabor's hand. "Good work," Jerry said.

"It is so frustrating," Gabor said. "Who knows is anyone listening. To speak of these things is like giving dancing lessons to fucking corpses. I am sorry, I am when I get vexated all the time saying fucking. Even speaking to audience I say, fucking this, fucking that. How did they translate 'fucking'?"

" 'Terrible,' " said Susanna.

" 'Terrible'?" Gabor laughed. "Oh, these Italians are too much. Always thinking the Pope is watching. You take your meals here at the hotel?"

"We have been," said Jerry, "though the food isn't great . . ."

"We have dinner," said Gabor. "At seven."

After her shower, Susanna put on her little white dress, then thought this was the wrong attire for lashing oneself to a whale, and changed into a black T-shirt and black jeans. "You're wearing that?" said Jerry.

Gabor and the girl were in their usual corner. When he saw them he lifted his glass and toasted them from across the room. The girl was even younger than she'd seemed—a brooding Slavic teen. She stuck out her hand and solemnly pumped theirs, once each, up and down hard.

Gabor said, "This is my wife, Maritsa. She is Yugoslavian. Unfortunately she has no English."

"She speaks Hungarian, no?" said Susanna. When had *she* begun framing sentences as if English weren't her language?

"No," said Gabor, smiling. "And I have no Slovenian."

"But they're similar languages?" said Jerry.

"Totally different," said Gabor. "We have no common speech. But we are only married three weeks."

"Obviously, that explains it," Jerry said. "Not long enough to have to talk. Anyway, congratulations. And here's an amazing coincidence—*we* were married three weeks ago, too."

"Good! Very good!" said Gabor, and lightly punched Jerry's arm. "The language is no problem—but food! Yugoslavians are the world's worst cooks!" He pulled Maritsa to him: she let herself be pulled. Gabor said, "Before we are married we know each other only one week. It is so sudden—like this!" He grabbed his T-shirt over his heart and bunched it up in his hand.

Susanna looked at Gabor, then at Maritsa, then down at the floor. "Great shoes," she said to Maritsa.

"Yugoslavian worker shoes," said Maritsa. She had a deep voice and an outthrust lower lip that gave her a permanent pout. Her skin was geisha white and on each cheek was a harsh smear of rouge, like a bruise. "You do speak English," Susanna said. Maritsa looked at Gabor.

"Everyone admire her shoes," he explained. "So that much at least she learns to say in every European language. Come now. Sit down. We must order."

Gabor stopped Jerry and Susanna from ordering the zuppa di pesce. "Mussels from Adriatic? Suicide!" he said.

Over their bruschetti and antipasti misti they talked about mutant algae. "We hear mutant," said Gabor, who turned out to be not just an ecoterrorist but also a biology professor at Budapest University. "But who knows? Even science news is manipulated. Until now. Wonderful! Everyone in Budapest is falling in love and buying electronic equipment! But algae we know is big." He held his hands out wide. "In Venice is big problem. This algae is big like—" He held up the hem of the tablecloth. "You say . . . ?"

"Tablecloth," said Susanna.

"Tablecloth," Maritsa repeated. Susanna and Jerry smiled encouragingly.

"Algae like tablecloth!" said Gabor.

Susanna said, "Where did you learn English?"

"In England," Gabor said. " 'Fifty-six. Someone put me on back of motorcycle. I am ten year old. They take me to England and put me with professor's family. Very *sympathique*. I stay five years, learn English, then the daughter gets pregnant, the professor has me deported back to Hungary."

"He deported you?" said Susanna.

"An ethics professor," Gabor said. He looked at Maritsa, then back at Susanna and Jerry. "Well, okay, anyway, there is more to life than algae like tablecloths."

"Amen!" said Jerry. Susanna leaned so far forward she pulled sharply back, afraid she might have singed her bangs in the candle. Maritsa touched Susanna's arm in a calming, maternal way.

"Not that you would know from this conference," Gabor said. "Speeches, speeches. I am sick. Like school. Tomorrow I am not going to panels. I am tired. Tomorrow we look at art. I know very well Milan museums. You will come?"

Jerry said, "I think I should stick around. Susanna can go if she wants."

The hotel lobby was glossy black with an atrium skylight admitting one dramatic shaft of light, like a Weimar nightclub crossed with a Mongolian yurt. Maritsa huddled in a corner of the black leather couch, practically hugging the standing ashtray. Gabor lounged beside her with his back to a mirrored column. "Did you sleep well?" he asked.

"Fine," Susanna said.

It felt good to be wearing blue jeans in this lobby full of Armani; crossing it, they fell into a companionable pack-like stride. Gabor hailed a cab and held the door for the women, then jumped in beside the driver and began gabbing in Italian. Maritsa stretched her legs till her feet touched the front seat. Susanna had never felt so stiff-backed and prim, it was a new experience. When Gabor stopped talking, the driver shrugged and hit the gas. Maritsa and Susanna went flying as they squealed around a curve.

Gabor wheeled around in his seat and said excitedly to Susanna, "Ayi, I love how these guys drive! They are the real cowboys. Not that pig John Wayne, your husband was right. Is nothing to ride a horse alone in desert. But to drive a hundred kilometers an hour in traffic! This trip will cost monthly salary of average Hungarian professor. Lucky, Milan is paying—" He broke off for an argument with the driver about directions.

"How do you know the city so well?" asked Susanna.

"On the way back from England I live awhile in Italy. Again, romantic trouble, is best for me to take off. Now that I have my Maritsa I am through with all that stuff." He twisted even further around so he and Maritsa could lock gazes.

Gabor did know the museums; he was a connoisseur of sorts. His taste ran to trompe l'oeil and dark late Renaissance narrative paintings of bizarre miracles. He was a great fan of Archimboldo's— "vegetable pipple," he called them.

"This is my favorite painting," he said, in front of an immense canvas entitled *The Miracle of the Bees*. In the painting a crowd was gathered around a baby from whose mouth issued a swarm of bees, curling up toward the ceiling. At least a dozen times he said, "This is my favorite painting," and hurried from favorite to favorite, ignoring everything else.

Nothing could have been further from Jerry's Michelin approach, and it exhilarated Susanna to be hustled past the tourists with their guidebooks. Gabor was eager to show them an elegant stiletto hidden in a Renaissance crucifix. He said, "This was made to be used only once. God, I love the Italians!"

They took cabs from museum to museum, like barhopping, thought Susanna. They wound up near the Duomo, Gabor yelling at the cabdriver as they hunted for the Ambrosian Library. Finally Gabor jumped out and grabbed Maritsa's hand and pulled her inside a building and up a long stone staircase. Susanna skipped along after. "What's the hurry?" she said.

"Hurry is because we are approaching my favorite painting," Gabor said. "Not my favorite. MY FAVORITE. Many times I say favorite but this I mean is my favorite. Astonishing, no?"

It was astonishing, all right—Bramantino's *The Virgin Enthroned with Saints*—an unexceptional Mother and Child, the ordinary saints, but on the floor at Mary's feet were two gigantic figures lying on their backs, drawn in showy perspective so you looked from behind their heads to their feet. On the left was a corpse—was it Christ?—and on the right was a human-sized dead frog. The corpse was naked but the frog was dressed in knee breeches and a livery jacket.

Maritsa pointed to the frog and said something in Slovenian. "Frog," said Susanna, and Gabor said the Hungarian word for frog.

"This is your favorite painting?" said Susanna. "Your favorite favorite?"

Gabor shrugged. "I like this frog. Is funny. It gives me a feeling. In all Milan is nothing gives me such strong feeling. Except maybe that Piero, that egg hanging from a string. But I think not as much as this frog."

Really, the most astonishing thing was how wretched this made Susanna. So Gabor liked a picture with a peculiar frog—why should that make her think her whole life was a misunderstanding and she would have to disassemble it all to begin to straighten it out? She had married the wrong person, ended up in the wrong place. It wasn't as if she'd trade Jerry for a crazy Hungarian whose favorite painting was a Virgin enthroned with Christ and a frog. But Gabor reminded her of what she had forgotten. Somehow she had forgotten that for some people it's fine, it's enough if something's funny and gives you a feeling. She was so tired of everything having to teach you a lesson, preferably a lesson about the end of the world.

"Coffee at once!" said Gabor. "Doctor Gabor's orders! That way, too, is art like food—too much can make you sleepy."

Not far from the Ambrosian they found a bar and went in and stood at the railing. Gabor ordered three espressos and three rakis. "You know raki?" he said. "Is Turkish. Very good for too much museum." He tossed back his raki and chased it with the espresso. Maritsa coolly did the same, and Susanna had no choice.

"Stamp-collector bar," Gabor said. "Sundays, stamp collectors set up tables in the square for buying and trading, and when they finish they come here and drink grappa." In fact, the walls were decorated with murals of giant stamps, and maybe on Sundays it drew a philatelist crowd, but right now it looked like a gay bar. Young men stood in couples and in little groups. Feeling better than she had in the museum, Susanna held up her raki glass. "Works like magic," she told Gabor.

"I tell you!" said Gabor and ordered another round of raki and another espresso. "Doctor Gabor prescribes!"

Both bartenders were peasant women, straight off the farm or the vineyard, still in housedresses and aprons, unusual in this city where everyone dressed like sales people in boutiques. They were chatting with a customer, a woman the size of a ten-year-old, dark-skinned, probably gypsy. Two braids hung to her waist. She wore a faded floor-length skirt and a kid's long-sleeved striped polo shirt. A curly-haired child clung to her skirt. Susanna recalled an older child they'd passed playing in the doorway. The woman puffed angrily on her cigarette as she chattered to the barmaids in Italian.

She kept pacing and turning sharply with little disdainful shakes of her hip.

"I love the gypsies," Gabor said. "They are tough people, believe me. After we fail, Greenpeace, conferences, all this blah-blah, everything failed, poisoned, civilization bye-bye, the gypsies will still be here when all of us are *finito*."

"Not cauliflowers?" said Susanna.

"Please?" Gabor said.

"The raki is something," she said. Even Maritsa, she noticed, was starting to look a bit green.

"One more. And espresso," said Gabor. "Then we will have the right dose."

After that round Susanna knew it had been a drastic mistake. The world around her got painfully loud, then syrupy and slow. All at once she was aware of the gypsy woman watching her. She felt as if she were watching herself, and she thought distinctly: "I am having a hallucination."

The vision couldn't have lasted more than a few seconds, but in that time she saw the end of the world, empty canyons of buildings in a depopulated city, like some post-nuclear Holly-wood set, except that it was Milan, deserted but for the gypsy woman and her children, sashaying idly in and out of empty restaurants and shops, bored and petulant, neither happy nor sad that all this was now theirs. Susanna watched for a while and then it rushed away, and she felt herself rising over Milan, over Italy, then above the earth, not the familiar earth, pockmarked, green and blue. This was a new earth, a bald earth, shining in the black sky, white and brilliant and polished, like a Ping-Pong ball lit from within.

The next thing Susanna knew, she was in her hotel bed looking up at Jerry. For a moment she saw his face as an Archimboldo: cauli-flower skin, carrot nose, greenbean eyeglass frames. He said, "Raki and espresso. Dynamite combination."

"Gabor?" she said.

"He was abject," said Jerry. "I gather it was quite a scene, him carrying you cave-man style through the lobby." Jerry was smiling at her. His voice was nasal with false urgency, like a forties news-reel announcer.

"I think I'm sick," said Susanna. "I was hallucinating."

Jerry said, "Raki isn't Dr Pepper."

Susanna said, "Jerry, the weirdest thing. I had a vision, a hallucination. But before that there was a moment . . . it was like sometimes we'd be in cathedrals with those machines you plug a hundred lire in to light up the frescoes for a minute. Always, just before the minute was up, I'd see something in the paintings. But when the light went out I would lose it and forget what it was. Well, there was a gypsy woman in the café, and just before I felt so strange, I looked at her and thought, She looks exactly like me. We could be twins and she knows it. Of course it was ridiculous. We looked nothing alike."

Jerry stretched out beside her and gazed down into her face. How old he looks, she thought guiltily, how unhappy and exhausted. Everything showed in his face, everything they both knew now, that they could not go on together, their marriage would have to end and she would have to leave him to face the death of the planet without her. She knew that Jerry was seeing in her the heartlessness of the young: unlike him, she still had time to fix some part of the world, and if it was ending, she still had the strength to enjoy what was left. And who was Jerry, really, to make her feel guilty about it?

"You don't look anything like a gypsy," said Jerry. "You look like Tinker Bell."

Tears came to Susanna's eyes. "I know that," she said, not because it was true but to fill the silence in which she might otherwise have to face the fact that she had married a man to whom she looked like Tinker Bell. An unpleasant buzzing in her head reminded her of Gabor's painting. Was the miracle the appearance of the bees or the getting them out of the baby? She said, "It was just a feeling I had that something was telling me something."

"Telling you something?" said Jerry. "Please. Keep your feet on the ground."

✍

For the Literary Traveler

One way to see Milan is in the spirit of Francine Prose's character Gabor Szekaly, the Hungarian Greenpeace activist whose approach to painting recalls William Blake: the material of art, he said, is particularities. "To generalize is to be an idiot." After searching out Milan's magnificent art collections with Blake in mind, the abstractions of Susanna's husband Jerry feel like a prescription for many dark nights of the soul, or, as Susanna suspects, of kinky sex in the mode of St. Sebastian's agonies.

Milan's galleries offer readers of Prose's story a chance to see exactly what Gabor found thrilling. From PIAZZA DELLA SCALA with its double monuments (LA SCALA opera house, Maria Callas's cathedral, and the statue of Leonardo da Vinci, whose arrival in 1483 marked Milan's birth as a center of art and humanism), it's a short walk north along VIA VERDI to the BRERA GALLERY (or PINACOTECA DI BRERA—*pinacoteca* means picture gallery) where such masterpieces as Veronese's *Supper in the House of Simon,* Caravaggio's *Supper at Emmaus,* Mantegna's *Dead Christ,* Piero della Francesca's *Madonna and Child with Saints and Federico da Montefeltro* (Gabor's almost favorite painting), and Raphael's *The Betrothal of the Virgin* display the erotic undercurrents and imagery of Italian mysticism. The Brera itself is a great light-filled space, originally a monastery, then a palazzo, now a fine-arts academy and gallery.

A few blocks northeast of La Scala, on Via Manzoni, the MUSEO POLDI-PEZZOLI, another gracious space, the former mansion of Signor Poldi Pezzoli, with a marble fountain at the base of a wide spiraling staircase, displays such treasure as Paollaiolo's *Lady of the Bardi Family* (more popularly known as *Profile of a Young Lady*), works of Mantegna, Bellini, Botticelli, Piero della Francesca, the charming Dante room (Saletta di Dante), and Cranach's portraits of Luther and his wife Katherine von Bora. (For all that the Protestant reformation abolished clerical celibacy, there is nothing even slightly playful in the faces of the reform's First Couple; rather, they recall Prose's pessimistic Jerry, sulking alone in the hotel.)

The PINACOTECA AMBROSIANA, where Gabor exults over the detail of the frog and the work of Bramantino, is undergoing, in 1996, extensive restorations. Gabor's adored Arcimboldi, along with other masters of the Northern Italian school, can be found in the Pinacoteca of CASTELLO SFORZESCO. (PARCO SEMPIONE, behind the Castello, with modern sculpture by De Chirico, seems a more likely hangout for the likes of Szekaly and Susanna than a hotel full of conventioneers.)

The nightscape of PIAZZA DEL DUOMO, the pulsing center of Milan, feels like an orchestrated celebration of sensory detail—the high frothing white fountains, the beat of drums and reggae backing up the crowd's noise and flirting, the glow of the gilded copper MADONNINA atop a cathedral spire that seems to touch the dark blue sky. Travelers true to the aesthetic of Gabor Szekaly—it's the details that arouse passion—will stop to look at the mosaic floor beneath the colossal glass-roofed GALLERIA VITTORIO EMANUELE, on the north side of the Piazza.

THE VENETO

VENICE

Mary Shelley

Mary Shelley (1797–1851) loved Italy. She would have been content to stay there forever when she returned with her son in the 1840s for the first time since the death of her husband, the poet Percy Bysshe Shelley, in a boating accident off the coast of Liguria in 1821. "The name of Italy has magic in its very syllables," she wrote in the preface to her book of travel writings Rambles in Germany and Italy *(1844). As a young woman she'd lived and traveled in Italy with Shelley. Now, after years of widowhood as a single mother, always needing money, often deeply depressed, she came back. The record she kept of their tour shows, in the words of her biographer Muriel Spark, "that she had lost none of her keen powers of observation and her receptivity to new experiences. She was happier, now, than she had been for many years, and this is apparent from the* Rambles *which have an 'intimate manner' and a 'frank autobiographical style,' combining 'descriptions of landscape,' people and works of art with practical information and advice." The daughter of feminist writer Mary Wollstonecraft and philosopher William Godwin, the wife of Shelley, the mother of four children only one of whom survived, the author of* Frankenstein *(1818) and many other novels (including* Valperga *[1823] a novel of medieval Italy, which Spark compares to George Eliot's* Romola—*see page 112), Mary Wollstonecraft Shelley sees Venice—"La Serenissima"—in tones of light and darkness that reflect her own complex life history.*

FROM *RAMBLES IN GERMANY AND ITALY*

LETTERS FROM VENICE

Can it, indeed, be true, that I am about to revisit Italy? How many years are gone since I quitted that country! There I left the mortal remains of those beloved—my husband and my children, whose loss changed my whole existence, substituting, for

happy peace and the interchange of deep-rooted affections, years
of desolate solitude, and a hard struggle with the world; which only
now, as my son is growing up, is brightening into a better day. The
name of Italy has magic in its very syllables. The hope of seeing it
again recalls vividly to my memory that time, when misfortune
seemed an empty word, and my habitation on earth a secure abode,
which no evil could shake. Graves have opened in my path since
then; and, instead of the cheerful voices of the living, I have dwelt
among the early tombs of those I loved. Now a new generation has
sprung up; and, at the name of Italy, I grow young again in their
enjoyments, and gladly prepare to share them.

LETTER VII.

The Ducal Palace.—The Accademia delle Belle Arti.

VENICE, SEPTEMBER

I miss greatly the view of the Canale Grande from my window;
however, the result, probably, of our being in a narrow canal will
be, that I shall see much more of Venice: for were we among its
most noble palaces, it would suffice and amply fill the hours,
merely to loiter away the day gazing on the scene before us. As it is,
though singularly Venetian—the wave-paved streets beneath, the
bridge close at hand—the peep we get at wider waters at the
opening,—it is but a promise of what we may find beyond, and
tempts us to wander.

There is something so different in Venice from any other place
in the world, that you leave at once all accustomed habits and
everyday sights to enter enchanted ground. We live in a palace;
though an inn, such it is: and other palaces have been robbed of
delicately-carved mouldings and elegant marbles, to decorate the
staircase and doorways. You know the composition with which
they floor the rooms here, resembling marble, and called everywhere in Italy Terrazi Veneziani: this polished uniform surface
whose colouring is agreeable to the eye, gives an air of elegance to
the rooms; then, when we go out, we descend a marble staircase to
a circular hall of splendid dimensions; and at the steps, laved by the
sea, the most luxurious carriage—a boat, invented by the goddess

of ease and mystery, receives us. Our gondolier, never mind his worn-out jacket and ragged locks, has the gentleness and courtesy of an attendant spirit, and his very dialect is a shred of romance; or, if you like it better, of classic history: bringing home to us the language and accents, they tell us, of old Rome. For Venice

> Has floated down, amid a thousand wrecks
> Uninjured, from the Old World to the New.*

With the world of Venice before us, whither shall we go? I would not make my letter a catalogue of sights; yet I must speak of the objects that occupy and delight me.

First, then, to the Ducal palace. A few strokes of the oar took us to the noble quay, from whose pavement rises the Lion-crowned column, and the tower of St. Mark. The piazzetta is, as it were, the vestibule to the larger piazza.

But I spare description of a spot, of which there are so many thousand—besides numerous pictures by Cannaletti and his imitators, which tell all that can be told—show all that can be shown: to know Venice, to feel the influence of its beauty and strangeness, is quite another thing; perhaps the vignettes to Mr. Rogers's Italy, by Turner, better than any other description or representation, can impart this.

From the piazzetta we entered a grass-grown court, once the focus of Venetian magnificence—for, at the top of that majestic flight of steps which rises from it, the Doges were crowned. The *cortile* is surrounded by arcades, decorated by two magnificent bronze reservoirs, and adorned by statues. The effect is light and elegant, even now that neglect has drawn a veil over its splendour. Yet Nature here is not neglectful; her ministrations may be said even to aid the work of the chisel and the brush, so beautiful are they in their effects.

The Scala de' Giganti was before us, guarded by two almost colossal figures of Mars and Neptune, the size of whose statues gives the name to the steps: ascending them, we found ourselves

[*Rogers's "Italy."—Au.]

in the open gallery that runs round three sides of the court, supported by the arcades. Yawning before us was the fatal lion's mouth, receiver of those anonymous accusations, the terror of all, and destroyer of many of the citizens. Ringing a bell, we were admitted into the palace.

We do not visit it once only; day after day we wander about these magnificent, empty halls—sometimes going in by the hall of audience, sometimes ascending the Scala d'Oro, we enter in by the library. Sometimes we give ourselves up to minute view of the many frescoes, which record the history, the glories, and even the legends of Venice. At the dawn of the art, the more than royal government caused the walls to be thus adorned by Gentile and Giovanni Bellini, and subsequently by Titian: a fire unfortunately destroyed their work in 1577; and the present paintings are by Tintoretto, Paul Veronese, and others. On an easel in the library, is a picture in oil by Paul Veronese,—the Queen of Cyprus, Catherine Cornaro, a daughter of Venice, resigning her crown to the Doge—an iniquitous act enough on the part of the republic; as others, heirs of Cyprus, with claims more legitimate than Catherine's, existed. There is the grace and dignity, characteristic of this painter, in the various personages of the group. It is to be raffled for, and the proceeds of the lottery are to be given to the infant schools; but the tickets are sold slowly, and the time when they are to be drawn is yet unfixed. There are marbles also, in this room, that deserve attention,—some among them are relics of antiquity; for the Rape of Ganymede is attributed to Phidias, and worthy of him. Sometimes we wander about, content only with the recollections called up by the spot; and we step out on the balconies which now command a view of the piazzetta, now of the inner courts, with a liberty and leisure quite delightful: and then again we pass on, from the more public rooms to the chambers, sacred to a tyranny the most awful, the most silent of which there is record in the world. The mystery and terror that once reigned, seems still to linger on the walls; the chamber of the Council of Ten, paved with black and white marble, is peculiarly impressive in its aspect and decorations: near at hand was the chamber of torture, and a door led to a dark staircase and the state dungeons.

The man who showed us the prisons was a character—he wanted

at once to prove that they were not so cruel as they were represented, and yet he was proud of the sombre region over whose now stingless horrors he reigned. A narrow corridor, with small double-grated windows that barely admit light, but which the sound of the plashing waters beneath penetrates, encloses a series of dungeons, whose only respiratories come from this corridor, and in which the glimmering dubious day dies away in "darkness visible." Here the prisoners were confined who had still to be examined by the Council. A door leads to the Ponte de' Sospiri—now walled up—for the prisons on the other side are in full use for criminals: years ago I had traversed the narrow arch, through the open work of whose stone covering the prisoners caught one last hasty glimpse of the wide lagunes, crowded with busy life. Many, however, never passed that bridge—never emerged again to light. One of the doors in the corridor I have mentioned leads to a dark cell, in which is a small door that opens on narrow winding stairs; below is the lagune; here the prisoners were embarked on board the gondola, which took them to the Canal Orfano, the drowning-place, where, summer or winter, it was forbidden to the fishermen, on pain of death, to cast their nets. Our guide, whom one might easily have mistaken for a gaoler, so did he enter into the spirit of the place, and take pleasure in pointing out the various power it once possessed of inspiring despair; this guide insisted that the Pozzi and Piombi were fictions, and that these were the only prisons. Of course, this ignorant assertion has no foundation whatever in truth. From the court, as we left the palace, he pointed to a large window at the top of the building, giving token that the room within was airy and lightsome, and said with an air of triumph, *Ecco la Prigione di Silvio Pellico!*—Was he to be pitied when he was promoted to such a very enviable apartment, with such a very fine view? Turn to the pages of Pellico, and you will find that, complaining of the cold of his first dark cell, he was at midsummer transferred to this airy height, where multitudinous gnats and dazzling unmitigated sunshine nearly drove him mad. Truly he might regret even these annoyances when immured in the dungeons of Spielburg, and placed under the immediate and *paternal* care of the Emperor—whose endeavour was to break the spirit of his *rebel children* by destroying the flesh; whose sedulous study how to discover means to torment and attenuate—to blight with disease and subdue to despair—puts to shame the fly-killing pastime of Dioclesian. Thanks to the noble hearts of the men who were his victims, he did not succeed. Silvio Pellico bowed with resignation to the will of God—but he still kept his foot upon the power of the tyrant. . . .

At other times, turning to the right, when we leave our canal, we are rowed up the Canale Grande to the Accademia delle Belle Arti, to feast our eyes on the finest works of Titian. The picture usually considered the *chef-d'oeuvre* of this artist, the *Martyrdom of St. Peter the Hermit,* has, for the purpose of being copied, been removed from the dark niche in which it is almost lost in the church of the Saints Giovanni and Paolo, and is here. The subject is painful, but conceived with great power. A deep forest, in which the holy man is overtaken by his pursuers, sheds its gloom over the picture; his attendant flies, the most living horror depicted on his face; the saint has fallen, cut down by the sword of the soldier; an angel is descending from above, and, opening heaven, sheds the only light that irradiates the scene. It is very fine; but in spite of the celestial messenger, there is wanting that connecting link with Heaven,—the rapture of faith in the sufferer's countenance, which alone makes pictures of martyrdom tolerable.

I was struck by the last picture painted by the venerable artist— Mary visiting the Tomb of Jesus. I was told that I ought not to admire it; yet I could not help doing so: there was something impressive in the mingled awe and terror in Mary's face, when she found the body of Jesus gone.

The Marriage at Cana, by Paul Veronese, adorns these walls, removed from the refectory of the suppressed Convent of San Giorgio Maggiore. It is the finest specimen of the feasts which this artist delighted to paint; bringing together, on a large scale, groups of high-born personages, accompanied by attendants, and sur-rounded by a prodigality of objects of architecture, dress, orna-ments, and all the apparatus of Patrician luxury. It is filled, Lanzi tells us, with portraits of princes and illustrious men then living.

We turned from the splendour of the feast to the more noble beauty of Titian's *Presentation of the Virgin*—a picture I look at

much oftener, and with far greater pleasure, than at the more celebrated Martyrdom. The Virgin, in her simplicity and youth; in the
mingled dignity and meekness of her mien, as she is about to ascend
the steps towards the High Priest, is quite lovely; the group of
women looking at her, are inimitably graceful: there is an old woman
sitting at the foot of the steps, marvellous from the vivacity and truth
of her look and attitude. In another large apartment is the *Assumption* of Titian.* The upper part is indeed glorious. The Virgin is rapt
in a paradisiacal ecstacy as she ascends, surrounded by a galaxy of
radiant beings, whose faces are beaming with love and joy, to live
among whom were in itself Elysium. Such a picture, and the "Paradiso" of Dante as a commentary, is the sublimest achievement of
Catholicism. Not, indeed, as a commentary did Dante write, but as
the originator of much we see. The Italian painters drank deep at the
inspiration of his verses when they sought to give a visible image of
Heaven and the beatitude of the saints, on their canvas. . . .

LETTER VIII.

VENICE, SEPTEMBER

Exactly opposite our canal, at the entrance from the Quay to the
Canale Grande, is the church of San Giorgio Maggiore; it is built
chiefly from a model of Palladio, and is the noblest in Venice. Our
gondola landed us at the spacious marble platform before the
church. Its situation is most happy. Looked at from the Piazzetta, it
is the most stately ornament of Venice. Looking from it, a view is
commanded of the towers, and domes, and palaces, that illustrate
the opposite shore. The church is immense, and adorned by several
pictures of Titian. A convent adjoined, now destroyed; but as we
rambled about, we found that they had kindly retained, and left
open for the visits of strangers, the celebrated cloister, surrounded
by an elegant colonnade of Ionic pillars, and the staircase, which is
one of the boasts of Venice.

Somewhat above, within the Canale Grande, is the church of
Santa Maria della Salute; this was built in 1631, a time when architecture had degenerated, and a multiplicity of ornaments was preferred

*Now in the *Frari.*

to that simple harmonious style, whose perfection has to my eye the effect of one of Handel's airs on the ear—filling it with a sense of exalted pleasure. Here was beauty, but it existed even in spite of the defects of the building; it sprang from its situation, its steps laved by the sea, its marble walls reflecting the prismatic colour of the waves, its commanding a view of great architectural beauty; within also it contains pictures of eminent merit. . . .

I cannot tell you of all we see, or it would take you as long to read my letter as we shall be at Venice. As we remain a month, we do not crowd our day with sights; our gondoliers come in the morning, and we pass our time variously. Sometimes, after visiting a single church, we are rowed over to Lido; and, crossing a narrow strip of sand, scattered with Hebrew tombstones, find ourselves on the borders of the ocean; we look out over the sea on vessels bound to the East, or watch the fishingboats return with a favourable wind, and glide, one after the other, into port, their graceful lateen sails filled by the breeze. We thus loiter hours away, especially on cold days, when we have been chilled at home; but Lido has a heat of its own—its sands receiving and retaining the sun's rays—which we do not enjoy among the marbles and pavements of Venice.

As the sun sinks behind the Euganean hills, we recross the lagune. Every Monday of this month is a holiday for the Venetian shopkeepers and common people; they repair in a multitude of gondolas to Lido, to refresh themselves at the little inn—to meet in holiday trim, and make merry on the seasands. We pass them in crowds as we return on that day. Our way is, sometimes (according as the tide serves,) under the walls of the madhouse, celebrated in Shelley's poem of Julian and Maddalo—

A windowless, deformed, and dreary pile.

Yet not quite windowless; for there are grated, unglazed apertures—against which the madmen cling—and gaze sullenly, or shout, or laugh, or sing, as their wild mood dictates.

We often allow our gondolier to take us where he will; and we see a church, and we say, what is that? and make him seek the sacristan, and get out to look at something strange and unexpected. . . .

Each day we grow more familiar with this delightful city—favourite of Amphitrite and the Nereids; the little roots, generated by sympathy and enjoyment, begin to strike out, and I shall feel the violence of transplanting when forced to go. I look wistfully on some of the palaces, thinking that here I might find a pleasant, peaceful home; nor is the idea, though impracticable for me, wholly visionary. Several of the palaces, bereft of their old possessors, are used for public offices, or are let at a low rent. It is easy to obtain a house, whose marble staircase, lofty halls, and elegant architecture, surpass anything to be found in France or England. Several English gentlemen have taken apartments, and fitted them up with old furniture, and find themselves, at slight cost, surrounded by Venetian grandeur. No one can spend much money in Venice:—a gondola is a very inexpensive carriage; hiring one, as we do, costs four swanzikers a day—about four pounds a month, with a *buona mano* of half a swanziker a day to the gondolier, on going away. . . .

The *gondolieri* often sing at their oars; nor are the verses of Tasso quite forgotten. One delicious calm moonlight evening, as we were walking on the Piazzetta, an old *gondoliere* challenged a younger one to alternate with him the stanzas of the "Gerusalemme." I have often wished to hear them. It was a double pleasure that I did not do so by command, but in the true old Venetian way, two challenging each other voluntarily, and taking up alternate stanzas, till one can remember no more, and the other comes off conqueror. We are told that the air to which they sing is monotonous: so it is; yet well adapted to recitation. The antagonists stood on the Piazzetta, at the verge of the laguna, surrounded by other *gondolieri*—the whole scene lighted up by the moon. They chanted the favourite passage, the death of Clorinda. I could only follow the general sense, as they recite in Venetian; but the subject of the verse, high and heroic, the associations called up—the beauty of the spot—a sort of dignity in the gestures of the elder boatman, and nothing harsh, though it might be monotonous, in their chaunt—the whole thing gave me inexpressible pleasure—it was a Venetian scene, dressed in its best; and the imagination was wrapped in perfect enjoyment.

The weeks pass away, and we are soon, I am sorry to say, about to leave Venice. We have taken our sight-seeing quietly, and each

day has had a novel pleasure. It is one of our amusements to visit
the piazza of San Marco at two in the afternoon, when, on the
striking of the hour on the great clock, the pigeons come down to
be fed. These birds are sacred to Saint Mark, and it is penal to kill
any. They lead a happy life, petted by all the citizens. Now and
then they may be served up at the dinner of a poor man; but they
are too many not to spare, without grudging, an individual or two
for the good of their maintainers. . . .

For the Literary Traveler

Wandering along the canals of Venice and back and forth across
bridges and campos quickens the mystery; there is a desire to get
lost. The pleasure of the place is the maze itself, not to be figured
out. Mary Shelley tells visitors to wander and "loiter." She is also partial to moving around by gondola. The vaporetto (water bus) is
another easy and practical method, younger than her Rambles in Germany and Italy (1844).

Her visits to the specific architectural gems of Venice—Henry
James described his visits here as "a perpetual love affair"—show her
originality as well as the autobiographical nuances of travel writing. In
the DUCAL PALACE (or the DOGE'S PALACE or the Palazzo Ducale), the
residence of the Doge and the center of the government that adjoins
the BASILICA OF SAN MARCO, she notes the magnificence of its decoration; its sculpture; the Scala d'Oro (the GOLDEN STAIRCASE); and the art
by the great Venetian painters Tintoretto, Titian, Veronese. On the
entrance wall to the enormous GRAND COUNCIL CHAMBER (Sala del
Maggior Consiglio) on the second floor—seating two thousand council
members—is Tintoretto's Vision of Paradise, inspired by Dante's Paradiso, Canto XXX—and the largest oil painting in the world. But Mary
Shelley gives her sharpest attention to the palace's sinister history as a
setting of the Inquisition and political oppression. She mentions the
dark cells where political prisoners were held, were tortured, and
died. (Shelley, too, had been obsessed with these dungeons, where

prisoners were "roasted to death or madness by the ardours of an Italian sun" or held "half up to their middles in stinking water.") Prisoners were taken from their cells along narrow passageways and then over the BRIDGE OF SIGHS (the Ponte dei Sospiri) to be interrogated in the Council Chamber of the Council of Ten (*La Serenissima*'s Secret Police). On the third floor of the Doge's Palace there is a staircase leading up from the Council of Ten's courtroom (Saletta dei Tre Inquisitori) to the torture room that is connected by a passage to the Bridge of Sighs. The name of the bridge comes from the sounds of grief the prisoners made as they returned to their cells and sentences.

As Muriel Spark's biography recounts, Mary Shelley knew first-hand the oppression and condemnation of men of power. As a widow with a child to support, she had long been the victim of her father-in-law's disapproval and stinginess; from him she received a life sentence of anxiety about money and security. Her references to the dark cells beneath the splendid Ducal Palace call to mind the circumstances that depressed her spirits and her potential as a writer. With neither money nor powerful friends to help her and as the object of the resentments and jealousy of several literary men, for more than half her life she was helpless to extricate herself from an abject financial dependence. She lived, in effect, as Sir Timothy Shelley's political prisoner.

Another reminder of the issue of powerlessness may have been the sorrow she would have remembered from her first visit to Venice in 1818. Though both Mary and her one-year-old daughter, Clara, had been ill and unfit to travel, her husband had insisted that they (and three-year-old William) join him in Venice. Two weeks after they arrived, the baby died. Mary was disconsolate, sunk in "a kind of despair," in Shelley's words. To distract her, Byron gave her some of his manuscripts to transcribe.

In her travel writings, Mary Shelley's voice has an independent ring. And her eye for the unusual detail—the evidence of both human callousness and ingenuity—belongs to the novelist who produced the masterpiece *Frankenstein* at the age of twenty. In the course of her visit to the ACCADEMIA DELLE BELLE ARTI—on the Grand Canal at the foot of the Accademia bridge in the DORSODURO section—she admires the superb collection of Venetian paintings, which includes

works of Bellini, Titian, Veronese, Tintoretto, Tiepolo, Canaletto, Giorgione, and Carpaccio's *The Dream of St. Ursula.* But, contrary to her
guide's orthodoxy, she expresses specific admiration for Titian's *Mary
Magdalene at the Tomb of Jesus:* "I was told I ought not to admire it;
yet I could not help doing so." And she tells why. On an excursion to
the LIDO, a strip of land dividing the Lagoon from the Adriatic (and the
setting of Thomas Mann's *Death in Venice*), she observes the "madhouse" Shelley had written about in his Venetian poem, "Julian and
Maddalo," and the imprisoned "madmen" gazing through the gratings
on the windows. Municipal institutions on the lagoon islands today are
the isolation hospital, the old people's home, a consumptive sanato-
rium, and Shelley's "madhouse" (renamed the lunatic asylum). On the
island of TORCELLO, Barbara Grizzuti Harrison spent a happy Easter
Sunday, beautifully described in *Italian Days*; Muriel Spark loved its
seventh-century CATHEDRAL, in particular the apse mosaic of the Madonna, considered one of the finest works of Byzantine art, "hypnotically radiant" in her words.

More than any prescribed route, Mary Shelley takes delight in the
random and spontaneous exploration of Venice. Though she had the
luxury of a month's visit, the traveler with less time can find many of
the places she admires. Especially lovely is the church of SANTA MARIA
DELLA SALUTE in DORSODURO, at the entrance to Venice, its white Istrian
marble dome dominating the view of the Grand Canal from the
lagoon ("Here was beauty.... it sprang from its situation, its steps
laved by the sea... commanding a view of great architectural beauty").
Salute was designed to honor the Madonna in her role as protector of
health and salvation after the plague of 1630. The interior has a Byzantine Madonna over the altar and Tintoretto's *Marriage Feast at Cana* in
the Sacristy.

In her lifetime, Mary Shelley's enemies accused her of snobbery. But
in Venice she sounds content with the common ground and ordinary
pleasures. The singing of the gondoliers, for instance, charms her, a
taste shared by many tourists according to Christopher Hibbert's
Venice: A Biography of a City: "Printed collections of [the gondoliers'
songs] were taken home by tourists and formed part of the library of
every musical collector of taste in Europe. Almost everyone sang, and
sang melodiously, expressing, so Goethe said, lament without melan-

choly. A lone voice far away across a canal in the dark would elicit a response, then another voice would join in, then others, until the night air rang in harmony." Mary Shelley's delight in the Venetians' infatuation with music contrasts sharply with George Eliot's reaction twenty years later. She found the singing under her window in the HOTEL DE L'EUROPE (on the Grand Canal, with full view of the Salute) "coarse," "much out of tune," "disgraceful to Venice and Italy." But she was suffering through a disastrous honeymoon, which is another story. In a better mood she remembered an "enchanting city where the glorious light . . . makes a Paradise much more desirable than that painted by Tintoretto." (Tintoretto, by the way, like many other painters of his time, was an accomplished musician.)

There is still music to be heard in public places. Bands (jazz, classical, schmaltz) play in the PIAZZA SAN MARCO; the bells toll in the CAMPANILE OF SAN MARCO (its elevator gives access to wonderful views of the lagoon and the city); and concerts are held weekly in the larger churches such as SAN MARCO and the FRARI. Vivaldi's music is performed in the CHURCH OF THE PIETÀ, where he was concert master (see page 55). A Vivaldi Festival is held there in September. And along the canals in the SAN POLO neighborhood of the CAMPO DI SANTA MARGHERITA and the CA' REZZONICO, the sound of music students practicing in the conservatory fills the autumn air in early afternoon.

Though she always said Rome was her favorite city, Mary Shelley, as a lover of the intensity and variety of life's colors, would have loved today's Venice. The crowds of tourists would not disgust her. Mary McCarthy, who came a century later, wrote in her classic study *Venice Observed*, "There is no use in pretending that the tourist Venice is not the real Venice." Both women, though tempered by loss, never lost their nerve or their taste for things as they are.

Jan Morris

Internationally praised as a brilliant travel writer, Jan Morris's range shows in the variety of places she has written about—Spain, New York, the Middle East, England, South Africa, and her home territory of Wales. Combining her passions for history, autobiography, and travel, she transforms travel writing into cultural studies of a rich and seductive texture. The World of Venice, *represented in the following pages by the chapter "On Women," is an original portrait that focuses with an astringent affection on "the loveliest city in the world." Morris supports her perspective with testimonials from many other writers and artists, among them the superlatives of Elizabeth Barrett Browning: "Nothing is like it, nothing equal to it, not a second Venice in the world." In a new introduction (the book was first published in 1960 in the persona of James Morris), Jan Morris defines* The World of Venice *as "a picture less of a city than of an experience," "highly subjective, romantic, impressionist."*

FROM *THE WORLD OF VENICE*

ON WOMEN

The women of Venice are very handsome, and very vain. They are tall, they walk beautifully, and they are often fair (in the sixteenth century Venetian ladies used to bleach their hair in the sunshine, training it through crownless hats like vines through a trellis). Their eyes are sometimes a heavy-lidded greenish-blue, like the eyes of rather despondent armadillos. Rare indeed is a dishevelled Venetian woman, and even the Madonnas and female saints of the old masters are usually elegantly dressed. The most slovenly people to be seen in the city are nearly always tourists—cranks and water-colour artists apart.

The Venetians are not, by and large, rich: but they have always spent a large proportion of their money on clothes and ornaments, and you will hardly ever see a girl dressed for pottering, in a sloppy sweater and a patched skirt, or in that unpressed dishabille that marks the utter emancipation of the Englishwoman. The girls at the University, who are either studying languages, or learning about Economics and Industrial Practices, look more like models than academics: and the housemaids, when they walk off in scented couples for their weekend pleasures, would hardly seem out of place at Ascot, or at a gala convention of the Women Lawyers' Association.

This love of dress is deep-rooted in the Venetian nature. The men are very dapper, too, and until quite recently used to cool themselves with little fans and parasols in the Public Gardens— "curious," as Augustus Hare observed austerely in 1896, "to English eyes." As early as 1299 the Republic introduced laws restricting ostentation, and later the famous sumptuary laws were decreed, strictly governing what people might wear, with a special magistracy to enforce them. They were never a success. When the Patriarch of Venice forbade the use of "excessive ornaments," a group of women appealed directly to the Pope, who promptly restored them their jewellery. When the Republic prohibited long gowns, the Venetian women caught up their trains in intricate and delicious folds, fastened with sumptuous clasps. When it was announced that only a single row of pearls might be worn, with a maximum value of 200 ducats, the evasions of the law were so universal, so ingenious and so brazen that the magistracy gave up, and turned its disapproving eyes elsewhere. In the eighteenth century Venetian women were the most richly dressed in Europe, and it took an Englishwoman, Lady Mary Wortley Montagu, to observe that since everybody wore masks at the opera anyway, there was consequently "no trouble in dressing."

Among the patrician ladies of old Venice, as among the women of Arabian harems, there was nothing much to think about but clothes and babies. Venetian *mores* were bred out of Byzantium, and respectable women were closely guarded and carefully circumscribed. Clamped in their houses out of harm's way, they were little more than tools or playthings, western odalisques: even the Doge's wife had no official position. No item of dress was more popular

among Venetian aristocrats than the absurd towering clogs, sometimes twenty inches high, which obliged their wives to totter about
with the help of two servants (and which, since they made great
height socially desirable, have perhaps left a legacy in the unshake-
able determination of modern Venetian women to wear the highest
possible heels in all circumstances).

Only two women have played parts of any prominence in
Venetian history. The first was Caterina Cornaro, who married the
King of Cyprus in 1472 and was officially adopted as a "daughter
of the Republic" in order to ensure Venetian control of the island:
her husband died a year after their marriage, the Venetians took
over, and poor Caterina languished away in gilded exile at Asolo,
signing herself to the last as "Queen of Cyprus, Jerusalem and
Armenia, Lady of Asolo." The second was Bianca Cappello,
daughter of a noble house, who ran away with a Florentine clerk in
1564: she was condemned to death *in absentia,* such was the dis-
grace of it all, but presently rose in the world to become Grand
Duchess of Tuscany, and was promptly re-clasped to the Venetian
bosom as another "daughter of the Republic." She died of poisoning in 1587, but the Republic did not go into mourning, just in
case it was the Grand Duke who had poisoned her.

It was only in the eighteenth century that the upper-class
Venetian woman came into her own, and even now a cloistered
feeling of anachronism often surrounds her. Sometimes a beautiful
young blonde is to be seen in Venice, gracefully rowing her own
boat: but the gondoliers do not even consider the possibility that she
might be Venetian, and airily point her out as English, American or
German, according to the nationality of their passengers. With her
maids, her always exquisite clothes, her waiting gondolier, and the
almost insuperable difficulty she has in getting out of one cushioned
gondola and into another, the Venetian lady is scarcely the kind to
go messing about in boats. She is often rich and often influential
("the flat downstairs," I was once told by a house agent, "is occupied
by a lady, with her husband"): but there are few professional women
in the city, and one sometimes pines, in an ambience so perfumed
and cosseted, for a hard-boiled New York career girl, with her
heart—or part of it, anyway—deep in the propagation of soap flakes.

Other classes of Venetian women were not so sheltered under the Republic. Burghers' wives and daughters were always freer and often better educated. Poor women lived a life of rugged equality, and Venetian working women today are often jolly gregarious characters, like figures from a Goldoni comedy, throwing hilarious ribaldries across the post-office counter, or sitting plumply at their knitting on the quaysides. Courtesans, in sixteenth-century Venice, were not only celebrated and honoured, but often people of cultivation, with a taste for art and poetry (though the law at one time decreed that each such girl must carry a red light at the prow of her gondola). In earlier centuries there was a celebrated brothel, the Casteletto, at the end of the Rialto bridge, famous throughout Europe for the beauty and skill of its girls. Later, when Venice was beginning her decline, the prostitutes became courtesans, increased in wealth and respectability, burst the confines of the bordels, and gave the city its lasting reputation for lascivious charm. At the end of the sixteenth century there are said to have been 2,889 patrician ladies in Venice, and 2,508 nuns, and 1,936 burgher women: but there were 11,654 courtesans, of whom 210 were carefully registered in a catalogue by a public-spirited citizen of the day, together with their addresses and prices—or, as the compiler delicately put it, "the amount of money to be paid by noblemen and others desirous of entering their good graces." The cheapest charged one *scudo,* the most expensive thirty, and the catalogue reckons that the enjoyment of them all would cost the intemperate visitor 1,200 gold *scudi.*

A scholarly Venetian once remarked that his city had fostered three bad practices hitherto unknown in Italy—adulation, Lutheranism and debauchery: but he did not sound altogether censorious. Venice in her heyday, despite a streak of salty puritanism in her character, was tolerant about sex. A favourite subject of the Venetian masters, it has been observed, was Christ Defending the Woman Taken in Adultery, and even the established church was fairly easygoing with libertines: it was only with reluctance and after long delay that the administration of the Basilica, in the seventeenth century, closed the chapel of San Clemente because of the scandalous things that were known to go on behind the altar. Gay young nuns were seen on visiting days in habits distinctly *décolletés,* and with clusters of pearls in their virginal hair. In the wildest days of carnival even the Papal Nuncio used to wear a domino. Family chaplains looked benignly upon the Venetian institution of the *cicisbeo,* the handsome young man who, in the dying years of the Republic, used to stand in constant attendance upon each great lady of Venice, even sometimes helping her maids to dress her. "The only honest woman in Venice," a wry husband remarked to a friend one day, "is that one there"—and he pointed to a little stone figure carved on a wall above a bridge: Venice took his point, and to this day the bridge, near the Frari church, is called The Bridge of the Honest Woman.

Today all is changed. Except at the more sophisticated levels of hotel society, sin is hard to come by in modern Venice. Brothels— "houses of toleration"—are no longer permitted by Italian law, and the police deal severely with harlots. When some modest bordel is uncovered, the newspapers make a great fuss about it—"an operation brilliant, delicate and complete," glowed the *Gazzettino* when the police recently pounced upon a backstairs stews in Dorsoduro. One distinguished foreign diplomat, it is true, discovered not long ago that his cook had been running a small but profitable brothel on the third floor of his consulate; but there is no red-light district in Venice. The sailors who wander through the city from their ships often look uncharacteristically lost and ill at ease, and you sometimes overhear disgruntled American business men trying to obtain guidance from reticent barmen ("My score so far is precisely zero, and I don't like it that way, see? *Comprenez, amico?* Hey?").

Venice nowadays is a regenerate city, free of public vice and aberrations, where a politic eye is still winked at the idiosyncrasies of foreigners, but where men are generally men, and women usually marry. The convent of the Penitents, reserved for remorseful harlots, has long since closed its doors—it stands on the Cannaregio, nearly opposite the slaughter-house, and offered a five-year reform course for its inmates. So has the home for fallen women, near San Sebastiano, that was founded by the most famous and cultured of all the courtesans, the prostitute-poetess Veronica Franco. This is not one of your smoky, hole-in-corner, juke-box cities, and here the Italo-American culture, that garish cross-breed, is kept at bay by water and tradition. A notice appeared on the walls of the city one recent summer day, sponsored by the Society for the Protection of Youth in Venice, begging citizens and visitors to wear garments "in accordance with the propriety of our city, which, being proud of its traditional standard of high morality, cannot approve of scanty or unbecoming clothes." I thought of the whoopee days of carnival as I read this sober appeal, of the masked Nuncio and the simpering *cicisbei,* the harlots and the hedonists, and *"O Tempora,"* I breathed as I hitched my trousers up, *"O Mores!"*

Family life flourishes in Venice. The birthrate is high, families are large and patriarchal. If you take a steamer to the station at about seven o'clock any evening, you may chance to see a touching sight at the Rialto stop. A workman catches this boat each night on his way home, keeping the seat beside him vacant: and every evening, when the steamer stops at the Rialto, his wife, who works nearby, hurries on board to join him. They have evidently been doing it for years, for she knows exactly where to find him, walks to her seat with calm and smiling certainty, and sits down beside him, instantly taking his hand in hers, without finding it necessary to say a word. They might be benign stone figures from a column of the Doge's Palace, representing Bliss.

But for all its reformation, Venice remains a sexy city still, as many a ravished alien has discovered. It is a city of seduction. There is sex and susceptibility in the very air of the place, in the mellow sunshine stones of its pavements, the shadows of its courtyards, the discretion of its silent black gondolas (which sometimes, as Byron remarked, "contain a deal of fun, like mourning coaches when the funeral's done"). In the summer evenings symmetrical pairs of lovers, neatly balanced, occupy each water-side seat of the Public Gardens: and the steps that lead down to the Grand Canal from the Courtyard of the Duke Sforza, almost opposite my window, are worn with moonlight ecstasies.

For the Literary Traveler

Seeing Venice in person is, of course, the best way to sift Jan Morris's impressions of Venetian women. But since her perspective is historical as well as experiential, the reader/traveler might also want to consider Venetian women from the angle of cultural history.

On the subject of the celebrated sixteenth-century courtesans, American scholar, Lynne Lawner, has studied Renaissance women writers, including two poets—Gaspara Stampa and Veronica Franco—thought to have been courtesans. Her book, *Lives of the Courtesans: Portraits of the Renaissance* (1987), weaves together letters and poems by courtesans and their patrons, and art works depicting them. As a Fulbright scholar living in Venice, Lawner found the neighborhood of the courtesans (that Morris refers to in "On Women") in the SAN POLO section at and around the PONTE DELLE TETTE—the "Bridge of the Teats." According to Lawner, some courtesans lived and worked at both the center and the edges of society. In the course of her research, she found a set of 400-year-old prints and accompanying bawdy sonnets (by Pietro Aretino) which she edited, translated, and published under the title, *I Modi* ("The Postures"): *The Sixteen Pleasures: An Erotic Album of the Italian Renaissance.*

Renaissance girls and women also provided Venice with its musical entertainment. The orchestras and choruses of the OSPEDALI GRANDI, the female charitable institutions-cum-conservatories of music for illegitimate, orphaned, and poor girls, thrilled audiences from all over Europe. The training at the four musical "convents"—the INCURABILI (on the Fondamenta Delle Zattere); the MENDICANTI; the OSPEDALETTO (east of the church of SANTI GIOVANNI E PAOLO in the San Marco district); and the PIETÀ (on the RIVA DEGLI SCHIAVONI)—as fine as was to be had anywhere in Europe (everyone was taught to play every instrument), produced "infinitely beautiful" voices in Goethe's words, young women whom many listeners said sang like angels—or earth angels, in their white dresses and with bunches of pomegranate blossoms over their ears.

The singing "nuns" without dowries who did not find husbands thought of themselves, in the words of music scholar Robert Craft, "as married to music, and thus metaphorically to Christ, music being the *ancilla religionis*, the art that mirrored the Divine Order and was practiced in Heaven, where angels sang and played instruments."

Composer Antonio Vivaldi (1678–1741), an ordained priest, was for thirty years the concert master and violin teacher at the Pietà, now the Hotel Metropole on the RIVA DEGLI SCHIAVONI (no. 4149), the wide promenade and paved embankment along the BACINO DI SAN MARCO from in front of the DOGE'S PALACE to the RIO CA'DIO. (At no. 4175 Tchaikovsky wrote his fourth symphony; at no. 4442 Petrarch lived; at no. 4161 Henry James completed *The Portrait of a Lady*). During Vivaldi's thirty years at the Pietà, his favorite singer, Anna Giraud, "La Girò," was thought to be his mistress. The *ospedali* were also homes to reformed and unreformed prostitutes. The superiors at the Pietà, in particular, supplied girls as mistresses to aristocrats and nuncios, according to Jane L. Baldauf-Berdes's *Women Musicians of Venice: Musical Foundations, 1525–1855* (1995). The adjoining CHURCH OF THE PIETÀ, by Massari, with splendid frescoes by Tiepolo, offers concerts of Vivaldi's music throughout the summer.

Though the church, according to Jan Morris, held an easy-going attitude toward libertines, the chapel of SAN CLEMENTE in the BASILICA OF SAN MARCO (to the right of the central apse, with a twelfth-century mosaic in white, blue, and gold) was finally shut down because, as Morris recounts, "scandalous things" were transpiring between "gay young nuns" and their visitors.

Renaissance tolerance about sex eventually changed. Aristocratic privilege lost ground to subversive notions of hygiene and democracy. If Byron showed up in Venice today, he'd find the new women sketched by Jan Morris disappointing, if not infuriating.

Marcella Hazan

When she first arrived in New York City from Italy, newly married, without English or relatives to turn to for advice, Marcella Hazan had only a cookbook and "the remembered taste of the food which had always nourished me." Over the years, following a process "more of discovery than of invention," while continuing to teach biology and mathematics, she learned to prepare her native food. In The Classic Italian Cookbook *(1973) and* More Classic Italian Cooking *(1978) she presents the art of her native country's cooking and eating. Considered "the most authentic" and best guide to Italian food ever written in the United States, Marcella Hazan herself, in the words of Craig Claiborne, is "a national treasure both in this country and in Italy. No one has done more than she to spread the gospel of fine Italian cookery in America." James Beard notes the "rare good humor" of her books.*

She now gives master classes in the art of la buona cucina *in Venice in the sixteenth-century palazzo where she and her husband Victor Hazan live for part of the year. A small group of students spend their time in classes and visiting the Rialto markets and the Hazans' favorite Venetian restaurants (a selection of which follows). The students' success is not guaranteed. "Music and cooking are so much alike," writes Marcella. "There are people who, simply by working hard at it, become technically quite accomplished at either art. But it isn't until one connects technique to feeling, turning it into the outward thrust of that feeling, that one becomes a musician, or a cook."*

FROM *THE CLASSIC ITALIAN COOKBOOK*

PREFACE

Nothing significant exists under Italy's sun that is not touched by art. Its food is twice blessed because it is the product of two arts, the art of cooking and the art of eating. While each nourishes the other, they are in no way identical accomplishments. The art of cooking produces the dishes, but it is the art of eating that transforms them into a meal.

Through the art of eating, an Italian meal becomes a precisely orchestrated event, where the products of the season, the traditions of place, the intuitions of the cook, and the knowledgeable joy of the participants are combined into one of the most satisfying experiences of which our senses are capable. . . .

ITALIAN COOKING:
WHERE DOES IT COME FROM?

The first useful thing to know about Italian cooking is that, as such, it actually doesn't exist. "Italian cooking" is an expression of convenience rarely used by Italians. The cooking of Italy is really the cooking of its regions, regions that until 1861 were separate, independent, and usually hostile states. They submitted to different rulers, they were protected by sovereign armies and navies, and they developed their own cultural traditions and, of course, their own special and distinct approaches to food.

The unique features of each region and of the individual towns and cities within it can still be easily observed when one travels through Italy today. These are living differences that appear in the physical cast of the people, in their temperament, in their spoken language, and, most clearly, in their cooking.

The cooking of Venice, for example, is so distant from that of Naples, although they are both Italian cities specializing in seafood, that not a single authentic dish from the one is to be found on the other's table. There are unbridgeable differences between Bologna and Florence, each the capital of its own region, yet only sixty miles apart. There are also subtle but substantial distinctions to be made between the cooking of Bologna and of other cities in its region, such as Cesena, fifty-two miles away, Parma, fifty-six miles, or Modena, just twenty-three miles to the north.

It isn't only from the inconstant contours of political geography that cooking in Italy has taken its many forms. Even more significant has been the forceful shaping it has received from the two dominant elements of the Italian landscape—the mountains and the sea.

Italy is a peninsula shaped like a full-length boot that has stepped into the Mediterranean and Adriatic seas up to its thigh. There it is fastened to the rest of Europe by an uninterrupted chain of the tallest mountains on the continent, the Alps. At the base of the Alps spreads Italy's only extensive plain, which reaches from Venice on the Adriatic coast westward through Lombardy and into Piedmont. This is the dairy zone of Italy, and the best-irrigated land. The cooking fat is butter, almost exclusively, and rice or corn mush (polenta) are the staples. Up to a few years ago, when thousands of workers from the south came north to find jobs in Turin and Milan, macaroni was virtually unknown here.

The northern plain gives out just before touching the Mediterranean shore, where it reaches the foothills of the other great mountain chain of Italy, the Apennines. This chain extends from north to south for the whole length of the country like the massive, protruding spine of some immense beast. It is composed of gentle, softly rounded hills sloping toward the seas on the eastern and western flanks and, in the central crest, of tall, forbidding stone peaks. Huddled within the links of this chain are countless valleys, isolated from each other until modern times like so many Shangri-las, giving birth to men, cultures, and cooking styles profoundly different in character.

To a certain extent, the Apennine range helps determine that variety of climates which has also favored diversity in cooking. Turin, the capital of Piedmont, standing in the open plain at the foot of the Alps, has winters more severe than Copenhagen. The Ligurian coast, just a few miles to the west, nestles against the Apennines, which intercept the cold Alpine winds and allow the soft Mediterranean breezes to create that mild, pleasant climate which has made the Riviera famous. Here flowers abound, the olive begins to flourish, and the fragrance of fresh herbs invades nearly every dish.

On the eastern side of the same Apennines that hug the Riviera coast lies the richest gastronomic region in Italy, Emilia-Romagna. Its capital, Bologna, is probably the only city in all Italy whose name is instantly associated in the Italian mind not with monuments, not with artists, not with heroes, but with food.

Emilia-Romagna is almost evenly divided between mountainous

land and flat, with the Apennines at its back and at its feet the last remaining corner of the northern plain rolling out to the Adriatic. This Emilian plain is extraordinarily fertile land enriched by the alluvial deposits of the countless Apennine torrents that have run through it toward the sea. It leads all Italy in the production of wheat, which perhaps explains why here it is almost heresy to sit down to a meal that doesn't include a dish of homemade pasta. The vegetables of Emilia-Romagna may well be the tastiest in the world, surpassing even the quality of French produce. The fruit from its perfumed orchards is so remarkable in flavor that local consumers must compete with foreign markets for it. Italy's best hams and sausages are made here and also some of its richest dairy products, among which is the greatest Italian cheese, Parmesan.

In Emilia-Romagna the sea has been as bountiful as the land. The Adriatic, perhaps because it contains less salt than the Mediterranean, perhaps because it is constantly purified by fresh waters from Alpine streams, produces fish famous in all Italy for its fine delicate flesh. When a restaurant in any part of Italy offers fish from the Adriatic it makes sure its patrons know it. Since the quality of the fish is so fine it requires little enhancement in the kitchen, and Adriatic fish cookery has become the essence of masterful simplicity. Nowhere else except perhaps in Japan is fish fried or broiled so simply and well.

In crossing Emilia-Romagna's southern border into Tuscany every aspect of cooking seems to have turned over and, like an embossed coin, landed on its reverse side. Tuscany's whole approach to the preparation of food is in such sharp contrast to that of Bologna that their differences seem to sum up two main and contrary manifestations of Italian character.

Out of the abundance of the Bolognese kitchen comes cooking that is exuberant, prodigal with precious ingredients, and wholly baroque in its restless exploration of every agreeable combination of texture and flavor. The Florentine, careful and calculating, is a man who knows the measure of all things, and his cooking is an austerely composed play upon essential and unadorned themes.

Bologna will sauté veal in butter, stuff it with the finest mountain ham, coat it with aged Parmesan, simmer it in sauce, and smother it with the costliest truffles. Florence takes a T-bone steak of noble size and grills it quickly over a blazing fire, adding nothing but the aroma of freshly ground pepper and olive oil. Both are triumphs.

From Tuscany down, the Apennines and their foothills in their southward march spread nearly from coast to coast so that the rest of Italy is almost entirely mountainous. As a result, two major changes take place in cooking. First, as it is cheaper and simpler on a hillside to cultivate a grove of olive trees than to raise a herd of dairy cows, olive oil supplants butter as the dominant cooking fat. Second, as we get farther away from the rich wheat fields of Emilia-Romagna, soft, homemade egg and flour pasta gives way to the more economical, mass-produced, eggless hard macaroni, the staple of the south.

From Naples south the climate becomes considerably warmer. A harsher sun bakes the land, inflames the temper of the inhabitants, and ignites their sauces. At the toe-tip of the peninsula and in the heart of Sicily there is little rainfall, and most of that only in the winter months. The lands are parched by harsh, burning winds and the temperatures are sometimes higher than in southern Florida and Texas. The food is as extreme as the climate. The colors of the vegetables are intense and violent, the pastas are so pungent that they often need no topping of cheese, and the sweets are of the most overpowering richness.

There is no need here and certainly there is no room to examine in greater detail all the richly varied forms that history and geography have pressed upon the cooking of Italy. What is important is to be aware that these differences exist and that behind the screen of the too-familiar term "Italian cooking" lies concealed, waiting to be discovered, a multitude of riches.

THE ITALIAN ART OF EATING

Not everyone in Italy may know how to cook, but nearly everyone knows how to eat. Eating in Italy is one more manifestation of the Italian's age-old gift of making art out of life.

The Italian art of eating is sustained by a life measured in nature's rhythms, a life that falls in with the slow wheelings of the seasons, a life in which, until very recently, produce and fish reached the table not many hours after having been taken from the soil or the sea.

It is an art that has also been abetted by the custom of shutting down the whole country at midday for two hours or more. Fathers come home from work and children from school, and there is sufficient time for the whole family to celebrate, not just the most important meal, but more likely also the most important event of the day.

There probably has been no influence, not even religion, so effective in creating a rich family life, in maintaining a civilized link between the generations, as this daily sharing of a common joy. Eating in Italy is essentially a family art, practiced for and by the family. The finest accomplishments of the home cook are not reserved like the good silver and china for special occasions or for impressing guests, but are offered daily for the pleasure and happiness of the family group.

The best cooking in Italy is not, as in France, to be found in restaurants, but in the home. One of the reasons that Italian restaurants here are generally so poor is that they do not have Italian home cooking with which to compete. The finest restaurants in Italy are not those glittering establishments known to every traveler, but the very small, family-run *trattorie* of ten or twelve tables that offer home cooking only slightly revised by commercial adaptations. Here the menus are unnecessary, sometimes nonexistent, and almost always illegible. Patrons know exactly what they want, and in ordering a meal they are evoking patterns established countless times at home.

Italian food may be a midnight spaghetti snack after the theater, a pizza and a glass of wine, a cool salad on a sultry summer noon. But an Italian *meal* is something else entirely; it is a many-layered experience far richer and more complete than this.

Out of the potentially infinite combinations of first and second courses, of side dishes, of sauces and seasonings, an Italian meal, whether it is set out at home for the entire family or consumed in solitary communion in a restaurant, emerges as a complex composition free of discordant notes. Its elements may vary according to the season and the unique desires of the moment, but their relationships are governed by a harmonious and nearly invariable arrangement.

There is no main course to an Italian meal. With some very rare exceptions, such as *ossobuco* with *risotto,* the concept of a single dominant course is entirely foreign to the Italian way of eating. There are, at a minimum, two principal courses, which are never, never brought to the table at the same time.

The first course may be pasta either in broth or with sauce, or it can be a risotto or a soup. *Minestra,* which is the Italian for "soup," is also used to mean the first course whether it is a soup or not. This is because, to the Italian mind, the first course, even when it is sauced pasta or *risotto,* is still a soup in the sense that it is served in a deep dish and that it always precedes and never accompanies the meat, fowl, or fish course.

After there has been sufficient time to relish and consume the first course, to salute its passing with some wine, and to regroup the taste buds for the next encounter, the second course comes to the table. The choice of the second course is usually a development of the theme established by the first. The reverse may also be true, when the first course is chosen in anticipation of what the second will be. If the second course is going to be beef braised in wine, you will not preface it with spaghetti in clam sauce or with a dish of *lasagne* heavily laced with meat. You might prefer a *risotto* with asparagus, with zucchini, or with plain Parmesan cheese. Or a dish of green *gnocchi.* Or a light potato soup. If you are going to start with *tagliatelle alla bolognese* (homemade noodles with meat sauce), you might want to give your palate some relief by following with a simple roast of veal or chicken. On the other hand, you would not choose a second course so bland, such as steamed fish, that it could not stand up to the impact of the first.

The second course is often attended by one or two vegetable side dishes, which sometimes may develop into a full course of their own. The special pleasures of the Italian table are never keener or more apparent than in this moment when the vegetables appear. In Italian menus the word for a vegetable side dish is *contorno,* which can be translated literally as "contour." This reveals exactly what role vegetables play, because it is the choice of vegetables that defines the meal, that gives it shape, that encircles it with the flavors, textures, and colors of the season.

The sober winter taste, the austere whites and gray-greens of artichokes, cardoons, celery, cauliflower; the sweetness and the tender hues of spring in the first asparagus, the earliest peas, baby carrots, young fava beans; the voluptuous gifts of summer: the luscious eggplant, the glossy green pepper, the sun-reddened tomato, the succulent zucchini; the tart and scented taste of autumn in leeks, finocchio, fresh spinach, red cabbage; these do more than quiet our hunger. Through their presence the act of eating becomes a way of sharing our life with nature. And this is precisely what is at the heart of the Italian art of eating.

An Italian meal is a story told from nature, taking its rhythms, its humors, its bounty and turning them into episodes for the senses. As nature is not a one-act play, so an Italian meal cannot rest on a single dish. It is instead a lively sequence of events, alternating the crisp with the soft and yielding, the pungent with the bland, the variable with the staple, the elaborate with the simple. . . .

In the relationships of its varied parts an Italian meal develops something very close to the essence of civilized life itself. No dish overwhelms another, either in quantity or flavor, each leaves room for new appeals to the eye and palate, each fresh sensation of taste, color, and texture interlaces a lingering recollection of the last.

Of course, no one expects that the Italian way of eating can be wholly absorbed into everyday American life. Even in Italy it is succumbing to the onrushing uniformity of an industrial society. In Blake's phrase, man's brain is making the world unlivable for man's spirit. Yet, it is possible even from the tumultuous center of the busiest city life to summon up the life-enhancing magic of the Italian art of eating. What it requires is generosity. You must give liberally of time, of patience, of the best raw materials. What it returns is worth all you have to give.

🍃

For the Culinary Traveler

A dominant theme of *The Classic Italian Cookbook* is the absolute necessity of fresh ingredients in *la buona cucina*. Thus the maestra's daily visits to the food markets of Venice, the RIALTO.

Venice was once the most powerful city in the world, mistress of the Mediterranean, Queen of the Adriatic, an international market and city of bazaars, with foreign communities of Turks, Greeks, Arabs, Jews, Armenians, and Germans trading at her quays, cooking their native foods, bearing spices. The Rialto was her ancient trading center, the commercial hub invoked in *The Merchant of Venice*—"What news on the Rialto?"

Today the wholesale food markets cover an area on the left bank or the San Polo side of the Grand Canal (moving in the direction of the railway station), extending from the foot of the RIALTO BRIDGE to the PESCHERIA (fish market), a Gothic market hall built on the site of the fourteenth-century fish market. (The underside of the broad span of the Rialto Bridge, until 1854 the only bridge over the Grand Canal, is the subject of one of John Singer Sargent's most brilliant water-colors, now in the Philadelphia Museum of Art.)

Fish, not meat, is the main fare of the lagoon city, which explains why the cooking of Venice is so uncomplicated. As in any city, the best time to visit the fish market is just before dawn when the live fish arrive on barges on the Grand Canal and go directly to the market stalls. Later in the day they turn up as antipasti—prawns, scampi, squid (*calamari*), baby octopus (*polpo*), soft-shelled crabs (*le moleche*) from the island of Murano, all served with olive oil, parsley, and lemon, or served together on a plate of mixed fried seafood (*pesce fritta mista*).

In between the Rialto Bridge and the Pescheria stretch the buildings of the food markets—open stalls in winding alleys and covered arcades. The bright reds and oranges, yellows, apricots, and shades of green displayed throughout the fruit and vegetable market (the ERBERIA) make the mounds of produce daily festivals of color and materiality, the fresh goods of the sacred table, itself a daily celebra-tion. (In a recent two-year survey of the living habits of forty thousand ordinary Italian families, 77.9 percent said that their main warm meal was eaten at midday, and 84.6 percent described it as home cooked and enjoyed with the family, underscoring the continuing pivotal role of Mamma and her *buona cucina*.)

There are a number of restaurants and wine bars in the market district where shoppers—and students from master classes in Italian cooking—may stop in late morning for *tramezzini* (they are especially good in Venice) and *prosecco*, the local sparkling white wine. Student cooks and regular travelers have a number of good Venetian restaurants and *trattorie* to choose from that come recommended and described by Marcella and Victor Hazan:

• DA FIORE, Campo S. Polo 2202 (Calle Scaleter)   721308
The place to go for Venice's most exquisite seafood. In Pat Wells's list of the world's ten best restaurants that appeared in the *International Herald Tribune,* Da Fiore placed fifth. Contact: Maurizio Martin, owner. Closed Sunday, Monday.

• DA IVO, S. Marco 1809 (Ramo dei Fuseri)   5285004
Owner-chef is Tuscan. Best *fiorentina* (firm but very tasty T-bone steak for two) in town, authoritative, herb-laden pastas, a sensational mussel soup, charcoal-grilled fish, fried soft-shell crabs, roast lamb, white truffles and grilled porcini in season. You might think twice about ordering the ossobuco, but you are not likely to be disappointed by anything else on the menu. Dinner served until 11:30 P.M. Contact: Ivo, owner. Closed Sunday.

• FIASCHETTERIA TOSCANA,
Cannaregio 5719 (S. Giovanni Grisostomo)   5285281
Despite the name, it has been an authentically Venetian restaurant for decades, with a varied menu that includes both fish and meat, all carefully prepared. Fine wine list and cheeses. Contact: Mariuccia or Albino, proprietors; try for Roberto or Claudio as your waiter; don't skip one of Mariuccia's lovely desserts. Closed Tuesday.

• AI MECANTI, S. Polo 1588 (Pescheria, Rialto)   5240282
Chef Bruno makes the best *spaghetti con le seppie* in Venice and excellent fried *scampi*. Good grilled fish, too. Pasta with mussels and basil late in the

Spring, pumpkin *gnocchi* and porcini sauce in the Fall. Small but choice wine list. Contact: Diego, owner. Closed Sunday.

• RIVIERA, Dorsoduro 1473 (Zattere, S. Basilio)   5227621
Lovely outdoor location on embankment facing Giudecca canal. Limited indoor seating. Simple pastas and *risottos,* good fish, chicken with cardoons sometimes, *fegato alla veneziana* usually. Contact: Franco, owner. Closed Monday.

• LA FURATOLA, Dorsoduro 2870 (Calle Lunga S. Barnaba)   5208594
At La Furatola, whose name in Venetian means small dark shop, you find the cozy, homey environment that used to be typical of *trattorie* throughout Italy and that has been largely replaced by more self-conscious, trendier décor. Come here for fish as fresh as any served in Venice, simply, but carefully, prepared. The assorted antipasti are exceptionally tasty, the spaghetti *alle vongole* (clams) or with fish sauce are delicious, and you round this off with your choice of grilled fish from the day's catch. You must book and be very punctual, or Sandro, the owner, may decide not to seat you even if the restaurant is empty. Closed Wednesday and Thursday.

• ALLA MADONNA, S. Polo 594 (Rialto market)   5223824
A large, lively, busy place, popular for decades for its reliable cooking and affable, but rather brisk service. We prefer more intimate surroundings and a kitchen that is geared to small production, but the restaurant can nonetheless be recommended for consistently good food. Closed Wednesday.

• AL MASCARON, Castello 5525 (Calle Lunga S. Maria Formosa) 5225995
Offers some of the best food served by a casual trattoria in Venice. Communal sitting at long wooden tables. Good wines. Closes Sunday and at midnight. Very popular, very busy, long waits are common.

THE BACARO EXPERIENCE

The sole aspect of authentically Venetian life that has yet to be altered by tourism is snacking at a bacaro. A bacaro is a small, cheery, crowded food and wine bar where, although tables are available, habitués usually stand by the counter and consume liberal amounts of young, good wine by the glass while maintaining sobriety with a variety of succulent, freshly made tidbits known as *cicheti* (*chee-kehtee*), a Venetian version of tapas. These may include *baccalà* whipped to a creamy consistency with olive oil and milk; tender braised baby octopus; sardines in saor; baked eggplant; artichoke bottoms; *risotto* with cuttlefish ink; *soppressa*— the indigenous soft Venetian salami; thick, hand-sliced prosciutto; *musetto*—the Venetian version of *cotechino*, an incredibly tender cooked salami; little meatballs; delicious tripe; *spienza*—spleen; spiced sliced tongue; *nervetti*—boiled, tenderly chewy bits of calf's feet served with olive oil, parsley, and sliced raw onion; and *tramezzini*, the Venetian sandwich which encloses between small triangles of soft bread an infinite variety of stuffings often laced with mayonnaise. Not every bacaro has all of these things; the assortment varies from place to place and each has some specialty it does better than anyone else. The visitor endowed with gastronomic curiosity and an unbiased palate will nowhere in Italy spend a more savory and convivial hour or two than in a Venetian bacaro. Most bacari open early in the morning, close for three hours or so in the afternoon, and reopen for what is usually a short evening, some closing as early as 8:30 P.M. There are exceptions however.

There are dozens of bacari in every neighborhood. Our current favorites are:

• VIVALDI, S. Polo 1457 (Calle Madonnetta)   5238185
Closed Sunday and in the evening at 10 P.M.

• MASCARETA,
Castello 5183 (Calle Lunga S. Maria Formosa)   5230744
Mascaron's little sister, down the street from its sibling. See Restaurants, above. No hot dishes, just snacks. You can also buy wine and olive oil here. Open 6 P.M. to 1 A.M.; closed Sunday.

• OSTERIA DA ALBERTO, Calle Gallina 5401   5238153
Alberto learned to cook at Da Fiore, and most would agree that he is today the most accomplished cook in the bacaro business. His meatballs,

pasta alla busara with scampi, grilled vegetables, liver Venetian style are the best examples of their kind in Venice. Good variety of simple wines by the glass. Open 9–2:30 A.M., 5:30–9 P.M., closed Sunday.

• ANTICO DOLO, S. Polo 778 (very near Rialto market)   5226546
One of the oldest and most atmosphere-laden bacari. Stays open until 11 P.M. or later, depending on business, and serves good hot food at table. Closed Sunday.

• DO MORI, S. Polo 429 (Calle dei do Mori, Rialto market)   5225401
Venice's most celebrated bacaro. Roberto, the owner, is famous for his superb red wines and for exquisite little toasts stuffed with truffles or goose breast or topped with musetto. Closes down at 8:30, and is closed Wednesday afternoon and all day Sunday.

• ALLA FRASCA, Cannaregio 5176
(Campiello della Carità, near Fondamente Nuove)   5285433
In warm weather, the most romantic of bacari, with tables under a luxuriant pergola in a stage-set little square. There is only one white and one red wine, both indifferent, but the expertly grilled fish and lovely risotto help overlook that failing. 9:30 A.M. to 8:30 P.M., closed Thursday.

• SACRO E PROFANO, S. Polo 502
(behind the porticoes near the Rialto food market)   5201931
Tasty little snacks and good wine, both Tuscan-inspired. It is as small as the smallest of Japanese noodle shops, but expands radiantly when Sylvie, a Frenchwoman, is behind the counter and smiles as she proffers bruschetta and a well-chosen glass of Chianti. 6 P.M. to 11 P.M. or later, closed Sunday.

GELATI

• HOTEL CIPRIANI, Giudecca   5207744
It would be worth going just for the extraordinary courtesy ride across St. Mark's basin on the hotel's 24-hour a day private launch. This is the only grand hotel in Venice worthy of the name and for a late night *grappa* or the best chocolate ice cream in the world the piano bar is the smart place to be. Men are expected to wear jackets. No jeans or sneakers.

• NICO, Dorsoduro 922 (Zattere embankment)
Venice is not much of a gelati town, but of what there is Nico has the best,

save of course for the Cipriani's chocolate ice cream. Try their *gianduiotto*.
Closed Thursdays.

❧

For information about the Hazans' master classes and other
cooking schools in Italy, *The Guide to Cooking Schools*, published by
Shaw Guides, is, according to *The New York Times*, "the bible of culi-
nary education."

❧

Muriel Spark

*Italy is home to Muriel Spark, who grew up in Edinburgh, the setting of her
best-known novel,* The Prime of Miss Jean Brodie. *She lives in Rome, near
the Campo dei Fiori (one of the city's liveliest markets and neighborhoods),
and also knows well Tuscany and the Veneto. Venice is the scene of her
novel* Territorial Rights *in which the canals, churches, campos, and pen-
siones have the specificity of human characters—Venice is a subtle but commanding presence in this story of intrigue and deception.*

*Critics have admired Muriel Spark's fiction as "compassionate and out-
rageously funny," as "mysterious as both Agatha Christie and Isak Dinesen
are mysterious," as "one of the genuine wonders of the contemporary British
literary world." She has also written critical biography, including a widely
praised portrait of Mary Shelley (see page 35), and edited the letters of the
Brontës and of John Henry Newman. Under the latter's influence, she con-
verted to Catholicism. In an address to the American Academy of Arts and
Letters, she declared that literature, "the only honorable weapon we have
left" in a ridiculous world, should be an instrument of "savage ridicule." In a
softer mood, she looks at Venice and almost makes us hear the beauty.*

VENICE IN FALL AND WINTER

Most people who write about Venice do not tell you what they
think of it but how they feel. Venice is a city not to inspire
thought but sensations. I think it is something to do with the

compound of air, water, architecture, and the acoustics. Like the effect of these elements on the ear, there are acoustics of the heart. One can think in Venice, but not about Venice. One absorbs the marvelous place, often while thinking about something else.

I have never been to Venice in summertime, or in festival time, nor at the time of any of the cinema and great art shows. My Venice belongs to late autumn and winter, the Venice of meager tourism, the Venetians' everyday city.

I have never known Venice to be crowded or hurried. Perhaps for this reason, when I published a novel set in autumnal Venice, someone was puzzled by the facility with which some of my characters encountered each other in the street. It transpired he had only been in Venice during the crowded and stifling tourist seasons, when you could not very likely meet the same face two days running. In the winter it is quite different. After a week of walking around Venice—and one does have to walk a lot—or of waiting at the landing stage for the diesel-run vaporetto, the same laughing students are there, the same solemn goodwives with their shopping bags and well-preserved fur collars, the same retired gentlemen with righteous blue eyes and brown hats. This is everyday Venice where the passersby are sparse, where eventually they say good morning.

My first visit to Venice was on a cold, bright morning in February, with a friend who had been there before. However much one has read and heard about the visual impact of Venice, it never fails to take one by surprise. After five visits I still gasp. It is not merely the architecture, the palaces, the bridges and the general splendor, it is the combination of architecture with water, space, light and color that causes amazement; especially, I think, the element of water. The first impression of the waterways of Venice is acoustic, so that normal sensations subliminally cease and new ones take their place. Voices, footsteps, bird cries, a cough from the window on the other side of the canal—all are different from the sounds of the land one has left. The traffic is entirely watery. A greengrocer's shop piled high with vegetables is a ship floating past your window.

After a few days of this estrangement from normal life I begin to feel at home with it. Some people tell me they can never settle down to a feeling of familiarity with Venice. Sometimes they are people who frequent the super hotels where everything is done to comfort and console the visitors who come with their usual bag of worries. I do not say that this is not a very good thing for a holiday. But the very nature of Venice is such that the things that usually preoccupy us, from which we are attempting to get away, undergo a shift of perspective after about three days.

I have known Venice in a mist and drizzle, where everything is depressed and soaking, every bridge is a bridge of sighs. But it is not the usual personal depression one is experiencing; it is something else, something belonging to Venice, it is collective. I think this is something like the reverse of Ruskin's Pathetic Fallacy in which he holds that artists and poets tend to attribute to nature our human responses; Venice would be "brooding" or "smiling," according to how we feel. On the contrary, I think we are sad when majestic Venice is in gloom; and if we are depressed already the fine thing about those gloomy days of Venice is that you forget what you are personally depressed about. Venice is a very good place to be sad. On days of mist, it is like a trip to the Shades. But winter often sparkles and these are the days one can sit warmly in Florian's Café while outside the hardy musicians perform their nostalgic Palm Court pieces.

Venice has been declining for some hundreds of years. Decline is now of its essence, and I do not think it would be anything like as attractive to ourselves if it were on the way up in the modern sense and flourishing. The Venetians themselves talk little about Venice, never unless you ask. They are proud of their native city and attached to it, but it does not go to their heads as it does with the rest of us.

There was a time when wealthy foreigners like Milly in Henry James's *The Wings of the Dove* could take on a romantic palace, and play at princesses. Poor Milly got what she demanded, and this was, of course, how James made fun of his contemporaries in Venice:

At Venice, please, if possible, no dreadful, no vulgar hotel; but, if it can be at all managed—you know what I mean—some fine old rooms, wholly independent, for a series of months. Plenty of them, too, and the more interesting the better; part of a palace, historic and picturesque, but strictly inodorous, where we shall be to ourselves, with a cook, don't you know?—with servants, frescoes, tapestries, antiquities, the thorough make-believe of a settlement.

Byron thought seriously of settling permanently in Venice to spend the winters there. Permanently is not a good idea; the city is bad for our bones, and also the sort of infatuation a foreigner feels about Venice cannot last. Henry James's American girlfriend,* if one can stretch a phrase, settled in Venice only to throw herself out of a window one dark night, to her death. Byron's Venetian girl, who threw herself into the canal, was careful to be rescued.

However, it is difficult not to be romantic about Venice. Myself, I arrived on one of my visits—it was early in November—close to midnight. All the river traffic including the taxis were on strike in solidarity with the gondoliers who had notices up demanding that gondoliers' claims should be dealt with "globally." There was a squall blowing in from the lagoon. It was quite a plight for me, there on the landing stage, for my luggage was heavy with some reference books (I was correcting the proofs of my Venetian novel *Territorial Rights*). But it was really exciting to strike a bargain with some men on a coal barge which rocked and plunged in the wind and surge, with me and my books among the sooty cargo, up the Grand Canal where doges and dowagers were once wont to ride in state.

The night porter at my lodgings showed no surprise; he merely came down to the landing stage to collect me and my goods, dripping rags that we were, and to make sure that the men had not overcharged me. I will always remember that midnight journey through the black water, and the calling of the bargemen, wild seabird noises, as every now and again they passed another laden vessel. The palaces were mostly in darkness, with the water splashing their sides, the painted mooring poles gleaming suddenly in the light of our passing; the few lights from the windows were dim and greenish, always from tiny windows at the top. Nobody

*Constance Fenimore Woolson.

walked on the banks, and yet a strange effect that I can only describe as water voices came from those sidewalks and landing stages. Perhaps they were ghosts, wet and cold.

I usually stay at a charming, fairly old pensione near the Accademia, which sits on an angle of the Grand Canal and a side canal. In time, after I had taken in day by day all the sights and spectacles of Venice, the incredible St. Mark's Church, the happy square with its shops full of expensive junk, the Tintorettos, museums, and galleries and all those already hyperdescribed stones of Venice, I began to form a Venice of my own. It is rather as one does with acquaintances when one goes to live for a length of time in a new country—eventually one whittles them down to an affectionate few. These I visit again and again in my winter walks and excursions, well wrapped up and wearing boots like everyone else. Most men and women wear warm hats, too.

Since one of the advantages of an off-season visit is that there are no crowds, it is possible to sit without interruption almost alone in the church of the Frari looking at Titian's *Assumption*. I love to walk around the Ducal Palace to see those four charming Tetrarchs, timid and proper and quietly influential, modestly embracing each other in a formal half-huddle. Giorgione's mysterious *Tempest* in the Accademia is another of my best-loved familiars. And I remember a sunny winter trip, and also a cold bleak one, with a friend in the ferryboat to Torcello, one of the islands in the Venetian lagoon where very little goes on now except the magnificent cathedral, part Gothic, part Byzantine. There is a vast biblical narrative done in seventh-century mosaics at one end, and a gold-backed mosaic of the Madonna behind the altar, hypnotically radiant. But going behind the altar to snoop we waded into a deep pool of water that had seeped into that glorious building. We were glad of our boots. In winter there are no restaurants on the smaller islands, no bars on the ferryboats. But sweet visitors do not care, and the sour ones do not matter.

The art treasures apart, what I return to again and again are the more homely friends of my walks through the windy *calles* and the placid, sometimes leafy squares of Venice. These include a men's hat shop standing all alone in a small square house on the canal near Santa Maria Formosa; in the windows, and piled up inside, is a vast variety of men's hats: straw boaters, Breton sailors' berets, felt hats, black velour hats, fedoras, Stetsons, hats for hunting, hats for going to funerals.

Funerals in Venice, of course, are a stately procession. The city lays on a great show, with gilt-edged barges and coffins carved within an inch of their lives. In vain have the last two Popes set the example of being buried in plain pinewood boxes, there in St. Peter's for all the world to see. Venice sails on regardless. In Venice the ambulance service too is interesting: It provides a sedan chair to run a less-than-stretcher case down to the boat.

Often, in Venice, getting lost, as everyone does, I have come across a type of that high blank wall of James's *The Aspern Papers*:

> . . . a high blank wall which appeared to confine an expanse of ground on one side of the house. Blank I call it, but it was figured over with the patches that please a painter, repaired breaches, crumblings of plaster, extrusions of brick that had turned pink with time; and a few thin trees, with the poles of certain rickety trellises, were visible over the top. The place was a garden and apparently it belonged to the house.

I like the term "apparently." Because, in Venice, anything can or might lie behind those high blank walls. It is well to say apparently. One never knows.

And the bridges on the side canals are something I can gaze at for hours. Sometimes they are set in groups, obliquely, for no immediately serviceable reason, and this is all the more enchanting.

It is true that, for myself, I never cease to feel a certain amazement that all that sheer visual goodness and aural sublimity was in fact based on commerce. Culture follows gold, somebody said. Indeed, in Venice, it apparently has done so. Today in Venice you could never live and follow a culture in the sort of style that gave birth to it. In a Venetian palace you could never live a modern life: You would have to be serving the walls, serving the servants, giving orders for your private riverboat to be repaired, the mooring posts to be painted, the crystal chandeliers to be cleaned piece by piece.

To own a Venetian palace must be simply awful. Some people still do it.

It was only quite lately, in a much-traveled life, that I made my first trip to Venice. That was in 1975. I was vaguely saving it up for a romantic occasion. Special and romantic occasions were not wanting in my life but they never coincided with the possibility of a trip to Venice. So in the winter of 1975 I suddenly went. Venice itself was the romantic occasion: the medium is the message.

For the Literary Traveler

"The Venice of my own"—the city Muriel Spark loves—encompasses some highlights of Mary Shelley's Venice—the DUCAL PALACE, the ACCADEMIA, ST. MARK'S. But mostly Spark suits herself. Inspired by the passionate intelligence of her attention, the reader/traveler gladly follows along.

She visits specific places, especially beloved off-season, when travelers can contemplate rather than glimpse the glories. The Franciscan church of the FRARI (in the San Polo district) holds a number of treasures (Bellini's triptych Madonna and Child in the sacristy, Titian's tomb and Pesoro Madonna, Donatello's statue of John the Baptist), but it is Titian's painting The Assumption in the apse of the sanctuary that draws Muriel Spark. The 1518 work of the Venetian High Renaissance established Titian's international reputation. It supposedly so enchanted Wagner, according to Christopher Hibbert, that he was inspired to compose the Meistersingers. The image in the painting is the focus of recent scholarship on women and Catholicism. According to writer Gertrud Mueller Nelson, the doctrine of the bodily assumption of Mary into heaven, proclaimed by Pope Pius XII in 1950, was, to Carl Jung, "the most important religious event since the Reformation." The Assumption, as he interpreted it, enacts an image out of the Church's own dream life; the papal proclamation brought it into the light of full consciousness. As Nelson puts it, "Mary, the archetypal feminine, once queen of all that was earthy, dark, unconscious ... she who had been left to the darkness, where all that is feminine is feared or honored, served or oppressed ... must now be raised into the light of our new understanding." Four centuries before papal recognition and Jungian psychology, Titian's vision coincided with the people's sense of the woman Mary as the radiant triumph of Italian Catholicism.

Another joy of Muriel Spark in Venice is walking the *calles*, exploring the campos. The campo of the FRARI was a favorite of the architect Le Corbusier. He considered "its quayside, its bridge with steps leading over the canal; the little square dominated by the facade of the church and the main square with its cross and fountain; the campanile and the perspective of the street" as so many examples of the subtleties of successful urban design.

Beside the Frari is the SCUOLA GRANDE DI SAN ROCCO where Tintoretto's masterpiece, *The Crucifixion*, hangs in the *Sala Dell'Albergo*. The easel painting of the Annunciation by Titian is another thrilling example of his bold and sensuous use of color to give vivacity and humanity to flesh and fabric and myth.

Walking Muriel Spark's Venice covers other large campos on the Frari side of the Grand Canal, the palatial CAMPO SAN POLO and the more neighborly CAMPO DI SANTA MARGHERITA, where local residents and lively children gather and play around the vegetable and flower markets.

Muriel Spark's Venetian novel, *Territorial Rights* (1979), has as one of its settings the beautiful church of SANTA MARIA FORMOSA, a short walk from St. Mark's and the Piazzetta Giovanni XXIII. The church is particularly admired for its side chapel paintings the *Madonna della Misericordia* and a womanly *St. Barbara* as well as for its location on a charming *campo*.

One way to enter into Spark's Venice is to settle in at a pensione and read the writers she mentions whose work reflects the city's spell: Henry James's *The Wings of the Dove* and *The Aspern Papers*; the fourth canto of Byron's *Childe Harold's Pilgrimage*, parts of *Don Juan*, and *Beppo* ("Didst ever see a Gondola?/ ... For sometimes they contain a deal of fun / Like mourning coaches when the funeral's done"); Mary Shelley's *Rambles in Italy and Germany* (see page 35); and Constance Fenimore Woolson's story, "Miss Grief," about the sad ending of a neglected woman writer and an arrogant male celebrity/artist. An American writer whose work (*Dorothy and Other Italian Stories*)

Henry James admired and whose friendship he valued, "Fenimore" committed suicide in Venice, jumping from a window of the Casa Semitecolo in Dorsoduro. Rowed out into the lagoon, James threw their correspondence overboard.

There is something Venetian about the art of Muriel Spark's novels. Like the city's great Baroque and Rococo paintings, their effect is often *veduta* and *capriccio*—a mix of straightforward views and views shuffled together: her plots seem fairly simple at the outset, but as they develop, boundaries shift and mysteries, suggesting unending curlicues of cosmic jokes, take hold, leaving the reader at once awed and amused.

LIGURIA

GENOA

PORTOFINO

Lady Mary Wortley Montagu

After eloping with Mr. Wortley Montagu, Lady Mary landed flat in the disappointment of an arid marriage. But she accompanied her husband to Turkey where he was ambassador and began to write letters about her travels in her inimitable clear voice. She also started the journal whose fifty years of details her chillingly conventional daughter Lady Bute burned in 1794. Hers was not the conviction her mother expressed at the age of twenty: "I believe more follies are committed out of complaisance to the world than in following our own inclinations. I am amazed to see that people of good sense in other things can make their happiness consist in the opinion of others."

An essayist, dramatist, and journalist whose personal correspondence fills three volumes, Mary Montagu bore two children and lived apart from her husband near Brescia, Italy. When the 52 Embassy Letters were published a year after her death (in 1763), against the wishes of her family, they drew a hugely enthusiastic audience and had to be reprinted again and again. Voltaire praised them in Europe, rating them superior to Madame de Sévigné's; Smollett, Dr. Johnson, and later Byron called them brilliant. Concurring, Lytton Strachey said, "Her wit has that quality which is the best of all preservatives against dullness—it goes straight to the point." In her introduction to a new edition of the letters, world bicyclist and travel-writer Dervla Murphy (herself a free spirit), recommends Lady Mary as above all an individual: *"strong-willed, warm-hearted, keen-witted, high-spirited, often unpredictable, sometimes downright eccentric"—a perfect travel companion.*

FROM *EMBASSY TO CONSTANTINOPLE*

TO LADY MAR—GENOA, 28 AUGUST 1718

I beg your pardon (my dear sister) that I did not write to you from Tunis (the only opportunity I have had since I left Constantinople), but the heat there was so excessive and the light so bad for the sight, I was half blind by writing one letter to the Abbé Conti and durst not go on to write many others I had designed, nor indeed, could I have entertained you very well out of that barbarous country. I am now surrounded with objects of pleasure, and so much charmed with the beauties of Italy I should think it a kind of ingratitude not to offer a little praise in return for the diversion I have had here. I am in the house of Mrs. Davenant at San Pietro d'Arena and should be very unjust not to allow her a share of that praise I speak of, since her good humour and good company has very much contributed to render this place agreeable to me. Genoa is situated in a very fine bay, and being built on a rising hill, intermixed with gardens and beautified with the most excellent architecture, gives a very fine prospect off at sea, though it lost much of its beauty in my eyes, having been accustomed to that of Constantinople. The Genoese were once masters of several islands in the archipelago and all that part of Constantinople which is now called Galata. Their betraying the Christian cause, by facilitating the taking of Constantinople by the Turk, deserved what has since happened to them, the loss of all their conquest on that side to those infidels. They are at present far from rich, and despised by the French since their Doge was forced by the late King to go in person to Paris to ask pardon for such a trifle as the Arms of France over the house of the envoy being spattered with dung in the night (I suppose) by some of the Spanish faction, which still makes up the majority here, though they dare not openly declare it.

The ladies affect the French habit and are more genteel than those they imitate. I do not doubt but the custom of *tetis beys* [*cicisbeismo*] has very much improved their airs. I know not whether you have ever heard of those animals. Upon my word, nothing but my own eyes could have convinced [me] there were any such upon earth. The fashion began here and is now received all over Italy, where the husbands are not such terrible creatures as we represent them. There are none among them such brutes to pretend to find fault with a custom so well established and so politically funded, since I am assured here that it was an expedient first found out by the Senate to put an end to those family hatreds which tore their state to pieces, and to find employment for those young men who were forced to cut one another's throats *pour passer le temps*, and it has succeeded so well that since the institution of *tetis beys* there has been nothing but peace and good humour amongst them. These are gentlemen that devote themselves to the service of a particular lady (I mean a married one, for the virgins are all invisible, confined to convents). They are obliged to wait on her to all public places, the plays, operas, and assemblies (which are called here conversations), where they wait behind the chair, take care of her fan and gloves if she plays, having the privilege of whispers, etc. When she goes out they serve her instead of lackeys, gravely trotting by her chair. 'Tis their business to present against any day of public appearance, not forgetting that of her name. In short, they are to spend all their time and money in her service who rewards them according to her inclination (for opportunity they want none), but the husband is not to have the impudence to suppose 'tis any other than pure plutonic friendship. 'Tis true they endeavour to give her a *tetis bey* of their own choosing, but when the lady happens not to be of the same taste (as that often happens) she never fails to bring it about to have one of her own fancy. In former times one beauty used to have eight or ten of these humble admirers but those days of plenty and humility are no more; men grow more scarce and saucy, and every lady is forced to content herself with one at a time. You see the glorious liberty of a republic, or more properly an aristocracy, the common people here as arrant slaves as the French but the old nobles pay little respect to the Doge, who is but two years in his office, and at that very time his wife assumes no rank above another noble lady. 'Tis true the family of Andrea Doria (that great man who restored them that liberty they enjoy) has some particular privileges; when the Senate found it necessary to put a stop to the luxury of dress, forbidding the wear of jewels and brocades, they left them at liberty to make what expense they pleased. I looked with great pleasure on the statue of that hero which is in the court belonging to the house of Duke Doria.*

This puts me in mind of their palaces, which I can never describe as I ought. Is it not enough that I say they are most of them of the design of Palladio? The street called Strada Nova here is perhaps the most beautiful line of building in the world. I must particularly mention the vast palace of Durazzo, those of two Balbi joined together by a magnificent (colonnade), that of the Imperiali at this village of San Pietro d'Arena, and another of the Doria. The perfection of architecture and the utmost profusion of rich furniture is to be seen here, disposed with most elegant taste and lavish magnificence, but I am charmed with nothing so much as the collection of pictures by the pencils of Raphael, Paulo Veronese, Titian, Carracci, Michelangelo, Guido, and Correggio, which two I mention last as my particular favourites. I own I can find no pleasure in objects of horror, and in my opinion the more naturally a crucifix is represented the more disagreeable it is. These, my beloved painters, show nature and show it in the most charming light. I was particularly pleased with a Lucretia in the House of Balbi. The expressive beauty of that face and bosom gives all the passion of pity and admiration that could be raised in the soul by the finest poem on that subject. A Cleopatra of the same hand deserves to be mentioned, and I should say more of her if Lucretia had not first engaged my eyes. Here are also some inestimable ancient bustos. The Church of St. Lawrence is all black and white marble, where is kept that famous plate of a single emerald,** which is not now permitted to be handled since a plot which (they say) was discovered to throw it on the pavement and break it, a childish piece of malice which they ascribe to the King of Sicily, to be revenged for their refusing to sell it to him. The Church of the Annunziata is finely

*Andrea Doria (1466–1560), of the great Genoese Doria family, was Genoa's greatest naval commander who wrote a constitution for the city which freed it from foreign rule.

**Long believed to be a present from the Queen of Sheba to Solomon, this emerald was later found to be a fake, after Napoleon appropriated it and had it analyzed in Paris.

lined with marble, the pillars of red and white marble, that of St. Ambrose very much adorned by the Jesuits; but I confess all those churches appeared so mean to me after that of Santa Sophia, I can hardly do them the honour of writing down their names; but I hope you'll own I have made good use of my time in seeing so much, since 'tis not many days that we have been out of the quarantine from which nobody is exempt coming from the Levant; but ours was very much shortened and very agreeably passed in Mrs. Davenant's company in the village of San Pietro d'Arena, about a mile from Genoa in a house built by Palladio, so well designed and so nobly proportioned 'twas a pleasure to walk in it. We were visited here only in the company of a noble Genoese commissioned to see we did not touch one another. I shall stay here some days longer and could almost wish it for all my life, but mine (I fear) is not destined to so much tranquillity.

For the Literary Traveler

When Lady Mary visited Genoa on her way back to England from Constantinople, she claims to have so enjoyed its tranquillity she could "almost" have stayed there for the rest of her life. She wasn't the first visitor to be carried away. Petrarch called the port city on a steep mountainside overlooking the bay "La Superba." Centuries later Charles Dickens remembered it as the scene of some of his happiest days in Italy. To explore the city's steep narrow streets and stairways in search of the places Lady Mary mentions in her letter to Lady Mar is to say at the end there is nothing in Genoa not to recommend. Walking it is pure delight. Yellow signs within the historic center—the CENTRO STORICO—make the high points easy to find.

(For the traveler with a car, the drive into the central city from the Autostrada leads, along Via XX Settembre and off to the left near PIAZZA DANTE, to a signposted public parking garage.)

A short walk along Via Dante, past the cloister ruins and the so-called house of Christopher Columbus, approaches through the dramatic twelfth-century PORTA SOPRANA a cluster of piazzas, palazzos, and churches, an enticing introduction to the city's rich heart. Rising with lordly magnificence over Piazza Matteotti is the PALAZZO DUCALE, a thirteenth-century building now beautifully restored as a cultural center with two spacious, light-filled interior courtyards. On the right side of the piazza is the Baroque church of SANTI AMBROGIO E ANDREA (or the GESÙ) with Rubens's splendid paintings of *The Circumcision* and *St. Ignatius Healing a Possessed Woman*. The Piazza de Ferrari, with a fountain and hundreds of vespas, borders both the Gesù and the Palazzo Ducale.

Further along, downhill from Piazza Matteotti, the DUOMO—the cathedral of SAN LORENZO—rises over its piazza to present a strikingly handsome facade of striped black and white marble decorated with thirteenth-century stone lions, sirens, and saints. Inside, in the south aisle, a shell still lodged in the wall since 1941 is a reminder of the heavy Allied bombing and naval bombardment the civilian population of Genoa suffered during World War II.

Continuing northeast, uphill (following the yellow signs or a *Pianta Generale of Genova*, available from newsstands), in the direction of the VIA GARIBALDI—called LA STRADA NUOVA in Lady Mary Wortley Montagu's time—the walk passes early medieval churches, workshops, houses, and piazzas where the handsome Genoese work, shop, eat, and enjoy themselves.

Having ascended through a maze of lanes from the bottom of the historic center to the jewel spread out above it, one sees at once the accuracy of Lady Mary's reference to *La Strada Nuova* as "perhaps the most beautiful line of building in the world." Closed to traffic, the gracious Renaissance thoroughfare—"one of the most handsome streets in Europe," according to another writer—invites the traveler to amble past one magnificent palazzo after another, stopping to look inside at their courtyards, fountains, and gardens. PALAZZO BIANCO (no. 11) and PALAZZO ROSSO (no. 18), both named for the color of their stone facades, are across the street from each other. Both are open to the public and house galleries of Genoa's finest paintings: the "pencils" of Raphael, Veronese, Titian, and Michelangelo that charmed Lady Mary.

"The perfection of architecture" continues to the northwest along Via Cairoli, across Piazza Nunziata (and past the CHURCH OF THE

ANNUNZIATA, which Lady Mary found "mean after that of Santa Sophia"), and onto VIA BALBI where on the right the University of Genoa occupies the splendid Palazzo Balbi. Its sunny interior court-yard and colonnades are filled on weekdays with students, professors, and palm trees. Across the street at the top of the wide staircase of the huge and lavish PALAZZO REALE (no. 10), there is a gallery with paintings by Tintoretto and van Dyck that requires all visitors be accompanied by a multilingual guide. Though the view from behind the palazzo is unscenic, the garden is quiet. For its statues of mythic figures such as Diana and its lively mosaic decorations, this retreat belongs on the itinerary of the city's visual treasures.

Returning to the foot of Via Balbi and bearing (ascending) left, the walk leads towards PIAZZA PORTELLO where a public elevator (ascensore) rises above the city to PIAZZA CASTELLETTO. From its height, the views of the city below—and the port and bay beneath the domes and terraces and moving veins of streets—make Lady Mary's description seem understated: "Genoa is situated in a very fine bay, and being built on a rising hill, intermixed with gardens and beautified with the most excellent architecture, gives a very fine prospect...." From Piazza Castelletto, it's Petrarch's words that come to mind—Genoa as La Superba.

Elizabeth von Arnim

Admired in her time as "one of the three finest wits of her day," novelist Elizabeth von Arnim (1866–1941) was traveling in Italy with her father when she met her first husband. Each of her twenty-one books displays the comic irreverence and descriptive power that has made The Enchanted April *(1922), set in Portofino on the Italian Riviera, so popular. Inspiring an emotional thaw in the lives of four unhappy English women travelers—Mrs. Lotty Wilkins, Mrs. Rose Arbuthnot, Mrs. Fisher, and Lady Caroline Dester—the novel's setting* is *the story. Saying she wanted to write a happy book, von Arnim worked on it while renting the Portofino* castello *during the month of April. Her cousin Katherine Mansfield mentioned Mozart when she thanked Elizabeth for her copy.*

FROM *THE ENCHANTED APRIL*

VI

When Mrs. Wilkins woke next morning she lay in bed a few minutes before getting up and opening the shutters. What would she see out of her window? A shining world, or a world of rain? But it would be beautiful; whatever it was would be beautiful.

She was in a little bedroom with bare white walls and a stone floor and sparse old furniture. The beds—there were two—were made of iron, enamelled black and painted with bunches of gay flowers. She lay putting off the great moment of going to the window as one puts off opening a precious letter, gloating over it. She had no idea what time it was; she had forgotten to wind up her watch ever since, centuries ago, she last went to bed in Hampstead. No sounds were to be heard in the house, so she supposed it was very early, yet she felt as if she had slept a long while,—so completely rested, so perfectly content. She lay with her arms clasped round her head thinking how happy she was, her lips curved upwards in a delighted smile. In bed by herself: adorable condition. She had not been in bed without Mellersh* once now for five whole years; and the cool roominess of it, the freedom of one's movements, the sense of recklessness, of audacity, in giving the blankets a pull if one wanted to, or twitching the pillows more comfortable! It was like the discovery of an entirely new joy.

Mrs. Wilkins longed to get up and open the shutters, but where she was was really so very delicious. She gave a sigh of contentment, and went on lying there looking round her, taking in everything in her room, her own little room, her very own to arrange just as she pleased for this one blessed month, her room bought with her own savings, the fruit of her careful denials, whose door she could bolt if she wanted to, and nobody had the right to come in. It was such a strange little room, so different from any she had known, and so sweet. It was like a cell. Except for the two beds, it suggested a happy austerity. "And the name of the chamber," she thought, quoting and smiling round at it, "was Peace."

Well, this was delicious, to lie there thinking how happy she was, but outside those shutters it was more delicious still. She jumped up, pulled on her slippers, for there was nothing on the stone floor but one small rug, ran to the window and threw open the shutters.

"*Oh!*" cried Mrs. Wilkins.

All the radiance of April in Italy lay gathered together at her feet. The sun poured in on her. The sea lay asleep in it, hardly stirring. Across the bay the lovely mountains, exquisitely different in colour, were asleep too in the light; and underneath her window, at the bottom of the flower-starred grass slope from which the wall of the castle rose up, was a great cypress, cutting through the delicate blues and violets and rose-colours of the mountains and the sea like a great black sword.

She stared. Such beauty; and she there to see it. Such beauty; and she alive to feel it. Her face was bathed in light. Lovely scents came up to the window and caressed her. A tiny breeze gently lifted her hair. Far out in the bay a cluster of almost motionless

*Mrs. Wilkins's husband.

fishing boats hovered like a flock of white birds on the tranquil sea. How beautiful, how beautiful. Not to have died before this . . . to have been allowed to see, breathe, feel this. . . . She stared, her lips parted. Happy? Poor, ordinary, everyday word. But what could one say, how could one describe it? It was as though she could hardly stay inside herself, it was as though she were too small to hold so much of joy, it was as though she were washed through with light. And how astonishing to feel this sheer bliss, for here she was, not doing and not going to do a single unselfish thing, not going to do a thing she didn't want to do. According to everybody she had ever come across she ought at least to have twinges. She had not one twinge. Something was wrong somewhere. Wonderful that at home she should have been so good, so terribly good, and merely felt tormented. Twinges of every sort had there been her portion; aches, hurts, discouragements, and she the whole time being steadily unselfish. Now she had taken off all her goodness and left it behind her like a heap of rain-sodden clothes, and she only felt joy. She was naked of goodness, and was rejoicing in being naked. She was stripped, and exulting. And there, away in the dim mugginess of Hampstead, was Mellersh being angry. . . .

VIII

Presently, when Mrs. Wilkins and Mrs. Arbuthnot, unhampered by any duties, wandered out and down the worn stone steps and under the pergola into the lower garden, Mrs. Wilkins said to Mrs. Arbuthnot, who seemed pensive, "Don't you see that if somebody else does the ordering it frees us?"

Mrs. Arbuthnot said she did see, but nevertheless she thought it rather silly to have everything taken out of their hands.

"I love things to be taken out of my hands," said Mrs. Wilkins.

"But we found San Salvatore," said Mrs. Arbuthnot, "and it *is* rather silly that Mrs. Fisher should behave as if it belonged only to her."

"What is rather silly," said Mrs. Wilkins with much serenity, "is to mind. I can't see the least point in being in authority at the price of one's liberty."

Mrs. Arbuthnot said nothing to that for two reasons,—first, because she was struck by the remarkable and growing calm of the hitherto incoherent and excited Lotty, and secondly because what she was looking at was so very beautiful.

All down the stone steps on either side were periwinkles in full flower, and she could now see what it was that had caught at her the night before and brushed, wet and scented, across her face. It was wistaria. *Wistaria and sunshine* . . . she remembered the advertisement. Here indeed were both in profusion. The wistaria was tumbling over itself in its excess of life, its prodigality of flowering; and where the pergola ended the sun blazed on scarlet geraniums, bushes of them, and nasturtiums in great heaps, and marigolds so brilliant that they seemed to be burning, and red and pink snapdragons, all outdoing each other in bright, fierce colour. The ground behind these flaming things dropped away in terraces to the sea, each terrace a little orchard, where among the olives grew vines on trellises, and fig-trees, and peach-trees, and cherry-trees. The cherry-trees and peach-trees were in blossom,—lovely showers of white and deep rose-colour among the trembling delicacy of the olives; the fig-leaves were just big enough to smell of figs, the vine-buds were only beginning to show. And beneath these trees were groups of blue and purple irises, and bushes of lavender, and grey, sharp cactuses, and the grass was thick with dandelions and daisies, and right down at the bottom was the sea. Colour seemed flung down anyhow, anywhere; every sort of colour, piled up in heaps, pouring along in rivers—the periwinkles looked exactly as if they were being poured down each side of the steps—and flowers that grow only in borders in England, proud flowers keeping themselves to themselves over there, such as the great blue irises and the lavender, were being jostled by small, shining common things like dandelions and daisies and the white bells of the wild onion, and only seemed the better and the more exuberant for it.

They stood looking at this crowd of loveliness, this happy jumble, in silence. No, it didn't matter what Mrs. Fisher did; not here; not in such beauty. Mrs. Arbuthnot's discomposure melted out of her. In the warmth and light of what she was looking at, of what to her was a manifestation, an entirely new side, of God, how could one be discomposed? If only Frederick* were with her, seeing it too, seeing as he would have seen it when first they were lovers, in the days when he saw what she saw and loved what she loved. . . .

She sighed.

"You mustn't sigh in heaven," said Mrs. Wilkins. "One doesn't."

"I was thinking how one longs to share this with those one loves," said Mrs. Arbuthnot.

"You mustn't long in heaven," said Mrs. Wilkins. "You're supposed to be quite complete there. And it *is* heaven, isn't it, Rose? See how everything has been let in together,—the dandelions and the irises, the vulgar and the superior, me and Mrs. Fisher—all welcome, all mixed up anyhow, and all so visibly happy and enjoying ourselves."

"Mrs. Fisher doesn't seem happy—not visibly, anyhow," said Mrs. Arbuthnot, smiling.

"She'll begin soon, you'll see."

Mrs. Arbuthnot said she didn't believe that after a certain age people began anything.

Mrs. Wilkins said she was sure no one, however old and tough, could resist the effects of perfect beauty. Before many days, perhaps only hours, they would see Mrs. Fisher bursting out into every kind of exuberance. "I'm quite sure," said Mrs. Wilkins, "that we've got to heaven, and once Mrs. Fisher realises that that's where she is, she's bound to be different. You'll see. She'll leave off being ossified, and go all soft and able to stretch, and we shall get quite—why, I shouldn't be surprised if we get quite fond of her." . . .

That last week the syringa came out at San Salvatore, and all the acacias flowered. No one had noticed how many acacias there were till one day the garden was full of a new scent, and there were the delicate trees, the lovely successors to the wistaria, hung all over among their trembling leaves with blossom. To lie under an acacia

*Rose Arbuthnot's husband.

tree that last week and look up through the branches at its frail leaves and white flowers quivering against the blue of the sky, while the least movement of the air shook down their scent, was a great happiness. Indeed, the whole garden dressed itself gradually towards the end in white, and grew more and more scented. There were the lilies, as vigorous as ever, and the white stocks and white pinks and white banksia roses, and the syringa and the jessamine, and at last the crowning fragrance of the acacias. When, on the first of May, everybody went away, even after they had got to the bottom of the hill and passed through the iron gates out into the village they still could smell the acacias.

THE END

For the Literary Traveler

The women in the novel do not hallucinate. Everywhere on the heights of Portofino, "the very heart of beauty," as Rose Arbuthnot thinks of it, the landscape displays the joy of Nature: the colors and scents of flowers, the bluegreen sea, gardens up and down the mountainsides dense with orange trees and cypresses and pines. The heavy tourist traffic below in the village is not the point and on foot can be quickly left behind on the ascent to the lighthouse *(il faro)*. The view of mountains and sea from the promontory beside the lighthouse makes von Arnim's insight palpable: the power of place to change hearts. Time spent in the sensual paradise of the Portofino peninsula could conceivably inspire the dreary soul to imagine life more generously: more blessing than duty, an adventure of love. Quite aptly, the house where the women come "unglued" is called San Salvatore.

The seaside town of SANTA MARGHERITA, five miles east, is also splendid and less crowded than Portofino. Walking at sundown along its waterside of blue distances and palm trees—there is a statue of Mary at the water's edge with arms extended to welcome homecoming fishermen—offers a tranquillity that can be hard for travelers to come by, especially on the Italian Riviera, which attracts more tourists than any other part of Italy. Sometimes they all seem to have arrived together, on bikes and vespas, along the narrow coast road that twists between Santa Margherita and Portofino.

TUSCANY

LUCCA

FLORENCE

SIENA

LA FOCE AND
MONTEPULCIANO

Francesca Alexander

The daughter of Boston portrait painter Francis Alexander and his devout wife, Lucia Grey Swett, Esther Frances Alexander (1837–1917)—known as "Francesca" and "Fanny"—moved with her parents from Boston to Italy in 1853, settling permanently in Florence, in the Piazza Santa Maria Novella. Folklorist, writer, and artist, Francesca traveled widely in northern Italy, collecting, translating, and illustrating popular and anonymous Tuscan writing— ballads, hymns, and stornelli *(ditties). Also known for her good works on behalf of the Tuscan peasantry, she gave the proceeds of her books to the poor as well as the profits she made from selling the woolen shawls and stockings knitted by local peasants to her American and English friends. In 1882, she met the art historian, critic, and social reformer John Ruskin, who became Alexander's friend and literary agent. The mutual affection of their correspondence—he addressed her as "Darling Sorella" (sister); she called him "Fratello" (brother)—signals their truly loving friendship. "I never knew such vivid goodness and innocence in any living creatures," he said of Fanny and her mother. To Fanny he wrote, "Every word you write . . . is joy and strength to me; and you are the more to me because my life has been strangely loveless till now."*

Impressed with her book The Story of Ida, *he edited it and helped get it published. He also wrote the introduction to* Roadside Songs of Tuscany *(1885) (published in America as* Tuscan Songs), *described by Francesca as "songs and hymns of the poor people . . . collected, little by little, in the course of a great many years which I have passed in constant intercourse with the Tuscan* contadini. *They are but the siftings . . . of the hundreds and hundreds which I have heard . . . mostly from old people: many of them have never . . . been written down before. . . . there are others who will collect and preserve the thoughts of the rich and great; and I have wished to make my book all of poor people's poetry. . . ."*

Both Fanny and Ruskin loved Lucca, he for its twelfth-century buildings— "so incorruptible"—which inspired him to begin his study of architecture—and

*she for its literary treasure, in particular the legend of the servant girl Zita of
Lucca, which she translated and illustrated as "The Ballad of St. Zita," using her
Tuscan friend Polissena from Abetone as a model of the saint. A portion of the
ballad follows here. In* The Lure of Italy: American Artists and The Italian
Experience, 1760–1914, *Karen Haas writes that Zita's story of self-sacrifice to
help the needy would have had particular meaning for Alexander, who was herself often described as a kind of modern-day saint for her work among the* contadini. *The Saint Zita sheets of the* Roadside Songs of Tuscany, *the illustrations
of which Ruskin held in "reverent admiration" and had a facsimile edition
printed, were recently exhibited at the Boston Museum of Fine Art and can be
seen in the special collections of the Wellesley College Library.*

FROM *ROADSIDE SONGS OF TUSCANY*

THE BALLAD OF SANTA ZITA
PROTECTRESS OF LUCCA.

ARRANGED IN OTTAVA RIMA BY GUASPARI DI BARTOLOMEO CASENTI,
OF LUCCA, IN THE YEAR 1616.

I.

O Light of lights, Redeemer of mankind,
Whose glory most in mercy shines displayed,
Concede Thy favour to my humble mind,
Increase my feeble memory with Thine aid,
My heart to-day some fitting words would find,
To tell of Zita, Lucca's holy maid:
That Christians all may read her life, and how
She sleeps in old San Frediano now.

II.

And so, O Light Divine, I turn to Thee.
Refuse me not the mercy I implore!
But grant me, all unworthy though I be,
To tell in rhyme the tale oft told before.
Without Thy help, too hard it were for me
Even to begin; oh give me from Thy store

A little wisdom; on Thy grace I wait,
While I this holy, humble life relate.

III.

So listen kindly, friends, and I will tell,
The story of our saint, now raised so high:
And first I pray you to remember well
Her birthplace. . . . To our city it lies nigh.
She who doth in the eternal glory dwell,
With other virgin saints above the sky,
Was born, long since, in Lucca's happy state,
At Monsagrato, so old books relate.

IV.

'Twas in the year twelve hundred and eighteen
This noble flower blossomed first on earth:
And in a poor man's household was she seen,
A household poor in gold, but rich in worth.
Her elder sister led a life serene
Within a convent, ere Saint Zita's birth.
Giovan Lombardo was the father styled,
A worthy parent of a saintly child.

V.

Her mother was so good, that every day
She loved her better, seeing how she grew
In fear of God, and walking in His way
From earliest childhood, with devotion true.
Prayer was her great delight, she loved to stay
In church alone, and dream of all she knew
Of how God lived on earth, and how He died;
Until her heart could hold no dream beside.

VI.

An uncle Zita had, of whom they tell,
That every virtue did his soul attire,

Faith, charity, and hope, did with him dwell,
And holy works were all his heart's desire.
Poor, yet content, God's name he honoured well,
Nor did to aught of earthly good aspire.
A man of humble life, and saintly fame;
And Graziano was this uncle's name.

VII.

Time passed, the girl grew older, well content
To do God's work, whate'er that work might be.
Her brightest hours on her knees were spent,
And little thought of worldly things had she.
One day to saddening care her mind was lent:
"I eat my father's bread, he works for me!"
She raised her heart in prayer: "O Lord," she said,
"To Lucca let me go, and earn my bread."

VIII.

And He who hears in secret, heard that prayer:
For both her parents came, the selfsame day,
And asked her, "Daughter, would'st thou now prepare
As servant in a noble house to stay?
For since to serve the Lord is all thy care,
In Lucca hath He marked thee out thy way.
There may'st thou live, there labour and there die."
"Thank God! So be it!" Zita made reply.

IX.

They reached the house for Zita's home designed,
And Casa Fantinelli was its name.
A family of noble life and mind
Dwelt in it, when the saintly maiden came.
Just to their servants,—to the needy, kind.
With them her life could pass, almost the same
As with her parents. She, rejoiced indeed,
Gave thanks to God who did such grace concede.

X.

The door once reached, she let her father go;
They said farewell, then parted; and this done,

She entered in, and bowed herself full low
Before the Fantinelli, every one:
Thenceforward toiling humbly; none might know
How long she worked before the morning sun:
Content each day, might only time remain
To hear the Mass; then back to work again.

XI.
At twelve years old she did to service go,
And ever after in that house she stayed,
With love unwearied, which no change could know:
Her master's word she never disobeyed.
A humble mind her very looks might show,
So poor was all the dress of this poor maid!
The meanest garment pleased her best to wear,
And all the whole year round her feet were bare. . . .

XV.
So would she visit in her loving care,
The hospital, and all who in it lay;
Or those in prison would her kindness share;
Or to some church, it might be far away,
At times with thankful heart she would repair,
Where, all unseen, unnoticed, she could pray.
For more she loved to be with God alone,
Than have by others her devotion known.

XVI.
And every morning, when but first awake,
To San Frediano straight her way she made,
For early matins, ere the day could break
('Twas near the house where she as servant stayed),
Her place there in a corner she would take,
And listen till the Service all was said.
In holy contemplation lost, until
'Twas time her morning duties to fulfil.

XVII.

It chanced one day,—and only one, 'tis said,—
That Zita lingered, being lost in prayer,
And quite forgot she had not made the bread,
Which on that morning should have been her care.
Till, service over, as she homeward sped,
She recollected and would now repair
Her error, so ran quickly all the way,
To make the bread, which must be baked that day.

XVIII.

But on the table what did she behold?
The loaves all there, a cloth above them laid.
At sight of which was Zita much consoled,
Not doubting but her mistress had them made:
But no, the house was silent; young and old
Had slept, while Zita in the church delayed.
She could but thank her Lord, with heart content,
Who by His Angels had this favour sent. . . .

A TUSCAN LULLABY

Maria lavava,
Giuseppe stendeva,
Suo Figlio piangeva
Dal freddo che aveva.
    —Sta zitto, mio figlio,
Chè adesso ti piglio!
Del latte t' ho dato,
Del pane 'un ce n' è.—
    La neve sui monti
Cadeva dal cielo:
Maria col suo velo
Copriva Gesù.

    Sweet Mary was washing,
While Joseph laid, drying,
The Baby was crying
For the cold that came on.

> Oh hush thee, my darling,
> I'll take thee this moment,—
> Of milk I have given thee,
> Of bread there is none.
> The snow on the mountains
> From heaven was falling:
> Then Mary her veil took
> and covered her Son.
> —*Roadside Song*

For the Literary Traveler

In the *Inferno* of *The Divine Comedy,* Dante's reference to St. Zita of Lucca evokes the city's reputation as a den of ruthless moneygrubbers. "Every man there is a swindler. . . .; there *No* is made *Ay* for cash" (XXI, 38). While other Tuscan city-states were wasting their resources in war, Lucca was trading silks and wool with northern Europe, creating jobs for the sculptors and stonemasons who built her seventy churches, and getting rich.

Zita's story turns this reputation upside down. She won sanctity—and Lucca's love (she is the city's patron saint)—by ignoring market values. Behind her master's back she distributed his wealth among the poor and the sick, enacting a medieval version of Bahktinian carnivalesque. Her body is preserved in a chapel within the spacious and lovely simplicity of SAN FREDIANO (early 1100s). In this Romanesque church, dedicated to the Irish saint "Frigidianus," or "Finnian,"—a sixth-century bishop of Lucca— Zita (d. 1278), according to the ballad, went to daily Mass. Down the nave rise Roman columns removed from the still intact site of the ROMAN AMPHITHEATRE between VIA FILLUNGO and VIA MORDINI. Near Zita's chapel in the south aisle (in 1996 her memorial space is as poorly maintained as she was in life) stands what is considered Tuscany's most beautiful baptismal font, bearing the stone heroics of Moses, Jesus, and the Apostles. Behind the font hangs a lyrical Annunciation by Andrea della Robbia.

Both traditions—business savvy and a generous spirit of life as play—animate Lucca today. Visitors who explore it on foot—the best and only way since its narrow streets are closed to traffic—sense an easy

coexistence of order and fun. The piazzas swell with markets of local arts
and crafts run by artisans even on Sundays; crowds stop to enjoy musicians, balloons, pigeons, and children in PIAZZA SAN MICHELE—the site of
the forum in ancient Roman "Luca" (admired by Julius Caesar) that surrounds the church of SAN MICHELE, whose gorgeous green, white, and
rose-colored marble facade Ruskin sketched and where Puccini (born
nearby) was a choirboy. The *passeggiatta* along the cobblestoned Via Fillungo flows thick with giddy and groping teenagers amidst lumbering
matrons in dignified outfits seeking good goods. In the shadows of the
low overhanging facades of medieval buildings broken by blasts of MTV
rock, the explosive teenagers and the sturdy ladies seem like timeless figures on the currents of history. Sunday Mass in San Frediano's as celebrated by a stern priest, served by altar girls in surplices and red
Converses, and sung by an especially lively folk choir of young and old,
men and women presents small dramas of gender and generational ten-
sions lit with humor. (When, on Pentecost, the priest sent a disapproving
frown in the choir's direction, a few singers giggled.) As Henry James
observed in *Italian Hours*, "I remember saying to myself...that no brown-
and-gold Tuscan city could *be* as happy as Lucca looked," [seeming]
"fairly to laugh." Even the heavy lore of its hagiography has a sense of
play: when St. Zita smuggled food to the poor it was miraculously
changed into flowers so that the servant girl would not get caught by her
master. Every year on April 26, the Lucchese remember Zita's holy con
game by filling the PIAZZA SAN FREDIANO with flowers.

Visiting the sick and the imprisoned, finding and feeding the poor,
going back and forth to Mass, the peripatetic Zita would have known a
number of the splendid twelfth-century churches that Ruskin praises in
his introduction to "Darling Sorella's" ballad. The DUOMO (SAN MARTINO
or ST. MARTIN'S CATHEDRAL), consecrated in 1070, has on its facade the
finest sculpture and reliefs in the city: Nicola Pisano's *Adoration of the
Magi*, for example (Ruskin calls it *Christ's Nativity*), is a notable work.
Inside there are windows of St. Zita and St. Frigidianus, paintings by
Ghirlandaio and Tintoretto, and in the north aisle, the VOLTO SANTO
("Holy Image")—famous throughout Europe as the wooden likeness of
Jesus supposed to have been carved by Nicodemus, who was present
at the crucifixion. Jacopo della Quercia's TOMB OF ILARIA DEL CARRETTO
GUINIGI, in the north transept, is an early Renaissance masterpiece.

For an overview of the city that Francesca and Ruskin admired for "the great fuss" it made "over her little Zita," the walk along the heights of the massive medieval walls, planted with chestnut and beech trees, is fine. But the most glorious prospect is from the roof garden of the TORRE GUINIGI (the tower next to the Guinigi family palace in Via Guinigi and Via Santa Andrea). The spread of the medieval city and the distant peaks of the Apuan Alps present a panorama of Lucca's material body and happy soul.

Elizabeth Barrett Browning

One wonders how "close to death" (as one scholar puts it) Elizabeth Barrett actually could have been when, approaching forty, she eloped and ran away to Italy with Robert Browning. After a winter in Pisa, they came to Florence in 1847 where they stayed for good and wrote the poems for which both are best known. Breaking free from the oppressions of Wimpole Street and embracing Italy in the period of its revolutionary heat made her the woman and writer she became: her passion was for the freedom of love, her theme was human rights. The causes of republicanism in Italy, abolition in the United States, child welfare laws in England, and full humanity for women focus her writings. Though her voice was sometimes cloying, she wrote as a serious social advocate and humanitarian. When George Eliot reread Casa Guidi* Windows *in 1862, she said, "I have lately read again with great delight Mrs. Browning's* Casa Guidi Windows. *It contains amongst other admirable things a very noble expression of what I believe to be the true relation of the religious mind to the Past." That relation is struck in the pages that follow—"We do not serve the dead—the past is past! God lives. . . ." Though the image of her past as captive, dutiful daughter is always at her back, the windows of the mature woman look out on the ardor and possibilities of freedom.*

*The name of the Brownings' home in Florence.

FROM *CASA GUIDI WINDOWS*

PART ONE

I heard last night a little child go singing
   'Neath Casa Guidi windows, by the church,
O bella libertà, O bella! stringing
   The same words still on notes he went in search
So high for, you concluded the upspringing
   Of such a nimble bird to sky from perch
Must leave the whole bush in a tremble green,
   And that the heart of Italy must beat,
While such a voice had leave to rise serene
   'Twixt church and palace of a Florence street!
A little child, too, who not long had been
   By mother's finger steadied on his feet,
And still *O bella libertà* he sang. . . .

   For me who stand in Italy to-day,
Where worthier poets stood and sang before,
   I kiss their footsteps, yet their words gainsay.
I can but muse in hope upon this shore
   Of golden Arno as it shoots away
Through Florence' heart beneath her bridges four!
   Bent bridges, seeming to strain off like bows,
And tremble while the arrowy undertide
 Shoots on and cleaves the marble as it goes,
And strikes up palace-walls on either side,
   And froths the cornice out in glittering rows,
With doors and windows quaintly multiplied,
   And terrace-sweeps, and gazers upon all,
By whom if flower or kerchief were thrown out
   From any lattice there, the same would fall
Into the river underneath no doubt,
   It runs so close and fast 'twixt wall and wall.

How beautiful! the mountains from without
   In silence listen for the word said next.
What word will men say,—here where Giotto planted
   His campanile, like an unperplexed

Fine question Heaven-ward, touching the things granted
    A noble people who, being greatly vexed
In act, in aspiration keep undaunted?
    What word will God say? Michel's Night and Day
And Dawn and Twilight wait in marble scorn,*
    Like dogs upon a dunghill, couched on clay
From whence the Medicean stamp's outworn,
    The final putting off of all such sway
By all such hands, and freeing of the unborn
    In Florence and the great world outside Florence. . . .

    We do not serve the dead—the past is past!
God lives, and lifts his glorious mornings up
    Before the eyes of men, awake at last,
Who put away the meats they used to sup,
    And down upon the dust of earth outcast
The dregs remaining of the ancient cup, . . .

You enter, in your Florence wanderings,
    The church of St. Maria Novella. Pass
The left stair, where at plague-time Macchiavel
    Saw One with set fair face as in a glass,
Dressed out against the fear of death and hell,
    Rustling her silks in pauses of the mass,
To keep the thought off how her husband fell,
    When she left home, stark dead across her feet,—
The stair leads up to what the Orgagnas save
    Of Dante's dæmons; you, in passing it,
Ascend the right stair from the farther nave,
    To muse in a small chapel scarcely lit
By Cimabue's Virgin. Bright and brave,
    That picture was accounted, mark, of old.
A king stood bare before its sovran grace,
    A reverent people shouted to behold
The picture, not the king, and even the place
    Containing such a miracle, grew bold,

*"Michel" is Michelangelo. His statues Night, Day, Dawn, and Twilight are in the New Sacristy of the church of San Lorenzo.

Named the Glad Borgo from that beauteous face,—
    Which thrilled the artist, after work, to think
His own ideal Mary-smile should stand
    So very near him,—he, within the brink
Of all that glory, let in by his hand
    With too divine a rashness! Yet none shrink
Who come to gaze here now—albeit 'twas planned
    Sublimely in the thought's simplicity.
The Lady, throned in empyreal state,
    Minds only the young babe upon her knee,
While sidelong angels bear the royal weight,
    Prostrated meekly, smiling tenderly
Oblivion of their wings; the Child thereat
    Stretching its hand like God. . . .

A noble picture! worthy of the shout
    Wherewith along the streets the people bore
Its cherub faces, which the sun threw out
    Until they stooped and entered the church door!—
Yet rightly was young Giotto talked about,
    Whom Cimabue found among the sheep,
And knew, as gods know gods, and carried home
    To paint the things he had painted, with a deep
And fuller insight, and so overcome
    His chapel-lady with a heavenlier sweep
Of light. For thus we mount into the sum
    Of great things known or acted. I hold, too,
That Cimabue smiled upon the lad,
    At the first stroke which passed what he could do,—
Or else his Virgin's smile had never had
    Such sweetness in 't. All great men who foreknew
Their heirs in art, for art's sake have been glad,
    And bent their old white heads as if uncrowned,
Fanatics of their pure ideals still
    Far more than of their triumphs, . . .

BELLOSGUARDO

I found a house at Florence on the hill
Of Bellosguardo.* 'Tis a tower which keeps
A post of double observation o'er
That valley of Arno (holding as a hand
The outspread city) straight toward Fiesole
And Mount Morello and the setting sun,
The Vallombrosan mountains opposite,
Which sunrise fills as full as crystal cups
Turned red to the brim because their wine is red.
No sun could die nor yet be born unseen
By dwellers at my villa: morn and eve
Were magnified before us in the pure
Illimitable space and pause of sky,
Intense as angels' garments blanched with God,
Less blue than radiant. From the outer wall
Of the garden, drops the mystic floating grey
Of olive trees (with interruptions green
From maize and vine), until 'tis caught and torn
Upon the abrupt black line of cypresses
Which signs the way to Florence. Beautiful
The city lies along the ample vale,
Cathedral, tower and palace, piazza and street,
The river trailing like a silver cord
Through all, and curling loosely, both before
And after, over the whole stretch of land
Sown whitely up and down its opposite slopes
With farms and villas.

🖋

For the Literary Traveler

Elizabeth Barrett Browning loved Florence with the same passion she
felt for her husband, Robert, and her son, Pen. Each enabled the
ecstasies of home and city, an amplitude of interior and exterior space

*Florence is encircled by the hills of Bellosguardo, Careggi, Fiesole, Settignano,
and Arcetri.

forbidden in her father's house. "O freedom! O my Florence!" The OLTRARNO, where they lived, on the south side of the ARNO, provides a welcome adagio amidst the *con fuoco* of the tourists in the central city. VIA MAGGIO leads from the PONTE SANTA TRINITA up to PIAZZA SAN FELICE and no. 8 CASA GUIDI (where the couple moved after lodging first in the VIA DELLE BELLE DONNE between PIAZZA SANTA MARIA NOVELLA and PIAZZA SANTA TRINITÀ). Originally "Palazzo" Guidi until the democratic-minded Mrs. Browning renamed it, the house is marked with a plaque that shows Elizabeth's love for Italy did not go unrequited: "Here wrote and lived Elizabeth Barrett Browning ... whose poems forged a golden ring between Italy and England." Her residence can be visited on Monday and Wednesday afternoons, the decor and furnishings having been restored to the appearance they had in the Brownings' time. Visitors may sit and use the library in Elizabeth's drawing room/study—she had no room of her own—the windows of which face out on the church of SAN FELICE. From the music school on the PIAZZA SAN FELICE the sound of singing, mentioned in her poetry, can still be heard from within the church's pretty interior, where Elizabeth attended services.

Further along the VIA ROMANA (the extension of Via Maggio), leaving the PITTI PALACE behind, is the ANNALENA ENTRANCE to the BOBOLI GARDENS (perhaps the best maintained park in Italy), where the Brownings and Pen often walked (their rent, a guinea a week, included admission to the Gardens), passing the grotto of Adam and Eve; further along, at the end of an avenue of tall hedges, is the charming and secluded ISOLOTTO, a small lake surrounding an island of roses and statues.

At the end of Via Romana, through the PORTA ROMANA, is the uphill turn and narrow road to BELLOSGUARDO, another beautiful hillside neighborhood (like SAN MINIATO AL MONTE and FIESOLE), more accessible by bus (number 42 from Porta Romana) than on foot. It is described in the preceding poem "Bellosguardo," and in *Aurora Leigh* and was visited frequently by the Brownings, Nathaniel and Sophia Hawthorne, and, in later years, Henry James and Violet Trefusis. Florence Nightingale, named after the city of her birth, was born in Bellosguardo.

From the small terrace outside the drawing room windows of Casa

Guidi Elizabeth watched the political demonstrations of 1848 in the piazza and streets below, and as the long poem shows, her sympathies (like those of Margaret Fuller in Rome, who introduced the Brownings' poetry to American readers in her dispatches to the *New York Tribune*) were ardently republican—Mazzini, Garibaldi, and at first Pio Nono (Pope Pius IX) were her heroes of the dream of a united and independent Italy. Her devotion to progressive politics colored her imagination of Florence's past and its monuments. Thus she imputes her own generosity of spirit to earlier artists: in *Casa Guidi Windows*, her description of the interior of SANTA MARIA NOVELLA (Henry James's favorite church in Florence) features Cimabue encouraging his own eclipse by Giotto. (GIOTTO'S BELL TOWER, in another part of the city, is, for her, another sign of the divine/human capacity for creative passion.) She also presents the ORCAGNA FRESCOES of scenes from Dante's *Inferno* and *Paradiso* in the STROZZI CHAPEL (up the steps in the north transept to the left of the magnificent GHIRLANDAIO FRESCOES in the SANCTUARY) as part of the glorious tradition of republican and artistic Florence. To the left of the church, the GREEN CLOISTERS and the SPANISH CHAPEL (inside the MUSEO) are among the loveliest and most peaceful places in her adopted city.

George Eliot

"There has been a crescendo of enjoyment in our travels," said George Eliot/Marian Evans ("Polly" to her life partner, G. H. Lewes) in a letter of 1860. "For Florence, from its relation to the history of modern art, has roused a keener interest in us even than Rome, and has stimulated me to entertain rather an ambitious project." The project was Romola, *a historical novel based on the life of the Florentine Dominican friar Savonarola (1452–1498) who, in fiery sermons between 1491 and 1494, attacked the immorality of Florentines, the power of Lorenzo de' Medici, and the corruption of Pope Alexander VI. For a while Savonarola was something of a religious hero; then the mood changed, and after his excommunication by the*

pope for heresy, the prior of San Marco was hanged and then burned at the
stake in Piazza della Signoria. Romola (1862), a success in its time, is rarely
read today. Henry James complained that "it smelled of libraries." (But critic
John Bayley believes that in the undervalued Romola, *Eliot is her most per-*
ceptive about the relations between men and women and that the wife
Romola, more than Dorothea Brooke in Middlemarch, *was in James's mind*
when he wrote the character of Isabel Archer in The *Portrait of a Lady.)*
The novel's prologue, evoking Florence at dawn from the hill of San
Miniato, can stand alone as evidence of the power that the city's beauty—
and history—held over Eliot's imagination.

FROM *ROMOLA*

PROEM

More than three centuries and a half ago, in the mid springtime
of 1492, we are sure that the angel of the dawn, as he travelled with broad slow wing from the Levant to the Pillars of Her-
cules, and from the summits of the Caucasus across all the snowy
Alpine ridges to the dark nakedness of the Western isles, saw nearly
the same outline of firm land and unstable sea—saw the same great
mountain shadows on the same valleys as he has seen to-day—saw
olive mounts, and pine forests, and the broad plains green with
young corn or rain-freshened grass—saw the domes and spires of
cities rising by the river-sides or mingled with the sedge-like masts
on the many-curved sea-coast, in the same spots where they rise today. And as the faint light of his course pierced into the dwellings
of men, it fell, as now, on the rosy warmth of nestling children; on
the haggard waking of sorrow and sickness; on the hasty uprising
of the hard-handed labourer; and on the late sleep of the night-
student, who had been questioning the stars or the sages, or his
own soul, for that hidden knowledge which would break through
the barrier of man's brief life, and show its dark path, that seemed
to bend no whither, to be an arc in an immeasurable circle of light
and glory. The great river-courses which have shaped the lives of
men have hardly changed; and those other streams, the life-
currents that ebb and flow in human hearts, pulsate to the same
great needs, the same great loves and terrors. As our thought

follows close in the slow wake of the dawn, we are impressed with the broad sameness of the human lot, which never alters in the main headings of its history—hunger and labour, seed-time and harvest, love and death.

Even if, instead of following the dim daybreak, our imagination pauses on a certain historical spot and awaits the fuller morning, we may see a world-famous city, which has hardly changed its outline since the days of Columbus, seeming to stand as an almost unviolated symbol, amidst the flux of human things, to remind us that we still resemble the men of the past more than we differ from them, as the great mechanical principles on which those domes and towers were raised must make a likeness in human building that will be broader and deeper than all possible change. And doubtless, if the spirit of a Florentine citizen, whose eyes were closed for the last time while Columbus was still waiting and arguing for the three poor vessels with which he was to set sail from the port of Palos, could return from the shades and pause where our thought is pausing, he would believe that there must still be fellowship and understanding for him among the inheritors of his birthplace.

Let us suppose that such a Shade has been permitted to revisit the glimpses of the golden morning, and is standing once more on the famous hill of San Miniato, which overlooks Florence from the south.

The Spirit is clothed in his habit as he lived: the folds of his well-lined black silk garment or *lucco* hang in grave unbroken lines from neck to ankle; his plain cloth cap, with its *becchetto*, or long hanging strip of drapery, to serve as a scarf in case of need, surmounts a penetrating face, not, perhaps, very handsome, but with a firm, well-cut mouth, kept distinctly human by a close-shaven lip and chin. It is a face charged with memories of a keen and various life passed below there on the banks of the gleaming river; and as he looks at the scene before him, the sense of familiarity is so much stronger than the perception of change, that he thinks it might be possible to descend once more amongst the streets, and take up that busy life where he left it. For it is not only the mountains and the westward-bending river that he recognises; not only the dark sides of Mount Morello opposite to him, and the long valley of the Arno that seems to stretch its grey low-tufted luxuriance to the far-off ridges of Carrara; and the steep height of Fiesole, with its crown of monastic walls and cypresses; and all the green and grey slopes sprinkled with villas which he can name as he looks at them. He sees other familiar objects much closer to his daily walks. For though he misses the seventy or more towers that once surmounted the walls, and encircled the city as with a regal diadem, his eyes will not dwell on that blank; they are drawn irresistibly to the unique tower springing, like a tall flower-stem drawn towards the sun, from the square turreted mass of the Old Palace in the very heart of the city—the tower that looks none the worse for the four centuries that have passed since he used to walk under it. The great dome, too, greatest in the world, which, in his early boyhood, had been only a daring thought in the mind of a small, quick-eyed man—there it raises its large curves still, eclipsing the hills. And the well-known bell-towers—Giotto's, with its distant hint of rich colour, and the graceful-spired Badia, and the rest—he looked at them all from the shoulder of his nurse.

"Surely," he thinks, "Florence can still ring her bells with the solemn hammer-sound that used to beat on the hearts of her citizens and strike out the fire there. And here, on the right, stands the long dark mass of Santa Croce, where we buried our famous dead, laying the laurel on their cold brows and fanning them with the breath of praise and of banners. But Santa Croce had no spire then: we Florentines were too full of great building projects to carry them all out in stone and marble; we had our frescoes and our shrines to pay for, not to speak of rapacious condottieri, bribed royalty, and purchased territories, and our façades and spires must needs wait. But what architect can the Frati Minori have employed to build that spire for them? If it had been built in my day, Filippo Brunelleschi or Michelozzo would have devised something of another fashion than that—something worthy to crown the church of Arnolfo."

At this the Spirit, with a sigh, lets his eyes travel on to the city walls, and now he dwells on the change there with wonder at these modern times. Why have five out of the eleven convenient gates

been closed? And why, above all, should the towers have been levelled that were once a glory and defence? Is the world become so
peaceful, then, and do Florentines dwell in such harmony, that
there are no longer conspiracies to bring ambitious exiles home
again with armed bands at their back? These are difficult questions: it is easier and pleasanter to recognise the old than to
account for the new. And there flows Arno, with its bridges just
where they used to be—the Ponte Vecchio, least like other bridges
in the world, laden with the same quaint shops where our Spirit
remembers lingering a little on his way perhaps to look at the
progress of that great palace which Messer Luca Pitti had set a-
building with huge stones got from the Hill of Bogoli close behind,
or perhaps to transact a little business with the cloth-dressers in
Oltrarno. The exorbitant line of the Pitti roof is hidden from San
Miniato; but the yearning of the old Florentine is not to see Messer
Luca's too ambitious palace which he built unto himself; it is to be
down among those narrow streets and busy humming Piazze where
he inherited the eager life of his fathers. Is not the anxious voting
with black and white beans still going on down there? Who are the
Priori in these months, eating soberly regulated official dinners in
the Palazzo Vecchio, with removes of tripe and boiled partridges,
seasoned by practical jokes against the ill-fated butt among those
potent signors? Are not the significant banners still hung from the
windows—still distributed with decent pomp under Orcagna's
Loggia every two months?

Life had its zest for the old Florentine when he, too, trod the
marble steps and shared in those dignities. His politics had an area
as wide as his trade, which stretched from Syria to Britain, but they
had also the passionate intensity, and the detailed practical interest,
which could belong only to a narrow scene of corporate action;
only to the members of a community shut in close by the hills and
by walls of six miles' circuit, where men knew each other as they
passed in the street, set their eyes every day on the memorials of
their commonwealth, and were conscious of having not simply the
right to vote, but the chance of being voted for. He loved his hon-
ours and his gains, the business of his counting-house, of his guild,
of the public council-chamber; he loved his enmities too, and

fingered the white bean which was to keep a hated name out of the *borsa* with more complacency than if it had been a golden florin. He loved to strengthen his family by a good alliance; and went home with a triumphant light in his eyes after concluding a satisfactory marriage for his son or daughter under his favourite loggia in the evening cool; he loved his game at chess under that same loggia, and his biting jest, and even his coarse joke, as not beneath the dignity of a man eligible for the highest magistracy. He had gained an insight into all sorts of affairs at home and abroad: he had been of the "Ten" who managed the war department, of the "Eight" who attended to home discipline, of the Priori or Signori who were the heads of the executive government; he had even risen to the supreme office of Gonfaloniere; he had made one in embassies to the Pope and to the Venetians; and he had been commissary to the hired army of the Republic, directing the inglorious bloodless battles in which no man died of brave breast wounds—*virtuosi colpi*—but only of casual falls and tramplings. And in this way he had learned to distrust men without bitterness; looking on life mainly as a game of skill, but not dead to traditions of heroism and clean-handed honour. For the human soul is hospitable, and will entertain conflicting sentiments and contradictory opinions with much impartiality. It was his pride besides, that he was duly tinctured with the learning of his age, and judged not altogether with the vulgar, but in harmony with the ancients: he, too, in his prime, had been eager for the most correct manuscripts, and had paid many florins for antique vases and for disinterred busts of the ancient immortals—some, perhaps, *truncis naribus*, wanting as to the nose, but not the less authentic; and in his old age he had made haste to look at the first sheets of that fine Homer which was among the early glories of the Florentine press. But he had not, for all that, neglected to hang up a waxen image or double of himself under the protection of the Madonna Annunziata, or to do penance for his sins in large gifts to the shrines of saints whose lives had not been modelled on the study of the classics; he had not even neglected making liberal bequests towards buildings for the Frati, against whom he had levelled many a jest.

For the Unseen Powers were mighty. Who knew—who was

sure—that there was *any* name given to them behind which there was no angry force to be appeased, no intercessory pity to be won? Were not gems medicinal, though they only pressed the finger? Were not all things charged with occult virtues? Lucretius might be right—he was an ancient, and a great poet; Luigi Pulci, too, who was suspected of not believing anything from the roof upward (*dal tetto in su*), had very much the air of being right over the supper-table, when the wine and jests were circulating fast, though he was only a poet in the vulgar tongue. There were even learned personages who maintained that Aristotle, wisest of men (unless, indeed, Plato were wiser?) was a thoroughly irreligious philosopher; and a liberal scholar must entertain all speculations. But the negatives might, after all, prove false; nay, seemed manifestly false, as the circling hours swept past him, and turned round with graver faces. For had not the world become Christian? Had he not been baptised in San Giovanni, where the dome is awful with the symbols of coming judgment, and where the altar bears a crucified Image disturbing to perfect complacency in one's self and the world? Our resuscitated Spirit was not a pagan philosopher, nor a philosophising pagan poet, but a man of the fifteenth century, inheriting its strange web of belief and unbelief; of Epicurean levity and fetichistic dread; of pedantic impossible ethics uttered by rote, and crude passions acted out with childish impulsiveness; of inclination towards a self-indulgent paganism, and inevitable subjection to that human conscience which, in the unrest of a new growth, was filling the air with strange prophecies and presentiments.

He had smiled, perhaps, and shaken his head dubiously, as he heard simple folk talk of a Pope Angelico, who was to come by-and-by and bring in a new order of things, to purify the Church from simony, and the lives of the clergy from scandal—a state of affairs too different from what existed under Innocent the Eighth for a shrewd merchant and politician to regard the prospect as worthy of entering into his calculations. But he felt the evils of the time, nevertheless; for he was a man of public spirit, and public spirit can never be wholly immoral, since its essence is care for a common good. That very Quaresima or Lent of 1492 in which he died, still in his erect old age, he had listened in San Lorenzo, not without a mixture of satisfaction, to the preaching of a Dominican

Friar, named Girolamo Savonarola, who denounced with a rare
boldness the worldliness and vicious habits of the clergy, and
insisted on the duty of Christian men not to live for their own ease
when wrong was triumphing in high places, and not to spend their
wealth in outward pomp even in the churches, when their fellow-
citizens were suffering from want and sickness. The Frate carried
his doctrine rather too far for elderly ears; yet it was a memorable
thing to see a preacher move his audience to such a pitch that the
women even took off their ornaments, and delivered them up to be
sold for the benefit of the needy.

"He was a noteworthy man, that Prior of San Marco," thinks
our Spirit; "somewhat arrogant and extreme, perhaps, especially in
his denunciations of speedy vengeance. Ah, *Iddio non paga il
Sabato*—the wages of men's sins often linger in their payment, and
I myself saw much established wickedness of long-standing prosperity. But a Frate Predicatore who wanted to move the people—
how could he be moderate? He might have been a little less defiant
and curt, though, to Lorenzo de' Medici, whose family had been
the very makers of San Marco: was that quarrel ever made up? And
our Lorenzo himself, with the dim outward eyes and the subtle
inward vision, did he get over that illness at Careggi? It was but a
sad, uneasy-looking face that he would carry out of the world
which had given him so much, and there were strong suspicions
that his handsome son would play the part of Rehoboam. How has
it all turned out? Which party is likely to be banished and have its
houses sacked just now? Is there any successor of the incomparable
Lorenzo, to whom the great Turk is so gracious as to send over
presents of rare animals, rare relics, rare manuscripts, or fugitive
enemies, suited to the tastes of a Christian Magnifico who is at once
lettered and devout—and also slightly vindictive? And what
famous scholar is dictating the Latin letters of the Republic—what
fiery philosopher is lecturing on Dante in the Duomo, and going
home to write bitter invectives against the father and mother of the
bad critic who may have found fault with his classical spelling? Are
our wiser heads leaning towards alliance with the Pope and the
Regno, or are they rather inclining their ears to the orators of
France and of Milan?

"There is knowledge of these things to be had in the streets below, on the beloved *marmi* in front of the churches, and under the sheltering Loggie, where surely our citizens have still their gossip and debates, their bitter and merry jests as of old. For are not the well-remembered buildings all there? The changes have not been so great in those uncounted years. I will go down and hear—I will tread the familiar pavement, and hear once again the speech of Florentines."

Go not down, good Spirit! for the changes are great and the speech of Florentines would sound as a riddle in your ears. Or, if you go, mingle with no politicians on the *marmi*, or elsewhere; ask no questions about trade in the Calimara; confuse yourself with no inquiries into scholarship, official or monastic. Only look at the sunlight and shadows on the grand walls that were built solidly, and have endured in their grandeur; look at the faces of the little children, making another sunlight amid the shadows of age; look, if you will, into the churches, and hear the same chants, see the same images as of old—the images of willing anguish for a great end, of beneficent love and ascending glory; see upturned living faces, and lips moving to the old prayers for help. These things have not changed. The sunlight and shadows bring their old beauty and waken the old heartstrains at morning, noon, and eventide; the little children are still the symbol of the eternal marriage between love and duty; and men still yearn for the reign of peace and right- eousness—still own *that* life to be the highest which is a conscious voluntary sacrifice. For the Pope Angelico is not come yet.

For the Literary Traveler

Whether or not the reader/traveler reads beyond the prologue of *Romola* is beside the point. The setting of its overture, SAN MINIATO AL MONTE, at any time of day or night, is possibly the most beautiful place in Florence. The walk up the mountain from the PONTE VECCHIO con- tributes a feeling of pilgrimage to the experience of the Tuscan

Romanesque basilica, with its exquisite interior and exterior. (Bus 13, following a roundabout route from Stazione di Santa Maria Novella, takes as long—about half an hour—as the hike.) Descending, one can rest in the PIAZZALE MICHELANGELO, viewing another magnificent panorama of the city—its "great dome, the greatest in the world," in Eliot's words—and the distant peaks of the Apennines.

Below San Miniato, in the historic city, the novel's settings are many. The PIAZZA and MUSEO DI SAN MARCO preserve the monastery where the visionary painter Fra' Angelico (1387–1455) was a monk—his frescoes appear throughout the buildings—and Girolamo Savonarola, the novel's historical focus, was made prior in 1491. Lewes took notes on the place for Marian since women were not admitted to the cloister. Savonarola's monastic cell (number 12) can be seen in the DORMITORY. (Lewes obtained a copy of a San Marco fresco by Fra' Angelico because "Polly" wished to hang one of his works before her as she wrote.) In the PIAZZA DELLA SIGNORIA, where Savonarola had once performed a bonfire of the vanities—observed by Eliot's protagonist Romola in vivid detail—a porphyry disc in the pavement in front of the huge NEPTUNE FOUNTAIN marks the site of his incineration.

Happier associations with this heart of Florence are found in the letters of Elizabeth Barrett Browning, who liked to sit in the Loggia of the piazza's PALAZZO VECCHIO and admire the statue of PERSEUS by Benvenuto Cellini (born behind San Lorenzo in Piazza dei Mercato). And Elizabeth Spencer's novel *A Light in the Piazza* uses the Piazza della Signoria as a metaphor of the crisscrossings and spaces of memory itself.

Mary McCarthy

"I can't help loving the Italians and not loving the French," Mary McCarthy *once wrote to her friend Hannah Arendt. On publication of McCarthy's* The Stones of Florence *(1959) Arendt sent her compliments: "You have made a*

city sit for its portrait." Other critics concurred with the praise: "A tri-
umphant jewel of a book," one said, "about one of the rarest jewels in Italy's
unique collection of cities." Carol Brightman, McCarthy's biographer,
defines the strength of her Florentine portrait as "the vigor of its characteri-
zations of both the artists and the art of the Italian Renaissance." Michelan-
gelo and "the tyranny of genius," da Vinci, Donatello, Brunelleschi, and
their relations with the popes and power families of their times, all receive
cold-eyed scrutiny. The Florentines invented the Renaissance, she declares,
"which is the same as saying that they invented the modern world." Seeing
Florence from Mary McCarthy's many-angled perspective enlarges the
reader/traveler's appreciation of both the city and its prominence within the
history of art. Her contribution to the art of travel writing is an impressive
mix of art history, social commentary, criticism, and gossip. Her attention to
the "jewel's" particularities signals her affection.

FROM *THE STONES OF FLORENCE*

V

. . . The Florentines, in fact, invented the Renaissance, which is the same as saying that they invented the modern world—not, of course, an unmixed good. Florence was a turning-point, and this is what often troubles the reflective sort of visitor today—the feeling that a terrible mistake was committed here, at some point between Giotto and Michelangelo, a mistake that had to do with power and megalomania, or gigantism of the human ego. You can see, if you wish, the handwriting on the walls of Palazzo Pitti or Palazzo Strozzi, those formidable creations in bristling prepotent stone, or in the cold, vain stare of Michelangelo's *David*, in love with his own strength and beauty. This feeling that Florence was the scene of the original crime or error was hard to avoid just after the last World War, when power and technology had reduced so much to rubble. "You were responsible for this," chided a Florentine sadly, looking around the Michelangelo room of the Bargello after it was finally reopened. In contrast, Giotto's bell tower appeared an innocent party.

But the invention of the modern world could not be halted, at Giotto's bell tower or Donatello's *San Giorgio* or the Pazzi Chapel or Masaccio's *Trinity*. The Florentines introduced dynamism into the arts, and this meant a continuous process of acceleration, a speed-up, which created obsolescence around it, as new methods do in industry. The *last word*, throughout the Renaissance, always came from Florence. When Cosimo il Vecchio, in 1433, arrived at Venice, an exile, with his architect, Michelozzo, and his court of painters and learned men, and was lodged, like a great prince, on the island of San Giorgio in the lagoon, the Venetians were amazed by these advanced persons, just as they were amazed, later, in Giorgione's time, by the arrival of Leonardo. The Romans, seeing the two young Florentines, Brunelleschi and Donatello, directing workmen to dig among the ruins of the old temples and baths, assumed that they were looking for buried treasure, gold and precious stones, and the measurements the two shabby young men were taking seemed to confirm this; it was thought that they must be practising geomancy or the art of divination by lines and figures, to find where the treasure lay hidden. A century later, the Romans themselves, having caught on to the lesson of the "treasure-hunters," were digging up the Laocoön.

Wherever the Florentines went, they acted as disturbers, agents of the new. . . .

In daring, the Florentines excelled; that is why their architecture and their sculpture and much of their painting have such a virile character. . . .

The Duomo, outside, still astonishes by its bulk, which is altogether out of proportion with the narrow streets that lead up to it. It sits in the centre of Florence like a great hump of a snowy mountain deposited by some natural force, and it is, in fact, a kind of man-made mountain rising from the plain of the city and vying with the mountain of Fiesole, which can be seen in the distance. Unlike St. Peter's in Rome, which is cleverly prepared for by colonnades, fountains, and an obelisk, the Duomo of Florence is stumbled on like an irreducible fact in the midst of shops, *pasticcerie*, and a wild cat's cradle of motor traffic. It startles by its size and also by its gaiety—the spread of its flouncing apse and tribune in their Tuscan marble dress, dark green from Prato, pure white from Carrara, pink from the Maremma. It is like a mountain but it is also like a bellying circus tent or festive marquee. Together with the Baptistery and Giotto's pretty bell tower, it constitutes a joyous surprise in the severe, dun, civic city, and indeed, throughout Tuscany there is always that characteristic contrast between the stone dread of politics and the marbled gaiety of churches.

Inside, Arnolfo's Duomo is very noble—sturdy, tall, grave, with great stone pillars rising like oaks from the floor to uphold massive arches so full they can hardly be called pointed. This splendid stone hall does not soar, like a Gothic cathedral; the upward thrust is broken by a strict, narrow iron gallery running around the whole interior, outlining the form. A few memorial busts; Uccello's clock; the two caparisoned knights on horseback in trompe l'œil; round, deep eyes of windows, set with large-paned stained glass, high in the thick walls; a small, sculptured bishop, blessing; a few faded images on gold backgrounds; a worn fresco of Dante; two statues of the prophet Isaiah; a holy-water stoup—that is almost all there is in this quiet, long room until it swells out into the vast octagonal tribune, surrounded by dim, almost dark chapels and topped by Brunelleschi's dome. There is nothing here but the essentials of shelter and support and the essentials of worship: pillars, arches, ribbing, walls, light, holy water, remembrance of the dead, a clock that still tells time.

The daring of Arnolfo, who was the first of the great Florentine master builders, lay not only in the scale of his undertaking but in the resolute stressing of essentials—what the Italians call the *membratura*, or frame of the building, a term that is drawn from anatomy (*i.e.*, from the human frame). Michelangelo, the last of the great builders in Arnolfo's tradition, considered architecture to be related to anatomy, and the Florentine Duomo, with its pronounced *membratura*, is like a building in the nude, showing its muscles and sinews and the structure of bone underneath. On the outside, it is a dazzling mountain, cased in the native marbles of Tuscany, and, inside, it is a man, erect. Arnolfo was a sculptor, too, and the sculptures he made for the old façade (now replaced by a Victorian façade) and interior of the Cathedral (they can be seen in the Museum of the Works of the Duomo) have an odd family resemblance to the interior of the Duomo itself, as though saints,

Madonnas, bishops, and building were all one breed of frontiersman—tall, sturdy, impassive. . . .

In the year 1418 a competition for the dome was announced to
which masters from all over Italy were invited. Such competitions
for public works were a regular feature of Florentine life, and the
young Filippo Brunelleschi, not long before, had lost a competition
in sculpture to Lorenzo Ghiberti, whose model for the second set
of bronze Baptistery doors had been accepted over his. Disappointed—so the story is told—he had gone off to Rome, with
Donatello, and made himself an architect, knowing that in this field
he could surpass everyone. He remained there several years, earning
his living as a goldsmith, while he examined Roman buildings, with
particular attention to the Pantheon and its dome. When the competition was announced, he came back to Florence, announcing
that he had found a way of raising the dome of Santa Maria del
Fiore without centring—a thing everyone believed to be impossible.
Faced, like Columbus, with an assembly of doubters, he anticipated Columbus with the egg trick. "He proposed," says Vasari's
version, "to all the masters, foreigners and compatriots, that he
who could make an egg stand upright on a piece of smooth marble
should be appointed to build the cupola, since, in doing that, his
genius would be made manifest. They took an egg accordingly, and
all those masters did their best to make it stand upright, but none
discovered the method of doing so. Wherefore, Filippo, being told
that he might make it stand himself, took it daintily into his hand,
gave the end of it a blow on the plane of marble and made it stand
upright." He vaulted the huge tribune by means of a double
cupola, one shell resting on another inside it and thus distributing
the weight—an idea he had probably got from the Pantheon.
This dome of Brunelleschi's, besides being a wonder, was
extremely practical in all its details. It had gutters for rain, little
ducts or openings to reduce wind pressure, iron hooks inside for
scaffolding so that frescoes could be painted if they were ever
wanted, light in the *ballatoio*, or gallery, that goes up to the top so
that no one would stumble in the dark, and iron treads to give a
footing in the steeper parts of the climb. While it was being built, it

even had temporary restaurants and wineshops provided by
Brunelleschi for the masons, so that they could work all day
without having to make the long trip down and up again at lunch
time. Brunelleschi had thought of everything.

In short, the dome was a marvel in every respect, and Michelangelo, when he was called on to do the dome of St. Peter's, paid his
respects to Brunelleschi's in a rhyming couplet:

> Io farò la sorella,
> Già più gran ma non più bella.
> (I am going to make its sister,
> Bigger, yes, but not more beautiful.)

Vasari said that it dared competition with the heavens. "This structure rears itself to such an elevation that the hills around Florence do not appear to equal it." Lightning frequently struck it, and
this was taken as a sign that the heavens were envious. When the
people of Florence learned that a lantern, on Brunelleschi's design
though not begun until after his death, was about to be loaded
onto the cupola, they took alarm and called this "tempting God."

Michelangelo was right, when he said that the dome of St.
Peter's would not be more beautiful. Brunelleschi's, moreover, was
the *first*. Michelangelo could be blunt and sarcastic about his
fellow-architects and sculptors. He dismissed Baccio d'Agnolo's
model for the façade of San Lorenzo as "a child's plaything," and
of the same architect's outside gallery on the Duomo he said that it
was "a cage for crickets" (crickets in little cages, like the ones he
meant, are still sold in the Cascine on Ascension Day, a spring festival corresponding to the old Roman Calends of May and called
in Florence the "Cricket's Feast"). But he was very much aware
of real greatness (he called Ghiberti's second set of Baptistery
doors the "Gates of Paradise," and to Donatello's *San Giorgio*
he said "March!"), and his architecture is always conscious of
Brunelleschi, long dead before he was born, whom he could not
surpass but only exceed: bigger, yes, but not more beautiful. The
portentous staging of the Medici Tombs, the staircase of the Laurentian Library, the dome of St. Peter's are Brunelleschi, only more

so. The heavy consoles and corbels of the Laurentian Library vestibule and staircase, with their strong, deep indentations, contrast of light and shade, their *pietra serena* and white plaster, are Brunelleschi, underscored or played *fortissimo*. Brunelleschi, like Arnolfo, had stressed the *membratura* of a building; in Michelangelo, there appears a false *membratura*, a fictive ensemble of windows, supporting pillars, brackets, and so on—in short, a display of muscle.

In Brunelleschi himself, the Florentine tradition reached its highest point. Here—in Santo Spirito, for instance, or the Pazzi Chapel or the Old Sacristy of San Lorenzo or the Badia at San Domenico di Fiesole—are the grave purity, simplicity, and peacefulness of the early Florentine churches. The germ of Brunelleschi can be found not in classical Rome but in the little church of Santi Apostoli that legend attributes to Charlemagne. All grey and white, the dark-grey stone that is called justly "serene" against white *intonaco*; three long aisles, one of which forms a nave; two processions of pillars with lovely Corinthian capitals marching down the church and upholding a rhythmic train of round arches; vaults interlacing like fans opening and closing; decorative motifs, always in dark-grey stone, of leaves, egg-and-dart pattern, scallop shells, and sun rays—these, generally speaking, are the elements of Tuscan classicism that are found, over and over, in the great Brunelleschi churches, sometimes with friezes and roundels added in the more frivolous parts, like the sacristy, by Donatello or Desiderio or Luca della Robbia: cherubs with rays like flower petals round their necks or with crossed wings like starchy bibs, the four Evangelists, or scenes from the life of Saint John.

The big churches of Brunelleschi, particularly San Lorenzo, which was the parish church of the Medici family, have been somewhat botched by later additions. The Pazzi Chapel, which was built for the Pazzi family as a kind of private oratory just outside the Franciscan church of Santa Croce, has not been tampered with, however, since the fifteenth century, and here you find the quintessential Brunelleschi. It is a small, square, yellowish, discreet temple, with projecting eaves, almost like a little mausoleum, from the outside, or like one of those little brown Etruscan funeral urns in the shape of a house, one of which can be seen in the Archaeological Museum—the "*aedes tuscanica.*" It has an atrium or pronaos supported by slender Corinthian columns, above which runs a frieze of cherubs' heads in little medallions, done by Desiderio. Under the eaves is an attic and above them a cupola with a very delicate tall lantern. A *tondo* in glazed terracotta by Luca della Robbia of Saint Andrew (the chapel was done for Andrea de' Pazzi) stands over the door.

The interior is a simple rectangle with four high narrow windows and bare white walls and at the end a small apse. In the four corners tall closed arches are drawn in dark-grey *pietra serena* on the white walls, like the memory of windows. Fluted pilasters with Corinthian capitals, also in *pietra serena*, are spaced along the walls, marking the points of support, and in the same way, the lunettes and supporting arches of the chapel are outlined in dark ribbons of stone against the white plaster, and the binding arches have stone rosettes enclosed in rectangles drawn on the white background. Arch repeats arch; curve repeats curve; rosette repeats rosette. The rectangles of the lower section are topped by the semi-circles of the lunettes and arches, which, in turn, are topped by the hemisphere of the cupola. The continual play of these basic forms and their variations—of square against round, deep against flat—is like the greatest music: the music of the universe heard in a small space.

The twelve Apostles, by Luca della Robbia, in dark-blue-and-white roundels framed in *pietra serena*, are seated about the walls, just below a frieze of cherubs' heads and lambs, in alternate blue-and-faded-pink terracotta. In the pendentives of the apse are wonderful immense grey scallop shells, and in the pendentives of the room itself, outranking the Apostles, sit the four Evangelists, cast in glazed terracotta by Luca della Robbia on Brunelleschi's designs, each with his attendant symbol and companion: Saint Luke with the Bull, Saint Mark with the Lion, Saint John with the Bird, and Saint Matthew with the Angel in the form of a Man. The colours of the terracotta glazes are clear and intensely beautiful in the severe gray-and-white room. The Bird is raven-black, the Lion chocolate, the Bull brown; the robes of the Evangelists are glittering, glassy white or yellow or translucent green; and these four great Teachers with their books are placed in wavy blue backgrounds, as though they were sitting comfortably at the bottom of the sea. In the blue cupoletta, above the little apse, with its plain altar, like a table, there is a Creation of Man and the Animals. The chapel is not large, but it seems to hold the four corners of the earth and all the winds securely in its binding of *pietra serena*. No more exquisite microcosm than the Pazzi Chapel could be imagined, for everything is here, in just proportion and in order, as on the Seventh Day of Creation, when God rested from His labours, having found them good.

The strong drama of Florentine life seems to have resulted, with Brunelleschi, in an art of perfect balance. The terrible struggles that took place in this city and in which the Pazzi family, a little later, took such a part had their reward in equilibrium—a reconciliation of forms. This same sabbath stillness can be felt in the hillside Abbey church of San Domenico di Fiesole, done for the old Cosimo on Brunelleschi's designs and in the Old Sacristy of San Lorenzo, where Brunelleschi had Donatello for his collaborator—a square white room with four great lunettes marked in *pietra serena*, a hemispheric cupola with a lantern or "eye," a dainty frieze of cherubs, four tablets in painted stucco of the life of Saint John the Evangelist, and four big roundels in coloured terracotta showing the four Evangelists deep in study at four classical desks. Above the altar in the tiny chapel at the back rises another cupola or playful cupoletta, painted a dark sky-blue in imitation of the heavens and sprinkled with the constellations in gilt, like a little planetarium. Santo Spirito, the Holy Ghost church in the big market square beyond the Arno, is grander in its orchestration of interior space, with its long lines of mighty grey pillars topped by Corinthian foliage treading down the church in solemn perspective recession like a vast forest (Birnam wood) on the move, but here, too, there is an elemental harmony and tranquil measure, as of an agon resolved. Michelangelo's agitation proceeds from the stillness of Brunelleschi.

Brunelleschi was a very down-to-earth person—simple, short, bald, plain. He disliked imbalance and exaggeration, and the story is told that when his friend Donatello showed him the wooden Crucifix, of a peasant-like, harshly suffering Christ, he had made for Santa Croce, Brunelleschi said to him sharply: "You have put a clown on the Cross." Donatello then asked him whether he thought he could do better, and Brunelleschi made no reply but went away and secretly made a wooden crucifix of his own (it is in a chapel of Santa Maria Novella) which so astonished Donatello by its beauty, when he finally saw it in his friend's studio, that he dropped some eggs he was carrying, in an apron, for their lunch.

The homely lives led by these artists, in which aprons and eggs figure as in the daily lives of ordinary workmen, are reflected in the character of their art, which is an art of essentials, of the bread-and-wine staples of the human construct. The big Brunelleschi churches—San Lorenzo and Santo Spirito—are almost free of tourists, as has been said; they belong, appropriately, to the people, and just outside them are the main Florentine markets, where the poor come to buy. Around Santo Spirito are the fruit and vegetable sellers of the Oltrarno quarter and old beggars, lame and halt, who sit in the sun, while across from San Lorenzo (the big covered market is just beyond) are the peddlars of cheap shoes, chiefly for men, hundreds and hundreds of rows of them, and displays of workmen's aprons and coveralls, hanging from clothes-hangers, like votive offerings, in brown, blue, and white—the colours of Saint Francis and the Madonna. Work and rest, weekday and Sunday, *pietra forte* and *pietra serena* make up the Florentine chiaroscuro, and the sense of their interplay, as of sphere and square, explains the unique ability of the Florentines to create cosmic myths in the space of a small chapel or a long poem. The unitary genius of the Florentines, that power of binding expressed in Brunelleschi's virile *membratura*, is evidently the product of a small world held in common and full of "common" referents. . . .

For the Literary Traveler

To use Mary McCarthy's *The Stones of Florence* as cicerone is to enter the architectural and sculptural heart of the Renaissance. Realistically, unless the traveler can stay awhile, you must follow her selectively.

One rewarding route is to locate, in her company, the work of the great Florentine sculptor and architect, Filippo Brunelleschi (1377–1446). (Obviously the stones of Michelangelo dominate most itineraries. Who visits Florence and fails to see the DAVID and the four PRISONERS in the ACCADEMIA, BACCHUS and the TONDO OF THE MADONNA AND CHILD WITH ST. JOHN in the BARGELLO, the two TOMBS in the MEDICI CHAPELS, and the PIETÀ in the MUSEO DEL DUOMO? Devotees of public libraries will want to see his LAURENTIAN LIBRARY, to the right and up the stairs from the cloister of the church of SAN LORENZO.)

But the city of Brunelleschi reveals the most beautiful spaces in Florence. McCarthy's commentary on his art, excerpted in the preceding pages, inspires a concrete sense of his genius: his love of balance and its effect—a transcendent serenity, a philosophical sense of the truth of things. She shows us that his was a poetry of stone and space.

Brunelleschi's masterpiece, the DOME of the DUOMO—SANTA MARIA DEL FIORE, the Madonna of Florence—is the city's majestic presence, presiding over Giotto's bell tower, the baptistery, and the people in the piazza. (The ascent of the dome is worth the time and energy.)

Nearby, the church of SAN LORENZO and its SAGRESTIA VECCHIA present more of Brunelleschi's powerful effects. A short walk from San Lorenzo and its lively market, past the amazing PALAZZO DEI PUCCI, and by way of the Via dei Servi, leads into PIAZZA SANTISSIMA ANNUNZIATA, generally revered as the most beautiful piazza in the city (though the presence of parked cars detracts). Brunelleschi designed it as well as the lovely Colonnade of the INNOCENTI (with its wonderful DELLA ROBBIA MEDALLIONS of babies in swaddling clothes above the arches), the first foundling hospital in Europe. The CONVENT AND CLOISTERS were also designed by Brunelleschi. (In the portico of the church of the Annunziata are frescoes by Andrea del Sarto, the subject of one of Robert Browning's most famous poems.)

In McCarthy's company, what is involved in the phenomenon of great architecture becomes clearer the longer you stay with her, especially in her responses to Brunelleschi's PAZZI CHAPEL and its two cloisters. (The entrance is immediately to the right of SANTA CROCE.)

Another delightful walk is across the Arno (by way of Ponte Santa Trinità and Via di Santo Spirito) to Brunelleschi's church of SANTO SPIRITO, where few tourists interrupt a quiet appreciation of the solemn interior. (The paintings in the many chapels are splendid, especially Alessandro Allori's *Christ and the Adulteress*, number 19.) The PIAZZA SANTO SPIRITO, an oasis of trees, a market, and outdoor cafes, is one instance that contradicts McCarthy's astringent point of view—"What irritates the modern tourist about Florence," she claims, "is that it makes no concession to the pleasure principle." This piazza is *about* pleasure and its low-key spirits don't feel like a concession.

In the same neighborhood, though not the work of Brunelleschi, the BRANCACCI CHAPEL (in the church of SANTA MARIA DEL CARMINE) with its FRESCOES by Masaccio is a stunning experience, drawing some of McCarthy's most astute comments. The effect of Masaccio, she says, is "absolute truthfulness," "an implacable candor of vision."

Recrossing the Arno, another gem that McCarthy visits (she calls it "the germ of Brunelleschi") is the church of SANTI APOSTOLI, near the river in the sunken PIAZZA DEL LIMBO, supposedly founded by Charlemagne. In this neighborhood are other treasures—SANTA TRINITÀ, for instance, which has GHIRLANDAIO FRESCOES in the church and sacristy.

❧

Kate Simon

"How splendid is Kate Simon, the incomparable Kate Simon, whom no one has ever rivaled in the long, long history of guidebooks. She has made of one of the dullest forms of literature a brilliant work of art"—the critic's voice (in this case, the English historian J. H. Plumb) on Simon as learned guide is one sustained accolade. Her meanderings through Siena, included in these pages (from Italy: The Places in Between*), reflect her good spirits—"To be in Siena only on a Palio day is to see it in orgasm and consequently at least a bit deceptive." Observing the contradictions within Italian culture, she refuses to force resolutions; she accepts—and enjoys—complexity. Readers of her other books on New York, Mexico, London, and Paris know the*

precision of her descriptions and her sensual evocation of atmosphere. Her force as a writer of memoir—Bronx Primitive *(1982),* A Wider World *(1986),* Etchings in an Hourglass *(1990)—positions her well as a subjective narrator of the subtleties and specifics of experience. In memoir, as in travel, place has a defining personality. It contributes to who and what a woman becomes.*

FROM *ITALY: THE PLACES IN BETWEEN*

SIENA

Many centuries ago, Siena rivaled Florence and continues to think so, after old defeats in battle and consequent losses of territory and lives and in spite of the Medici shields on many walls. Although Florence is in Tuscany, the cradle of Italian literary speech, the Florentines have hideous, grunting accents, say the Sienese, while theirs is pure, exquisite. This sentiment is often spoken in something like Arabic-Italian; all "c" sounds are lacking or slightly aspirated, so that *casa* becomes *hasa,* a *coppa* of *gelato* brightens to *hoppa,* although cultivated Sienese speech is as musical as they say it is. You will probably hear that Giotto copied from Duccio, that Florentine painting is a decayed imitation of the Sienese, and so on. Don't argue; it is impolite and useless to fight one of the endearing faults of a delightful people. . . .

The light must have its dark and the honey its blood; Siena inflicted injuries and the oppression of conquest on surrounding towns. She was a mighty power, as ruthless as she could afford to be, the home of warriors and bankers to the papacy, of medieval wheelers and dealers who could turn loyalties on and off with lightning speed, and yet she was an extraordinarily long-lived free commune. The essence of the belligerence, the intense rivalry, the fanfares and battle colors, the marching, the drums and war chariots, the splendors of Renaissance costumes, the unseen but never quite secret deals and counterdeals and the commune spirit remain in the Palios and the passions they trigger.

The Palio is actually a long silk banner, currently a painting of the Assumption of the Virgin (for the August 16 race) in a timid late-cubist manner. To possess this, to hang it in a *contrada* church or museum, a short, brutal and crooked race is run. To be in Siena only on a Palio day is to see it in orgasm and consequently at least a bit deceptive. See it before, see it after, although between the hithering and thithering mounting like a dancing madness, the spiraling hysteria of a Children's Crusade (medieval allusions come easily in Siena), it is possible, with enough resolution, to explore the city.

It may not clarify the frenzy altogether, but it should help to follow the Good Government mural with a visit to the house-museum of the *contrada* Torre, on the via Salicotto behind the Palazzo Pubblico. As you might know, a *contrada* is, sociologically and emotionally, an expanded family with all that means in a culture whose only meaningful unit is the family. The members of a *contrada* may not all be crazy about each other, but making the best of proximity, interdependence, joint traditions and the financial responsibility and team effort required by the Palio produces an abstract affection that works better, in the long run, than love. They have no wish to escape each other and often take vacations together, and when one Sienese introduces himself to another he will designate his *contrada* as if it were part of his name. During the waxing, exploding and reluctantly waning time of the Palio the *contrada*, traditionally an almost autonomous townlet within the city, is controlled by a *capo*, who is in complete charge of all Palio activities, including judgment of turbulent disputes concerning who is to be taxed how much to make up the millions of lire spent and for what purpose.

The Palio race is a development of ancient games harking back to the Romans—some say to the Etruscans—through changes that echoed courtly games, such as bucolic imitations of jousting, the goading of buffaloes, which suggests early bullfighting, and long hazardous races through the city.

Torre, one of the prosperous *contrade*, has a varied and largish museum, attractively arranged to keep great memories vivid: its first win in 1599; the summer, two hundred years ago, when it won both Palios; the great silver platters won as awards for the skill, beauty and fine comportment of its group. In the section set apart for matters of horse and jockey, the silver-studded trappings and the evolutions of the jockey's costume and equipment: the spiked iron maces they once used (the knives sometimes used later are not in evidence) and the hard helmet since replaced by a less conspicuous protective cap. Surrounded by the flourish of banners—about one hundred and fifty of them—the shine of metal on fifty carefully preserved drums, the coats of armor and the velvets and furs, two local boys, quite young, are brought in by the keeper of the house to demonstrate the use of the drums and flags. Their work is profoundly serious, adept, unhurried, priestly. These boys practice every night—drummers, beginning as early as six, the flag boys at ten or eleven—in total, obsessed dedication, as Spanish and Mexican boys practice veronicas with a rag cape.

The *contrada* church has its own specialized characteristics. The sixteenth and seventeenth centuries saw the first changes in neighborhood churches, which led to the present Palio-adapted structures. There are no stairs, or very few, and no side aisles; the organ is placed high in the back, the altar is shallow and there are no choir stalls; in short, a box with churchly trappings, arranged to allow maximum space and no impediments to horse, jockey and *contrada* crowd. The priest is of the church but primarily of the *contrada*, and it is he who appears in Siena's newspapers at the side of the horse, under the heading, "Ritorna Vincitor." Except for baptisms, also frequently performed at the *contrada* fountain, the church is rarely used at other times of the year; it belongs to the Palio. . . .

The Duomo is as overwhelmingly full of too much to see as other great cathedrals, and like many of them (except the unrivaled peak, Saint Peter's in Rome), dedicated equally to the greater glory of the Virgin Mary and rivalry with some other cathedral. Pisa has Nicola and Giovanni Pisano? We hire them for Siena. Rome has Bernini? Let's bring him to work here. Donatello? Michelangelo? Get them out of Florence. Nothing but the best and, if possible, better and bigger. Not the most altruistic way to build and fill a church, this competitive drive has produced magnificent collections of church art, however.

The Duomo complex is best seen from the side of the church of

San Domenico, where its compact gray and white presence appears large and calm, a Lorenzetti Virtue who expresses the non-Palio mood and conduct of the city. This indirect approach continues through the tortuous streets devoted to Saint Catherine and the Goose, into the via di Città, then the via del Castoro. Above, the extravagant height of the double-arched Facciatone (big façade), a blind giant that was meant to be the façade of a cathedral grand enough to rival that of Florence. The Black Plague of 1348, financial reverses and the perilous weakness of the disproportionately slender columns—among other reasons—called a halt to the building and left a unique, evocative piazza.

The prehistory of the church probably followed the usual pattern: a temple on a height, very likely Etruscan; later, Roman, replaced by a small Christian church. The site might thus be considered the core, the oldest part, of Siena, the oldest houses those that slope away from the ecclesiastical prominence. The ecclesiastical center was to have been linked, as a symbol of accord between church and civic powers, with the Campo by a long, regal stairway continuing from the steps that now drop to the baptistry, another fantasy of grandeur that faded with other city planning. The only present evidence of balanced lay and church influence is the fact that the Mangia tower of the government and the campanile of the Cathedral are carefully of the same height.

Other than by sheer size and pride framed in winged space, and its accretion of mosaics and detail in the style of Orvieto, the Duomo façade attracts as a combination of Gothic imposed on Romanesque; a peaceable low, wide movement pulling against the surging vertical, and since this is Italy, the spiritual soaring quickly arrested. The lower Romanesque section of rounded arches, in recessed, carved bands topped by the animal symbols of the Evangelists, is reminiscent of churches in Puglia and for good reason. It was the work of Giovanni Pisano, whose father, Nicola, was originally "di Puglia" and may easily have been among the numerous artists in the Pugliese courts of that extraordinary, pre-Renaissance "Renaissance" prince, Frederick II. From that long distance, via Pisa, come the Oriental abstractions and the practice of enlivening monochrome stone with bands of contrast. The French Gothic was introduced by restless artists and craftsmen, the bees who carried the pollen of innovation from one region to another; here, particularly, a group of Cistercian monks who directed the building of the later (fourteenth-century) sections of the Duomo. Although the façade seems perfectly balanced at first glance, a slower look reveals two pink blocks, probably from the first church, on the left side, not repeated on the right, and one end pier narrower than the other, testimony of various ideas, hands and patchings that affected the church in its long time of building, beginning in the late twelfth century.

The conflict between Gothic flight and flat, squared space is noticeable again in the interior as numerous iron bars, probably meant for a ceiling or a broad rail to contain the foreign-inspired urge toward uncomfortable height. There was a change of mind or taste, obviously, and the clusters of pillars, tall and fiercely rigid in their alternations of black and white, stretch up and up, into distant starry vaults. The famous incised and inlaid marble floor is also a product of centuries (from the fourteenth into the sixteenth). The choicest sections are kept covered except for the period between August 15 and September 15 (roughly) but there is always visible an ample stretch to exemplify the early and straightforward, the later concentrations on virtuosity, the still later whirlwinds of distortion in the excessive lights and darks of mannerism.

Above the biblical figures and pagan sibyls and the shields of Siena are riches of other masterworks: the incredible pulpit created by the Pisanos, father and son, and Arnolfo di Cambio; the handsome Piccolomini altar with a figure, in a niche, believed to be the work of the young Michelangelo, and several figures by Bernini; a tomb figure and a wonderfully shaky John the Baptist by Donatello; the inlaid woodwork in the choir stalls, finely worked even under the seats, the ultimate of art for art's sake; the Piccolomini library and its sleek, infinitely charming frescoes of Pinturicchio bound in bravura perspectives and bands of Pompeian ornament.

The splendors of the church reach their climax in the Museo dell'Opera at the side of the Facciatone, where there is a room

devoted to the Duccio Maestà and the smaller panels that surrounded it and were attached to its reverse side. It was originally
hung in a central area of the Duomo, before the altar, but the
expansion of the Duomo made its position impractical and it was
retired for a period to be rehung as two panels, back and front. A
later expansion caused the paintings to be removed and discarded—cut up, sold, stolen. A few of the panels seem irrevocably
gone; a few remain in England and the United States. After a stubborn, difficult task of searching out, authenticating, buying back
and restoring, the almost complete set—some forty-odd of sixty—
hang in the hushed, mellow illumination of an air-controlled room.
If you have seen the Giotto frescoes in the Scrovegni chapel in
Padua, these will seem a repetition in miniature of the life of Jesus
and Mary, and there are superficial resemblances. Siena's pride as
womb of language and art—the pride that causes marble quota-
tions from Dante to speak from many streets in the city, sometimes
a bit out of context, sometimes implying a love for the city that
Dante did not always feel—insists that Duccio was Giotto's predecessor, an indisputable fact. But the Scrovegni frescoes were
painted a few years before the Maestà, and furthermore there is
hardly any way of claiming a "predecessor" between two men so
close in age who both drew from a varied, rich world of church art;
who both made brilliant, arresting places in a long line of continuity, Duccio to bring the traditional Byzantine-Gothic to its
richest, warmest culmination, Giotto to deflect it to paths that ran
toward the Renaissance. . . .

It is a rough guess but there seem to be ten thousand Etruscan sar-
cophagi of repetitious design, many of them markedly unbeautiful,
throughout Italy, and Siena's archaeological museum has its share.
However, it doesn't exaggerate, and among the rubber stamps, a
few are worth a pause. Look for the lively meeting of Paris and his
goddess friends; another still shows its terra-cotta paint and, below
its warriors, swords and shields, the teasing Etruscan inscription,
scratched in crudely and backward as if by a child learning its letters. One multicolored stone box seems to have emerged from a
chromo factory yesterday; another appears to have been the work

of an Indian artist to judge from the plump drapery and shape of a lady whose jewelry sets off her naked breasts in the Indian fashion.

Some is cooky-cutter art, some of it highly refined, the sort of thing called "decadent" by purists, and certainly not all of it is worth prayerful concentration. The museum is well arranged, not discouragingly crowded, not heaped, and it might interest you to look at a few of the unusual pieces. For one, an Arianna with a few rosebuds in her hair, slightly tousled, her mouth a bit crooked, a touch that brings her completely to life and lends a knowing, flirtatious slyness to her almond-shaped eyes; a girl born two thousand years ago and as sturdily real as the shoes on your tired feet. One of her companions is a beguilingly arrogant little Aphrodite, and another wears a far-fetched Mayan headdress. It can't be, this linkage of cultures, you think, until you see, as you leave, a photo of a stone snake found in Etruscan country and easily mistaken for a Mexican snake god.

Return to the Campo, observe the duet of light and shade on the piazza, the shadow of the tower turning with the sun. At about 11:00 A.M., the shadow is a long, diagonal stripe that cuts the shell, and in the dark ray people shelter and talk, the pigeons bobbing near their feet; the small children dart, stray and gather like fish in a narrow stream. At the fruit stalls the local housewives and the international young are buying their luncheon grapes, the cafés are filling with tourists and summer students. As the shadow tower diminishes, the indefatigable talkers—and how much there is to say out of the wisdoms of a provincial town in the course of frequently daily encounters!—meet at the round edge of the piazza fan, and the old ladies whose domain is the sides of the fountain talk and talk while one of them, never dropping a word, turns to shave a piece of stale bread for the spoiled, demanding pigeons.

More than in most Italian cities, to turn a corner in Siena is to be presented with a gift. You might climb up the via della Sapienza to the Banchi di Sopra to see again the mighty palaces of two rival banking firms, the Palazzo Tolomei of the early thirteenth century and the Palazzo Salimbeni of the fourteenth century, and their

Gothic and Renaissance neighbors. Or, return to the Costa Sant'-
Antonio, facing the great strange red and white chunk in the sky
above the angles of roofs: once more, the Facciatone that haunts
Siena as the Mangia tower sings to it. A complex of loggie and
arcades above the vicolo del Tiratoio introduces the enclave
devoted to Saint Catherine, a confusing mixture of old house and
numerous chapels heavily laden with scenes of her life and works.
One chapel sells, another begs; one is luminous with Pompeian
design, another is a dank room of closets and a samovar that acts as
a fountain. The most interesting unit in the prodigious hagiography
is that painted by Sodoma, and shared, at least equally, by the *contrada* goose who stands in all its proud foolishness of yellow bill
and yellow feet in an inlaid marble shield set in the center of the
floor of the church. The light fixtures are conspicuously attached to
golden geese; below the stern saint (and one yields her the right to
be disapproving of this forced coupling with a goose), at either side
of the main altar, two large geese preen and expand their wings,
their curvaceous bodies immortalized in white marble set off by
black. Each wears a crown. Saint Catherine, who sacrificed, fasted
and flagellated herself, who took perilous journeys on behalf of
the church, who castigated noble sinners without fear, who was
wounded and blessed with Christ's stigmata and exchanged her
heart with that of Christ, wears a white cowl and sometimes a halo,
never a crown.

If one symbol had to suffice (and it speaks for many Italians) for
the not at all disconcerting light fidelity to religion combined with
contempt, the love for the traditional manipulated to serve present
purposes, the Saint Catherine–Goose complex might serve. To
spice up the minestra of total skepticism that doesn't quite accept
or discard anything ("Why take a chance? There may be something
in religion, who knows?"), this hard-working neighborhood turns
in a substantial Communist vote, as does most of the province.
"Contradictions? No. Why? You must know that although we are
officially Catholic we have been passionately anticlerical for centuries and still are. Communists? Naturally. It is only recently in
our history that we emerged from the serf-lord class system; some
of us may even be the descendants of slaves brought from the East

to serve Tuscan princes in that glorious enlightenment, the Renaissance. It is about time we began to respect our own labor and control our own lives. Tradition? Religion? Why throw them out? We can manage it all."

For the Literary Traveler:

Walking Siena in the company of Kate Simon covers both a number of key sites that no visitor would want to miss and the hidden byways that inspired her title—*Italy: The Places in Between*. Some historical details add texture to her major and minor interests.

The city's many statues of Romulus and Remus suckling a she-wolf express the tradition that Siena was founded by the sons of Remus (brother of Romulus)—Senius who rode a black horse and Ascius who rode a white horse, and thus the shield of black and white halves that is another symbol seen throughout Siena. Legends aside, evidence of Etruscan and (even earlier, Celtic) settlements has been found in the area around Siena and throughout Tuscany. (The name Tuscany comes from the inhabitants of ancient Etruria known as *Tusci* or *Tyrrheni* who landed in Italy in about the eighth century B.C.E.) Kate Simon's sense of the Etruscan images in the ARCHAEOLOGICAL MUSEUM (Via della Sapienza) recalls D. H. Lawrence's interpretation of Italy's ancient people in *Etruscan Places*. The material remains of that civilization, said Lawrence, suggest the Etruscans' instinct to "preserve the natural humour of life," their "queer stillness and curious peaceful repose," and their lingering "homeliness and happiness." Visitors walking Siena's streets of hills and arches, past and around its many fountains, have remarked upon this smiling serenity. The sensibility of a place, the odd hint and glimpse of it, counts as one of the best "rewards of meandering" available to readers and travel companions of Kate Simon. (For afficionados of the Etruscan smile, the VILLA GIULIA in Rome—on the Viale delle Belle Arti—has a large collection of amazing artifacts found in excavations further south.)

Kate Simon's account of the PALIO (from *pallium*, the Latin word for banner), the prize given to the winner of the annual horse race held on July 2 and August 16 in the CAMPO, catches the historical and psychological threads of the event that make Siena such a colorful weave. Siena's violence, its fierce passion to triumph (whether over the enemy city-state of Florence or another horse doesn't matter) conjoins with its passionate religious devotion to the Virgin Mary, Mother of God, Mother of Sorrows, Mother of Mercy. Her image is embroidered on the pallium. August 16, the date of the Palio, is the season of the feast of Mary's Assumption into heaven, celebrated on August 15 (*Ferragosto*). The horse's triumph is considered her doing.

The counterpoint of cruelty and compassion shows up again amidst the splendors of the DUOMO. High above the columns of the nave and the spectacular marble floor, in the clerestory wall, are perched the severed heads of centuries of popes, a cold collective presence signifying a tradition of institutional power and authority; but elsewhere, throughout the interior, the peaceful face of holiness presents itself— in the images of the Carrara marble pulpit carved by Nicola Pisano (the sculptor of the Duomo's façade in Lucca), in statues, in stained glass, in frescoes. Next to the Duomo, off the right transept, the MUSEO DELL' OPERA DEL DUOMO contains more treasure: images of spiritual beauty and freedom, especially Duccio's masterpiece, the *Maestà*, a painting of the Virgin Enthroned, that is a Sienese favorite. A stairway leads to the top of the FACCIATONE and a panoramic view of Siena and Tuscany, a good prospect from which to contemplate the contradictory and multiple perspectives of Sienese tradition, of what Kate Simon refers to as its "light fidelity to religion combined with contempt."

Her comments on the house of ST. CATHERINE OF SIENA (Santuario e Casa di Santa Caterina on Vicolo del Tiratoio) give final expression to the swirl or simply the diversity of cultural currents to be felt in Siena. Catherine's life itself (1347–1380) demonstrates both the extreme asceticism of medieval religion and a bold, moral courage: Catherine talked back to the pope, in public, scolding him for the corruption rotting his institution, and she actually lived the life of the poor people she and her women followers—*la bella brigata*—served. A mystic activist and a wise woman, Catherine, and her legacy, seem more opaque than clear in the pious shrine on Vicolo del Tiratoio. Perhaps

FONTE BRANDA, a short walk down Via di Santa Caterina from the Casa, the simple eleventh- and thirteenth-century fountain where Catherine drew water for her father's dyeshop and for her large family (she was the twenty-fourth of twenty-five children) is a more suggestive memorial. In her *Dialogues*, the fountain was a source of rich imagery, its waters a sign of divine life always renewing itself. On the hill above Fonte Branda, the church of SAN DOMENICO, where she worshipped, rises dramatically. It contains the only portrait of Catherine— "a moving figure painted with awe and love," in Simon's words—and in the CAPPELLA SANTA CATERINA, there is a series of murals by Sodoma of the saint in ecstasy.

Iris Origo

Iris Cutting Origo, the daughter of an American father and an Anglo-Irish mother, spent her youth mostly in Florence. She came to the Tuscan country southeast of Siena as a bride, undertaking with her husband, Antonio Origo, the reclamation of a dilapidated house, ruined farm buildings, and uncultivated land. Over the course of fifty-two years of marriage, they transformed a barren wilderness into the beautiful La Foce described in her luminous autobiography Images and Shadows *(1970). The Origos also opened a school and a health clinic for the local children as well as a home for children orphaned during World War II. As* War in Val D'Orcia: An Italian War Diary 1943–1944 *shows, La Foce was an important center of the network of resistance operating in the mountains and valleys of southern Tuscany against the native Italian and occupying German fascists. An intellectually curious and well-read woman, Iris Origo also published the highly esteemed* The Merchant of Prato, The World of San Bernardino, *and biographical portraits of Ignazio Silone, Lauro de Bosis, Ruth Draper, and Gaetano Salvemini collected under the title* A Need To Testify *(1984). Place, the physical and historical context of an individual's world, figures in all her books with the intensity of an unforgettable human character.*

FROM *IMAGES AND SHADOWS*

LA FOCE

. . . superata tellus Sidera donat.*

—Boethius

It was on a stormy October afternoon in 1923, forty-seven years ago, that we first saw the Val d'Orcia and the house that was to be our home. We were soon to be married and had spent many weeks looking at estates for sale, in various parts of Tuscany, but as yet we had found nothing that met our wishes.

We knew what we were looking for: a place with enough work to fill our lifetime, but we also hoped that it might be in a setting of some beauty. Privately I thought that we might perhaps find one of the fourteenth- or fifteenth-century villas which were then almost as much a part of the Tuscan landscape as the hills on which they stood or the long cypress avenues which led up to them: villas with an austere façade broken only by a deep loggia, high vaulted rooms of perfect proportions, great stone fireplaces, perhaps a little court-yard with a well, and a garden with a fountain and an overgrown hedge of box. (Many such houses are empty now, and crumbling to decay.) What I had not realised, until we started our search, was that such places were only likely to be found on land that had already been tilled for centuries, with terraced hillsides planted with olive-trees, and vineyards that were already fruitful and trim in the days of the Decameron. To choose such an estate would mean that we would only have to follow the course of established custom, handing over all the hard work to our *fattore*,** and casting an occasional paternal eye over what was being done, as it always had been done. This was not what we wanted.

We still had, however, one property upon our list: some 3,500 acres on what we were told was very poor farming-land in the south of the province of Siena, about five miles from a new little watering-place which was just springing up at Chianciano. It was

[*Earth overcome gives the stars.—Au.]
**Farmer.

from there that we drove up a stony, winding road, crossed a ford, and then, after skirting some rather unpromising-looking farm buildings, drove yet farther up a hill on a steep track through some oak coppices. From the top, we hoped to obtain a bird's-eye view of the whole estate. The road was nothing more than a rough cart-track up which we thought no car had surely ever been before; and the woods on either side had been cut down or neglected. Up and up we climbed, our spirits sinking. Then suddenly we were at the top. We stood on a bare, windswept upland, with the whole of the Val d'Orcia at our feet.

It is a wide valley, but in those days it offered no green welcome, no promise of fertile fields. The shapeless rambling river-bed held only a trickle of water, across which some mules were picking their way through a desert of stones. Long ridges of low, bare clay hills—the *crete senesi*—ran down towards the valley, dividing the landscape into a number of steep, dried-up little water-sheds. Tree-less and shrubless but for some tufts of broom, these corrugated ridges formed a lunar landscape, pale and inhuman; on that autumn evening it had the bleakness of the desert, and its fascination. To the south, the black boulders and square tower of Radicofani stood up against the sky—a formidable barrier, as many armies had found, to an invader. But it was to the west that our eyes were drawn: to the summit of the great extinct volcano which, like Fujiyama, dominated and dwarfed the whole landscape around it, and which appeared, indeed, to have been created on an entirely vaster, more majestic scale—Monte Amiata.

The history of that region went back very far. There had already been Etruscan villages and burial-grounds and health-giving springs there in the fifth century B.C.; the chestnut-woods of Monte Amiata had supplied timber for the Roman galleys during the second Punic war, while, from the eighth to the eleventh century, both Lombards and Carolingians had left their traces in the great Benedictine abbeys of S. Antimo and Abbadia San Salvatore, in the *pieve* of S. Quirico d'Orcia and in innumerable minor Romanesque churches and chapels—some still in use, some half-ruined or used as granaries or storehouses—and the winding road we could just see across the valley still followed

almost the same track as one of the most famous mediaeval pilgrims' roads to Rome, the *via francigena*, linking this desolate
valley with the whole of Christian Europe. Then came the period
of castle-building, of violent and truculent nobles—in particular,
the Aldobrandeschi, Counts of Santa Fiora, who boasted that
they could sleep in a different castle of their own on each night
in the year—and who left as their legacy to the Val d'Orcia the
half-ruined towers, fortresses and battlements that we could see
on almost every hilltop. And just across the valley—its skyline
barely visible from where we stood—lay one of the most perfect
Renaissance cities, the creation of that worldly, caustic man of letters, Aeneas Silvius Piccolomini, Pope Pius II, the first man of
taste in Italy to enjoy with equal discrimination the works of art
and those of nature, who would summon, in the summer heat, his
Cardinals to confer with him in the chestnut woods of Monte
Amiata, "under one tree or another, by the sweet murmur of the
stream."

But of all this we knew nothing then, and still less could we
foresee that, within our lifetime, those same woods on Monte
Amiata, as well as those in which we stood, which for centuries had
been a hiding-place for the outlawed and the hunted, would again
be a refuge for fugitives: this time for anti-Fascist partisans and for
Allied prisoners of war. We only knew at once that this vast, lonely,
uncompromising landscape fascinated and compelled us. To live in
the shadow of that mysterious mountain, to arrest the erosion of
those steep ridges, to turn this bare clay into wheat-fields, to
rebuild these farms and see prosperity return to their inhabitants,
to restore the greenness of these mutilated woods—that, we were
sure, was the life that we wanted.

In the next few days, as we examined the situation more closely,
we were brought down to earth again. The estate was then of
about 3,500 acres, of which the larger part was then woodland
(mostly scrub-oak, although there was one fine beech-wood at the
top of the hill) or rather poor grass, while only a small part con-
sisted of good land. Even of this, only a fraction was already
planted with vineyards or olive-groves, while much of the arable
land also still lay fallow. The buildings were not many: besides the

villa itself and the central farm-buildings around it, there were twenty-five outlying farms, some very inaccessible and all in a state of great disrepair and, about a mile away, a small castle called Castelluccio Bifolchi. This was originally the site of one of the Etruscan settlements belonging to the great lucomony of Clusium (as is testified by the fine Etruscan vases found in the necropolis close to the castle, and which now lie in the museum of Chiusi), but the first mention of it in the Middle Ages as a "fortified place" dates only from the tenth century, and we then hear no more about it until the sixteenth, when it played a small part in the long drawn-out war between Siena and Florence for the possession of the Sienese territory—a war which gradually reduced the Val d'Orcia to the state of desolation and solitude in which we found it. In this war Siena was supported by the troops of Charles V and Florence by those of François I of France, and Pope Clement VII (who was secretly allied with the French) made his way one day by a secondary road from the Val d'Orcia to Montepulciano and, on arriving at the Castelluccio, expressed a wish to lunch there. But the owner of the castle, a staunch Ghibelline, refused him admittance, "so that the Pope was obliged, with much inconvenience and hunger, to ride on to Montepulciano."*

This castle, which held within its walls our parish church, dedicated to San Bernardino of Siena, and which owned some 2,150 acres, had once formed a single estate with La Foce; when we first saw it it was still inhabited by an old lady who (even if we had had the money) did not wish to sell. It was not until 1934 that we were able to buy it and thus bring the whole property together again.

As for the villa of La Foce itself, it is believed to have served as a post-house on the road up which Papa Clemente passed, but this is unconfirmed, and the only thing certain is that in 1557 its lands, together with those of the Castelluccio, were handed over to the Sienese hospital of Santa Maria della Scala, as is testified by

[*Verdiani Bandi, I Castelli della Val d'Orcia, quoting the chronicler Malavolti. Subsequently the castle was occupied in turn by the troops of the Emperor and of the French and after the fall of Montalcino passed, like all the rest of this territory, into the hands of Cosimo de' Medici, Grand Duke of Tuscany.—Au.]

a shield on the villa and on the older farms, bearing this date, with the stone ladder surmounted by a cross which is the hospital's emblem. The home itself was certainly not the beautiful villa I had hoped for, but merely a medium-sized country-house of quite pleasant proportions, adorned by a loggia on the ground floor, with arches of red brick and a façade with windows framed in the same material. Indoors it had no especial character or charm. A steep stone staircase led straight into a dark central room, lit only by red and blue panes of Victorian glass inserted in the doors, and the smaller rooms leading out of it were papered in dingy, faded colours. The doors were of deal or yellow pitch-pine, the floors of unwaxed, half-broken bricks, and there was a general aroma of must, dust, and decay. There was no garden, since the well was only sufficient for drinking-water, and of course no bathroom. There was no electric light, central heating or telephone.

Beneath the house stood deep wine-cellars, with enormous vats of seasoned oak, some of them large enough to hold 2,200 gallons, and a wing connected the villa with the *fattoria* (the house inhabited by the agent or *fattore* and his assistants) while just beyond stood the building in which the olives were pressed and the oil made and stored, the granaries and laundry-shed and wood-shed and, a little further off, the carpenter's shop, the blacksmith's and the stables. The small, dark room which served for a school stood next to our kitchen; the ox-carts which carried the wheat, wine, and grapes from the various scattered farms were unloaded in the yard. Thus villa and *fattoria* formed, according to old Tuscan tradition, a single, closely-connected little world.

When, however, we came to ask the advice of the farming experts of our acquaintance, they were not encouraging. To farm in the Sienese *crete*, they said, was an arduous and heart-breaking enterprise: we would need patience, energy—and capital. The soil-erosion of centuries must first be arrested, and then we would at once have to turn to re-afforestation, road-building, and planting. The woods, as we had already seen, had been ruthlessly cut down, with no attempt to establish a regular rotation; the olive trees were ill-pruned, the fields ill-ploughed or fallow, the cattle underfed. For thirty years practically nothing had been spent on any farm implements, fertilisers or repairs. In the half-ruined farms the roofs leaked, the stairs were worn away, many windows were boarded up or stuffed with rags, and the poverty-stricken families (often consisting of more than twenty souls) were huddled together in dark, airless little rooms. In one of these, a few months later, we found, in the same bed, an old man dying and a woman giving birth to a child. There was only the single school in the *fattoria*, and in many cases the distances were so great and the tracks so bad in winter, that only a few children could attend regularly. The only two roads—to Chianciano and Montepulciano—converged at our house (which stood on the watershed between the Val d'Orcia and Val di Chiana, and thence derived its name), and also ended there. The more remote farms could only be reached by rough carttracks and, if we wished to attempt intensive farming, their number should at least be doubled. We would need government subsidies, and also the collaboration of our neighbours, in a district where few landowners had either capital to invest, or any wish to adopt new-fangled methods, and we would certainly also meet with opposition from the peasants themselves— illiterate, stubborn, suspicious, and rooted, like countrymen all the world over, in their own ways.

We had no lack of warnings. Was it courage, ignorance or mere youth that swept them all away? Five days after our first glimpse of the Val d'Orcia, in November 1923, we had signed the deed of purchase of La Foce. In the following March we were married and, immediately after our honeymoon, we returned to the Val d'Orcia to start our new life.

How can I recapture the flavour of our first year? After a place has become one's home, one's freshness of vision becomes dimmed; the dust of daily life, of plans and complications and disappointments, slowly and inexorably clogs the wheels. But sometimes, even now, some sudden trick of light or unexpected sound will wipe out the intervening years and take me back to those first months of expectation and hope, when each day brought with it some new small achievement, and when we were awaiting, too, the birth of our first child.

For the first time, in that year, I learned what every country

child knows: what it is to live among people whose life is not regulated by artificial dates, but by the procession of the seasons: the
early spring ploughing before sowing the Indian corn and clover;
the lambs in March and April and then the making of the delicious
sheep's-milk cheese, *pecorino*, which is a speciality of this region,
partly because the pasture is rich in thyme, called *timo sermillo* or
popolino. ("*Chi vuol buono il caciolino*," goes a popular saying,
"*mandi le pecore al sermolino*."*) Then came the hay-making in
May, and in June the harvest and the threshing; the vintage
in October, the autumn ploughing and sowing; and finally, to con-
clude the farmer's year, the gathering of the olives in December,
and the making of the oil. The weather became something to be
considered, not according to one's own convenience but the
farmer's needs: each rain-cloud eagerly watched in April and May
as it scudded across the sky and rarely fell, in the hope of a kindly
wet day to swell the wheat and give a second crop of fodder for the
cattle before the long summer's drought. The nip of late frosts in
spring became a menace as great as that of the hot, dry summer
wind, or, worse, of the summer hail-storm which would lay low the
wheat and destroy the grapes. And in the autumn, after the sowing,
our prayers were for soft sweet rain. "*Il gran freddo di gennaio*,"
said an old proverb, "*il mal tempo di febbraio, il vento di marzo, le
dolci acque di aprile, le guazze di maggio, il buon mietere di giugno,
il buon battere di luglio, e le tre acque di agosto, con la buona sta-
gione, valgon più che il tron di Salmone*."** . . .

I still felt myself, however, very much a stranger in this new world
and was not very good at fitting into it. The solid, tradition-bound
group of people living in the *fattoria*—the *fattore* and his wife
and children, his three assistants and the *fattoressa* (who was never,

according to custom, the *fattore's* wife, but a woman who cooked and did the baking and the housekeeping and looked after the barn-yard) so deeply rooted in the customs laid down centuries ago, so certain that nothing could or should be changed—made me feel as shy and foreign as the peasant-women who, on certain feast-days, came from their farms on foot or by ox-cart, to place in my hands a couple of squawking fowls, a brace of pigeons or a dozen eggs—and often, too, a flow of grievances, tales of all the family illnesses, or requests for advice and help. But what advice could I give them, when I knew so little myself? Nothing that I had learned at Villa Medici or I Tatti was of any use to me now; I doubt whether any young married woman has started upon her new life more ill-equipped for the particular job she had to do. I did not even know, though Antonio told me that it was my business to concern myself with the *fattoria* linen-cupboard and the barn-yard, that the sheets, to be durable, should be made of a mixture of cotton and hemp, however scratchy, and that a part of our wool should be laid aside each year, after washing and bleaching, to make new mattresses; I could not distinguish a Leghorn hen from a Rhode Island Red. Nor did I succeed, for a long time, in being as easily cordial as Antonio with everyone we met, nor realise the fine hierarchical distinctions between the *fattore* and his assistants, the keepers and the foreman, the *contadini* and the day-labourers. I learned day by day, but never fast enough, always hampered by self-consciousness and shyness, seeming most aloof when I most wished to be friendly, I would walk or ride with Antonio from farm to farm and, while he was busy in the fields or stables, would go into the house and try to make friends with the women and children. It was uphill work. The women were polite—and wary. They offered me fresh raw eggs to drink, or a little glass of sweet home-made liqueur; they showed me the sheep-cheese that they had made, their furniture and their children. But I did not know the right questions to ask; I felt it an impertinence to comment on the way they kept their house, as Antonio said was expected of me; I could not tell one cheese from another; I had no idea whether the baby had measles or chicken-pox, and on the only occasion on which I attempted to give an injection to an old woman with asthma,

I broke the syringe. I did better with the children and, when the new schools were opened, I spent a lot of time there—playing with the children during recess, looking at their copy-books, providing them with a small library, admiring their little vegetable- or wheat-plots and giving prizes at the end of the school year—and through the children I gradually got to know the women a little better. It was always a very one-sided relationship though, and hampered by the whole framework of the *fattoria* between us. If a woman came to ask for her sink to be repaired or for her child to be taken to hospital it had to be referred to the *fattore*, and sometimes I found that incautious promises I had made had not been carried out. I think, now, that one of the fundamental evils of the *mezzadria* system was the presence and influence of these middlemen—tougher with the *contadini* than any landowner, because conscious of being only one step above them, and often shielding the *padrone* from what they thought it was inconvenient or undesirable for him to know. In our particular case, Antonio was fortunate, particularly in later years, in being surrounded by a group of loyal and devoted collaborators, who have become his close friends, but I still think that the system was a bad one, though perhaps an inevitable consequence of the whole structure of the *mezzadria*. Always, too, I was distressed by a sense of injustice, by the worn, tired faces of women only a little older than myself, and by the contrast—though certainly at that time we did not live in great luxury—between their life and my own. It is now one of my greatest regrets that inexperience, shyness, and my own other interests so often led me to take the path of least resistance and to leave things as they were. . . .

During the Nazi occupation of Italy, at considerable personal risk, the Origos turned their farm and villa into a safe haven for children from Genoa and Turin who had lost their homes and families in the bombings. They also helped escaped Allied war prisoners. In War in Val d'Orcia: An Italian War

Diary, 1943–1944, Origo chronicles the crises and confusion of anti-fascist resistance at a time when Tuscany was crawling with Nazis, Italian black-shirts loyal to Mussolini, Italian partisans (underground fighters against Hitler and Mussolini), escaped prisoners of war, citizen collaborators, and ordinary Tuscans waiting for deliverance by the American army making its way up the peninsula from Sicily and Naples. When La Foce became known as a beacon of rescue to the partisans and soldiers hiding in the hills of Monte Amiata, the local fascist newspapers demanded the Anglo-Irish-American Iris Origo be deported to Germany.

FROM *WAR IN VAL D'ORCIA: AN ITALIAN WAR DIARY,*
1943–1944

The experiences recorded in this diary have been in no way exceptional: thousands of other Italians have had similar ones, and many have had far worse. Indeed, the events here described are, as the reader will see, singularly undramatic and unheroic. Although in the last months of the German occupation the shadow of the Gestapo was never far away, and their spies and punitive expeditions did several times reach this valley, our anxieties were far less intense, far less continuous, than those borne by the people who hid Allied prisoners and partisans in their houses in the very heart of Rome or Milan, who concealed munitions or transmitted information, to whom every telephone call was a peril, every footstep on the stairs a menace. Nor did any active fighting or destruction of enemy property by the partisans of this district compare with that achieved by the partisans of the north, in Piemonte or Lombardy. No, our problems (and those of our neighbours) were of a different nature: they arose from a continual necessity to weigh, not between courage and cowardice or between right and wrong, but between conflicting duties and responsibilities, equally urgent. Every day the need for deciding between them would arise: the request for a lodging of a p.o.w. would have to be weighed against the danger to the farm which sheltered him, the dressing of a partisan's wound against the risk to the nurse and to the other patients in her charge, the pleas of the starving townsfolk who, in the last weeks before the liberation of Rome, came all the way from the city to beg for food, against the needs of the children and partisans whom we must go on feeding here. And when some hot-headed partisans would shoot at a *carabiniere* behind a hedge, or disarm two German soldiers in a village pub, disappearing themselves into the woods and leaving the helpless villagers at the mercy of German reprisals, it was our unpleasing task to attempt to point out the consequences of these methods, or (subsequently) to try to protect the villagers therefrom. Moreover, these were problems which—since the local situation was continually changing, with the arrival of different officials, and with the fluctuations of the military situation—could never be solved: every day each incident had to be met on its own merits. This became, in the long run, distinctly fatiguing, since it was impossible not to conduct a perpetual cross-examination of one's own conscience. At the end of each day prudence inquired, "Have I done too much?"—and enthusiasm or compassion, "Might I not, perhaps, have done more?"

What, it may be asked, under such circumstances, was the motive underlying the generous help given to the hunted Allied prisoners of war by the Italian countryfolk, often at the risk of their own lives, from the Garigliano to the Po, from the mountains of Piemonte and the Abruzzi to the fishing-villages of Liguria and Emilia? It would be a mistake, I think, to attribute it to any political—or even patriotic—motive. There was, it is true, a certain amount of anti-German and anti-Fascist feeling, especially among those peasants whose sons had been in the army against their will, or else were still attempting to avoid conscription by the Fascist Republican Army. But the true motive was a far simpler one: it has been described by an Italian partisan as "the simplest of all ties between one man and another; the tie that arises between the man who asks for what he needs, and the man who comes to his aid as best he can. No unnecessary emotion or pose."* And an English officer, himself an escaped prisoner of war, who owes his life to the help given him in this manner, has expressed his views in almost identical words: "The peasants' native sympathy with the underdog and the outcast asserted itself. Simple Christianity impelled them to befriend those complete strangers, feed them, clothe them,

[*Roberto Battaglia: *Un uomo, un partigiano*, Edizioni U., 1945.—Au.]

and help them on their way . . . All over Italy this miracle was to be seen, the simple dignity of humble people who saw in the escaped prisoners not representatives of a power to be withstood or placated, but individuals in need of their help."*

Of the 70,000 Allied p.o.w.s at large in Italy on September 8th, 1943, nearly half escaped, either crossing the frontier to Switzerland or France, or eventually rejoining their own troops in Italy; and each one of these escapes implies the complicity of a long chain of humble, courageous helpers throughout the length of the country. "I can only say," wrote General O'Connor to me, "that the Italian peasants and others behind the line were magnificent. They could not have done more for us. They hid us, escorted us, gave us money, clothes and food—all the time taking tremendous risks . . . We English owe a great debt of gratitude to those Italians whose help alone made it possible for us to live, and finally to escape."**

There is a passage in *The Pool of Vishnu* in which L. H. Myers, in attacking certain forms of self-protective egotism, maintains that they are not natural to men, but produced by the structure of organized society. "If one sees," he says, "a man struggling at the bottom of a well, one's natural impulse is to pull him out. If a man is starving, one's natural impulse is to share one's food with him. Surely it is only on second thoughts that we *don't* do these things? Society seems to me to be like an organized system of rather mean second-thoughts." During those crucial months of shared apprehension and danger, when the structure of society did not seem very important, that "organized system of mean second-thoughts" also, mercifully, disappeared into the background. For a short time all men returned to the most primitive traditions of ungrudging hospitality, uncalculating brotherhood. At most, some old peasant-woman, whose son was a prisoner in a far-away camp in India or Australia, might say—as she prepared a bowl of soup or made the bed for the foreigner in her house—"Perhaps someone will do the same for my boy."

[*Major P. Gibson.—Au.]
[**General Sir Richard O'Connor, K.C.B., D.S.O., M.C.—Au.]

* *

The actual keeping of the diary was not always an easy matter. During the first months, when a search of the house did not seem likely (though always possible), it usually lay among the pages of the children's picture-books; since I believed that the nursery bookshelf would probably be one of the last places to be searched. Later on, most of it (together with various propaganda leaflets and my jewellery) was buried in tin boxes in the garden. But the current pages were naturally always in the process of being written—even up to the end, with the Germans in the house, and (since even in times of danger the careless remain careless) were apt to be lying about in undesirable places. During the most eventful periods, too, it was often difficult to find time to write at all. Some passages were hurriedly scribbled at night, others with twenty children in the room—and some in the cellar, during the shelling.

But I felt at the time, and feel now, that any interest this diary might have would come from its being an immediate, first-hand account. I put down each day's events as they occurred, as simply and truthfully as I could, and (though I did report stories and rumours that reached us, since they were part of the queer mental colouring of our daily life) I tried not to make statements of which I had not had first-hand knowledge. And now, on re-reading, I have refrained from "touching up" the photograph, from changing the colour of events in the light of subsequent knowledge.

I have tried to avoid political bias and national prejudice. But we are all affected, far more deeply than we know—not by the theories, but by the mental climate of the world in which we live. Even our reactions against it show that we are not immune. I have no doubt that to those living in a different climate and seeing the same events from a different peep-hole, many of my judgments will appear mistaken, naive, prejudiced and even wrong. Most certainly I have swallowed propaganda without realizing it; but may I be permitted to ask my readers—are they quite certain that they have never done so, too?

It will, I think, be obvious that I love Italy and its people. But I have become chary of generalizations about countries and nations; I believe in individuals, and in the relationship of individuals to one another. When I look back upon these years of tension and

expectation, of destruction and sorrow, it is individual acts of kindness, courage or faith that illuminate them; it is in them that I trust.
I remember a British prisoner of war in the Val d'Orcia helping the
peasant's wife to draw water from the well, with a ragged, beaming
small child at his heels. I remember the peasant's wife mending his
socks, knitting him a sweater, and baking her best cake for him, in
tears, on the day of his departure.

These—the shared, simple acts of everyday life—are the realities
on which international understanding can be built. In these, and in
the realization that has come to many thousands, that people of
other nations are, after all, just like themselves, we may, perhaps,
place our hopes.

LA FOCE

JUNE 22ND

The day begins badly. During the first lull in the firing a tragic procession begins to struggle down to our cellar: those of our farmers
who, until then, have preferred to take shelter in the woods. All
night they have been under fire, and their drawn, terrified faces
bear witness to what they have been through. They thankfully
take refuge in the cellar and the vat-room—old men, women and
children—about sixty more people to shelter and feed. An old
grandmother from a neighbouring farm is among them; half para-
lysed, with a weak heart, she has been dragged along by her son
and daughter, and now collapses, utterly exhausted. The babies
whimper from cold and hunger. The older children go and whisper
to ours, frightening them with the tales that I have tried to spare
them until now. We go up to the kitchen (since fortunately the
lull still continues) and produce hot barley-coffee and bread-and-
milk, the keeper having succeeded in finding and milking the
cows. The farmers' account of their nights in the woods is not such
as to encourage us to try to get through to the Allied lines with the
children, a plan which again, this morning, we had considered.
Sporadic firing goes on all through the morning.

This glimpse of a tiny segment of the front increases my conviction of the wastefulness of this kind of warfare, the disproportion
between the human suffering involved and the military results

achieved. In the last five days I have seen Radicofani and Contig-
nano destroyed, the countryside and farms studded with shell
holes, girls raped, and human beings and cattle killed. Otherwise
the events of the last week have had little enough effect upon either
side: it is the civilians who have suffered.

LATER

The above reflections were written during a lull in the shelling, in
the kitchen, while boiling some milk for the children. But, in the
midst of them, a louder burst of shell-fire than any we had experienced brought me down to the cellar, where we turned on the
gramophone and started songs with the children, and waited.
"Now," we felt, "it really is beginning." It had already been evident
for some hours that shells of larger calibre were now being used,
and both Antonio and I (though fortunately no one else) realized
that the cellar was by no means proof against them. After a while, in
another slight lull, the door opened, and a German sergeant came
in: space would at once be required, he said, in the cellar (already
filled to overflowing) for some German troops. A few minutes later
an officer appeared: "You must get out," he said, "and get the children away. You can't keep them here. And we need the cellar."
(That same morning we had again asked this officer what we should
do with the children, and he had said emphatically, "Stay on!") "If
you get out at once," he added, "you may be able to get out of range
during this lull." There followed a few minutes of considerable confusion. Antonio and I were besieged by a crowd of terrified people,
asking when and where they should go, what they should take with
them, what they should leave behind, and so on. We could only
answer: "At once. To Montepulciano or Chianciano, wherever you
have friends. Take only what you can carry with you—the clothes
on your back, and some food." The babies were howling, and, with
Donata in my arms, I couldn't help Schwester much, but we managed to pack a basket with the babies' food, and the pram with
some of their clothes and nappies. I took a tiny case, which we had
in the cellar, containing a change of underclothes for Antonio and
me, a pair of shoes, some soap and eau de cologne and face powder,
my clock and Giorgio's photographs; and that is all that we now

possess. Each of the children carried his own coat and jersey. The grown-ups each carried a baby, or a sack of bread. And so, in a long, straggling line, with the children clutching at our skirts, half walking, half running, we started off down the Chianciano road.

I did not think, then, that we should get all the children through safely. We had been warned to stick to the middle of the road, to avoid mines, and to keep spread out, so as not to attract the attention of Allied planes. German soldiers, working at mine-laying, looked up in astonishment as we passed. *"Du lieber Gott!* What are those children still doing here?"· Some corpses lay, uncovered, by the roadside. A German Red Cross lorry came tearing up the hill, nearly running over us. And all the time the shells were falling, some nearer, some farther off, and the planes flew overhead. The children were very good, the older ones carrying whatever they could, the smaller ones stumbling along as fast as their small legs could carry them. Donata shouted with glee on Antonio's shoulder. No one cried except the tiny babies, but now and again there was a wail: "I can't go so fast!" and someone would pick up that child for a few hundred yards. The sun was blazing overhead, the hill very steep, and none of us had had any food since early breakfast. But every stumbling, weary step was taking us farther away from the cellar, and from what was still to come.

When we got to the top of the hill before Chianciano we divided into two parties. Those who had friends in Chianciano went on there, the rest of us, sixty in all (of whom four were babies in arms, and twenty-eight others children) started across country towards Montepulciano. The road itself was, we knew, under continual shell-fire, but we hoped to be able to cut across to the Villa Bianca cross-roads. The first part went well, and when at last we had a ridge between us and La Foce, we called a first halt. The children fell exhausted and thankful on the ground, only to rise again hastily, having sat down on an ant-hill. They made, indeed, much more fuss about the ants than about the shells.

The shelling seemed farther off, the mined path was behind us, and a peasant brought us glasses of water. Until then, there had been no moment in which to stop and think, but now we began to realize, with dismay, all that we had left behind. The people in the vat-room—had they been warned? No one knew, and we looked at each other in horror. Then at last Assunta remembered: "Yes, she had seen the fattore go in to warn them." But what they could do next it was difficult to imagine, for the old grandmother who was with them was unable to walk, and there were also several children. Probably they would merely hide in terror in a ditch. One could only pray that none of them would be killed.

And then there was Giorgio's body. We had hoped to bury him the night before, so that at least we could show his grave to his family when we are able to trace them, but the firing on the road to the cemetery prevented us from getting there. So we had had to leave him in that little room, unburied.*

And then the dogs—they, too, had been forgotten. We fed them up to yesterday, but in the hurry of leaving we did not remember to go up to the kennels (five hundred yards away, and under shell fire) to fetch them. And poor Gambolino, the poodle, is terribly gun-shy. Even if he is not killed he will go almost mad with fear. It does not bear thinking of.

After a brief rest (too brief, but as long as we dared) we went on again—Antonio and the keeper, Porciani, taking the longer and more dangerous road, on which the pram could be pushed, and the rest of us scrambling along a rough track up and down steep gulleys. The children were getting very tired, but struggled manfully on, and we lifted them over the steepest places. Twice planes came hovering over us, and we all crouched down in a ditch. Then when we came out into the open cornland, beyond Pianoia, came the worst part of the journey. The shelling had begun again, and on the Montepulciano road, a few hundred yards below us, shells were bursting with a terrific din. The children were afraid to go on, but on we must. Some more planes came over, and we lay down for cover in the tall corn. I remember thinking at that moment, with Benedetta lying beside me and two other children clutching at my skirts: "This can't be real—this isn't really happening."

[*When we got home we found the room empty, and under the cypresses, a few yards away, a fresh grave with a rough cross, on which was written *Unbekannter Italiäner* (Unknown Italian). It was many months before we were at last able to trace his family in Bergamo.—Au.]

At last we reached a farm on the road, occupied by a German Red Cross unit, and there again we got some water and a short rest. But the officer came out and, hearing that it was a *Kinderheim*, gave us disconcerting advice: take refuge at once in the Capuchin convent on the hill, he said, and don't push on to Montepulciano. "What is happening at La Foce to-day, will happen there to-morrow." For a minute we hesitated, but the convent, we knew, had no food and no sort of shelter, so we decided to risk it and push on. From this point onward, the Germans said, the road was safe, and so we took it, a long, straggling, foot-sore procession. Half an hour after we had passed, that very stretch of the road was shelled.

After four hours we got to San Biagio, at the foot of the Montepulciano hill, and there sat down in a ditch for a breather before the last pull. We were very tired now, and a dreadful thought came over us: "What if the Braccis should have left?" "What if we find no shelter here?" But as we sat there, a little group of Montepulciano citizens appeared, then yet another: they had seen us from the ramparts, and were coming down to meet us with open arms. Never was there a more touching welcome. Many of them were partisans; others were refugees themselves from the south whom we had helped; yet others old friends among the Montepulciano workmen. They shouldered the children and our packages, and in a triumphant procession, cheered by so much kindness, we climbed up the village street, Antonio at the head, with Donata on his shoulder. Bracci and his wife Margherita came out to meet us, the children were at once settled on cushions on the terrace, and the Montepulcianesi vied with each other in offering accommodation. Antonio and I acted as billeting officers. Three went to one house, four to another, and the Braccis nobly took in not only our whole family, but all the refugee children as well. The Braccis' mattresses and blankets, which had been walled up, were pulled out again and laid on the ground, the children (after a meal of bread and cheese) put to bed, and at last we were able to wash and rest. Only one child was the worse for the terrible experience: Rino, who had a touch of the sun and suddenly fainted. Benedetta (sharing a bed with me) woke up, when I came to bed, to say: "We've left the bangs behind at last, haven't we?" and then fell into a twelve hours' sleep.

We have left behind everything that we possess, but never in my life have I felt so rich and so thankful as looking down on all the children as they lay asleep. Whatever may happen to-morrow, to-night they are safe and sound! . . .

~

For the Literary Traveler

Roughly an hour's drive southeast of Siena on S2, passing the turn-off to SAN QUIRICO D'ORCIA, and winding left along S146 through the VAL D'ORCIA, leads eventually (after more winding right and then left), to LA FOCE, still the private home of the Origo family. Local people know the place (and its location is printed on the map of *Toscana* of the Touring Club Italiano). In his biography of Edith Wharton, R. W. B. Lewis, noting Wharton's visit to La Foce in 1930, describes it as "the magnificent estate" that the Origos carved "out of a desolate, stony stretch of land below Siena, and which would eventually resemble the beautifully receding landscape of a fifteenth-century Sienese painting." On the left at the top of the hill as you enter the Montepulciano/Chianchiano crossroads is the health clinic, *Ambulatorio*, built in memory of the Origos' young son, Gianni, who died suddenly at the age of seven. To the right, about half-a-mile down the road from the villa, is a small graveyard where local partisans, workers, and the Origos and their son are buried, a place more quiet and green than any formal cloister. The inscription on Iris Origo's headstone comes from St. Catherine of Siena: *"Chi più conosce più ama, più amando più gusta"*—"The more you know the more you love, and by loving more, the more you enjoy."

Returning to the crossroads, the narrow back mountain road along which the Origos, their young daughters, and their sixty orphans and neighbors fled the Nazis and the Allies' bombings in 1944 (described in these pages), leads to Montepulciano. (This mountain road between cypresses, the streets of Montepulciano, and Origo's story of herding children at night through mined countryside bring to mind the

Taviani brothers' beautiful film, *The Night of the Shooting Stars [La Notte di San Lorenzo)* about Italians in northern Tuscany running from the Germans and looking for the Americans in August 1944.)

Originally an Etruscan settlement, Montepulciano today is a lovely hill town, warm with the serenity and good humor attributed to Etruscan civilization, a pleasure to explore, especially in the evening. The townspeople still practice the caring tradition implicit in Montepulciano's hospitality to the war orphans described in Iris Origo's *War Diary*. Homes for infants and children in need of medical care and shelter can be found in the quiet PIAZZA DI SANTA LUCIA (where Garibaldi and Anita stayed) and in the larger PIAZZA SAN FRANCESCO. The panoramic prospect from this piazza, of the valleys beneath MONTE AMIATA ("beloved mountain") in the distance, the highest point in southern Tuscany, suggests an emblem out of nature of the magnanimity of the Poliziani partisans, the Origos as rescuers of orphans, and the nuns who care for the babies today in the clinic that faces the mountain.

References to Montepulciano recur in a number of Iris Origo's books. She would have known well the landmark statue of PUCINELLA, tolling the time atop the old tower at the bottom of the town near PIAZZA MICHELOZZO; the steep walk up along VIA DI GRACCIANO and VIA VOLTAIA to the PIAZZA GRANDE where men and boys play soccer in rosy twilight and music students practice at the open windows of a Renaissance mansion (the PALAZZO CONTUCCI); and the DUOMO, both its plain façade and austere interior enhanced with the magnificent TRIPTYCH OF THE ASSUMPTION on the high altar. The place seems like an equivalent in stone of the straightforwardness and elegance that make the tone of Iris Origo's prose linger in the reader's mind. You want to linger in Montepulciano and read more of her.

UMBRIA

CORTONA AND THE UMBRIAN APENNINES

ASSISI

Lisa St. Aubin de Terán

*Prize-winning author of eight novels (*The Slow Train to Milan; *Venice;* Joanna*), as well as a volume of poetry and a collection of short stories, Lisa St. Aubin de Terán calls her search for a castle in Italy her most abiding romantic obsession.* A Valley in Italy *recounts her and her artist husband's infatuation on sight with the ruin the Villa Orsola, a potentially magnificent house in Umbria, "the green heart of Italy." It also offers a portrait of the highly amusing process of an Italian restoration against the rhythms of a bohemian family life in a remote Italian village where "all things are made to be as enjoyable as possible." The head carpenter Imolo, for instance, takes regular times out to get Lisa upstairs to admire, among other things, "the pools of pink sunlight that settled on pockets of hillslope, highlighting the intensity of green that is so characteristic of Umbria. Imolo was in love with the crest of a hill. . . . I watched him watching it with rapture, and the lifting of the veil of constant sorrow that seemed to hang over his face."*

The protagonist of this memoir is as much the spirit of a place as the individual people. Both have a vitality and a still center that the traveler desires to read more closely.

FROM *A VALLEY IN ITALY: THE MANY SEASONS OF A VILLA IN UMBRIA*

I

For years before I came to settle here in Umbria, the name conjured up for me a strange, wild, contradictory place. Despite travelling the length and breadth of mainland Italy numerous times, tunnelling through as many veins and arteries as its railway system dictated, I never reached the lungs: the self-seeded Umbrian forests. I had heard that there were bears and wolves in Umbria, and hideaways in the woods where kidnap victims were held by their Sardinian captors. It was said to be a poor, infertile place where life was hard for the *contadini* who slaved for their feudal overlords, who were, in turn, the bastard sons of cardinals and popes.

My family and I were in Italy house-hunting. We had been looking for a suitably dilapidated villa for three years. With such a serious task before us, we had no time for sightseeing, so the old Papal States remained a mystery on the periphery of our half-hearted search. Half-hearted in the sense that we rarely visited a house, villa, tower or farm. Most of our efforts centred on bars, where we would sit and discuss what we were looking for. Each winter, this dream house would be taken back to whichever ill-heated rented place we were then living in, and used to fan the meagre flames of the fire we huddled around.

I had a mental picture of my ideal house which I had been carrying around with me like a piece of luggage since my schooldays. It had been to Venezuela and back through the Caribbean. It had travelled with me to North America and Canada and as far south as Patagonia. I took it from frontier to frontier across Europe. I wanted a house so huge that I could move from room to empty room without disturbing anyone. The design of the house was as fickle as most young loves, and changed in shape and layout all the time. The only constant features in my dream image were a pillared loggia, a stone arch, a terracotta balustrade and a line of sentinel cypresses. . . .

I grew up on a diet of Byron, Keats and Shelley; I worshipped Italy as a pilgrim might worship Mecca from afar, determined someday to go there. As a girl, I had married for the chance to live in Italy. I can hardly remember a time when I wasn't in love with the idea of it. Sitting out on the Corso Vanucci, with the pastel pink and ivory Umbrian marble warming in the morning sun, surrounded by palatial banks and offices, with grey-green hills at one end and the great Renaissance Fontana Maggiore at the other, I fell in love with Umbria. But then, I fall in love with places readily. I have been in love with so many places that, like old lovers, I can no longer remember all their names. . . .

* *

The sight of any beautiful house or garden makes my heart miss a beat. I grew up making Sunday visits to the botanical gardens at Kew. Holidays were spent visiting the great English country houses (for a small fee and a couple of hours at a time), and Sunday evenings were spent in Clapham poring over the property advertisements in the *Sunday Times* with my mother and our mutual delusions of grandeur. We used to fantasize constantly about buying and moving into now this castle, now that. Superimposed on these childhood memories was my own dream house; as our cortège of cars turned into a drive past a triple row of venerable black cypresses, I saw the house I had been looking for all my life. It was standing like a jilted beauty still dressed in its ancient best. The abandoned façade was groaning under tons of sculpted terracotta. There was row upon row of long, graceful windows reaching down to white marble sills, there were dozens of arches, a loggia, a roof, a balcony and a cascade of wisteria. . . .

VI

San Orsola crouches on the edge of a road that once stopped a few miles beyond the village boundary, petering into an almost impassable mule track. Thus no one ever went to San Orsola by accident or because they were passing through. It remained isolated from most of what was good and bad in the rest of Umbria, let alone the rest of Italy. It became close-knit and interbred. Unmolested by travellers, bandits or even taxmen, the Orsolani developed no fear or suspicion of strangers. During the Second World War, their open, easy ways were sorely tried, but few reprisals were enforced upon them, despite the Partisan enclave, and the bombs that fell mainly by accident, intended for larger, vaguely similar targets.

Towards the end of the war, the village sheltered two American airmen and an RAF officer for over a year. These airmen taught the local children to sing "She'll be coming round the mountain when she comes," so that when the Allied armies arrived they could sing it and thus disclose their act of kindness under German occupation. To this day, I catch many a strain of "Singing aye aye yippie yippie aye," and I've often been asked to translate the refrain, which has enormous significance to many a sixty-year-old. It is always a disappointment to them that there is not more poetry in the lyric.

The hills around San Orsola were full of Partisans. Men from the village lived out with them; the local barman was their message runner. As work on the house moved forward, more and more stories unfolded and more and more false walls emerged and were knocked down. Some of them still had mouse-chewed cobs left behind them from the days of the hidden grain.

Everyone who came to work on the house had a theory about it and another scrap of narrative to add to the ill-fitting jigsaw of its history. Soon, the workmen's visitors outnumbered our own. People came from all around to see Imolo's reconstruction of the villa. Each newcomer announced himself in the same way, yodelling up from the forecourt, "O, Imolo!"

Everyone seemed to be connected in some way to the villa, which they called *il palazzo*. Dozens of local people were reared in the big kitchen, and so many people either claim to have been born here, or to be related to someone who was, that visions of a massive rural maternity ward take shape. However, the director of the telephone company was definitely born here—many witnesses stepped forward to corroborate his claim—and in honour of this, he jumped us along the queue for a new telephone line.

The *palazzo* also seems to have been a labour-intensive farm since the last war. The shepherds who kept sheep on the first floor came visiting, as did the swineherds of the pigs that once roamed on the ground floor, or those who fed the quail on the second floor. Others, looking as though they wouldn't know one end of a farm animal from another, wandered around nostalgically. These, I was told, just used to make love in the open spaces of the vertiginous attic, with its fourteen window holes open to the air, on a granulated mattress of bat droppings.

Imolo and the workmen speak of the past here as though it were tangible. They prize it the way the best wild *funghi* are prized and stored away to be savoured at will. Their memories are hoarded, pored over and then bottled up again. They are communal memories, stored in the *cantinas* under all the houses and cottages with the barrels of wine, and it's usually the wine that brings them out.

Imolo explains that the days of poverty have come to an end in this part of Umbria, but they are often remembered. Tobacco has changed their fortune. Until 1945, the local men had to emigrate or work a six-day week as day labourers, charcoal burners or wood-cutters in the endless forests. His family, who scraped a living as agricultural workers under the few local landlords, were the lucky ones, able to live with their families, and the women and children helped bring in the crops.

The land around excelled in no single crop, producing only infe-rior versions of what neighbouring Tuscany grew. Then the tobacco began to catch on, and from 1953 onwards there was a boom which by 1980 had provided every family in San Orsola with their own house, a piece of land, and at least one car. So the wolf is far from each door, but psychologically it is still there, hovering in the garden, somewhere between the lilies and the lettuces.

The older generation all have bowed backs and gnarled, scarred hands. Many of them wear the black and dark-blue garb of 1900. The old women wear headscarves and thick wrinkled wool stock-ings, regardless of the heat. They gather immense bundles of fag-gots to stoke their stoves and bread ovens. At dawn and dusk they can be seen hobbling along the edge of the road with these bundles on their backs, while their grandchildren whizz by in their new Fiats. These grandparents are all quite well-to-do, despite appear-ances, but their wealth has arrived too late to change their ways. They live in the same houses as their grown-up children, sur-rounded by luxuries and all the gadgetry of modern technology, but they cling to their old cycles of ritual behaviour, working long hours on their own allotments and vineyards.

San Orsola is an organized village, run by a junta of local men and women who form the *proloco*. The *proloco* raises money from within the village and then spends it on dances and banquets, pic-nics, concerts and fireworks. The women gather mostly in each other's houses. The teenagers travel in packs of cars and mopeds, cruising from disco to disco, while the men congregate at the four local bars and play cards. They play a game called *briscola*, and another called 151, both governed by strict rules that include (Italian fashion) rules about permissible cheating. Four players sit around a table thumping their cards down dramatically, while a group of advisers and detractors stand by them, shouting advice and recrimination. On Sunday afternoons, the men dress up to play Italian bowls—*bocce*—with heavy balls which they roll down a long sandpit. No game is complete without its crowd of loudly arguing umpires.

The parish of San Orsola sprawls across a long river valley and straggles up the wooded slopes of the hills to either side. There are dozens of hamlets, or *frazioni*, all belonging to the village. The centre of the village is enclosed in a triangle formed by the church, the bar and the *campo sportivo*. After a few glasses of the local San Giovese wine, anyone will tell you the secret that they share at San Orsola: Umbria is the centre of the world, and San Orsola itself is the good heart of Umbria. This is not strictly, geographically, true, but the point is not worth arguing. The vicinity of the Tuscan border is irrelevant, just as the vicinity of lovely cities and the approach of the twenty-first century are irrelevant. I thought when I lived in Venice that I had found the proudest people in the world, but here, without any of the Venetians' snobbery, are the proudest people. They make no concessions to other places (mostly un-known); this is the best, the first and finest. As an essay in positive thinking, it seems to have worked. The village has such a pleasant atmosphere that all over the neighbourhood, potential rivals will say quite spontaneously, "San Orsola *è bello*, eh, there's no place like it."

Despite my years of brainwashing here, I have to say that it is not actually the most aesthetically pleasing village in Umbria. But its spirit is *bello* and I happily concur that there really is no place like it.

In the 1950s and '60s when work was still scarce, and all but the landowners were grindingly poor, dozens of men and boys emi-grated to Switzerland to work. Thus it is sometimes called a Swiss village (of which there are many, hereabouts). Imolo told me:

"I went to Switzerland too. It was there that I learnt my preci-sion. It's a cold place there, people are cold inside. I was lucky, I met a family who took me in. I think I would have died if I'd had to cope on my own. It was hard.

"After Switzerland, I moved to Milan. I used to work on old *palazzos* and churches.

"Most of the villagers who went away suffered out there. Our children will never *have* to leave, like we did."

Imolo has two children, as do all the couples in San Orsola. The families are planned (in strict defiance of the Pope). He told me one evening, down at Regina's bar, toying with his empty wine glass and a battered cigarette,

"In other villages, the children leave now not because they have to, but because they want to. That is what we're trying to balance here, I suppose."

For the Literary Traveler

Cortona is another ancient cobblestone hill town—it's more of a mountain than a hill—perched on the steep border of Tuscany and Umbria. Visiting it makes the perfect introduction to the love song Lisa St. Aubin de Terán has written to the beauty of Umbria. Cortona is one of the places where she and her children stop on their way to settling in at their villa-in-progress.

Among the town's major attractions is the PIAZZA DELLA REPUB-BLICA, the reward of space, operatic architecture, and restful steps beneath the PALAZZO COMUNALE that awaits walkers making the ascent of Via Nazionale from the main gate of the city's wall. Just behind the Palazzo Comunale with its huge clock tower is the second main square, PIAZZA SIGNORELLI, and the PALAZZO CASALI, which houses the ETRUSCAN ACADEMY and the MUSEO OIVICO. Travelers interested in the Etruscan traces of Italy's past will be delighted with the erotic dance of metal sirens, satyrs, and dolphins on the famous *lampadario*, a bronze chandelier from the fifth-century B.C.E., when Cortona was one of the largest and most important Etruscan cities in the north. To the right and slightly downhill from the Palazzo Casali is the small PIAZZA DEL DUOMO where, as R. W. B. Lewis suggests in *The City of Florence*, "one can sit and look over a waist-high rampart at the dark plain of the Chianti River Valley, and, to the right, at the hills, covered with gray olive trees, rising above the Val d'Arno." It is here that Lewis's sense of Cortona's "heart-restoring tranquillity" is most palpable.

The genius of this place is in its effect—the easy communality of the expansive piazzas, with their processions of schoolchildren and affable schoolteachers. Cortona liberates space. It quickens the desire for more of it, for the dimensions, physical and existential, that space represents. One simply wants to stay here, and sit and watch, and later on to follow the mysteries of the narrow medieval streets leading into and off the piazzas. No wonder so many writers (Ann Cornelisen), artists, and scholars have come here and moved in.

But Lisa St. Aubin de Terán traveled on to her valley in Umbria. The route into the lonely world she found and celebrates is as glorious as the introduction provided by this cityscape. The most curvy but beautiful road is the one going to MERCATALE (and eventually to UMBERTIDE), to the left and signposted, midway along the descent from the heights of Cortona. Climbing its high twists leads to visions of castles and towns on clifftops, vast meadows of poppies, rainbows after sudden showers, sunlit steep slopes planted lushly with olive trees—the road seems to leave the modern world behind and discover a paradise. Umbria is the place where St. Benedict, the founder of monasticism, imagined the unity of prayer and work, and Francis of Assisi saw creation as God's handiwork—a work of love—conceiving a spiritual revolution by the power of his visions. What Lisa St. Aubin de Terán understood when she chose Umbria as a womb of life was a down-to-earth and sensual version of a similar insight. The more one sees along these high green roads and dark valleys the stronger the desire grows to spend time there. If you can't, reading A Valley in Italy from beginning to end is a good substitute.

Patricia Hampl

Place is a dominant passion in all of Patricia Hampl's writing: St. Paul and Prague in A Romantic Education *(1981), Assisi, Lourdes, and a Benedictine retreat in California in* Virgin Time *(1992). Poet, memoirist, and travel writer, Hampl loves the world and it comes through in her vigorous, attentive prose. The sensuality of her vision is not incompatible with the experience of Assisi. The power of the place derives from its multiple and interacting personalities: it's an amazingly beautiful medieval hill town built steeply into the side of Mount Subasio; a rich resource of superb art by Cimabue, Giotto, and Martini; the birthplace of St. Francis and St. Clare, and of their revolutionary religious foundations; and the destination of pilgrims seeking an encounter with the beauty and freedom inspired by all these resonances. Hampl, with a Catholic convent school background and the mystical instincts of a poet, understands all this. Her essay also shows the strong autobiographical slant of the most engaging travel writing.*

UMBRIAN SPRING

At one time, the little mustard-colored room in my high school where I was sent after lunch to practice playing the piano had been a dormitory room. Years before, farmers and bankers as far away as the Dakotas had sent their daughters to the nuns in St. Paul to be finished—as the rather sinister phrase of the day put it.

But by 1964 the boarders were long gone. We were all day pupils, studying trig, hoping to score high on the SAT's. Most of the old dorm rooms, opening onto a long, dim corridor, had been turned into practice rooms. One, used for storage, was filled with Singer treadle sewing machines from some ghostly home-ec class of yore. And one room, always locked, at the darkest end of the corridor, remained a mystery.

The room was next to a door on which a white cardboard sign announced in stern block letters: ENCLOSURE.

It might just as well have read STOP. No girl was allowed past this door or past any other "enclosure" signs posted throughout the building. Such markers indicated the border, strictly observed, between school and cloister.

The whole place, even the big, walled courtyard, was divided in half like that. Them and Us. "I'll fetch it, dear," a nun would say affably when one of us lobbed a tennis ball out of range into the cloister garden behind the tall hedge called The Maze. It was unthinkable that one of *us* might trespass Over There.

The building was romantic, made of red brick and laid out in an L-shape, with a great bell tower from which the Angelus tolled. There was an arched walk, a reflecting pool, statues, a grotto—the works.

Though it was only a few blocks from my own house, it seemed—and was—foreign. The design of the building had been taken from that of an old French monastery. The fact that the nuns casually referred to their own rooms in the cloister as *cells* only heightened the romance, the oddity of the place. There is something tantalizing about what can never be seen, especially when it's nearby. Even more so when those deadpan "enclosure" signs were posted on every floor, teasing.

So complete was the injunction against entering the cloister that no one flirted with the idea of a raid. It was impossible to imagine putting a hand on the doorknob of an enclosure door.

Yet, the cloister calm reached us. I loved the cramped, yellowed room on the fourth floor where, truth be told, I did precious little practicing. After a few swipes at "The Jolly Farmer" and "Für Elise," I threw myself on the flowered daybed behind the black grand piano (said to belong to the archbishop, who stopped by at times and spent an hour playing things like "Begin the Beguine" and "Sweet Georgia Brown"). The long window rattled in its sash, and I stared down upon the courtyard. I was so high up that no enclosure sign could deny a view of the cloister garden below. It proved to be disappointingly ordinary.

I lounged on the daybed in my blue serge uniform and brown oxfords and considered my future. I had many airy castles in mid-construction. I would travel, I would see the world. It was some kind of oversight, a mistake, that I'd been born in St. Paul, Minn., in the first place. I was really destined for. . . .

One afternoon, emerging from the practice room and my fine plans, I saw that the door to the always-locked room was open. A shaft of light fell across the dark corridor. There was a window in the room, south-facing, and the sun was flooding in.

It's strange, the places that strike one as perfect. They needn't be beautiful. But they must somehow *register*, must touch a core of harmony. A room, after all, is an *interior*: it speaks to the inner self.

The floor was maple, golden, highly polished. Nun's work. There was a small, blue rag rug, a plain table meant to be a desk, a chair. No crucifix; instead, a print of a painting of a ship at sea. Behind it, someone had stuck a dried frond—from Palm Sunday— that curled around the wooden frame.

But it was the bed, I think, that did it. The narrow, white bed, the candlewick spread, the great wafer of sunlight cast upon it from the window.

I wanted to go in there, lie down and sleep for maybe a hundred years. The entire cube (it was tiny, another former dorm room) was engulfed in the light. It seemed not part of the school, not part of the cloister, but belonged to some middle ground of utter serenity.

Sister Marie Therese was placing a vase of lilacs on the table. She had a bundle of bedding under her other arm. She gave the white bedspread a final flick as she came to the door. What was this room for, I asked.

"This room dear? This is for visitors."

"Visitors?" Who, I wondered, ever came here to visit.

Sister Marie Therese took a final look around the little chamber: it seemed to pass inspection. She stepped outside, near me. "Strangers, dear," she said, closing the door, which left us suddenly in the dark again. "We must always have a room for strangers."

Then she opened the enclosure door and went on her way into the cloister, out of my part of the world, the bundle of laundry balanced on her hip like a baby.

Hospitality is one of the oldest missions of the monastic life, one largely forgotten by the modern secular world. We tend to think of monasteries, reasonably enough, as places apart, hidden, off limits.

And it's true: The primary work of a contemplative monastery is the *Opus Dei*—the Work of God. That is—pure and simple—prayer.

But the tradition of monastic hospitality is an old one, providing lodging for "pilgrims and strangers," as St. Francis of Assisi called himself and his followers. There was a lot of wandering about during the Middle Ages, much of it by pilgrims and itinerant monks attached to no specific monastery. Such wandering monks, called *gyrovagi*, were a social embarrassment, trading on the commitment to hospitality that governed the great monastic houses. "Concerning their miserable way of life," St. Benedict wrote, "it is better to be silent than to speak."

Today's monastery inns can be anything from a few rooms along a convent wing to a great monastic complex with a separate visitors' *auberge*. Maintaining some kind of hostelry is an obvious way for monastic communities to earn some money. But when Soeur Ste. Agathe at Santa Coletta in Assisi handed me the change from my American Express travelers check after I had spent three nights (private room with breakfast), I knew—if I'd ever doubted—that something besides a healthy entrepreneurial spirit was running the show there.

Italy—no surprise—is especially rich in monasteries that take in travelers. In Umbria, "the mystical province," home of St. Benedict, St. Francis and St. Clare, it seems easy to find convents and monasteries offering hospitality in the little hill towns.

Late last spring, on a hiking trip in the region (destination: Assisi), I stayed one night at the Benedictine monastery in Bevagna. The entrance faced a dark, cramped street littered with cars parked every which way. The place looked as unpromising as the front of a warehouse. Once inside, though, the blank façade gave way to a labyrinthine series of white, hushed hallways that—best of all—formed a square facing a flagstoned courtyard covered with vines and bright flowers. At the center was a fountain. Tucked under one portion of the arched walk was a cash bar tended in the evening by a novice who bore down forcefully on the chrome handle of the espresso machine and urged me to try the local liqueur, made from truffles sniffed out by dogs trained for that purpose.

In Todi, the most beautifully situated of the medieval towns I visited, I stayed at the Hotel Bramante—not a monastery but a *former* monastery. There again were the mustard-colored walls, a foot thick, the unmistakable solidity that is a feature of monastic architecture, as though the work of prayer, being so effervescent, requires especially fortified housing.

In the morning, I swung open the inner louvered wooden shutters of the casement windows. The room, which had been dark, was pierced with sunshine. The sharp black-white of a southern landscape. The keen distinction between cloister and world. Outside, the mist that gives Umbria its mystical reputation strayed over the distant hills and the camel-colored medieval towns clinging to them.

After trekking through the region, the final hike brought me into Assisi. From Spello, up and then steeply down Monte Subasio, was a glory of wind and wildflowers. The wind was fierce—not cold, but as if a part of the sun had detached itself and become all blast, no heat. Easy to imagine St. Francis tearing around this exposed exultant spot.

The wildflowers clung bravely to the rocky soil of the sheer rise, then grew lush in the greener, protected dips. A lot of screaming orange from poppies in great profusion. Also wild gladioli, convolulus, grape hyacinth, and a lovely china-blue flower with black markings called, in English, love-in-a-mist. Here and there, lizards sunned themselves on the gravel path; the bleached white pebbles made a dry ticking sound as they were dislodged and skittered down the path in little landslides.

Assisi presented itself, finally, as part monastery, part carnival. The twisting streets leading to the Basilica of St. Francis were chockablock with concession stands selling souvenirs. I looked up from a plaster beer mug made in the shape of a friar to see, walking by, a sandaled friar in the shape of a beer mug.

I stayed at the Poor Clare monastery of Santa Colleta on the Borgo San Pietro—a community from France; the language of the house is French. The monastery has a strict cloister as well as common rooms (a pleasant, shadowy lounge and library with easy chairs and a piano, and a breakfast room with many small tables).

The bedrooms, each named for a saint or some part of the liturgical year, are located in a wing of the main monastery and in a separate building that overlooks, on one side, the convent garden and, on the other, the Plain of Spoleto and Church of Santa Maria degli Angeli. That was my view from L'Annunciation—the Annunciation, my room. Next door, in La Joie (Joy), a man I never saw coughed a racking smoker's cough most of the first night and then was gone—or dead. I never heard him again. I seemed to have the whole suite of little rooms to myself the rest of my stay.

At breakfast I sat with a once-beautiful woman, a retired professor of French literature from Nice. After our first *café crème* in the breakfast room, she said she could tell that I was well trained. Trained? I felt like a dog.

"Chez les soeurs," she said. "By the good sisters." Oh yes, that.

I wandered around by myself, in between the proper sightseeing of churches and Franciscan places. I bought a pair of shoes and tried, without success, to use my phrase book to get enzyme tablets to clean my soft contact lenses. I drank coffee at an outdoor cafe by the Temple of Minerva, a refreshingly pagan site in the middle of town—a building that proved, however, to have been turned into a Catholic church. I lit a candle for world peace in the dark interior and again wandered out into the sunlight.

But the truth was, I wasn't much of a tourist. I spent most of my time not viewing the Giottos, guidebook in hand, but sitting on the little balcony of my room, gazing down at the nuns who were cultivating the garden, dressed in their heavy habits, which were hitched up slightly. They had broad straw hats over their veils. Birds dipped and paused, twittering and scolding, very busy about their own business.

I read. I slept—maybe a small version of the hundred-years sleep I wished for that day in high school when I saw, briefly, the flood of light coming from the locked room for strangers.

I was content. I had bought some ham and cheese, a loaf of crusty bread, some figs and wine, and a bar of chocolate at a local store. *"Bien sûr, bien sûr,"* Soeur Ste. Agathe said. Of course I could have a picnic in the garden. I stayed all afternoon. The light began to fade, going toward Vespers. At five, the bells started up all over town, from church to convent to monastery, a wild cuckoo-clock-shop effect.

I could hear the nuns' voices coming from the choir, chanting a long, wavering line of a psalm in French. I had no desire to go anywhere.

I gathered up my picnic things and turned toward my room, where the simple bed with the white spread, the plain table and chair and the long French window were waiting, just as they'd always been, just as they would when the sun would come flooding in. Just as I would be, letting the bright light fall on my face, clear as a ringing bell.

ꗉ

For the Literary Traveler

In her travel memoir *Virgin Time*, Patricia Hampl writes, "It was integral to the fundamental inspiration of Christianity that Jesus was poor, that he was born in a stable, homeless. He was not a prince like the Buddha. He was nothing and nobody." St. Francis founded his order of friars to live in imitation of Christianity's origin story. Considering himself wedded to Lady Poverty (their marriage is depicted above the high altar in the lower church of the Basilica), he and the Franciscans lived and traveled without money, shoes, or a home to return to. But in the town where Francis grew up to reject his father's wealth, travelers and pilgrims find an overwhelming richness of art and landscape. Giotto transformed the life story of the reformer and mystic in the magnificent frescoes that cover the walls of the upper church of the BASILICA OF ST. FRANCIS. In the lower church, in the transept to the right of the high altar, is Cimabue's famous representation of *Il Poverello* in the company of Mary enthroned with four angels. In every vault and chapel and transept, on both levels, there is treasure. Images of women saints, Mary Magdalene, and the Virgin Mary abound.

The women whom St. Francis inspired to follow his way of life called themselves the "Poor Clares" after their founder, Clare Faverone (the subject of Joan Mowat Erikson's "The Lady Clare, His Daughter" in her renowned *St. Francis and His Four Ladies*). In the church of SANTA CHIARA in the eastern end of Assisi, a contemplative order of nuns still follows the rule of the original thirteenth-century community, chanting the hours of the Divine Office and the Mass, behind the grille in the CHAPEL OF THE SACRAMENT. (Visitors may attend at 6:15 A.M.) In the light and silence of dawn (and again at sunfall), the pink and white and pale reddish stone of Santa Chiara's façade, its rose window and flying buttresses, present a harmony of color and space and air that brings to mind Umbria's well-deserved reputation as "the mystical province."

A steep path outside the town's walls leads down to SAN DAMIANO, "the lyric, sunny place," as Patricia Hampl describes it, where Clare lived with her nuns for forty-two years. The convent—refectory, choir, dormitory, chapel, garden, fountain, and cloister—is set deep in a valley surrounded by cypresses, olive groves, and flowering trees in spring. Here St. Francis wrote his "Canticle of the Creatures," a love poem to the glory of creation. Simple and beautiful, San Damiano is, in Joan Erikson's words, "the most eloquent monument to the early spirit of the Franciscan movement." Its seclusion and the obvious austerity of the life the women lived there provoke questions about what marriage was like that medieval women chose this penitential alternative. But that may be the wrong question to ponder at San Damiano. Maybe these women were not escapists or masochists or peasants looking for security. Their model, after all, was the countercultural Francis. Perhaps they, too, were rebels.

Above, within the walls of Assisi, people sit enjoying "Brother Sun" and "Our Sister, Mother Earth," in the words of Francis's "Canticle of the Creatures," in the friendly and spacious PIAZZA DEL COMUNE midway between the church of Santa Chiara and the Basilica of St. Francis. In the portico of the pagan TEMPLE OF MINERVA (now a Catholic church), even the clerical fashion police are friendly.

ROME

I wouldn't live anywhere else but in Rome, if you would give me the Gates of Paradise and all the Apostles thrown in. . . .

—Harriet Hosmer (1830–1908), the first American woman to make her career in Italy as a sculptor

The wonder and beauty of Italy later brought healing and some relief to the paralyzing sense of the futility of all artistic and intellectual effort when disconnected from the ultimate test of the conduct it inspired. The serene and soothing touch of history also aroused old enthusiasms, although some of their manifestations were such as one smiles over more easily in retrospection than at the moment. I fancy that it was no smiling matter to several people in our party, whom I induced to walk for three miles in the hot sunshine beating down upon the Roman Campagna, that we might enter the Eternal City on foot through the Porta del Popolo, as pilgrims had done for centuries. To be sure, we had really entered Rome the night before, but the railroad station and the hotel might have been anywhere else, and we had been driven beyond the walls after breakfast and stranded at the very spot where the pilgrims always said "Ecco Roma," as they caught the first glimpse of St. Peter's dome. This melodramatic entrance into Rome, or rather pretended entrance, was the prelude to days of enchantment. . . .

—Jane Addams, from *Twenty Years at Hull House*

Florence Nightingale

Florence Nightingale spent the winter of 1847–48 in Rome, when she was still trying to figure out what her life's work was going to be. Ten years earlier, revealing her mystical bent, she claimed that "On February 7, 1837, God spoke to me and called me to His service." Eventually, the Crimean War (1854) provided the object for that service. But in the years before that legendary commitment, her energies went mostly to resisting the life she didn't want: marriage, dinner parties, idle privilege. She also enjoyed herself traveling in Italy. "I never enjoyed any time in my life so much as my time in Rome," she wrote in 1869.

FROM *FLORENCE NIGHTINGALE IN ROME*

LETTER VI

ROME. NOVEMBER 11, 1847

Yes, my dears, here we are, I can hardly believe it. On Tuesday, the 9th of November, 1847, we came here from Civita Vecchia. The last 3 hours were in the dark, and I felt as if we were passing through the Valley of the Shadow of Death, on our way to the Celestial City. I looked out every five minutes to see the lights of the city on the hill, but in vain—the earth was sending forth her fragrance of night like an incense to heaven, for the Campagna is covered with thyme—the stars were all out—there was a solemn silence, not a trace of habitation, all desert solitude, and we were feverish and very tired, which increased the likeness of the Valley of the Shadow. At last, without the least preparation, not a house, not a suburb, we knocked at a little gate—"Chi è la?" "Carrozza." "Venga," was all that passed—the door opened quietly—not a word at the guard house—we took up the Doganiere on the carriage—just a little stop

184

during which I heard the sound of the fountains of St. Peter's, softly plashing in the stillness of night, and in a moment we were passing the colonnades slowly au petit pas. I saw the Obelisk, the Dome, the Vatican, dimly glooming in the twilight, then the Angel of the Last Judgment. We crossed Ponte Sant'Angelo. Oh Tiber, father Tiber, to whom the Romans pray, a Roman's life, a Roman's arms, take thou in charge this day. Though it was hardly 9 o'clock, not a carriage, scarcely a living being, as we drove slowly up Via di Ripetta, (all was solemn and still like a city of times gone by) to Piazza del Popolo, where we silently and stilly went to bed.

I could not sleep for knowing myself in the Eternal City and towards dawn I got up, scoured myself, and cleaned myself from the dust of many days, and as soon as it was daylight, (forgive an ancient fool who found herself for the first time in her old age in the land of Rome) I went out, and I almost ran till I came to St. Peter's. I would not look to the right or left, (I know I passed through Piazza Navona,) till I came to the Colonnades, and there was the first ray of the rising sun just touching the top of the fountain. The Civic Guard was already exercising in the Piazza. The dome was much smaller than I expected. But that enormous Atrio. I stopped under it, for my mind was out of breath, to recover its strength before I went in. No event in my life, except my death can ever be greater than that first entrance into St. Peter's, the concentrated spirit of the Christianity of so many years, the great image of our Faith which is the worship of grief. I went in. I could not have gone there for the first time except alone, no, not in the company of St. Peter himself, and walked up to the Dome. There was hardly a creature there but I. There I knelt down. You know I have no art, and it was not an artistic effect it made on me—it was the effect of the presence of God.

❧

For the Literary Traveler

Though she apologizes for her prose style, Florence Nightingale's letters from Italy ring with genuine feeling. Rome overwhelmed her, inspiring her to want to live a life worthy of such a place, this historic repository of centuries of sensual and spiritual experience. Though she describes many places with affection, the letter of November 1847 mentions the splendid PIAZZA DEL POPOLO and PIAZZA NAVONA glancingly, as mere references en route to the heart of the city: SAINT PETER'S—the PIAZZA, the BASILICA, the PIETÀ. Though an Anglican Christian, she only expresses reverence toward this monument of Roman Catholicism.

At sunrise, she first stood awed in "the enormous Atrio"—her words for Piazza San Pietro. Another of Bernini's masterpieces, it is distinguished by two COLONNADES of 284 columns and 140 statues; the OBELISK with a cross on top, in the center of the piazza (originally brought from Alexandria and placed in a Roman circus by Caligula); and two FOUNTAINS, their waters flowing abundantly. The interior of The Basilica, the largest church in the world, has its quiet spaces, depending on the season. Florence Nightingale's first visit in November was propitious. In the winter months the place is peaceful and its wonders—the Pietà; Bernini's BALDACCHINO over the high altar, decorated with the BARBERINI BEES; the colored marble of his walls and floor; Michelangelo's DOME—seem radiant in the afternoon sunlight touching the stone columns and visitors.

The ASCENT OF THE DOME, by elevator and stairs, leading first to a close-up view of the mosaics inside the cupola, and then to the roof to see the huge statues of the apostles on top of the façade (as if protecting the life in the piazza below them), and finally up to the LANTERN with its magnificent view of Rome, is, without qualification, worth every strenuous step. This perspective on the city and its river, never to be forgotten, raises the question of what "a sense of place" can actually mean to the experience of an individual traveler. (In his description of the climb in his Italian Journey, Goethe, too, remembers great beauty. So, too, does Margaret Fuller—see page 187—in her letters.)

And, though it wasn't open in the nineteenth century, the well-preserved NECROPOLIS with ST. PETER'S TOMB beneath the basilica may now be seen. Again, in winter, one may join a group by entering through the Swiss-guarded gate to the left of the basilica and applying at the UFFICIO SCAVI (excavation office) on the right. In high-tourist season, applying in advance is recommended. The tour offers an informed and lively introduction to the science of archaeology and to events and personalities from ancient Roman and early Christian history.

Florence Nightingale, an energetic and curious traveler who walked good distances in the months of her Roman visit, would, one guesses, have enjoyed both the ascent and the descent, had the latter been available.

Margaret Fuller

"Had I only come ten years earlier," Margaret Fuller wrote Emerson from Rome in 1847. After leaving New England (and Puritanism and Transcendentalism) for New York in the 1840s, the first self-supporting American woman journalist had then traveled to Italy as a reporter for the New York Tribune. *There she covered the war for the Roman Republic and worked as a nurse during the city's bombardment by the French and its defense by Garibaldi and his red-shirted army. The articles she sent back to America— collected under the title* These Sad But Glorious Days: Dispatches from Europe 1846–1850—*are now considered the best writing she ever did. Her* Woman in the Nineteenth Century, *respected by European intellectuals when it was published in 1845, remains an important feminist text. (Emerson and Hawthorne, by turns, patronized and ridiculed her.) Her personal history in Italy coincided with the momentum of upheaval. With her lover, Giovanni Angelo Ossoli, she had a son whom she kept hidden during the war in a mountain village of Umbria.*

A few years earlier she'd written in her journal: "Once I was almost all intellect; now I am almost all feeling. Nature vindicates her rights, and I feel all Italy glowing beneath the Saxon crust. This cannot last long; I shall burn to ashes if all this smoulders here much longer." When they returned to America in 1850, after the defeat of the republican army and the exile of

Mazzini and Garibaldi, she and Ossoli and baby Angelo drowned in a ship-wreck within sight of land off the coast of Long Island.

FROM *DISPATCHES FROM EUROPE*
TO THE NEW YORK TRIBUNE, *1846–1850*

DISPATCH 14

ROME, MAY 1847

There is very little that I can like to write about Italy. Italy is beautiful, worthy to be loved and embraced, not talked about. Yet I remember well that when afar I liked to read what was written about her; now all thought of it is very tedious.

The traveler passing along the beaten track, vetturinoed from inn to inn, ciceroned from gallery to gallery, thrown, through indolence, want of tact, or ignorance of the language, too much into the society of his compatriots, sees the least possible of the country; fortunately, it is impossible to avoid seeing a great deal. The great features of the past pursue and fill the eye.

Yet I find that it is quite out of the question to know Italy; to say anything of her that is full and sweet, so as to convey any idea of her spirit, without long residence, and residence in the districts untouched by the scorch and dust of foreign invasion, (the invasion of the dilettanti I mean,) and without an intimacy of feeling, an abandonment to the spirit of the place, impossible to most Americans; they retain too much of their English blood; and the traveling English, as a tribe, seem to me the most unseeing of all possible animals. There are exceptions; for instance, the perceptions and pictures of Browning seem as delicate and just here on the spot as they did at a distance;* but, take them as a tribe, they have the vulgar familiarity of Mrs. Trollope without her vivacity, the cockneyism of Dickens without his graphic power and love of the odd corners of human nature. I admired

---

*In a letter to a friend, Fuller wrote, "Admirable as Browning's sketches of Italian scenery and character seemed before, they seem far finer now that I am close to their objects. The best representation of the spirit of Italy which our day affords. It is difficult to speak with any truth of Italy: it requires *genius, talent* . . . "

the English at home in their island; I admired their honor, truth, practical intelligence, persistent power. But they do not look well in Italy; they are not the figures for this landscape. I am indignant at the contempt they have presumed to express for the faults of our semi-barbarous state. What is the vulgarity expressed in our tobacco-chewing, and way of eating eggs, compared to that which elbows the Greek marbles, guide-book in hand—chatters and sneers through the Miserere of the Sistine Chapel, beneath the very glance of Michel Angelo's Sibyls,— praises St. Peter's as *"nice,"* talks of *"managing"* the Colosseum by moonlight,—and snatches *"bits"* for a *"sketch"* from the sublime silence of the Campagna. . . .

I have heard owls hoot in the Colosseum by moonlight, and they spoke more to the purpose than I ever heard any other voice upon that subject. I have seen all the pomps and shows of Holy Week in the Church of St. Peter, and found them less imposing than an habitual acquaintance with the place with processions of monks and nuns stealing in now and then, or the swell of vespers from some side chapel. I have ascended the dome and seen thence Rome and its Campagna, its villas with their cypresses and pines serenely sad as is nothing else in the world, and the fountains of the Vatican Garden gushing hard by. I have been in the Subterranean to see a poor little boy introduced, much to his surprise, to the bosom of the Church; and then I have seen by torchlight the stone Popes where they lie on their tombs, and the old mosaics, and Virgins with gilt caps. It is all rich and full,—very impressive in its way. St. Peter's must be to each one a separate poem. . . .

DISPATCH 19

ROME, DEC. 17, 1847

This seventeenth day of December I rise to see the floods of sunlight blessing us as they have almost every day since I returned to Rome—two months and more; with scarce three or four days of rainy weather. I see the fresh roses and grapes still each morning on my table, though both these I expect to give up at Christmas.

This autumn is *"something like,"* as my country men say at

home. Like *what*, they do not say, so I always supposed they meant like the ideal standard. Certainly this weather corresponds with mine, and I begin to believe the climate of Italy is really what it has been represented. Shivering here last Spring in an air no better than the cruel east wind of Puritan Boston, I thought all the praises lavished on

Italia, O Italia!*

would turn out to be figments of the brain, and that even Byron, usually accurate beyond the conception of plodding pedants, had deceived us when he says you have the happiness in Italy to

See the sun set sure he'll rise to-morrow,

and not according to a view which exercises a withering influence on the enthusiasm of youth in my native land be forced to regard each pleasant day as a *"weather-breeder."*

How delightful, too, is the contrast between this time and the Spring in another respect! Then I was here, like travelers in general, expecting to be driven away in a short time. Like others, I went through the painful process of sight-seeing, so unnatural everywhere, so counter to the healthful methods and true life of the mind. You rise in the morning knowing there are around you a great number of objects worth knowing, which you may never have a chance to see again. You go every day, in all moods, under all circumstances; you feel, probably, in seeing them, the inadequacy of your preparation for understanding or duly receiving them; this consciousness would be most valuable if you had time to think and study, being the natural way in which the mind is lured to cure its defects—but you have no time, you are always wearied, body and mind, confused, dissipated, sad. The objects are of commanding beauty or full of suggestion, but you have no quiet to let that beauty breathe its life into your soul—no time to follow up these suggestions and plant for your proper harvest. Many persons run about Rome for nine days and then go away; they might as well

*"Childe Harold's Pilgrimage."

expect to see it so, as to appreciate the Venus by throwing a stone at it. I stayed in Rome nine weeks and came away unhappy as he who, having been taken in the visions of night through some wondrous realm, wakes unable to recall anything but the hues and outlines of the pageant, the real knowledge, the recreative power induced by familiar love, the assimilation of its soul and substance—all the true value of such a revelation—is wanting, and he remains a poor Tantalus, hungrier even when he most needed to be fed.

No; Rome is not a nine-days' wonder, and those who try to make it such lose the ideal Rome (if they ever had it) without gaining any notion of the real. For those who travel, as they do everything else—only because others do—I do not speak to them; they are nothing. Nobody counts in the estimate of the human race who has no character.

For one, I now really live in Rome, and I begin to see and feel the real Rome. She reveals herself now; she tells me some of her life. Now I never go out to see a sight, but I walk every day, and here I cannot miss of some object of consummate interest to end a walk. In the evenings, which are long now, I am at leisure to follow up the inquiries suggested by the day. . . .

From 1847 until she left Rome in 1850, Margaret Fuller kept her American readers informed about the rapid developments of the Roman revolution led by Mazzini and Garibaldi. She also wrote many letters home to friends, including Ralph Waldo Emerson.

DISPATCH 30

ROME, MAY 27, 1849

. . . The struggle is now fairly, thoroughly commenced between the principle of democracy and the old powers, no longer legitimate. That struggle may last fifty years, and the earth be watered with the blood and tears of more than one generation, but the result is sure. All Europe, including Great Britain, where the most bitter resistance of all will be made, is to be under republican government in the next century.

God moves in a mysterious way.

Every struggle made by the old tyrannies, all their Jesuitical deceptions, their rapacity, their imprisonments and executions of the most generous men, only sow more dragon's teeth; the crop shoots up daily more and more plenteous.

When I first arrived in Italy, the vast majority of this people had no wish beyond limited monarchies, constitutional governments. They still respected the famous names of the nobility; they despised the priests, but were still fondly attached to the dogmas and ritual of the Roman Catholic Church. It required King Bomba, the triple treachery of Charles Albert, Pius IX, and the "illustrious Gioberti," the naturally kind-hearted, but, from the necessity of his position, cowardly and false Leopold of Tuscany, the vagabond "serene" meannesses of Parma and Modena, the "fatherly" Radetzsky, and, finally, the imbecile Louis Bonaparte, "would-be Emperor of France," to convince this people that no transition is possible between the old and the new.*
The work is done; the revolution in Italy is now radical, nor can it stop till Italy becomes independent and united as a republic. Protestant she already is, and though the memory of saints and martyrs may continue to be revered, the ideal of woman to be adored under the name of Mary, yet Christ will now begin to be a little thought of; *his* idea has always been kept carefully out of sight under the old *régime*; all the worship being for the Madonna and saints, who were to be well paid for interceding for sinners;—an example which might make men cease to be such, was no way coveted. Now the New Testament has been translated into Italian; copies are already dispersed far and wide; men calling themselves Christians will no longer be left entirely ignorant of the precepts and life of Jesus. . . .

*All these, in their various roles and for their many betrayals, the republicans considered the enemies of the revolution.

* *

War near at hand seems to me even more dreadful than I had fancied it. True, it tries men's souls, lays bare selfishness in undeniable deformity. Here it has produced much fruit of noble sentiment, noble act; but still it breeds vice too, drunkenness, mental dissipation, tears asunder the tenderest ties, lavishes the productions of Earth, for which her starving poor stretch out their hands in vain, in the most unprofitable manner. And the ruin that ensues, how terrible! Let those who have ever passed happy days in Rome grieve to hear that the beautiful plantations of Villa Borghese—that chief delight and refreshment of citizens, foreigners, and little children—are laid low, as far as the obelisk. The fountain, singing alone amid the fallen groves, cannot be seen and heard without tears; it seems like some innocent infant calling and crowing amid dead bodies on a field which battle has strewn with the bodies of those who once cherished it. The plantations of Villa Salvage on the Tiber, also, the beautiful trees on the way from St. John Lateran to La Maria Maggiore, the trees of the Forum, are fallen. Rome is shorn of the locks which lent grace to her venerable brow. She looks desolate, profaned. I feel what I never expected to,—as if I might by and by be willing to leave Rome.

Then I have, for the first time, seen what wounded men suffer. The night of the 30th of April I passed in the hospital, and saw the terrible agonies of those dying or who needed amputation, felt their mental pains and longing for the loved ones, who were away; for many of these were Lombards, who had come from the field of Novarra to fight with a fairer chance,—many were students of the University, who had enlisted and thrown themselves into the front of the engagement.* The impudent falsehoods of the French general's despatches are incredible. The French were never decoyed on in any way. They were received with every possible mark of hostility. They were defeated in open field, the Garibaldi legion rushing out to meet them; and though they suffered much from the walls, they sustained themselves nowhere. They never put up a white flag till they wished to surrender. The vanity that strives to cover over these facts is unworthy of men. . . .

*The Janiculum Hill was the scene of the bloodiest fighting.

But to return to the hospitals: these were put in order, and have been kept so, by the Princess Belgioioso. The princess was born of one of the noblest families of the Milanese, a descendant of the great Trivalzio, and inherited a large fortune. Very early she compromised it in liberal movements, and, on their failure, was obliged to fly to Paris, where for a time she maintained herself by writing, and I think by painting also. A princess so placed naturally excited great interest, and she drew around her a little court of celebrated men. After recovering her fortune, she still lived in Paris, distinguished for her talents and munificence, both toward literary men and her exiled countrymen. Later, on her estate, called Locate, between Pavia and Milan, she had made experiments in the Socialist direction with fine judgment and success. Association for education, for labor, for trans-action of household affairs, had been carried on for several years; she had spared no devotion of time and money to this object, loved, and was much beloved by, those objects of her care, and said she hoped to die there. All is now despoiled and broken up, though it may be hoped that some seeds of peaceful reform have been sown which will spring to light when least expected. The princess returned to Italy in 1847–8, full of hope in Pius IX and Charles Albert. She showed her usual energy and truly princely heart, sustaining, at her own expense, a company of soldiers and a journal up to the last sad betrayal of Milan, August 6th. These days undeceived all the people, but few of the noblesse; she was one of the few with mind strong enough to understand the lesson, and is now warmly interested in the repub-lican movement. From Milan she went to France, but, finding it impossible to effect anything serious there in behalf of Italy, returned, and has been in Rome about two months. Since leaving Milan she receives no income, her possessions being in the grasp of Radetzky, and cannot know when, if ever, she will again. But as she worked so largely and well with money, so can she without. She pub-lished an invitation to the Roman women to make lint and bandages, and offer their services to the wounded; she put the hospitals in order; in the central one, Trinita de Pellegrini, once the abode where the pilgrims were received during holy week, and where foreigners were entertained by seeing their feet washed by the noble dames and dignitaries of Rome, she has remained day and night since the 30th

of April, when the wounded were first there. Some money she pro-
cured at first by going through Rome, accompanied by two other
ladies veiled, to beg it. . . .

TO RALPH WALDO EMERSON, JUNE 10, 1849

. . . I received your letter amid the round of cannonade and mus-
ketry. It was a terrible battle fought here from the first to the last
light of day. I could see all its progress from my balcony. The Italians
fought like lions. It is a truly heroic spirit that animates them. They
make a stand here for honor and their rights, with little ground for
hope that they can resist, now they are betrayed by France.

Since the 30th of April, I go almost daily to the hospitals, and
though I have suffered, for I had no idea before how terrible gun-
shot wounds and wound-fevers are, yet I have taken pleasure, and
great pleasure, in being with the men. There is scarcely one who is
not moved by a noble spirit. Many, especially among the Lombards, are the flower of the Italian youth. When they begin to get
better, I carry them books and flowers; they read, and we talk.

The palace of the Pope, on the Quirinal, is now used for convales-
cents. In those beautiful gardens I walk with them, one with his sling,
another with his crutch. The gardener plays off all his water-works for
the defenders of the country, and gathers flowers for me, their friend.

A day or two since, we sat in the Pope's little pavilion, where he
used to give private audience. The sun was going gloriously down
over Monte Mario,* where gleamed the white tents of the French
light-horse among the trees. The cannonade was heard at intervals.
Two bright-eyed boys sat at our feet, and gathered up eagerly every
word said by the heroes of the day. It was a beautiful hour, stolen
from the midst of ruin and sorrow, and tales were told as full of
grace and pathos as in the gardens of Boccaccio, only in a very different spirit,—with noble hope for man, and reverence for woman.

The young ladies of the family, very young girls, were filled
with enthusiasm for the suffering, wounded patriots, and they
wished to go the hospital, to give their services. Excepting the three

---

*Beautifully visible from the Gallery of Pius IV in Castel Sant' Angelo, Monte
Mario rises above the Tiber on the northwest outskirts of the city.

superintendents, none but married ladies were permitted to serve there, but their services were accepted. Their governess then wished to go too, and, as she could speak several languages, she was admitted to the rooms of the wounded soldiers, to interpret for them, as the nurses knew nothing but Italian, and many of these poor men were suffering because they could not make their wishes known. Some are French, some Germans, many Poles. Indeed, I am afraid it is too true that there were comparatively few Romans among them. This young lady passed several nights there.

Should I never return, and sometimes I despair of doing so, it seems so far off,—so difficult, I am caught in such a net of ties here,—if ever you know of my life here, I think you will only wonder at the constancy with which I have sustained myself,—the degree of profit to which, amid great difficulties, I have put the time,—at least in the way of observation. Meanwhile, love me all you can. Let me feel that, amid the fearful agitations of the world, there are pure hands, with healthful, even pulse, stretched out toward me, if I claim their grasp.

I feel profoundly for Mazzini. At moments I am tempted to say, "Cursed with every granted prayer,"—so cunning is the demon. Mazzini has become the inspiring soul of his people. He saw Rome, to which all his hopes through life tended, for the first time as a Roman citizen, and to become in a few days its ruler. He has animated, he sustains her to a glorious effort, which, if it fails this time, will not in the age. His country will be free. Yet to me it would be so dreadful to cause all this bloodshed,—to dig the graves of such martyrs!

Then, Rome is being destroyed; her glorious oaks,—her villas, haunts of sacred beauty, that seemed the possession of the world for ever,—the villa of Raphael, the villa of Albani, home of Winck-elmann and the best expression of the ideal of modern Rome, and so many other sanctuaries of beauty,—all must perish, lest a foe should level his musket from their shelter. I could not, could not!

I know not, dear friend, whether I shall ever get home across that great ocean, but here in Rome I shall no longer wish to live. O Rome, *my* country! could I imagine that the triumph of what I held dear was to heap such desolation on thy head!

Speaking of the republic, you say, "Do you not wish Italy had a

great man?" Mazzini is a great man. In mind, a great, poetic
statesman; in heart, a lover; in action, decisive and full of resource
as Cæsar. Dearly I love Mazzini. He came in, just as I had finished
the first letter to you. His soft, radiant look makes melancholy
music in my soul; it consecrates my present life, that, like the Magdalen, I may, at the important hour, shed all the consecrated oint-
ment on his head. . . .

For the Literary Traveler

During the siege of Rome, Margaret Fuller wrote her dispatches about
the war and worked in the hospitals with the Principessa Cristina
Trivulzio Belgioioso—"the revolutionary princess." Every day they
nursed the wounded and dying at the TRINITÀ DEI PELLEGRINI (still a hos-
pice) next to the church of the same name (off Via dei Pettinari
leading to the Ponte Sisto and Trastevere); and at the FATEBENEFRATELLI
("do good, brothers"). This hospital, founded by monks in 1548, is
located on the ISOLA TIBERINA, the pretty island in the Tiber shaped like
a ship that has been associated with healing since 293 B.C.E. when a
temple to the Greek god of healing, Aesculapius, stood here. The two
original Roman bridges leading to the island are still intact, and the
hospital still occupies most of the island. As the siege began in 1849,
Margaret received a note from the Principessa: "Dear Miss Fuller: You
are named *Regolatrice* of the Hospital of the *Fatebenefratelli*. Go there
at twelve if the alarm bell does not ring before. . . . May God help us."
A friend described Margaret's ministry with the soldiers: "I have seen
the eyes of the dying as she moved among them meet in commenda-
tion of her unwearied kindness. And I have heard those who recov-
ered speak, with all the passionateness and fervor of Italian natures, of
her whose sympathy and compassion throughout their long illness ful-
filled all the offices of love. . . ." In memory of her service for the cause
of Italian freedom, a road on the Janiculum Hill is named the "Viale
Margaret Ossoli Fuller."

George Eliot

Foreign travel was always a panacea for George Eliot. She said she always felt better the minute she crossed the channel. But on entering the Eternal City for the first time in 1860 at the start of Holy Week, George Eliot and George Henry Lewes expressed disappointment. "There was nothing imposing to be seen" except "dirty uninteresting streets," and "unimpressive" St. Peter's dome, and too many tourists. After the "hateful shams" of Holy Week, however, and a rainy Easter Sunday, the couple began to warm up. Rapturous enthusiasm—St. Peter's as "magically beautiful"—is soon recorded in their journals.

In her masterpiece, Middlemarch *(1871), Eliot sends the beautiful Dorothea Brooke and dour Mr. Casaubon to Rome on their wedding journey, an ironic setting, as the following chapters show, for a marriage of conflicting traditions and temperaments. The groom's monkish obsession with antique manuscripts and his patriarchal authoritarianism bode misery for the bride, who, in Eliot's words, exemplifies the "sensuous force" and "spiritual passion" of a "Christian Antigone" and a Teresa of Avila. Roman ruins provide an apt, if ominous, backdrop for this marriage made in a library.*

FROM *MIDDLEMARCH*

THE WEDDING JOURNEY

CHAPTER 19

> L'altra vedete ch'ha fatto alla guancia
> Della sua palma, sospirando, letto,
> —*Purgatorio,* vii*

*"See the other, who couches his cheek on his hand and sighs."

198

When George the Fourth was still reigning over the privacies of Windsor, when the Duke of Wellington was Prime Minister, and Mr. Vincy was mayor of the old corporation in Middlemarch, Mrs. Casaubon, born Dorothea Brooke, had taken her wedding journey to Rome. In those days the world in general was more ignorant of good and evil by forty years than it is at present. Travellers did not often carry full information on Christian art either in their heads or their pockets; and even the most brilliant English critic of the day* mistook the flower-flushed tomb of the ascended Virgin for an ornamental vase due to the painter's fancy. Romanticism, which has helped to fill some dull blanks with love and knowledge, had not yet penetrated the times with its leaven and entered into everybody's food; it was fermenting still as a distinguishable vigorous enthusiasm in certain long-haired German artists at Rome, and the youth of other nations who worked or idled near them were sometimes caught in the spreading movement.

One fine morning a young man whose hair was not immoderately long, but abundant and curly, and who was otherwise English in his equipment, had just turned his back on the Belvedere Torso in the Vatican and was looking out on the magnificent view of the mountains from the adjoining round vestibule. He was sufficiently absorbed not to notice the approach of a dark-eyed, animated German who came up to him and placing a hand on his shoulder, said with a strong accent, "Come here, quick! else she will have changed her pose."

Quickness was ready at the call, and the two figures passed lightly along by the Meleager towards the hall where the reclining Ariadne, then called the Cleopetra, lies in the marble voluptuousness of her beauty, the drapery folding around her with a petal-like ease and tenderness. They were just in time to see another figure standing against a pedestal near the reclining marble: a breathing blooming girl, whose form, not shamed by the Ariadne, was clad in Quakerish grey drapery; her long cloak, fastened at the neck, was thrown backward from her arms, and one beautiful ungloved hand pillowed her cheek, pushing somewhat backward the white beaver

*William Hazlitt.

bonnet which made a sort of halo to her face around the simply braided dark-brown hair. She was not looking at the sculpture, probably not thinking of it: her large eyes were fixed dreamily on a streak of sunlight which fell across the floor. But she became conscious of the two strangers who suddenly paused as if to contemplate the Cleopatra, and, without looking at them, immediately turned away to join a maid-servant and courier who were loitering along the hall at a little distance off.

"What do you think of that for a fine bit of antithesis?" said the German, searching in his friend's face for responding admiration, but going on volubly without waiting for any other answer. "There lies antique beauty, not corpse-like even in death, but arrested in the complete contentment of its sensuous perfection: and here stands beauty in its breathing life, with the consciousness of Christian centuries in its bosom. But she should be dressed as a nun; I think she looks almost what you call a Quaker; I would dress her as a nun in my picture. However, she is married! I saw her wedding-ring on that wonderful left hand, otherwise I should have thought the sallow *Geistlicher** was her father. I saw him parting from her a good while ago, and just now I found her in that magnificent pose. Only think! he is perhaps rich, and would like to have her portrait taken. Ah! it is no use looking after her—there she goes! Let us follow her home!"

"No, no," said his companion, with a little frown.

"You are singular, Ladislaw. You look struck together. Do you know her?"

"I know that she is married to my cousin," and Will Ladislaw, sauntering down the hall with a preoccupied air, while his German friend kept at his side and watched him eagerly.

"What, the *Geistlicher*? He looks more like an uncle—a more useful sort of relation."

"He is not my uncle. I tell you he is my second cousin," said Ladislaw, with some irritation.

"*Schön, schön.* Don't be snappish. You are not angry with me for thinking Mrs. Second-Cousin the most perfect young Madonna I ever saw?"

*Minister of religion.

"Angry? nonsense. I have only seen her once before, for a couple of minutes, when my cousin introduced her to me, just before I left England. They were not married then. I didn't know they were coming to Rome."

"But you will go to see them now—you will find out what they have for an address—since you know the name. Shall we go to the post? And you could speak about the portrait."

"Confound you, Naumann! I don't know what I shall do. I am not so brazen as you."

"Bah! that is because you are dilettantish and amateurish. If you were an artist, you would think of Mistress Second-Cousin as antique form animated by Christian sentiment—a sort of Christian Antigone—sensuous force controlled by spiritual passion."

"Yes, and that your painting her was the chief outcome of her existence—the divinity passing into higher completeness and all but exhausted in the act of covering your bit of canvas. I am amateurish if you like: I do *not* think that all the universe is straining towards the obscure significance of your pictures."

"But it is, my dear!—so far as it is straining through me, Adolf Naumann: that stands firm," said the good-natured painter, putting a hand on Ladislaw's shoulder, and not in the least disturbed by the unaccountable touch of ill-humour in his tone. "See now! My existence pre-supposes the existence of the whole universe—does it *not*? and my function is to paint—and as a painter I have a conception which is altogether *genialisch,** of your great-aunt or second grandmother as a subject for a picture; therefore, the universe is straining towards that picture through that particular hook or claw which is put forth in the shape of me—not true?"

"But how if another claw in the shape of me is straining to thwart it?—the case is a little less simple then."

"Not at all: the result of the struggle is the same thing—picture or no picture—logically." Will could not resist this imperturbable temper, and the cloud in his face broke into sunshiny laughter.

"Come now, my friend—you will help?" said Naumann, in a hopeful tone.

*Brilliant.

"No; nonsense, Naumann! English ladies are not at everybody's service as models. And you want to express too much with your painting. You would only have made a better or worse portrait with a background which every connoisseur would give a different reason for or against. And what is a portrait of a woman? Your painting and Plastik are poor stuff after all. They perturb and dull conceptions instead of raising them. Language is a finer medium."

"Yes, for those who can't paint," said Naumann. "There you have perfect right. I did not recommend you to paint, my friend."

The amiable artist carried his sting, but Ladislaw did not choose to appear stung. He went on as if he had not heard.

"Language gives a fuller image, which is all the better for being vague. After all, the true seeing is within; and painting stares at you with an insistent imperfection. I feel that especially about representations of women. As if a woman were a mere coloured superficies! You must wait for movement and tone. There is a difference in their very breathing: they change from moment to moment.—This woman whom you have just seen, for example: how would you paint her voice, pray? But her voice is much diviner than anything you have seen of her."

"I see, I see. You are jealous. No man must presume to think that he can paint your ideal. This is serious, my friend! Your great-aunt! 'Der Neffe als Onkel'* in a tragic sense—ungeheuer!"

"You and I shall quarrel, Naumann, if you call that lady my aunt again."

"How is she to be called then?"

"Mrs. Casaubon."

"Good. Suppose I get acquainted with her in spite of you, and find that she very much wishes to be painted?"

"Yes, suppose!" said Will Ladislaw, in a contemptuous under-tone, intended to dismiss the subject. He was conscious of being irritated by ridiculously small causes, which were half of his own creation. Why was he making any fuss about Mrs. Casaubon? And yet he felt as if something had happened to him with regard to her. There

---

*Title of a play by Schiller in which the hero disguises himself as his uncle to win the woman he loves; ungeheuer means monstrous.

are characters which are continually creating collisions and nodes for themselves in dramas which nobody is prepared to act with them. Their susceptibilities will clash against objects that remain innocently quiet.

CHAPTER 20

> A child forsaken, waking suddenly,
> Whose gaze afeard on all things round doth rove,
> And seeth only that it cannot see
> The meeting eyes of love.

Two hours later, Dorothea was seated in an inner room or boudoir of a handsome apartment in the Via Sistina.

I am sorry to add that she was sobbing bitterly, with such abandonment to this relief of an oppressed heart as a woman habitually controlled by pride on her own account and thoughtfulness for others will sometimes allow herself when she feels securely alone. And Mr. Casaubon was certain to remain away for some time at the Vatican.

Yet Dorothea had no distinctly shapen grievance that she could state even to herself; and in the midst of her confused thought and passion, the mental act that was struggling forth into clearness was a self-accusing cry that her feeling of desolation was the fault of her own spiritual poverty. She had married the man of her choice, and with the advantage over most girls that she had contemplated her marriage chiefly as the beginning of new duties: from the very first she had thought of Mr. Casaubon as having a mind so much above her own, that he must often be claimed by studies which she could not entirely share; moreover, after the brief narrow experience of her girlhood she was beholding Rome, the city of visible history, where the past of a whole hemisphere seems moving in funeral procession with strange ancestral images and trophies gathered from afar.

But this stupendous fragmentariness heightened the dreamlike strangeness of her bridal life. Dorothea had now been five weeks in Rome, and in the kindly mornings when autumn and winter seemed to go hand in hand like a happy aged couple one of whom would presently survive in chiller loneliness, she had driven about at first with Mr. Casaubon, but of late chiefly with Tantripp and

their experienced courier. She had been led through the best galleries, had been taken to the chief points of view, had been shown
the greatest ruins and the most glorious churches, and she had
ended by oftenest choosing to drive out to the Campagna where
she could feel alone with the earth and sky, away from the oppressive masquerade of ages, in which her own life too seemed to
become a masque with enigmatical costumes.

To those who have looked at Rome with the quickening power
of a knowledge which breathes a growing soul into all historic
shapes, and traces out the suppressed transitions which unite all
contrasts, Rome may still be the spiritual centre and interpreter of
the world. But let them conceive one more historical contrast: the
gigantic broken revelations of that Imperial and Papal city thrust
abruptly on the notions of a girl who had been brought up in
English and Swiss Puritanism, fed on meagre Protestant histories
and on art chiefly of the hand-screen sort; a girl whose ardent
nature turned all her small allowance of knowledge into principles,
fusing her actions into their mould, and whose quick emotions
gave the most abstract things the quality of a pleasure or a pain; a
girl who had lately become a wife, and from the enthusiastic acceptance of untried duty found herself plunged in tumultuous preoccupation with her personal lot. The weight of unintelligible Rome
might lie easily on bright nymphs to whom it formed a background
for the brilliant picnic of Anglo-foreign society; but Dorothea had
no such defence against deep impressions. Ruins and basilicas,
palaces and colossi, set in the midst of a sordid present, where all
that was living and warm-blooded seemed sunk in the deep degen-
eracy of a superstition divorced from reverence; the dimmer but
yet eager Titanic life gazing and struggling on walls and ceilings;
the long vistas of white forms whose marble eyes seemed to hold
the monotonous light of an alien world: all this vast wreck of ambitious ideals, sensuous and spiritual, mixed confusedly with the
signs of breathing forgetfulness and degradation, at first jarred her
as with an electric shock, and then urged themselves on her with
that ache belonging to a glut of confused ideas which check the
flow of emotion. Forms both pale and glowing took possession of
her young sense, and fixed themselves in her memory even when

she was not thinking of them, preparing strange associations which remained through her after-years. Our moods are apt to bring with them images which succeed each other like the magic-lantern pictures of a doze; and in certain states of dull forlornness Dorothea all her life continued to see the vastness of St. Peter's, the huge bronze canopy, the excited intention in the attitudes and garments of the prophets and evangelists in the mosaics above, and the red drapery which was being hung for Christmas spreading itself everywhere like a disease of the retina.

Not that this inward amazement of Dorothea's was anything very exceptional: many souls in their young nudity are tumbled out among incongruities and left to "find their feet" among them, while their elders go about their business. Nor can I suppose that when Mrs. Casaubon is discovered in a fit of weeping six weeks after her wedding, the situation will be regarded as tragic. Some discouragement, some faintness of heart at the new real future which replaces the imaginary, is not unusual, and we do not expect people to be deeply moved by what is not unusual. That element of tragedy which lies in the very fact of frequency, has not yet wrought itself into the coarse emotion of mankind; and perhaps our frames could hardly bear much of it. If we had a keen vision and feeling of all ordinary human life, it would be like hearing the grass grow and the squirrel's heart beat, and we should die of that roar which lies on the other side of silence. As it is, the quickest of us walk about well wadded with stupidity.

However, Dorothea was crying, and if she had been required to state the cause, she could only have done so in some such general words as I have already used: to have been driven to be more particular would have been like trying to give a history of the lights and shadows; for that new real future which was replacing the imaginary drew its material from the endless minutiae by which her view of Mr. Casaubon and her wifely relation, now that she was married to him, was gradually changing with the secret motion of a watch-hand from what it had been in her maiden dream. It was too early yet for her fully to recognize or at least admit the change, still more for her to have readjusted that devotedness which was so necessary a part of her mental life that she was almost sure sooner or later to recover it. Permanent rebellion, the disorder of a life without some loving reverent resolve, was not possible to her; but she was now in an interval when the very force of her nature heightened its confusion. In this way, the early months of marriage often are times of critical tumult—whether that of a shrimp-pool or of deeper waters—which afterwards subsides into cheerful peace.

But was not Mr. Casaubon just as learned as before? Had his forms of expression changed, or his sentiments become less laudable? O waywardness of womanhood! did his chronology fail him, or his ability to state not only a theory but the names of those who held it; or his provision for giving the heads of any subject on demand? And was not Rome the place in all the world to give free play to such accomplishments? Besides, had not Dorothea's enthusiasm especially dwelt on the prospect of relieving the weight and perhaps the sadness with which great tasks lie on him who has to achieve them?—And that such weight pressed on Mr. Casaubon was only plainer than before.

All these are crushing questions; but whatever else remained the same, the light had changed, and you cannot find the pearly dawn at noonday. The fact is unalterable, that a fellow-mortal with whose nature you are acquainted solely through the brief entrances and exits of a few imaginative weeks called courtship, may, when seen in the continuity of married companionship, be disclosed as something better or worse than what you have preconceived, but will certainly not appear altogether the same. And it would be astonishing to find how soon the change is felt if we had no kindred changes to compare with it. To share lodgings with a brilliant dinner-companion, or to see your favourite politician in the Ministry, may bring about changes quite as rapid: in these cases too we begin by knowing little and believing much, and we sometimes end by inverting the quantities.

Still, such comparisons might mislead, for no man was more incapable of flashy make-believe than Mr. Casaubon: he was as genuine a character as any ruminant animal, and he had not actively assisted in creating any illusions about himself. How was it that in the weeks since her marriage, Dorothea had not distinctly observed but felt with a stifling depression, that the large vistas and

wide fresh air which she had dreamed of finding in her husband's
mind were replaced by ante-rooms and winding passages which
seemed to lead nowhither? I suppose it was that in courtship everything is regarded as provisional and preliminary, and the smallest
sample of virtue or accomplishment is taken to guarantee
delightful stores which the broad leisure of marriage will reveal.
But the door-sill of marriage once crossed, expectation is concentrated on the present. Having once embarked on your marital
voyage, it is impossible not to be aware that you make no way and
that the sea is not within sight—that, in fact, you are exploring an
enclosed basin.

In their conversation before marriage, Mr. Casaubon had often
dwelt on some explanation or questionable detail of which Dorothea
did not see the bearing; but such imperfect coherence seemed due to
the brokenness of their intercourse, and, supported by her faith in
their future, she had listened with fervid patience to a recitation of
possible arguments to be brought against Mr. Casaubon's entirely
new view of the Philistine god Dagon and other fish-deities, thinking
that hereafter she should see this subject which touched him so
nearly from the same high ground whence doubtless it had become
so important to him. Again, the matter-of-course statement and tone
of dismissal with which he treated what to her were the most stirring
thoughts, was easily accounted for as belonging to the sense of haste
and preoccupation in which she herself shared during their engagement. But now, since they had been in Rome, with all the depths of
her emotion roused to tumultuous activity, and with life made a new
problem by new elements, she had been becoming more and more
aware, with a certain terror, that her mind was continually sliding
into inward fits of anger or repulsion, or else into forlorn weariness.
How far the judicious Hooker or any other hero of erudition would
have been the same at Mr. Casaubon's time of life, she had no means
of knowing, so that he could not have the advantage of comparison;
but her husband's way of commenting on the strangely impressive
objects around them had begun to affect her with a sort of mental
shiver: he had perhaps the best intention of acquitting himself
worthily, but only of acquitting himself. What was fresh to her mind
was worn out to his; and such capacity of thought and feeling as had

ever been stimulated in him by the general life of mankind had long shrunk to a sort of dried preparation, a lifeless embalmment of knowledge.

When he said, "Does this interest you, Dorothea? Shall we stay a little longer? I am ready to stay if you wish it,"—it seemed to her as if going or staying were alike dreary. Or, "Should you like to go to the Farnesina, Dorothea? It contains celebrated frescoes designed or painted by Raphael, which most persons think it worth while to visit."

"But do you care about them?" was always Dorothea's question.

"They are, I believe, highly esteemed. Some of them represent the fable of Cupid and Psyche, which is probably the romantic invention of a literary period, and cannot, I think, be reckoned as a genuine mythical product. But if you like these wall-paintings we can easily drive thither; and you will then, I think, have seen the chief works of Raphael, any of which it were a pity to omit in a visit to Rome. He is the painter who has been held to combine the most complete grace of form with sublimity of expression. Such at least I have gathered to be the opinion of cognoscenti."

This kind of answer given in a measured official tone, as of a clergyman reading according to the rubric, did not help to justify the glories of the Eternal City, or to give her the hope that if she knew more about them the world would be joyously illuminated for her. There is hardly any contact more depressing to a young ardent creature than that of a mind in which years full of knowledge seem to have issued in a blank absence of interest or sympathy.

On other subjects indeed Mr. Casaubon showed a tenacity of occupation and an eagerness which are usually regarded as the effect of enthusiasm, and Dorothea was anxious to follow this spontaneous direction of his thoughts, instead of being made to feel that she dragged him away from it. But she was gradually ceasing to expect with her former delightful confidence that she should see any wide opening where she followed him. Poor Mr. Casaubon himself was lost among small closets and winding stairs, and in an agitated dimness about the Cabeiri,* or in an exposure of

*Samothracian fertility gods.

other mythologists' ill-considered parallels, easily lost sight of any purpose which had prompted him to these labours. With his taper stuck before him he forgot the absence of windows, and in bitter manuscript remarks on other men's notions about the solar deities, he had become indifferent to the sunlight.

These characteristics, fixed and unchangeable as bone in Mr. Casaubon, might have remained longer unfelt by Dorothea if she had been encouraged to pour forth her girlish and womanly feeling—if he would have held her hands between his and listened with the delight of tenderness and understanding to all the little histories which made up her experience, and would have given her the same sort of intimacy in return, so that the past life of each could be included in their mutual knowledge and affection—or if she could have fed her affection with those childlike caresses which are the bent of every sweet woman, who has begun by showering kisses on the hard pate of her bald doll, creating a happy soul within that woodenness from the wealth of her own love. That was Dorothea's bent. With all her yearning to know what was afar from her and to be widely benignant, she had ardour enough for what was near, to have kissed Mr. Casaubon's coat-sleeve, or to have caressed his shoe-latchet, if he would have made any other sign of acceptance than pronouncing her, with his unfailing propriety, to be of a most affectionate and truly feminine nature, indicating at the same time by politely reaching a chair for her that he regarded these manifestations as rather crude and startling. Having made his clerical toilette with due care in the morning, he was prepared only for those amenities of life which were suited to the well-adjusted stiff cravat of the period, and to a mind weighted with unpublished matter.

And by a sad contradiction Dorothea's ideas and resolves seemed like melting ice floating and lost in the warm flood of which they had been but another form. She was humiliated to find herself a mere victim of feeling, as if she could know nothing except through that medium: all her strength was scattered in fits of agitation, of struggle, of despondency, and then again in visions of more complete renunciation, transforming all hard conditions into duty. Poor Dorothea! she was certainly troublesome—to herself chiefly; but this morning for the first time she had been troublesome to Mr. Casaubon.

She had begun, while they were taking coffee, with a determination to shake off what she inwardly called her selfishness, and turned a face all cheerful attention to her husband when he said, "My dear Dorothea, we must now think of all that is yet left undone, as a preliminary to our departure. I would fain have returned home earlier that we might have been at Lowick for the Christmas; but my inquiries here have been protracted beyond their anticipated period. I trust, however, that the time here has not been passed unpleasantly to you. Among the sights of Europe, that of Rome has ever been held one of the most striking and in some respects edifying. I well remember that I considered it an epoch in my life when I visited it for the first time; after the fall of Napoleon, an event which opened the Continent to travellers. Indeed I think it is one among several cities to which an extreme hyperbole has been applied—'See Rome and die': but in your case I would propose an emendation and say, See Rome as a bride, and live thenceforth as a happy wife."

Mr. Casaubon pronounced this little speech with the most conscientious intention, blinking a little and swaying his head up and down, and concluding with a smile. He had not found marriage a rapturous state, but he had no idea of being anything else than an irreproachable husband, who would make a charming young woman as happy as she deserved to be.

"I hope you are thoroughly satisfied with our stay—I mean, with the result so far as your studies are concerned," said Dorothea, trying to keep her mind fixed on what most affected her husband.

"Yes," said Mr. Casaubon, with that peculiar pitch of voice which makes the word half a negative. "I have been led farther than I had foreseen, and various subjects for annotation have presented themselves which, though I have no direct need of them, I could not pretermit. The task, notwithstanding the assistance of my amanuensis, has been a somewhat laborious one, but your society has happily prevented me from that too continuous prosecution of thought beyond the hours of study which has been the snare of my solitary life."

"I am very glad that my presence has made any difference to you," said Dorothea, who had a vivid memory of evenings in which she had supposed that Mr. Casaubon's mind had gone too deep during the day to be able to get to the surface again. I fear there was a little temper in her reply. "I hope when we get to Lowick, I shall be more useful to you, and be able to enter a little more into what interests you."

"Doubtless, my dear," said Mr. Casaubon, with a slight bow. "The notes I have here made will want sifting, and you can, if you please, extract them under my direction."

"And all your notes," said Dorothea, whose heart had already burned within her on this subject so that now she could not help speaking with her tongue. "All those rows of volumes—will you not now do what you used to speak of?—will you not make up your mind what part of them you will use, and begin to write the book which will make your vast knowledge useful to the world? I will write to your dictation, or I will copy and extract what you tell me: I can be of no other use." Dorothea, in a most unaccountable, darkly-feminine manner, ended with a slight sob and eyes full of tears.

The excessive feeling manifested would alone have been highly disturbing to Mr. Casaubon, but there were other reasons why Dorothea's words were among the most cutting and irritating to him that she could have been impelled to use. She was as blind to his inward troubles as he to hers; she had not yet learned those hidden conflicts in her husband which claim our pity. She had not yet listened patiently to his heart-beats, but only felt that her own was beating violently. In Mr. Casaubon's ear, Dorothea's voice gave loud emphatic iteration to those muffled suggestions of consciousness which it was possible to explain as mere fancy, the illusion of exaggerated sensitiveness: always when such suggestions are unmistakably repeated from without, they are resisted as cruel and unjust. We are angered even by the full acceptance of our humiliating confessions—how much more by hearing in hard distinct syllables from the lips of a near observer, those confused murmurs which we try to call morbid, and strive against as if they were the oncoming of numbness! And this cruel outward accuser was there in the shape of a wife—nay, of a young bride, who, instead of observing his abundant pen scratches and amplitude of paper with the uncritical awe of an elegant-minded canary-bird, seemed to present herself as a spy watching everything with a malign power of inference. Here, towards this particular point of the compass, Mr. Casaubon had a sensitiveness to match Dorothea's, and an equal quickness to imagine more than the fact. He had formerly observed with approbation her capacity for worshipping the right object; he now foresaw with sudden terror that this capacity might be replaced by presumption, this worship by the most exasperating of all criticism,—that which sees vaguely a great many fine ends and has not the least notion what it costs to reach them.

For the first time since Dorothea had known him, Mr. Casaubon's face had a quick angry flush upon it.

"My love," he said, with irritation reined in by propriety, "you may rely upon me for knowing the times and the seasons, adapted to the different stages of a work which is not to be measured by the facile conjectures of ignorant onlookers. It had been easy for me to gain a temporary effect by a mirage of baseless opinion; but it is ever the trial of the scrupulous explorer to be saluted with the impatient scorn of chatterers who attempt only the smallest achievements, being indeed quipped for no other. And it were well if all such could be admonished to discriminate judgments of which the true subject-matter lies entirely beyond their reach, from those of which the elements may be compassed by a narrow and superficial survey."

This speech was delivered with an energy and readiness quite unusual with Mr. Casaubon. It was not indeed entirely an improvisation, but had taken shape in inward colloquy, and rushed out like the round grains from a fruit when sudden heat cracks it. Dorothea was not only his wife: she was a personification of that shallow world which surrounds the ill-appreciated or desponding author.

Dorothea was indignant in her turn. Had she not been repressing everything in her except the desire to enter into some fellowship with her husband's chief interests?

"My judgment *was* a very superficial one—such as I am capable of forming," she answered, with a prompt resentment, that needed no rehearsal. "You showed me the rows of notebooks—you have often spoken of them—you have often said that they wanted digesting. But I never heard you speak of the writing that is to be published. Those were very simple facts, and my judgment went no farther. I only begged you to let me be of some good to you."

Dorothea rose to leave the table and Mr. Casaubon made no reply, taking up a letter which lay beside him as if to reperuse it. Both were shocked at their mutual situation—that each should have betrayed anger towards the other. If they had been at home, settled at Lowick in ordinary life among their neighbours, the clash would have been less embarrassing: but on a wedding journey, the express object of which is to isolate two people on the ground that they are all the world to each other, the sense of disagreement is, to say the least, confounding and stultifying. To have changed your longitude extensively, and placed yourselves in a moral solitude in order to have small explosions, to find conversation difficult and to hand a glass of water without looking, can hardly be regarded as satisfactory fulfilment even to the toughest minds. To Dorothea's inexperienced sensitiveness, it seemed like a catastrophe, changing all prospects; and to Mr. Casaubon it was a new pain, he never having been on a wedding journey before, or found himself in that close union which was more of a subjection than he had been able to imagine, since this charming young bride not only obliged him to much consideration on her behalf (which he had sedulously given), but turned out to be capable of agitating him cruelly just where he most needed soothing. Instead of getting a soft fence against the cold, shadowy, unapplausive audience of his life, had he only given it a more substantial presence?

Neither of them felt it possible to speak again at present. To have reversed a previous arrangement and declined to go out would have been a show of persistent anger which Dorothea's conscience shrank from, seeing that she already began to feel herself guilty. However just her indignation might be, her ideal was not to claim justice, but to give tenderness. So when the carriage came to the door, she drove with Mr. Casaubon to the Vatican, walked with him through the stony avenue of inscriptions, and when she parted with him at the entrance to the Library, went on through the Museum out of mere listlessness as to what was around her. She had not spirit to turn round and say that she would drive anywhere. It was when Mr. Casaubon was quitting her that Naumann had first seen her, and he had entered the long gallery of sculpture at the same time with her; but here Naumann had to await Ladislaw, with whom he was to settle a bet of champagne about an enigmatical medieval-looking figure there. After they had examined the figure, and had walked on finishing their dispute, they had parted, Ladislaw lingering behind while Naumann had gone into the Hall of Statues, where he again saw Dorothea, and saw her in that brooding abstraction which made her pose remarkable. She did not really see the streak of sunlight on the floor more than she saw the statues: she was inwardly seeing the light of years to come in her own home and over the English fields and elms and hedge-bordered highroads: and feeling that the way in which they might be filled with joyful devotedness was not so clear to her as it had been. But in Dorothea's mind there was a current into which all thought and feeling were apt sooner or later to flow—the reaching forward of the whole consciousness towards the fullest truth, the least partial good. There was clearly something better than anger and despondency.

CHAPTER 21
> Hire facounde eke full womanly and plain,
> No contrefeted termes had she
> To semen wise.
>
> —Chaucer

It was in that way Dorothea came to be sobbing as soon as she was securely alone. But she was presently roused by a knock at the door, which made her hastily dry her eyes before saying, "Come in." Tantripp had brought a card, and said that there was a gentleman waiting in the lobby. The courier had told him that only Mrs. Casaubon was at home, but he said he was a relation of Mr. Casaubon's: would she see him?

"Yes," said Dorothea, without pause; "show him into the salon." Her chief impressions about young Ladislaw were that when she had seen him at Lowick she had been made aware of Mr. Casaubon's generosity towards him, and also that she had been interested in his own hesitation about his career. She was alive to anything that gave her an opportunity for active sympathy, and at this moment it seemed as if the visit had come to shake her out of her self-absorbed discontent—to remind her of her husband's goodness, and make her feel that she had now the right to be his helpmate in all kind deeds. She waited a minute or two, but when she passed into the next room there were just signs enough that she had been crying to make her open face look more youthful and appealing than usual. She met Ladislaw with that exquisite smile of goodwill which is unmixed with vanity, and held out her hand to him. He was the elder by several years, but at that moment he looked much the younger, for his transparent complexion flushed suddenly, and he spoke with a shyness extremely unlike the ready indifference of his manner with his male companion, while Dorothea became all the calmer with a wondering desire to put him at ease.

"I was not aware that you and Mr. Casaubon were in Rome, until this morning, when I saw you in the Vatican Museum," he said. "I knew you at once—but—I mean, that I concluded Mr. Casaubon's address would be found at the Poste Restante, and I was anxious to pay my respects to him and you as early as possible."

"Pray sit down. He is not here now, but he will be glad to hear of you, I am sure," said Dorothea, seating herself unthinkingly between the fire and the light of the tall window, and pointing to a chair opposite, with the quietude of a benignant matron. The signs of girlish sorrow in her face were only the more striking. "Mr. Casaubon is much engaged; but you will leave your address—will you not?—and he will write to you."

"You are very good," said Ladislaw, beginning to lose his diffidence in the interest with which he was observing the signs of weeping which had altered her face. "My address is on my card. But if you will allow me I will call again to-morrow at an hour when Mr. Casaubon is likely to be at home."

"He goes to read in the Library of the Vatican every day, and you can hardly see him except by an appointment. Especially now. We are about to leave Rome, and he is very busy. He is usually away almost from breakfast till dinner. But I am sure he will wish you to dine with us."

Will Ladislaw was struck mute for a few moments. He had never been fond of Mr. Casaubon, and if it had not been for the sense of obligation, would have laughed at him as a Bat of erudition. But the idea of this dried-up pendant, this elaborator of small explanations about as important as the surplus stock of false antiquities kept in a vendor's back chamber, having first got this adorable young creature to marry him, and then passing his honeymoon away from her, groping after his mouldy futilities (Will was given to hyperbole)—this sudden picture stirred him with a sort of comic disgust: he was divided between the impulse to laugh aloud and the equally unseasonable impulse to burst into scornful invective. For an instant he felt that the struggle was causing a queer contortion of his mobile features, but with a good effort he resolved it into nothing more offensive than a merry smile.

Dorothea wondered; but the smile was irresistible, and shone back from her face too. Will Ladislaw's smile was delightful, unless you were angry with him beforehand: it was a gush of inward light illuminating the transparent skin as well as the eyes, and playing about every curve and line as if some Ariel were touching them with a new charm, and banishing for ever the traces of moodiness. The reflection of that smile could not but have a little merriment in it too, even under dark eyelashes still moist, as Dorothea said inquiringly, "Something amuses you?"

"Yes," said Will, quick in finding resources. "I am thinking of the sort of figure I cut the first time I saw you, when you annihilated my poor sketch with your criticism."

"My criticism?" said Dorothea, wondering still more. "Surely not. I always feel particularly ignorant about painting."

"I suspected you of knowing so much, that you knew how to say just what was most cutting. You said—I daresay you don't remember it as I do—that the relation of my sketch to nature was quite hidden from you. At least, you implied that." Will could laugh now as well as smile.

"That was really my ignorance," said Dorothea, admiring Will's good humour. "I must have said so only because I never could see any beauty in the pictures which my uncle told me all judges thought very fine. And I have gone about with just the same ignorance in Rome. There are comparatively few paintings that I can really enjoy. At first when I enter a room where the walls are covered with frescoes, or with rare pictures, I feel a kind of awe—like a child present at great ceremonies where there are grand robes and processions; I feel myself in the presence of some higher life than my own. But when I begin to examine the pictures one by one, the life goes out of them, or else is something violent and strange to me. It must be my own dullness. I am seeing so much all at once, and not understanding half of it. That always makes one feel stupid. It is painful to be told that anything is very fine and not be able to feel that it is fine—something like being blind, while people talk of the sky."

"Oh, there is a great deal in the feeling for art which must be acquired," said Will. (It was impossible now to doubt the directness of Dorothea's confession.) "Art is an old language with a great many artificial affected styles, and sometimes the chief pleasure one gets out of knowing them is the mere sense of knowing. I enjoy the art of all sorts here immensely; but I suppose if I could pick my enjoyment to pieces I should find it made up of many different threads. There is something in daubing a little one's self, and having an idea of the process."

"You mean perhaps to be a painter?" said Dorothea, with a new direction of interest. "You mean to make painting your profession. Mr. Casaubon will like to hear that you have chosen a profession."

"No, oh no," said Will, with some coldness. "I have quite made up my mind against it. It is too one-sided a life. I have been seeing a great deal of the German artists here: I travelled from Frankfort with one of them. Some are fine, even brilliant fellows—but I should not like to get into their way of looking at the world entirely from the studio point of view."

"That I can understand," said Dorothea, cordially. "And in Rome it seems as if there were so many things which are more wanted in the world than pictures. But if you have a genius for painting, would it not be right to take that as a guide? Perhaps you might do better things than these—or different, so that there might not be so many pictures almost all alike in the same place."

There was no mistaking this simplicity, and Will was won by it into frankness. "A man must have a very rare genius to make changes of that sort. I am afraid mine would not carry me even to the pitch of doing well what has been done already, at least not so well as to make it worth while. And I should never succeed in anything by dint of drudgery. If things don't come easily to me I never get them."

"I have heard Mr. Casaubon say that he regrets your want of patience," said Dorothea, gently. She was rather shocked at this mode of taking all life as a holiday.

"Yes, I know Mr. Casaubon's opinion. He and I differ."

The slight streak of contempt in his hasty reply offended Dorothea. She was all the more susceptible about Mr. Casaubon because of her morning's trouble.

"Certainly you differ," she said, rather proudly. "I did not think of comparing you: such power of presevering devoted labour as Mr. Casaubon's is not common."

Will saw that she was offended, but this only gave an additional impulse to the new irritation of his latent dislike towards Mr. Casaubon. It was too intolerable that Dorothea should be worshipping this husband: such weakness in a woman is pleasant to no man but the husband in question. Mortals are easily tempted to pinch the life out of their neighbour's buzzing glory, and think that such killing is no murder.

"No, indeed," he answered, promptly. "And therefore it is a pity that it should be thrown away, as so much English scholarship is, for want of knowing what is being done by the rest of the world. If Mr. Casaubon read German he would save himself a great deal of trouble."

"I do not understand you," said Dorothea, startled and anxious.

"I merely mean," said Will, in an offhand way, "that the Germans have taken the lead in historical inquiries, and they laugh at results which are got by groping about in the woods with a pocket-compass while they have made good roads. When I was with Mr. Casaubon I saw that he deafened himself in that direction: it was almost against his will that he read a Latin tretise written by a German. I was very sorry."

Will only thought of giving a good pinch that would annihilate that vaunted laboriousness, and was unable to imagine the mode in which Dorothea would be wounded. Young Mr. Ladislaw was not at all deep himself in German writers; but very little achievement is required in order to pity another man's shortcomings.

Poor Dorothea felt a pang at the thought that the labour of her husband's life might be void, which left her no energy to spare for the question whether this young relative who was so much obliged to him ought not to have repressed his observation. She did not even speak, but sat looking at her hands, absorbed in the piteousness of that thought.

Will, however, having given that annihilating pinch, was rather ashamed, imagining from Dorothea's silence that he had offended her still more; and having also a conscience about plucking the tail-feathers from a benefactor.

"I regretted it especially," he resumed, taking the usual course from detraction to insincere eulogy, "because of my gratitude and respect towards my cousin. It would not signify so much in a man whose talents and character were less distinguished."

Dorothea raised her eyes, brighter than usual with excited feeling, and said, in her saddest recitative, "How I wish I had learned German when I was at Lausanne! There were plenty of German teachers. But now I can be of no use."

There was a new light, but still a mysterious light, for Will in Dorothea's last words. The question how she had come to accept Mr. Casaubon—which he had dismissed when he first saw her by saying that she must be disagreeable in spite of appearances—was not now to be answered on any such short and easy method. Whatever else she might be, she was not disagreeable. She was not coldly clever and indirectly satirical, but adorably simple and full of feeling. She was an angel beguiled. It would be a unique delight to wait and watch for the melodious fragments in which her heart and soul came forth so directly and ingenuously. The Æolian harp again came into his mind.

She must have made some original romance for herself in this marriage. And if Mr. Casaubon had been a dragon who had carried her off to his lair with his talons simply and without legal forms, it would have been an unavoidable feat of heroism to release her and fall at her feet. But he was something more unmanageable than a

dragon: he was a benefactor with collective society at his back, and
he was at that moment entering the room in all the unimpeachable
correctness of his demeanour, while Dorothea was looking animated with a newly aroused alarm and regret, and Will was looking
animated with his admiring speculation about her feelings.

Mr. Casaubon felt a surprise which was quite unmixed with
pleasure, but he did not swerve from his usual politeness of
greeting, when Will rose and explained his presence. Mr. Casaubon was less happy than usual, and this perhaps made him look
all the dimmer and more faded; else, the effect might easily have
been produced by the contrast of his young cousin's appearance.
The first impression on seeing Will was one of sunny bright-
ness, which added to the uncertainty of his changing expression.
Surely, his very features changed their form; his jaw looked sometimes large and sometimes small; and the little ripple in his nose
was a preparation for metamorphosis. When he turned his head
quickly his hair seemed to shake out light, and some persons
thought they saw decided genius in this coruscation. Mr. Casaubon, on the contrary, stood rayless.

As Dorothea's eyes were turned anxiously on her husband she
was perhaps not insensible to the contrast, but it was only mingled
with other causes in making her more conscious of that new alarm
on his behalf which was the first stirring of a pitying tenderness fed
by the realities of his lot and not by her own dreams. Yet it was a
source of greater freedom to her that Will was there; his young
equality was agreeable, and also perhaps his openness to conviction. She felt an immense need of some one to speak to, and she
had never before seen any one who seemed so quick and pliable, so
likely to understand everything.

Mr. Casaubon gravely hoped that Will was passing his time
profitably as well as pleasantly in Rome—had thought his intention
was to remain in South Germany—but begged him to come and
dine to-morrow, when he would converse more at large: at present
he was somewhat weary. Ladislaw understood, and accepting the
invitation immediately took his leave.

Dorothea's eyes followed her husband anxiously, while he sank
down wearily at the end of a sofa, and resting his elbow supported

his head and looked on the floor. A little flushed, and with bright eyes, she seated herself beside him, and said,

"Forgive me for speaking so hastily to you this morning. I was wrong. I fear I hurt you and made the day more burdensome."

"I am glad that you feel that, my dear," said Mr. Casaubon. He spoke quietly and bowed his head a little, but there was still an uneasy feeling in his eyes as he looked at her.

"But you do forgive me?" said Dorothea, with a quick sob. In her need for some manifestation of feeling she was ready to exaggerate her own fault. Would not love see returning penitence afar off, and fall on its neck and kiss it?

"My dear Dorothea—'who wish repentance is not satisfied, is not of heaven nor earth'—You do not think me worthy to be banished by that severe sentence," said Mr. Casaubon, exerting himself to make a strong statement, and also to smile faintly.

Dorothea was silent, but a tear which had come up with the sob would insist on falling.

"You are excited, my dear. And I also am feeling some unpleasant consequences of too much mental disturbance," said Mr. Casaubon. In fact, he had it in his thought to tell her that she ought not to have received young Ladislaw in his absence; but he abstained, partly from the sense that it would be ungracious to bring a new complaint in the moment of her penitent acknowledgment, partly because he wanted to avoid further agitation of himself by speech, and partly because he was too proud to betray that jealousy of disposition which was not so exhausted on his scholarly compeers that there was none to spare in other directions. There is a sort of jealousy which needs very little fire; it is hardly a passion, but a blight bred in the cloudy, damp despondency of uneasy egoism.

"I think it is time for us to dress," he added, looking at his watch. They both rose, and there was never any further allusion between them to what had passed on this day.

But Dorothea remembered it to the last with the vividness with which we all remember epochs in our experience when some dear expectation dies, or some new motive is born. To-day she had begun to see that she had been under a wild illusion in expecting a response to her feeling from Mr. Casaubon, and she had felt the waking of a presentiment that there might be a sad consciousness in his life which made as great a need on his side as on her own.

We are all of us born in moral stupidity, taking the world as an udder to feed our supreme selves: Dorothea had early begun to emerge from that stupidity, but yet it had been easier to her to imagine how she would devote herself to Mr. Casaubon, and become wise and strong in his strength and wisdom, than to conceive with that distinctness which is no longer reflection but feeling—an idea wrought back to the directness of sense, like the solidity of objects— that he had an equivalent centre of self, whence the lights and shadows must always fall with a certain difference.

For the Literary Traveler

Rome, the city of *la dolce vita*, would seem the perfect ground for the newly married, a fertile place to explore the pleasures of romantic love. "Here," wrote Goethe, "everything is new." Thus the bitter irony of Eliot's fictional bridegroom holing up alone for five weeks in the VATICAN LIBRARY. (Open to students with a letter of introduction, it now holds one million printed books.)

Dorothea passes her time brooding in the MUSEO PIO CLEMENTINO'S GALLERY OF STATUES, near the SLEEPING ARIADNE (number 548), which is also called *Cleopatra* in the novel. Next to this copy of a Greek original, Dorothea is observed and admired by Will Ladislaw's German artist-friend Naumann.

Eliot situates Ladislaw at that moment in the adjacent OCTAGONAL COURTYARD, his attention to the graceful sensuality of the APOLLO BELVEDERE suggesting an affinity between this masterpiece of classical sculpture and the novel's romantic hero.

Eliot repeats the ironic juxtaposition of character and work of art by having Mr. Casaubon ask his bride if she'd like to see RAPHAEL'S CUPID AND PSYCHE in the Farnesina, an expedition toward which he is clearly indifferent. Visiting the VILLA FARNESINA in TRASTEVERE (across the street from the fine galleries in the PALAZZO CORSINI), one sees the irony of this reference to Raphael. On the ground floor of the Renaissance palace (the sixteenth-century home of the banker Agostino Chigi "the Magnificent" whose Chigi Chapel can be seen in the church of Santa Maria del Popolo) is Raphael's exuberant *Loggia of Cupid and Psyche* and his extraordinary *Galatea*, a gorgeous image of yearning eroticism. The FARNESINA—its art, gardens, and views of the river—is an ideal destination for lovers. The Casaubons do not go.

Instead Dorothea takes her solitary drives out to the CAMPAGNA— the plains outside the city, sites of ancient tombs, ruins, and, in Eliot's time, of undrained swamp that bred malarial disease. (For Isabel Archer, the troubled young wife of Gilbert Osmond in Henry James's *The Portrait of a Lady*, the Campagna was "almost a daily habit.")

And although she tells Ladislaw of her love of the sunset from the PINCIAN HILL, the summit of Via Sistina where the Casaubons are staying, there are no heights of passion or friendship between the honeymooning couple on Sistina. Rather, a more apt emblem of their miserable marriage suggests the buried life of the lonely bride: in the church of SANTA MARIA DELLA VITTORIA on Via Venti Settembre, Bernini's famous statue *SAINT TERESA IN ECSTASY* in the CORNARO CHAPEL calls to mind Eliot's reversal of the eroticism of mystical experience. Dorothea, as the vowed wife of sterile intellectualism in post-religious England, is "a modern-day Saint Theresa, foundress of nothing, whose loving heartbeats and sobs after an unattained goodness tremble off and are dispersed ..."

Rereading *Middlemarch* in 1934, the same year she wrote "Roman Fever" (see page 224), Edith Wharton argued with friends about whether the marriage of Casaubon and Dorothea was ever consummated.

Edith Wharton

There have long been rumors about Edith Jones Wharton's possible illegitimacy. Was her real father a young Englishman employed by Wharton's mother, Lucretia Jones, to tutor her sons? Biographer R. W. B. Lewis doubts it. But, as the following story shows—one of Wharton's best—toward the uncertainties of paternity and the philandering of the upper classes she paid a keen and subtle attention. About her passion for Rome, where she remembered seeing tulips on the Spanish Steps and playing on the Pincian Hill as a four-year-old, she was straightforward: Why live anywhere else? she remarked to friends in 1932.

ROMAN FEVER

I.

From the table at which they had been lunching two American ladies of ripe but well-cared-for middle age moved across the lofty terrace of the Roman restaurant and, leaning on its parapet, looked first at each other, and then down on the outspread glories of the Palatine and the Forum, with the same expression of vague but benevolent approval.

As they leaned there a girlish voice echoed up gaily from the stairs leading to the court below. "Well, come along, then," it cried, not to them but to an invisible companion, "and let's leave the young things to their knitting"; and a voice as fresh laughed back: "Oh, look here, Babs, not actually *knitting*—" "Well, I mean figuratively," rejoined the first. "After all, we haven't left our poor parents much else to do. . . ." and at that point the turn of the stairs engulfed the dialogue.

The two ladies looked at each other again, this time with a tinge of smiling embarrassment, and the smaller and paler one shook her head and colored slightly.

· "Barbara!" she murmured, sending an unheard rebuke after the mocking voice in the stairway.

The other lady, who was fuller, and higher in color, with a small determined nose supported by vigorous black eyebrows, gave a good-humored laugh. "That's what our daughters think of us!"

Her companion replied by a deprecating gesture. "Not of us individually. We must remember that. It's just the collective modern idea of Mothers. And you see—" Half-guiltily she drew from her handsomely mounted black handbag a twist of crimson silk run through by two fine knitting needles. "One never knows," she murmured. "The new system has certainly given us a good deal of time to kill; and sometimes I get tired just looking—even at this." Her gesture was now addressed to the stupendous scene at their feet.

The dark lady laughed again, and they both relapsed upon the view, contemplating it in silence, with a sort of diffused serenity which might have been borrowed from the spring effulgence of the Roman skies. The luncheon hour was long past, and the two had their end of the vast terrace to themselves. At its opposite extremity a few groups, detained by a lingering look at the outspread city, were gathering up guidebooks and fumbling for tips. The last of them scattered, and the two ladies were alone on the air-washed height.

"Well, I don't see why we shouldn't just stay here," said Mrs. Slade, the lady of the high color and energetic brows. Two derelict basket chairs stood near, and she pushed them into the angle of the parapet, and settled herself in one, her gaze upon the Palatine. "After all, it's still the most beautiful view in the world."

"It always wil be, to me," assented her friend Mrs. Ansley, with so slight a stress on the "me" that Mrs. Slade, though she noticed it, wondered if it were not merely accidental, like the random underlinings of old-fashioned letter writers.

"Grace Ansley was always old-fashioned," she thought; and added aloud, with a retrospective smile: "It's a view we've both been familiar with for a good many years. When we first met here we were younger than our girls are now. You remember?"

"Oh, yes, I remember," murmured Mrs. Ansley, with the same

undefinable stress. "There's that headwaiter wondering," she interpolated. She was evidently far less sure than her companion of herself and of her rights in the world.

"I'll cure him of wondering," said Mrs. Slade, stretching her hand toward a bag as discreetly opulent-looking as Mrs. Ansley's. Signing to the headwaiter, she explained that she and her friend were old lovers of Rome, and would like to spend the end of the afternoon looking down on the view—that is, if it did not disturb the service? The headwaiter, bowing over her gratuity, assured her that the ladies were most welcome, and would be still more so if they would condescend to remain for dinner. A full-moon night, they would remember. . . .

Mrs. Slade's black brows drew together, as though references to the moon were out of place and even unwelcome. But she smiled away her frown as the headwaiter retreated. "Well, why not? We might do worse. There's no knowing, I suppose, when the girls will be back. Do you even know back from *where*? I don't!"

Mrs. Ansley again colored slightly. "I think those young Italian aviators we met at the Embassy invited them to fly to Tarquinia for tea. I suppose they'll want to wait and fly back by moonlight."

"Moonlight—moonlight! What a part it still plays. Do you suppose they're as sentimental as we were?"

"I've come to the conclusion that I don't in the least know what they are," said Mrs. Ansley. "And perhaps we didn't know much more about each other."

"No; perhaps we didn't."

Her friend gave her a shy glance. "I never should have supposed you were sentimental, Alida."

"Well, perhaps I wasn't." Mrs. Slade drew her lids together in retrospect; and for a few moments the two ladies, who had been intimate since childhood, reflected how little they knew each other. Each one, of course, had a label ready to attach to the other's name; Mrs. Delphin Slade, for instance, would have told herself, or anyone who asked her, that Mrs. Horace Ansley, twenty-five years ago, had been exquisitely lovely—no, you wouldn't believe it, would you? . . . though, of course, still charming, distinguished. . . . Well, as a girl she had been exquisite; far more beautiful than her daughter Barbara, though certainly Babs, according to the new standards at any rate, was more effective—had more *edge*, as they say. Funny where she got it, with those two nullities as parents. Yes; Horace Ansley was—well, just the duplicate of his wife. Museum specimens of old New York. Good-looking, irreproachable, exemplary. Mrs. Slade and Mrs. Ansley had lived opposite each other—actually as well as figuratively—for years. When the drawing-room curtains in No. 20 East 73rd Street were renewed, No. 23, across the way, was always aware of it. And of all the movings, buyings, travels, anniversaries, illnesses—the tame chronicle of an estimable pair. Little of it escaped Mrs. Slade. But she had grown bored with it by the time her husband made his big *coup* in Wall Street, and when they bought in upper Park Avenue had already begun to think: "I'd rather live opposite a speakeasy for a change; at least one might see it raided." The idea of seeing Grace raided was so amusing that (before the move) she launched it at a woman's lunch. It made a hit, and went the rounds—she sometimes wondered if it had crossed the street, and reached Mrs. Ansley. She hoped not, but didn't much mind. Those were the days when respectability was at a discount, and it did the irreproachable no harm to laugh at them a little.

A few years later, and not many months apart, both ladies lost their husbands. There was an appropriate exchange of wreaths and condolences, and a brief renewal of intimacy in the half-shadow of their mourning; and now, after another interval, they had run across each other in Rome, at the same hotel, each of them the modest appendage of a salient daughter. The similarity of their lot had again drawn them together, lending itself to mild jokes, and the mutual confession that, if in old days it must have been tiring to "keep up" with daughters, it was now, at times, a little dull not to.

No doubt, Mrs. Slade reflected, she felt her unemployment more than poor Grace ever would. It was a big drop from being the wife of Delphin Slade to being his widow. She had always regarded herself (with a certain conjugal pride) as his equal in social gifts, as contributing her full share to the making of the exceptional couple they were: but the difference after his death was irremediable. As the wife of the famous corporation lawyer, always with an international case or two on hand, every day brought its exciting and unexpected obligation: the impromptu entertaining of eminent colleagues from abroad, the hurried dashes on legal business to London, Paris or Rome, where the entertaining was so handsomely reciprocated; the amusement of hearing in her wake: "What, that handsome woman with the good clothes and the eyes is Mrs. Slade—*the* Slade's wife? Really? Generally the wives of celebrities are such frumps."

Yes; being *the* Slade's widow was a dullish business after that. In living up to such a husband all her faculties had been engaged; now she had only her daughter to live up to, for the son who seemed to have inherited his father's gifts had died suddenly in boyhood. She had fought through that agony because her husband was there, to be helped and to help; now, after the father's death, the thought of the boy had become unbearable. There was nothing left but to mother her daughter; and dear Jenny was such a perfect daughter that she needed no excessive mothering. "Now with Babs Ansley I don't know that I *should* be so quiet," Mrs. Slade sometimes half-enviously reflected; but Jenny, who was younger than her brilliant friend, was that rare accident, an extremely pretty girl who somehow made youth and prettiness seem as safe as their absence. It was all perplexing—and to Mrs. Slade a little boring. She wished that Jenny would fall in love—with the wrong man, even; that she might have to be watched, out-maneuvered, rescued. And instead, it was Jenny who watched her mother, kept her out of drafts, made sure that she had taken her tonic. . . .

Mrs. Ansley was much less articulate than her friend, and her mental portrait of Mrs. Slade was slighter, and drawn with fainter touches. "Alida Slade's awfully brilliant; but not as brilliant as she thinks," would have summed it up; though she would have added, for the enlightenment of strangers, that Mrs. Slade had been an extremely dashing girl; much more so than her daughter, who was pretty, of course, and clever in a way, but had none of her mother's—well, "vividness," someone had once called it. Mrs. Ansley would take up current words like this, and cite them in quotation marks, as unheard-of audacities. No; Jenny was not like her mother. Sometimes Mrs. Ansley thought

Alida Slade was disappointed; on the whole she had had a sad life. Full of failures and mistakes; Mrs. Ansley had always been rather sorry for her. . . .

So these two ladies visualized each other, each through the wrong end of her little telescope.

II

For a long time they continued to sit side by side without speaking. It seemed as though, to both, there was a relief in laying down their somewhat futile activities in the presence of the vast Memento Mori which faced them. Mrs. Slade sat quite still, her eyes fixed on the golden slope of the Palace of the Caesars, and after a while Mrs. Ansley ceased to fidget with her bag, and she too sank into meditation. Like many intimate friends, the two ladies had never before had occasion to be silent together, and Mrs. Ansley was slightly embarrassed by what seemed, after so many years, a new stage in their intimacy, and one with which she did not yet know how to deal.

Suddenly the air was full of that deep clangor of bells which periodically covers Rome with a roof of silver. Mrs. Slade glanced at her wristwatch. "Five o'clock already," she said, as though surprised.

Mrs. Ansley suggested interrogatively: "There's bridge at the Embassy at five." For a long time Mrs. Slade did not answer. She appeared to be lost in contemplation, and Mrs. Ansley thought the remark had escaped her. But after a while she said, as if speaking out of a dream: "Bridge, did you say? Not unless you want to. . . . But I don't think I will, you know."

"Oh, no," Mrs. Ansley hastened to assure her. "I don't care to at all. It's so lovely here; and so full of old memories, as you say." She settled herself in her chair, and almost furtively drew forth her knitting. Mrs. Slade took sideway note of this activity, but her own beautifully cared-for hands remained motionless on her knee.

"I was just thinking," she said slowly, "what different things Rome stands for to each generation of travelers. To our grand-mothers, Roman fever; to our mothers, sentimental dangers—how we used to be guarded!—to our daughters, no more dangers than the middle of Main Street. They don't know it—but how much they're missing!"

The long golden light was beginning to pale, and Mrs. Ansley lifted her knitting a little closer to her eyes. "Yes; how we were guarded!"

"I always used to think," Mrs. Slade continued, "that our mothers had a much more difficult job than our grandmothers. When Roman fever stalked the streets it must have been comparatively easy to gather in the girls at the danger hour; but when you and I were young, with such beauty calling us, and the spice of disobedience thrown in, and no worse risk than catching cold during the cool hour after sunset, the mothers used to be put to it to keep us in—didn't they?"

She turned again toward Mrs. Ansley, but the latter had reached a delicate point in her knitting. "One, two, three—slip two; yes, they must have been," she assented, without looking up.

Mrs. Slade's eyes rested on her with a deepened attention. "She can knit—in the face of *this*! How like her. . . ."

Mrs. Slade leaned back, brooding, her eyes ranging from the ruins which faced her to the long green hollow of the Forum, the fading glow of the church fronts beyond it, and the outlying immensity of the Colosseum. Suddenly she thought: "It's all very well to say that our girls have done away with sentiment and moonlight. But if Babs Ansley isn't out to catch that young aviator—the one who's a Marchese—then I don't know anything. And Jenny has no chance beside her. I know that too. I wonder if that's why Grace Ansley likes the two girls to go everywhere together? My poor Jenny as a foil—!" Mrs. Slade gave a hardly audible laugh, and at the sound Mrs. Ansley dropped her knitting.

"Yes—?"

"I—oh, nothing. I was only thinking how your Babs carries everything before her. That Campolieri boy is one of the best matches in Rome. Don't look so innocent, my dear—you know he is. And I was wondering, ever so respectfully, you understand . . . wondering how two such exemplary characters as you and Horace had managed to produce anything quite so dynamic." Mrs. Slade laughed again, with a touch of asperity.

Mrs. Ansley's hands lay inert across her needles. She looked straight out at the great accumulated wreckage of passion and splendor at her feet. But her small profile was almost expression-less. At length she said: "I think you overrate Babs, my dear."

Mrs. Slade's tone grew easier. "No; I don't. I appreciate her. And perhaps envy you. Oh, my girl's perfect; if I were a chronic invalid I'd—well, I think I'd rather be in Jenny's hands. There must be times . . . but there! I always wanted a brilliant daughter . . . and never quite understood why I got an angel instead."

Mrs. Ansley echoed her laugh in a faint murmur. "Babs is an angel too."

"Of course—of course! But she's got rainbow wings. Well, they're wandering by the sea with their young men; and here we sit . . . and it all brings back the past a little too acutely."

Mrs. Ansley had resumed her knitting. One might almost have imagined (if one had known her less well, Mrs. Slade reflected) that, for her also, too many memories rose from the lengthening shadows of those august ruins. But no; she was simply absorbed in her work. What was there for her to worry about? She knew that Babs would almost certainly come back engaged to the extremely eligible Campolieri. "And she'll sell the New York house, and settle down near them in Rome, and never be in their way . . . she's much too tactful. But she'll have an excellent cook, and just the right people in for bridge and cocktails . . . and a perfectly peaceful old age among her grandchildren."

Mrs. Slade broke off this prophetic flight with a recoil of self-disgust. There was no one of whom she had less right to think unkindly than of Grace Ansley. Would she never cure herself of envying her? Perhaps she had begun too long ago.

She stood up and leaned against the parapet, filling her troubled eyes with the tranquilizing magic of the hour. But instead of tran-quilizing her the sight seemed to increase her exasperation. Her gaze turned toward the Colosseum. Already its golden flank was drowned in purple shadow, and above it the sky curved crystal clear, without light or color. It was the moment when afternoon and evening hang balanced in midheaven.

Mrs. Slade turned back and laid her hand on her friend's arm. The gesture was so abrupt that Mrs. Ansley looked up, startled.

"The sun's set. You're not afraid, my dear?"

"Afraid—?"

"Of Roman fever or pneumonia? I remember how ill you were that winter. As a girl you had a very delicate throat, hadn't you?"

"Oh, we're all right up here. Down below, in the Forum, it does get deathly cold, all of a sudden . . . but not here."

"Ah, of course you know because you had to be so careful." Mrs. Slade turned back to the parapet. She thought: "I must make one more effort not to hate her." Aloud she said: "Whenever I look at the Forum from up here, I remember that story about a great-aunt of yours, wasn't she? A dreadfully wicked great-aunt?"

"Oh, yes; great-aunt Harriet. The one who was supposed to have sent her young sister out to the Forum after sunset to gather a night-blooming flower for her album. All our great-aunts and grandmothers used to have albums of dried flowers."

Mrs. Slade nodded. "But she really sent her because they were in love with the same man—"

"Well, that was the family tradition. They said Aunt Harriet confessed it years afterward. At any rate, the poor little sister caught the fever and died. Mother used to frighten us with the story when we were children."

"And you frightened *me* with it, that winter when you and I were here as girls. The winter I was engaged to Delphin."

Mrs. Ansley gave a faint laugh. "Oh, did I? Really frightened you? I don't believe you're easily frightened."

"Not often; but I was then. I was easily frightened because I was too happy. I wonder if you know what that means?"

"I—yes . . ." Mrs. Ansley faltered.

"Well, I suppose that was why the story of your wicked aunt made such an impression on me. And I thought: 'There's no more Roman fever, but the Forum is deathly cold after sunset—especially after a hot day. And the Colosseum's even colder and damper.' "

"The Colosseum—?"

"Yes. It wasn't easy to get in, after the gates were locked for the night. Far from easy. Still, in those days it could be managed; it *was* managed, often. Lovers met there who couldn't meet elsewhere. You knew that?"

"I—I dare say. I don't remember."

"You don't remember? You don't remember going to visit some ruins or other one evening, just after dark, and catching a bad chill? You were supposed to have gone to see the moon rise. People always said that expedition was what caused your illness."

There was a moment's silence; then Mrs. Ansley rejoined: "Did they? It was all so long ago."

"Yes. And you got well again—so it didn't matter. But I suppose it struck your friends—the reason given for your illness, I mean— because everybody knew you were so prudent on account of your throat, and your mother took such care of you. . . . You *had* been out late sight-seeing, hadn't you, that night?"

"Perhaps I had. The most prudent girls aren't always prudent. What made you think of it now?"

Mrs. Slade seemed to have no answer ready. But after a moment she broke out: "Because I simply can't bear it any longer—!"

Mrs. Ansley lifted her head quickly. Her eyes were wide and very pale. "Can't bear what?"

"Why—your not knowing that I've always known why you went."

"Why I went—?"

"Yes. You think I'm bluffing, don't you? Well, you went to meet the man I was engaged to—and I can repeat every word of the letter that took you there."

While Mrs. Slade spoke Mrs. Ansley had risen unsteadily to her feet. Her bag, her knitting and gloves, slid in a panic-stricken heap to the ground. She looked at Mrs. Slade as though she were looking at a ghost.

"No, no—don't," she faltered out.

"Why not? Listen, if you don't believe me. 'My one darling, things can't go on like this. I must see you alone. Come to the Colosseum immediately after dark tomorrow. There will be some- body to let you in. No one whom you need fear will suspect'—but perhaps you've forgotten what the letter said?"

Mrs. Ansley met the challenge with an unexpected composure.

Steadying herself against the chair she looked at her friend, and replied: "No; I know it by heart too."

"And the signature? 'Only *your* D.S.' Was that it? I'm right, am I? That was the letter that took you out that evening after dark?"

Mrs. Ansley was still looking at her. It seemed to Mrs. Slade that a slow struggle was going on behind the voluntarily controlled mask of her small quiet face. "I shouldn't have thought she had herself so well in hand," Mrs. Slade reflected, almost resentfully. But at this moment Mrs. Ansley spoke. "I don't know how you knew. I burnt that letter at once."

"Yes; you would, naturally—you're so prudent!" The sneer was open now. "And if you burnt the letter you're wondering how on earth I know what was in it. That's it, isn't it?"

Mrs. Slade waited, but Mrs. Ansley did not speak.

"Well, my dear, I know what was in that letter because I wrote it!"

"You wrote it?"

"Yes."

The two women stood for a minute staring at each other in the last golden light. Then Mrs. Ansley dropped back into her chair. "Oh," she murmured, and covered her face with her hands.

Mrs. Slade waited nervously for another word or movement. None came, and at length she broke out: "I horrify you."

Mrs. Ansley's hands dropped to her knee. The face they uncovered was streaked with tears. "I wasn't thinking of you. I was thinking—it was the only letter I ever had from him!"

"And I wrote it. Yes; I wrote it! But I was the girl he was engaged to. Did you happen to remember that?"

Mrs. Ansley's head drooped again. "I'm not trying to excuse myself . . . I remembered. . . ."

"And still you went?"

"Still I went."

Mrs. Slade stood looking down on the small bowed figure at her side. The flame of her wrath had already sunk, and she wondered why she had ever thought there would be any satisfaction in inflicting so purposeless a wound on her friend. But she had to justify herself.

"You do understand? I'd found out—and I hated you, hated

you. I knew you were in love with Delphin—and I was afraid; afraid of you, of your quiet ways, your sweetness . . . your . . . well, I wanted you out of the way, that's all. Just for a few weeks; just till I was sure of him. So in a blind fury I wrote that letter . . . I don't know why I'm telling you now."

"I suppose," said Mrs. Ansley slowly, "it's because you've always gone on hating me."

"Perhaps. Or because I wanted to get the whole thing off my mind." She paused. "I'm glad you destroyed the letter. Of course I never thought you'd die."

Mrs. Ansley relapsed into silence, and Mrs. Slade, leaning above her, was conscious of a strange sense of isolation, of being cut off from the warm current of human communion. "You think me a monster!"

"I don't know. . . . It was the only letter I had, and you say he didn't write it?"

"Ah, how you care for him still!"

"I cared for that memory," said Mrs. Ansley.

Mrs. Slade continued to look down on her. She seemed physically reduced by the blow—as if, when she got up, the wind might scatter her like a puff of dust. Mrs. Slade's jealousy suddenly leapt up again at the sight. All these years the woman had been living on that letter. How she must have loved him, to treasure the mere memory of its ashes! The letter of the man her friend was engaged to. Wasn't it she who was the monster?

"You tried your best to get him away from me, didn't you? But you failed; and I kept him. That's all."

"Yes. That's all."

"I wish now I hadn't told you. I'd no idea you'd feel about it as you do; I thought you'd be amused. It all happened so long ago, as you say; and you must do me the justice to remember that I had no reason to think you'd ever taken it seriously. How could I, when you were married to Horace Ansley two months afterward? As soon as you could get out of bed your mother rushed you off to Florence and married you. People were rather surprised—they wondered at its being done so quickly; but I thought I knew. I had an idea you did it out of *pique*—to be able to say you'd got ahead of Delphin and me. Girls have such silly reasons for doing the most serious things. And your marrying so soon convinced me that you'd never really cared."

"Yes. I suppose it would," Mrs. Ansley assented.

The clear heaven overhead was emptied of all its gold. Dusk spread over it, abruptly darkening the Seven Hills. Here and there lights began to twinkle through the foliage at their feet. Steps were coming and going on the deserted terrace—waiters looking out of the doorway at the head of the stairs, then reappearing with trays and napkins and flasks of wine. Tables were moved, chairs straightened. A feeble string of electric lights flickered out. Some vases of faded flowers were carried away, and brought back replenished. A stout lady in a dust coat suddenly appeared, asking in broken Italian if anyone had seen the elastic band which held together her tattered Baedeker. She poked with her stick under the table at which she had lunched, the waiters assisting.

The corner where Mrs. Slade and Mrs. Ansley sat was still shadowy and deserted. For a long time neither of them spoke. At length Mrs. Slade began again: "I suppose I did it as a sort of joke—"

"A joke?"

"Well, girls are ferocious sometimes, you know. Girls in love especially. And I remember laughing to myself all that evening at the idea that you were waiting around there in the dark, dodging out of sight, listening for every sound, trying to get in—Of course I was upset when I heard you were so ill afterward."

Mrs. Ansley had not moved for a long time. But now she turned slowly toward her companion. "But I didn't wait. He'd arranged everything. He was there. We were let in at once," she said.

Mrs. Slade sprang up from her leaning position. "Delphin there? They let you in?—Ah, now you're lying!" she burst out with violence.

Mrs. Ansley's voice grew clearer, and full of surprise. "But of course he was there. Naturally he came—"

"Came? How did he know he'd find you there? You must be raving!"

Mrs. Ansley hesitated, as though reflecting. "But I answered the letter. I told him I'd be there. So he came."

Mrs. Slade flung her hands up to her face. "Oh, God—you answered! I never thought of your answering. . . ."

"It's odd you never thought of it, if you wrote the letter."

"Yes. I was blind with rage."

Mrs. Ansley rose, and drew her fur scarf about her. "It is cold here. We'd better go . . . I'm sorry for you," she said, as she clasped the fur about her throat.

The unexpected words sent a pang through Mrs. Slade. "Yes; we'd better go." She gathered up her bag and cloak. "I don't know why you should be sorry for me," she muttered.

Mrs. Ansley stood looking away from her toward the dusky secret mass of the Colosseum. "Well—because I didn't have to wait that night."

Mrs. Slade gave an unquiet laugh. "Yes; I was beaten there. But I oughtn't to begrudge it to you, I suppose. At the end of all these years. After all, I had everything; I had him for twenty-five years. And you had nothing but that one letter that he didn't write."

Mrs. Ansley was again silent. At length she turned toward the door of the terrace. She took a step, and turned back, facing her companion.

"I had Barbara," she said, and began to move ahead of Mrs. Slade toward the stairway.

&

For the Literary Traveler

The conversation of "Roman Fever" takes place on the JANICULUM HILL, accessible from Trastevere via a vigorous climb up Via Garibaldi, leading past the TEMPIETTO DI BRAMANTE and the fountain of the ACQUA PAOLA to the PASSEGGIATA DEL GIANICOLO and the famous views of Rome, especially of the PALATINE HILL: gazing down on its ancient FORUM and the COLOSSEUM (where Henry James's Daisy Miller caught a deadly strain of "Roman fever"), Mrs. Ansley and Mrs. Slade feel the stir of old erotic memories.

Wharton wrote this story in 1934 in the last years of her life (she died in 1937) at a time when, while visiting Rome, she showed a more than aesthetic interest in Roman Catholicism. She visited the early Christian CATACOMBS OF SAINT SEBASTIAN on the Via Appia Antica (the old Appian Way) still open to visitors. Her attendance at Mass in ST. PETER'S, SANTA MARIA SOPRA MINERVA and TRINITÀ DEI MONTI (at the top of the Spanish Steps), and her love of the Benedictine monks' Gregorian chant at SANT' ANSELMO on the AVENTINE (still a part of the 9:30 A.M. Sunday liturgy), made some friends suspect she was experiencing a religious conversion.

Though she never sought formal baptism, Wharton admired, as much as Catholic ritual, the intricacies of the Baroque, a kind of Counter-Reformation liturgy in stone. In *Italian Villas and Their Gardens* she names her favorite Roman examples. Like Elizabeth Bowen (see page 248), she knew well the VILLA BORGHESE, housing the MUSEUM OF SCULPTURE in which many masterpieces by Bernini are exhibited (*David, Apollo and Daphne*, the *Rape of Proserpine, Aeneas and Anchises*) as well as statues of the goddess Isis, the poet Sappho, and the biblical Susanna and the Elders. She loved, too, the vast BORGHESE GARDENS, a park of meadows, flowers, umbrella pines, oak groves, fountains, statues of Goethe and Byron, lovers, and families wheeling strollers and bicycles.

Eleanor Clark

The novelist (and wife of the novelist Robert Penn Warren), Eleanor Clark lived and traveled in Italy for many years. Her familiarity with Italian history and art, like her command of the language, has a fluency that has made her Rome and a Villa *(1952) one of the most respected books about the culture of place. Her chapter on "The Fountains of Rome," excerpted here, presents the communal space of the piazza—its play of water and people amidst the fixities of stone—as a metaphor of identity, a point where the private self encounters a larger human presence, and, losing separateness, changes. Cur-*

*rents of individuality and community converge, producing a new complex
wholeness and holiness. For an engaging dialogue with her vision, lovers of
fountains (and history) might also read Simon Schama's chapter "Streams of
Consciousness" in* Landscape and Memory. *Under his brilliant gaze, Bernini's
Fountain of the Four Rivers in the Piazza Navona comes alive as history and
autobiography. All his life, Bernini said, he felt he'd been* "un amici dell'
acqua" *(a friend of water). In Clark's view and in Schama's words, Navona,
as "the greatest water spectacle in any urban space in Europe" bears witness
to the exuberant friendship of artist, water, stone, and space, the unfailing
delight of travelers.*

FROM *ROME AND A VILLA*

FOUNTAINS

You walk close to your dreams. Sometimes it seems that these
pulsing crowds, with their daily and yearly rhythms established
so long ago none of it has to be decided any more, with their
elbows and knees and souls and buttocks touching and rubbing
and everybody most pleased and agreeable when it is like that, in a
bus for instance, will in another minute all be naked, or will have
fish tails or horses' behinds like the characters of the fountains. For
the Anglo-Saxon mind, ruled by conscience and the romantic, rigid
in its privacies, everything here is shocking—an endless revelation
and immersion; this is the vocabulary of our sleep; and the key
image is always water.

That is the great assault of Rome, and it is total and terrible. It is
really strange that foreigners of the polite centuries always used to
wax so romantic about the fountains of Rome, and the music supposed to represent them was such as any young girl could listen to.
The truth is, they are extremely indecent, in various ways. Their
number is indecent, much as the lives of the Caesars were;
common reason expires here; it is of their nature too to make those
lives quite ordinary, nothing surprises you beside them. Their settings are apt to be extravagant; they can have sprung up anywhere,
be tacked anywhere on the sides of buildings or are themselves a
whole house wall; and their details have the candid, smiling sadism

of dreams. But the worst is the life around them, and their part in it. They are not only memory, or the living singleness of time, though they are that too and the city would have fallen apart under the weight of its past a long time ago without them; this is easy to see; you notice at once when there is a drought and the fountains become quiet and stale, or empty, how old everything begins to look. But there is another unity or community within every single moment to which they are essential, and that is where the real outrage comes.

The romantic, the idealist, the tender-minded of any vein dies a thousand deaths in these fountains; their every dolphin is his nemesis.

The very genius spent on them makes them shocking. They are not *objets d'art* held off from life and treated with respect as they would be anywhere else; there is a closeness, an imminence of touch around them that nothing in our life has except dreams and sex, whence the awful burden on those. They are always being drunk from and splashed in and sat on, everybody dips into them as into his own private memory and quite often they have all kinds of rubbish in their lovely basins, because although the street cleaners of Rome are many and hard-working they cannot be everywhere at once.

The churches likewise; it is all physical and close; God is not up in any Gothic shadows but to be touched and smelled and fondled, reached into up to the armpit. The Anglo-Saxon, hunting everywhere for French cathedrals, feels his mind threatened like a lump of sugar in a cup of tea.

The spaces are shocking. They are close too, and give no warnings, so that suddenly the Pantheon or the huge volutes of Sant' Ignazio are crowding right over you; you are not allowed to stand off, it seems you are not allowed to admire at all; it is as though a giant mother were squashing you to her breast. Besides those freakish squares and the narrow streets around them, most vividly in the old quarters, Trastevere and all the part between the Corso and the Tiber, do not constitute an *outside* in our sense, but a great rich withinness, an interior, and running water is its open fire. Even a tourist can tell in a Roman street that he is in something and not

outside of something as he would be in most cities. In Rome to go
out is to go home.

There are no sidewalks in these sections. The walls rise from the
cobbles as from lagoons, only people are out all along them, under
the laundry which is a drastic exposure in itself, more than for any
Kinsey or Gallup, and unless they are playing football they are
most often mending something. That is one of three occupations
you see anywhere in Europe that are no longer known in America:
people walk, they carry, and they mend. Not only women; men are
mending too, in thousands of dark bicycle and mattress shops and
tiny individual foundries opening on to the same streets, and which
may be the family's windowless kitchen and bedroom as well.
What makes these streets Roman, and not those of any old European city, is the demonic energy that goes into everything, and the
divine disregard for any other form of life, especially in the football
players; also an element of miracle in the way the motorcycles and
other traffic get through, shooting straight from hell, without
anyone's changing his expression or pace or direction at all. . . .

The big spaces are distressing too. There is nothing French
about them, none of that spacious public elegance of the Place de
la Concorde or the views up past the Tuileries. Big Piazza del
Popolo, where the great political mass meetings are held among
trees and flowing streams and Egyptian tigers, was even designed
by a Frenchman, but the Roman look soon grew over it, like the
weeds and wild flowers in the crevices of its twin churches.

Piazza San Pietro, so splendidly reasonable as architecture, if you
forget the Via della Conciliazione, is not a place for reasonable individuals to stroll with a happy sense of partaking in the achievement
and somehow corresponding to it, as they would in such a square in
Paris. It is a place for people to congregate in the terrific force of
their gregariousness, their mass cravings, like cattle around a water-
hole; and when it is empty, when there is no saint being made or
other spectacle, it is lifeless: very admirable in its lines but cold, with
a hollow look, like the scene of a dream in which after standing with
a great crowd one has suddenly been left alone. But then as suddenly
you find it filled another way; another sequence has begun. It is a
sunny winter afternoon, and now even this enormous space has

become a living room, or public nursery. The Dome, announcing itself for miles around as the center of the world, is actually presiding like a hen over thousands of babies and mothers and lovers and very ancient people strewn all over the steps of Bernini's colonnade and the awesome area it encloses, not as if they owned it but really owning it. It is where they live. The fountains, those two high waving flags of world Catholicism, are as local as a barnyard pump. There is no distance; there is no awe of anything.

It is like a party all the time; nobody has to worry about giving one or being invited; it is going on every day in the street and you can go down or be part of it from your window; nobody eats alone in the cafeteria, reading a book. . . .

It is a deluge. You are in life way over your head, there is no getting out of it, except in the *beaux quartiers* which are not *beaux* at all but only pretentious; taste never functioned here on anything between the hovel and the grand palazzo. There are distances there but they are the result of a failure, not a natural way of being. Those sections are always sad and on the big party days, about a dozen a year though some percolate into a season of two or three weeks, seem marked more than ever with the black sign of the sickness of the middle class. The health of the city is elsewhere, around the fountains, where the private soul is in ceaseless disintegration; nothing is held back; the only secrecy is of the city itself.

Of course the fountains are not all for every purpose and time of day; it depends on the space. Piazza del Popolo is a fascinating crossroads, a place to sit a while, but far too big and unprotective really to live in; the little square around the lovely Tortoise Fountain is more like a back stoop. For general all-day use, but especially at l'ora della passeggiata and in the evening, two of the best are beautiful Piazza Navona with its three fountains—"godless Navona" the angry reformers of the Middle Ages called it—and the cobbled square of Santa Maria in Trastevere, which is not much less beautiful although only one of its buildings is a true palazzo. But the others are massive and handsome too, of a comfortable height, and have the weathered stucco colors of embers, ochre to rose, darker under the ledges, that are the characteristic ones of the city and help to give the walls their mysterious organic relation to people, nothing one could think of clearing away in a hurry. The main beauty of the piazza, as of most of the others, is that in spite of its superb proportions it seems not to have been planned but to have come about as a widening in a cow path does, so that nobody has that unpleasant feeling of doing what is expected of him, though in fact they are doing in nearly every detail what has been done in the same place for a great many generations. The fountain here is large and central, as it needs to be. It is not a sculptured one but a high impersonal form, a real flowing goblet, chattery but serene, which both fosters and absolves all the immense amount of *being*, being then and there, not waiting, not conceiving or imagining, that goes on around it. All water has an aspect of holy water; you feel it most strongly in these unfigured basins, not shooting up great rousing banners of liquid light as at Saint Peter's but the stiller ones, especially where life is so thick around them. The main feeling around this one is of a perpetual wiping out of experience; continuity is all in the water.

The church is essential in the same way. It was the first one dedicated to Mary and has kept the modest, authentic dignity of its great age beneath its tatters and strange accretions—or not so strange: there has been no serious change since the 12th Century square tower and mosaic across the façade. It gives the square its deep subtlety of color and line, and is part of its other spaciousness too, along with the moving water, and as a view of the mountains would be.

The place itself is voyage; that is why there is no restlessness. Neither is there anything for the tender heart, neither pity nor self-pity; for the delicate sensibility it is all scandal and continual death.

The most startling people are the children; no other Italians have quite that look. These are the boys painted by Caravaggio, with all the tough seductive wisdom of the city, the toying challenge miles beyond any illusion, in their eyes; painted sometimes, in their careless open shirts, as child saints, when all their sublimity is of the rock bottom. They have been spared nothing, nobody ever changed the subject when they came into the room; by the age of seven it seems there is no human temptation or degradation they have not walked through the boiling center of, no vice they have not made up their own minds about, and they can have the manners of mule drivers or of cardinals as they happen to choose; only they cannot dissemble; they have the appalling candor of all Rome, and when you see it in a child's face you do not know if you are looking at fish or at angels. You see something else in their eyes; it is themselves as very old men, then their children and great-grandchildren standing before you at the age of seven and of seventy or a hundred, all with the same two huge eyeballs looking at you in what might be a smile. . . .

It is in Pasquin's district, down across the Tiber in the neighborhood of another great fountain, that you find the truest Romans, though some will tell you that none are left in that category but the statue-wits Pasquin, Marforio and The Foot. "Noialtri siamo dei fessi. All the rest of us are horses' asses." The central fountain of this district is Bernini's one of the four rivers in Piazza Navona. Many of the streets around are named for guilds; they are of the butchers, the bakers, and so on, and at the trattorie you are likely to come on a tableful of carpenters or ironworkers having their evening wine. A peculiar thing is how often they are talking about Rome and themselves its inhabitants, in those terms; i romani, noialtri romani are like this or that, behave this way or that; there never was a city at the same time so unexclusive and so fascinated by its own character, although if it were threatened like Paris at the Marne it is hard to imagine that many Romans would willingly give up their motorcycles to help defend it. It would not seem very vital, and by the same token the 1943–44 German occupation, which was as vicious as anywhere else though in some ways no more galling than the French ones of the last century, left no sense of human breakage, none of that cracking and splintering that occurred in some places; and so the city was saved better than most after all; there were not even many collaborationists; it must have been maddening. . . .

The design of that fountain* is Bernini's. Other sculptors did the river figures, representing the Nile, the Ganges, the Danube and

*In Piazza Navona.

the Rio de la Plata, or the four corners of the world—good sign-
posts to the esoteric expansion of spirit in the baroque. Most of
their fingers were broken off by American soldiers for souvenirs
during the war and the replacements are a little whiter than the
rest. The favorite story about the fountain, referring to the rivalry
between Bernini and Borromini who designed the church alongside, is that the Plata is holding up his hand to keep the church
façade from falling on him and the Nile is hiding his head so as not
to see such a hideous building. Actually the church, though not
Borromini's best, does a good deal for the fountain in the way of
setting; so does Palazzo Madama, just visible on a parallel avenue
on the other side.

A few other fountains:

TORTOISE FOUNTAIN

At the edge of the Jewish quarter. Paths of royal gardens could
have been designed to lead to it, but its Romanness and half its
beauty are from the sudden little cobble-paved clearing it is in; one
thinks of the copies of such works put up in garden courts in the
Berkshires in the 1890's, and how sad they have become. This has
lost nothing. But it is alone in its genre in Rome, and too exquisite
to be Roman; the figures are the work of a Florentine. The life-size
bronze tortoises at the upper rim were removed for safety during
the German occupation. The water moves up in two or three ways
and down in three or four, through marble cockleshells and over
the gleaming bodies of the boys, whose lifted arms and raised
knees make opposing circular patterns through the water. The
problematic part is their smiles; they are almost exactly that of the
Mona Lisa; it is very striking.

FOUNTAIN OF THE PONTE SISTO

Formerly at the other end of that delightful bridge, at the head of
the Via Giulia; built by the architect of the Fontana Paola up the
hill. The shrine theme again, but this is more strictly a shrine, and
really it is not very beautiful but it is tall and necessary and gives an
impression of the beautiful. There is a crescent piazza there which
is the formal anteroom or visitors' entrance to Trastevere and this
requires a particular dignity of water; however there is another

such water-shrine at the back of the district, where it is only a road-side one; like the Madonna, they could be anywhere. In this one water falls the full length of the recess, among monster heads and portaled by Ionic columns, a grave and pleasant concept, which has lent itself to various pompous imitations, notably in the fascist era. There is one parody of it, still with the imprint of the ripped-off fasci, out toward the Baths of Caracalla.

A large number of Christian martyrs were thrown off the adjacent bridge. . . .

For the Literary Traveler

In the narrow Roman streets winding off in all directions from the fountains and piazzas Eleanor Clark describes, whoever loves meandering and surprise will find the most exquisite satisfaction.

On the way in from the Corso to PIAZZA NAVONA, the ancient neighborhood west of it invites exploration. Begin just off the Corso on Via di San Pantaleo, on the left side of PALAZZO BRASCHI (the Museo di Roma). In the small PIAZZA PASQUINO stands the statue of Pasquino, a stone torso to which politically conscious citizens have for centuries attached comments expressing their contempt of a corrupt status quo. Art and antiques workshops/galleries line the narrow Via del Governo Vecchio, which winds past splendid palazzos through the PIAZZA DELL'OROLOGIO with Borromini's clock tower, eventually opening out (you might need the help of the *Nuova Pianta di Roma*—New Map of Rome) into Piazza Navona and its glorious fountains.

Then, to the east of Piazza Navona, along the streets clustering around the PANTHEON and the fountain in PIAZZA DELLA ROTONDA, one comes upon the tucked away treasures of PIAZZA SAN EUSTACHIO and, nearby, the church of SANTA MARIA SOPRA MINERVA in which works of Michelangelo, the bodies of Fra' Angelico and St. Catherine of Siena, and the frescoed narratives of the Annunciation and Mary's Assumption give the interior a sense of real presences. In lodgings on the jumbled streets behind the Pantheon, the nineteenth-century

American writer Constance Fenimore Woolson set her sad stories about a woman painter ("The Street of the Hyacinth") and a writer ("Miss Grief"), reflecting the writer's problematic friendship with Henry James. Via di Seminario leads further east of the Pantheon into the lovely PIAZZA DI SANT'IGNAZIO, "Rome's most perfect little outdoor 'drawing room,'" in the words of Elizabeth Bowen.

Radiating from the corners of the small PIAZZA MATTEI and the exquisite TORTOISE FOUNTAIN (FONTANA DELLE TARTARUGHE)—the most beloved fountain in the city for some cognoscenti—across or south of the Corso and the Largho Argentina, are streets leading to the serenity of PIAZZA CAMPITELLI and the church of SANTA MARIA IN CAMPITELLI (honoring Mary as healer), the vines of PIAZZA MARGANA, and down the hill along VIA SANT'ANGELO IN PESCHERIA to the medieval and labyrinthine byways of the GHETTO where the Jews were segregated after 1556. Portions of Elsa Morante's powerful novel *History* are set in this neighborhood during the years of the Nazi occupation. The SYNAGOGUE, one of the monumental landmarks of the Roman skyscape, welcomes visitors and worshippers. Just across from it is the ancient bridge leading to ISOLA TIBERINA where Margaret Fuller, lover of freedom, nursed the wounded in 1849 (See page 197). Bearing right from the Synagogue along the peaceful LUNGOTEVERE CENCI, the enchanted itinerary of Eleanor Clark's piazzas and fountains leads to and across PONTE SISTO, into Trastevere, and another fountain. But by now the secret is clear: there are rays upon rays of treasure—ancient, medieval, and modern—extending outwards from every fountain in the city. Tracing their routes on foot is one of the chief pleasures of time in Rome.

Elizabeth Bowen

To this Dublin-born writer of Anglo-Irish parentage, Rome is, quite simply, the Beloved. Bowen gathered her impressions over a period of three months, mostly on foot—the best way to explore the city (though the public transportation system is quite efficient)—as she describes in these pages. Author of the masterpiece The Death of the Heart *(1938) and many other novels, Elizabeth Bowen ends her learned portrait,* A Time in Rome *(1959), with a cry of the heart: "My darling, my darling, my darling." Visitors/readers similarly* inamorata *will understand.*

FROM *A TIME IN ROME*

THE SMILE

To the sun Rome owes its underlying glow, and its air called golden—to me, more the yellow of white wine; like wine it raises agreeability to poetry. One remembers the glow as a constant, the city as a succession of bright distances—there can be blindness to what is harsh or hideous, sprawlingness, raggedness at the edges. There can be days when the eye appeases the ear, diverting it somehow from noisiness—Rome, less excruciating than Paris or Madrid, has inevitably its hell's cauldrons, such as the Piazza Barberini, but I have known those to be endurable, if only for the pleasure of getting out of them: round any corner may be a sudden hush. The February, March and April I was there, winter was like spring, spring like summer. A mild year, everybody remarked. February, almond and judas trees fluffed the Borghese and other gardens with pink and purple; pavements gave off what (to me, coming from the Atlantic) was almost a Mediterranean glare; soil was hard underfoot, and flags out or washing drying flicked at the sunshine like tinted fires. This, a wintry version of what was still in store, acted on me like an extra season grafted into the calendar, a bonus. By April I found myself thinking twice, round noon, about any ascent of steps—roses began; round me buildings deepened from blonde to honey. While it lasts, such weather seems everlasting.

But there is no constant, rather a range of changes which are extreme, theatrical. (The only neutral I know of is a drained-away day, such as that of my February arrival, when the sky fades over a Rome fatigued and unreal.) There are onslaughts which have the character of reprisals—such as when, under an iron cloud-ceiling, grit begins by blowing in weird puffs, then gales mount up into ferocity, spattering bent fountains, clawing at awnings, ruffling the dull Tiber, dementing the shutters on their hooks. My first Sunday, wind wrenched a glass transome out of a public building and dashed it on to the street across the way, all but decapitating a pair of lovers. Rome has also an anti-weather which makes for lassitude, through heaviness, or tension—nothing is more ominous than when clouds pile up, fulvous and inky, behind livid buildings on the hills. Thunder grumbles more angrily here than elsewhere. Rain crashes down so hard that it rebounds, making everything dark, clammy and stuffy indoors or out; there may be Venice-like reflections in the watery tarmac, and rain is to be admired inside the Pantheon, where, falling through the round aperture in the top of the dome, it forms a diaphanous central pillar, running away at the base through the slots cut for it. Otherwise, nothing is so demoralizing, unedifying and indeed dangerous as a Roman wet day: everything goes slippery underfoot, traffic makes lunges at you half-blindedly, for on streaming windscreens wipers cannot work fast enough. Write off such a day, if you can afford to: settle for a cinema, or, in a corner of a café, puzzle over the blank back pages of a neglected diary. The insides of many churches you deem this an opportunity to visit will be blotted out. As for museums and galleries, those merit better than to be resorts or refuges, surely?

Yet nothing is more quickly forgotten than a Roman wet day. It vanishes like a quickly-retrieved mistake—one which has been, anyway, out of character. Sometimes in the middle of a night I have been wakened by rain stopping: when one has fallen asleep to it, one misses it. Most often, it is over in time for sunset—then, pavements steam up into the long, late rays; in the sunshot aftermath stone, stucco and ironwork glisten as though new-varnished, and the final drip-drops from trees and balconies flash like trembling prisms before falling. Colour comes rushing back, to be caught up in this burst of compensatory brilliance before nightfall. Air smells of gutters and gardens, sodden newspapers, shellac, refreshed dust. Quite soon, nobody coming indoors will leave behind them a wet footprint. An hour later, rain is a finished story.

How can Rome, with this physical volatility, be tragic? Enact tragedy, yes; live it out, no. So many disavowals, inconstancies, changes of face! One comes to see something climatic about history. In spite of all the monuments, busts and statues, inscriptions on the arches, I had the sense, often, of being in a city of oblivion. Or does Rome wear this carelessness like an outer coat? I doubt it: there can be a saturation-point with regard to feeling, an instinctive reaction against memory—could one wonder, here, if those had been reached? Yet, for centuries of the generality of people, *was* feeling more than that of the moment? The gravity, the passion for the conception, the resoluteness that forged Rome into Roman-ness, one must associate with the great few, the minority who stood out against the undertow—successive legislators, administrators, writers and orators, campaigners. Those gave scale to the Roman destiny. Uncompromisingness created a moral pattern; to be of the *élite* was to bear its stamp. The rest, the others, being voluble and fickle were also malleable; to the point required they could be worked on. Rome knows tragedies, but they were individual; there is a stone-coldness about great Roman thought, alone in the warm weather of the senses. As things went, the worst happened so many times: was there not to come to be something saving about the general fluidity of the temperament, its rebounds, its power to throw off violences and distresses by forgetting them? Often has fire consumed Rome; it would appear that grief never has—were history felt, could it be survived? There have been all but incredible recoveries. The overall of Rome is the golden glow. . . .

* *

It becomes Rome to be open to the sun, open to the eye. One rejoices in positive spaces, like giant ballrooms, connected by corridors of perspective. The longer the distances to look down, the greater the pleasure. This is realized by "Sistine" Rome, which, extending from the Esquiline to the Quirinal, also to the Pincian, is so called because it was evolved by Pope Sixtus V (1585–1590). One marvels at how much this inspired man carried out within so short a reign—one must think, he rushed into being, once come to power, what he had had in mind most of his life. Also this particular time of his accession presented him with an idealist's opportunity: Rome, devastated in 1527 by the Imperial rabble armies and the incendiarism witnessed by Cellini, cried out for reconstruction and re-embellishment. Restoration was needed by pride laid low. By no means all of the city had been wiped out—note the happy escape of the Via Giulia so near the embattled riverfront, the early-Renaissance palaces of the Campus Martius, and churches everywhere; but all Rome had felt the blow to morale. The Esquiline-Quirinal area would appear to have been among those surviving, for Sixtus V began by sweeping away medieval streets which, otherwise, would have balked his project. (He had what is yearned for by city-planners: absolute, ungainsayable authority.) Sistine Rome, therefore, did not replace earlier glories gone up in smoke; it was an addition, eloquent and timely.

Since 1527, there had begun and ended the lengthy Council of Trent; with, as outcome, re-definition and affirmation of the Church of Rome's lately-challenged authority. Charles V's somewhat guarded attempt to gain hearing for the forces of Reformation, from whom he might, in return, again be glad of support, had been foiled at the outset. It did emerge, however, that the strengthened Vatican must be above reproach; laxities and resultant scandals were not any longer to be countenanced. Secular magnificence, accorded, was to link with spiritual austerity. Sixtus V, as Pope, perfectly answered this fresh requirement: only in one particular did he not conform. Rome of the late sixteenth century and of the century to follow was the Rome of the counter-reformation; with that, the architectural association is Baroque—Sixtus V still thought on other lines; his tastes preserved the classicism of the Renaissance. He was for the stretching, the aerial and the uphill. Planning, he launched streets as one might let off arrows. He so built as never to be oppressive. Sistine Rome is to be thought of as a beautiful, geometrical spiders-web, spun from hilltop to hilltop. The web dips in the middle, but without slackening or losing pattern. On the Esquiline side, it takes in two great basilicas of the Lateran and Santa Maria Maggiore: these, we are caused to see from as many angles and distances as possible.

Sistine Rome has stood up, where need be, to modern pressure. Organically part of a living city, it has in places assented to business centres, shopping vortexes, and streets widened for heavy commercial traffic. But in what still is the greater part, little of the character has been forfeited. Sistine lay-out survives where buildings do not; elsewhere, tracts seem in a conspiracy to remain as they are, at whatever cost—I fancy, sometimes a high one. And, walking through the area's whole extent, one finds oneself ending as one began, in considered spaciousness.

You begin upon an elating, enormous plateau, the sun-polished Piazza di San Giovanni in Laterano—having ascended to it (let us imagine) by a street of the same name, from the Colosseum. You enter the *piazza* at one corner—each time I did so, I caught a breath. You behold the obelisk, highest in the world, oldest in Rome, whose shadow, were you to stay and watch, could be seen to move round the day like a single clock-hand. The openness you confront is in shape irregular, being cut into by the Lateran Palace, now museum, which protrudes from and hides the flank of the church. One of the church's impressive entrances is in an enclave between the palace and the baptistry. San Giovanni itself, Rome's second cathedral, acts, from here, chiefly, on the imagination—its major portico faces another way, and seems to me to belong to another picture. The Piazza's other side is bonded by a line of assorted buildings; rival cafés invite you. Here and there occur gaps which are heads of streets—Via Merulana, the first you come to, you take.

Merulana, today somewhat drab, was a masterpiece leadthrough of Sixtus V's—in whose time it was known as the Via Gregoriana.

Framed at its end, small with distance but nearer with every step, is a segment of Santa Maria Maggiore, and the wonderful church as a whole waits to reward you. I suggest that, having reached it, you walk straight through—in at the near door, out again at the far. (By "straight" I do not, as you will understand, mean hurriedly, blindly or disrespectfully: how long you stay, *en route*, and how much you absorb, this time, of Santa Maria's glimmering marble interior is for you to say. Simply, I mean "straight" in terms of the walk.) The church is an elevated island in a sea of traffic—emerging from it, standing in the doorway, you gaze across into the Piazza del Esquilino, set back in a comparative hush. Out of the centre-back end of the Esquilino opens a street: yours—now you have ahead of you Sixtus V's lengthiest arrow-shot. In spite of name-changes along its course, this street is unbroken in continuity, for exactly how great a distance I cannot say. It can hypnotize by its scenic risings-and-fallings, its never-deflectedness, its unendingness. Beginning as the Via Depretis, it becomes (after one busy intersection) the Via Quattro Fontane; finally, after its dip down toward the Piazza Barberini it goes up the Pincian hill as the Via Sistina. Where that comes out, at the Trinità dei Monti, you are again at a height. The greater part of Rome stretches below you: you have been carried to the head of the Spanish Steps.

Another plateau tops Rome's highest hill, the Quirinal. This area, though it may be reached from below, is best entered from the Via Quattro Fontane, at the point marked by the "Four" fountains. Turn down the corridor which is the Via del Quirinale—discreet, full of official silence, often empty but for the pacing sentries, overlooked by the half-shuttered flank of the palace; with, across the way, Bernini's oval gem of a church, Sant' Andrea (not in the Sistine picture) together with a stretch of the formal gardens to which much of this high ground is given over. Though you see ahead of you, there is to be a suddenness about the entire burst of sky, Rome and space which is the Piazza del Quirinale—which is why I say, enter at one corner. This is another "ballroom," launched out, at an angle, over the city. On its outer sides, there is nothing but a low balustrade.

The great floor tips downward (which, now I think of it, would be a dancing problem). At the top, gaze fixed on far-off St. Peter's, is the Palazzo del Quirinale—long, low, the façade keeps its initial simplicity, though Sixtus V's successors did what they could to variegate or adorn it, adding an end tower, a Bernini portal. The building is of a yellow no other Roman yellow approaches; it has a melon underglow. This *piazza* atones by colour, and dazzlingness, for what it lacks in order—as to the latter, it is inferior to the Laterano. Awkwardly close together, its major ornaments look like objects dumped, at random, out on the floor during a house-cleaning. They comprise two colossal statues, one obelisk, one fountain with extra-capacious basin. The Dioscuri—Castor and Pollux, each with his rearing steed—were, at the outset, brought by Sixtus V from the near-by remains of the Baths of Constantine, and here "placed" with the usual Sistine flair, their bases the ideal distance apart. So far, so good. But a later Pope, less inspired, fancied the fountain dug from the Roman Forum, and succeeded in having its scalloped granite lip shoved up as close as possible to the Dioscuri, on the palace side. The effect, still bearable, may be seen in the painting of the Piazza del Quirinale by Gaspar van Wittel (1647–1736). Nagel's guide-book attributes the error to Pius VII, but that Pope's dates were 1800–1823, so we have as counter-evidence the Van Wittel picture. Pius VI (1775–1799) is charged—in *this* case, dependably?—with the obelisk. His eye having lit upon one to spare, in the Mausoleum of Augustus, he had it hauled here, and caused its substantial pediment to be wedged between the bases of the twin statues. You cannot, the good man may have thought, go wrong with an obelisk. You can. Monumental chaos remains a monument to inability to let well alone.

These and other not always happy Papal attentions and additions to the Quirinal are accounted for by its having been the summer residence of the Popes, up to the changes of 1870. From then, up to the deposition of Italy's King Umberto, it was, as we all know, the Royal palace; since 1946, it has been the residence of the President of the Italian Republic. Indifferent, as must be any great theatre, to the changing portent of dramas played upon its stage, it continues to offer setting for ceremonials. What I think of, when I look at the yellow palace, is, that it was here, while there were still only the Dioscuri, alone in colossal innocence under the windows, that

Sixtus V died. God is praised in His works, praised in the instrumentality He has given man. Sixtus V brought Rome's extravagant distances and bewildering contours into a discipline which is beautiful. Art harmonizes. His *piazze* add wonder and size to daylight by containing it—so do lakes to water—and in the joy set up one's spirit dances like David before the Lord. Nor was this all; he re-erected obelisks, bestowing them where the Rome reincarnating itself beneath his eyes came to require that they should be (Piazza di San Pietro, Piazza del Popolo, Piazza di San Giovanni in Laterano, or where you will) and arriving each time at miraculous rightness in the relation between the height reached and the space dominated. (The nerve-cracking tensity of the operation, the actual getting into the perpendicular of the huge thing, hauled to the spot, recumbently waiting, is borne in by the St. Peter's story or legend—the enjoined silence, death to be the penalty for the onlooker who so much as caught a breath or whispered a word, the sailor's irrepressible cry of warning, the wetted ropes . . .)* Further, Sixtus V brought in, or rather brought back, water, partly repairing, partly diverting, one of the many derelict ancient aqueducts of the Campagna, so that flow was resumed from the hills around Palestrina to feed Sistine-Roman fountains, twenty-seven in all. The play of aquatic plumes in front of St. Peter's, triumphantly misting the colonnades, is the most spectacular of his living memorials (water lives, stone not) but the naive Esquiline fountains are the most intimate: the laughed-at Moses statue, the beaming lions commemorate a metaphorical striking of the rock—here the water-giver stood watching the first gush. He had been of humble birth, a country lad, Felice Peretti: the name was his throughout his years in the Church, till old age saw him Sixtus V. The waters piped into this part of Rome are therefore called the Aque Felice: it is likely that the people in general honoured him more for this benefit than for any other. . . .

Above ground, pleasure and palaces. . . . One or another desire or curiosity shaped my courses for runs of days. The pursuit through Rome of one artist, such as Bernini, or tracking down of the vestiges

*The sailor who cried out *"Acqua alle funi"* was not executed. Sixtus V awarded his family with the privilege of supplying St. Peter's with palms on Palm Sunday.

of some epoch, or search for the answer to some enigma exciting or troubling to my mind, but not, it seemed, to anyone else's— anything of that sort could be enough to keep me zigzagging about the city, not so much at random as might appear. What meant little yesterday could be a clue today. A hunt, with the disregard for everything else that it sets up, is itself pleasure. Nor does one know where one may not be landed up—I got to know Rome as a hunter gets to know country. Equally, there were moods, which I gave way to. A relationship cannot stand still; there are phases and develop- ments and it may be setbacks in one's having to do with a place, par- ticularly if it be Rome. As for going about, I know I do not care for being conducted, for more than a few steps or a few minutes, how- ever well. Nothing, that is to say no one, can be such an inexorable tour-conductor as one's own conscience or sense of duty, if one allows either the upper hand: the self-bullying that goes on in the name of sightseeing is grievous. Fatigue, rebellious distaste due to satiation, may ruin Rome for you—should *you* lay Rome in ruins over again? Enjoy yourself, I say—having in mind that there is always the matter of learning how to. This book is not even my foot- note to your guide-book; it is my scribblings on the margins of mine. I claim to be little help to anyone else.

It seemed to me hopeless to make a methodical round of all Rome's churches. I admired many simply for their façades; I entered, and very often, the same few, and those less on account of the merits for which they might be starred than because they drew me. Some meant journeys, others grew dear through familiarity, from being in parts of Rome where I often found myself. Those in which I spent most time were, Santa Maria in Cosmedin, down by the Tiber, not far from the foot of the Aventine; San Gregorio, overlooking the street of that name, which runs under a flank of the Palatine to the Arch of Constantine; Santa Sabina, on top of the Aventine; Santa Maria in Domenica (or, dell Navicella) on top of the Caelian, with in front of it the small marble ship; Santa Maria Maggiore; St. Peter's; Sant' Andrea del Quirinale; San Giovanni in Porta Latina, near the gate of that name, peacefully shaded by an enormous cedar; San Pietro in Vincoli, on the Esquiline near the Via Cavour, up alleys and flights of steps, containing the Michelangelo Moses. I went into more

others than I can number; I name only those I cannot forget. Three
(each, it happens, unique in beauty) are set apart by their hidden-
ness—these are "secret" churches, to be sought as one seeks for a
cabinet's secret drawer: Santi Quattro Coronati, back behind two
deep courtyards, themselves led to by out-of-the-way streets, uphill
off the Via San Giovanni in Laterano, on your right as you walk from
the Colosseum; ancient Santa Prassede, darker inside than most,
tucked away off the Via Merulana at the Santa Maria Maggiore end;
and Santa Costanza, circular, having within it Rome's oldest known
Christian, also most lyrical, mosaics. Santa Costanza lies at the back
of another church, Sant' Agnese fuori le Mure, whose claims it (for
me) unfairly eclipses; the two are in an enclave off the populous Via
Nomentana. A "horror" church is San Stefano Rotondo, on the
Caelian, close to the Navicella: it has frescoes, photographic in detail,
of unspeakable tortures suffered by Christian martyrs. Too much
more has happened since last I saw them, in the days of my youth;
this time the church, in a state of prolonged repair, was closed—
should it perhaps remain so? One which, within, resembles a music-
room, pretty, secular-looking (but for its apse mosaics) and a shade
prim, is Santa Cecilia in Trastevere: this marks the site of the saint's
home and somewhat inhuman young married life, and one still sees
her atrium, now a courtyard quartered into beds of virginal lilies. She
is not, for some reason, my favourite saint, but the place offers
pleasant shelter from Trastevere dust-storms.

Many Baroque façades tend to run into one in my memory—
wrongly, for no two are really alike. In retrospect, I cannot distinguish between (for instance) Sant' Andrea della Valle, San Mar-
cello, Sant' Agostino, Santa Maria della Vittoria, San Carlino alle
Quattro Fontane, though I could tell you the site on which each is
found. Sant' Ignazio (just off the Corso) I would not fail to identify,
for this reason: the tiny *piazza* it commands is architected in elegant
unity with the church's frontage: here is Rome's most perfect little
outdoor "drawing-room"—as distinct from ballroom—in which, at
a restaurant table under an awning, one may while away hours of
noon or evening. (A major drawing-room is the Piazza del Popolo.)
In the main, my liking was wedded to what is simple—such as
Santa Maria della Pace's semi-circular portico, on the Campus

Martius. Exception, the glorious virtuosity of Sant' Agnese in
Agonia, Borromini's façade on the Piazza Navona—dome flanked
by pillared campanili, doorway sadly blocked from the eye by the
"Rivers" fountain. In much of Rome one is hampered, in the
taking-in of effect, by crowdedness; seldom is one seeing from far
away. How immense the gain may be if one can and does, how
enhanced may be noble theatricality, is shown by San Giovanni in
Laterano—which launches its statue-topped portico into the air
from the head of ascent after ascent of lawns and steps; visible for
miles, this is one of Rome's dominant silhouettes.

One Roman pleasure, I found, is the holiday from Rome to be
had in gardens. Apart from the Pincian and the Borghese, many are
open to you and me—public. Private they formerly were, and they
still seem so. Ownership now goes to whoever loves them. Nothing
is stone in them but the benches, the fountain-basins, the statues
mysteriously located in glades, by grottoes, or at the turns of leafy
serpentine walks. Your few living companions are in worlds of
their own—lovers, fingertips touching, pause by the pools seriously
to contemplate their reflections, as though being photographed;
old people sit in dignity in the sun; infants totter and children play
with an absorption which keeps them all but silent. . . .

What many people remember about the Aventine is the magnificent, iron-plated locked gate through whose keyhole you obtain
the keyhole-shaped, minute view of St. Peter's. But elsewhere the
hill is more generous: alongside Santa Sabina is the gladelike Parco
Savello, garden in feeling, with nothing beyond its parapet but sky.
I associate the Savello with singing birds, the columnar lines of the
slender trees, and reposefulness—here in so green a space, at so
great a height, above Rome. . . .

While I stand and regard it, the indifference to myself shown by a
work of art in itself is art. In Rome, I was more drawn to statues
than paintings. But, whether it was a statue or a painting, I came
to recognize first a disturbance and then a lessening of the confusion within me as I beheld. Partly there was a liberation from the
thicket of the self, partly some equivalent of St. Paul's sensation of

scales falling from the eyes. In Rome, it was extraordinary how I woke up in the mornings to realize how much was near me, how near the edges of vision I had been sleeping. When it came to going round some of the churches and galleries to say good-bye, I found the saddest good-byes to be, sometimes, those to things I had loved more for my reasons than for their own. Perhaps "love" settles more quickly on what is mortal, rather than immortal? What I cared for now, I might not care for so much if I came back again—*if* I came back again? There, in the Villa Borghese, I faced it that I might in a sense be looking my last on the snarl of David, twisted by the instant before the letting go of the sling, or that other Bernini, Daphne writhing within the clutch at once of Apollo and her metamorphosis—while you watch, bark rushes up her thighs and her twig-fingers separate into leaves. But there need be no end to the shimmer of the rooms' ever-reflecting floors, the marble halls in which one has the right to dream that one dwells. The halls, the galleries—whatever they were called, Vatican, Borghese, Conservatori, however far apart they might be in Rome—ran together into the unbroken chain which had led me, and had led others and would lead others, on and on, in and out of the many Romes. So what matter? All the same, I looked out of a Borghese window at the flowers in the garden and began to cry.

After Easter, there were two more Sundays, the second my last. Before that, I had the honour of being taken by a friend to the Beatification, in St. Peter's, of the Christian Chinese martyrs, massacred during the Boxer rising. There were more people than, seeing St. Peter's empty, one could have pictured even it capable of holding. Not only length and width but great parts of the inconceivable height were thronged, tiers upon tiers of galleries having been constructed. Half the lights in the world were already blazing, hanging in torrents from the roof, clustered against the carmine brocades clothing the columns, when on the ungated river of congregation we surged in, scaled to our places, waited. Then, to a burst of music—organ and silver trumpets— the other half of the lights in the world blazed out. The Pope's procession was moving up the aisle. Before Pius XII was carried a scarlet spiked tree of gladioli. This was his first other than brief appearance after the long bout of illness he had fought: no so tumultuous and rejoicing a wave of love of thousands for one could ever have been imagined breaking, gathering up again, again breaking. Nothing could contain it. Drowning the loudening organ, the clapping and crying aloud went on and on, as Pius XII was borne slowly forward to the high altar, turning to bless us from side to side.

The last Sunday was very blue all day, very hot all night. The yellow of evening brightened on the upper parapets of the Pincio, making the dusk in the Piazza del Popolo below by contrast bluer and, though watery-clear, mysterious. Above, many coloured balloons afire with sun could be seen trailing against the sky, and a band was playing—loudly enough for those who preferred to circulate down in the *piazza* to be able to do so, also, to music. As shadow travelled up the face of the Pincio, I also climbed the ramps and staircases to the festive terrace, to continue moving restlessly about. By now I was anxious to be gone, so as to have going away over. Crossing the gravel to an empty table, I sat down, soon to find myself drinking something I had never drunk, a glassful of some sort of coloured syrup. The waiter had misunderstood my order. Dust from the trodden gravel was filling the summery, tired air: as evening deepened, ilexes ran together ahead of it into the ink of midnight. Lovers wandered away from parties, deeper into the glades to await darkness, in which, when it came, their presences would be felt in the zones between lamps wakening in branches. I walked to the bridge spanning the deep gulch, one side of it the Aurelian Wall, between the Pincio and Borghese gardens, and looked over. Under me passed cars returning to Rome, people with elbows out of the open windows in what was already an August languor.

Two days later I left, taking the afternoon train to Paris. As before, I had too much baggage to go by air. Such a day, when it does come, has nothing particular about it. Only from the train as it moved out did I look at Rome. Backs of houses I had not ever seen before wavered into mists, stinging my eyes. My darling, my darling, my darling. Here we have no abiding city.

❧

For the Literary Traveler

Elizabeth Bowen's explorations of Rome have a graceful, meditative rhythm; in actual fact, they can easily be followed on foot. The pattern of SISTINE ROME etched so elegantly in her pages makes for a delightful, if arduous, walking tour: from ST. JOHN'S LATERAN, down and up the leafy MERULANA, to SANTA MARIA MAGGIORE; then down the ESQUILINE along Via Depretis and Via delle Quattro Fontane (bearing left at the FOUR FOUNTAINS crossroads along Via Venti Settembre to the PIAZZA DE QUIRINALE—glorious under floodlights at night), and then returning to the crossroads and the descent of the Esquiline. (One block down the Esquiline hill from the Four Fountains, to the left of Palazzo Barberini is VIA RASELLA where partisans attacked and killed ten Nazi soldiers during the German occupation in 1944, leading to the massacre of 335 civilians at Ardeatine Fosse. In the Via Ardeatina on the outskirts of the city along the Via Appia Antica, the atrocity is memorialized in the ARDEATINE CAVES—FOSSE—Rome's monument of the Holocaust and the Italian Resistance. Eleanor Clark calls it "the most moving war memorial in Europe.")

Sistine Rome continues across Piazza Barberini (past Bernini's FONTANA DEL TRITONE), following VIA SISTINA for the ascent to TRINITÀ DEI MONTI and then the promenade along the walls of the PINCIAN HILL (passing the VILLA MEDICI—now the French Academy, where musicians practice under open windows) up to the terrace of the PIAZZALE NAPOLEONE on the Pincian Hill. Its splendid views of the always wonderful PIAZZA DEL POPOLO below and ST. PETER'S DOME and all of Rome in the distance corroborate, like everything else along this long route, Bowen's perception of the "smile" of the mortal city.

Some of the "hidden" churches she loves occur along this route of Sistine Rome. Behind Santa Maria Maggiore on Via Santa Prassede is the church of SANTA PRASSEDE, named for the early Christian woman Praxedes, the daughter of the Roman Senator Pudens who knew and entertained St. Peter on the site of the church of SANTA PUDENZIANA, a few blocks further down the Esquiline, bearing left onto Via Urbana. In Santa Prassede's well-known CHAPEL OF ST. ZENO are ancient images of women saints and leaders. On its left wall are the mosaics of four female images. Of special interest is the image of Theodora "Episcopa" crowned with the square nimbus. Karen Jo Torjesen argues in her book *When Women Were Priests* that this mosaic square is evidence that women acted as bishops in the early church. (Clerical tour guides omit Theodora from the details on St. Zeno's walls that they point out to tourists.) Southwest of the Esquiline, at the foot of the Circus Maximus and the Aventine, the church of SANTA MARIA IN COSMEDIN incorporates another ancient structure, an early Christian welfare center—a *diaconia*—where the poor, the sick, and the dispossessed found food, clothing, and shelter.

Bowen's portraits of Rome's public gardens include the lovely PARCO SAVELLO, a few minutes walk up the hill from Santa Maria in Cosmedin, high on the AVENTINE HILL, next to the fifth-century Dominican church of SANTA SABINA and down the street from the famous keyhole on PIAZZA DEI CAVALIERI DI MALTA. Parco Savello is a "gladelike" space, full of singing birds at twilight, orange trees, children, and the sky over the Tiber, the green Janiculum, and the domes of the city, flaming sunlight.

Elizabeth Spencer

Eudora Welty describes her fellow Mississippian Elizabeth Spencer as "a kind of smiling sibyl," writing fiction of "width, depth, and shapeliness." Her settings range from her native South to Venice, Florence, Rome, and Montreal. In the Introduction to her best-known novel, The Light in the Piazza, *a love story in which the chiaroscuro of Florence is a main character, she remembers her first encounter with the country that also figures as the romantic center of the story set in Rome, "The White Azalea." "There's a second country for everybody," she says, "one way or another. First and last, for me it was Italy."*

FROM *THE LIGHT IN THE PIAZZA*

INTRODUCTION

The first time I saw Italy was in August of 1949, and I was half-asleep. It was the third, final month of my first summer abroad, my first trip to Europe. I had undertaken the venture on the modest proceeds of my first novel and the invitation from a close friend to visit her in Germany, where she had been working for three years with the American occupation. Except for a happy time I had spent in Paris while waiting for my permit to enter Germany, I had had so far little to rejoice about. To my friend and her fiancé, who tried their best to see that I "had a good time," I must have seemed hopelessly uninitiated to the moral rigors of postwar Europe. To them I must have been like a chirpy sparrow, flitting by accident through the horrors of a Max Ernst painting. I can see that now. My country training, for instance, had made me view all visits as a little like house parties—a bad mistake. While they worked daily in their government offices, in cloudy Bad Nauheim, I hung around the empty apartment a friend of theirs had lent me, reading, or walked in the village, knowing scarcely a word of German. I shivered at the pool. What, besides the temperature, was the difference between this and a dull summer in some little Southern town? There, at least, friends might call and come. I took to riding horses at a local stable, and so met a young Viennese who began to ask me out. He, too, was at loose ends, waiting for a work permit. My friends rose up with disapproval and suspicion. Who was he? What did he want? Mississippi old maids a dozen years back had cut up this way. I had to give up a pleasant friendship. My friends had worked in Nuremberg during the trials, and in this and many other episodes, they must have been right, as my life so far, they pointed out, had not got me prepared for things there.

All miseries end. This one ended for us all three when my pass ran out. I had a month to spend somewhere. What to do? Drearily (Germany had got to me, too) I agreed that the best choice was Italy. There might at least, I thought, be some sun. I came down on the night train to Milan.

Sun.

In the predawn light, I crept by taxi through the kind of bombed-out area I had become used to seeing in German towns. I wondered, as I locked the door to my hotel room in a bare new structure that still smelled of fresh cement, if I shouldn't go back to Paris after a few days and see people there again before my return. It had been the one happy time, with little French restaurants to discover and the sights to see, picnics in the Bois de Fontainebleau and evenings at the Deux Magots. With this resolve, I slept and woke. Breakfast came up. Coffee such as I had never known before—rich, smooth and hot. Tender croissants. Gobs of butter and jam. I pulled a blind. Sun poured into the room. I opened a window. Singing came up from the streets. All this in a vanquished city whose horrors of so short a time ago must linger still! Still unbelieving, I went out, found my way to the cathedral, bought a guidebook, wandered, fed pigeons at a café in a piazza. I smiled and talked to beautiful, smiling people without knowing a word they said. Well, maybe a little. *"Americana?" "Si."* That was easy.

As was much else. That entire month I never carried my own bag, or lacked for a guide. Waiters guessed what I might like and brought it; workmen stopped building new walls to show the way to galleries and palaces. Sitting in the sun at that happy day's end, I felt that life had begun once more. If my friends in Germany had been stationed in Italy, I wondered, would things have been different? So pondering, I walked around till a certain truth dawned. I could think whatever I liked about anybody or anything, but everywhere around me Italy was making its first great statement. If I have dwelt too much here on that unfortunate time in Germany, it was only as a preface to Italy, only to show that there was never a heart more ready for Italy to impress it. And the measure of what Italy could do was astounding, and simply cannot to this day be taken.

From Milan I went to Verona, to another hotel, breakfast and guidebook—but this time as I went about the streets of that softly lyrical town, I became at every step more aware of what beauty was being cast up at me, regular and almost as rhythmic as the waves of the sea, on every side, at every turning. And all in the open, outside! A small-town Southerner is not apt to be ignorant of architecture, but I had never before thought of statues and fountains as accepted ornaments of life—its daily dress—to be enjoyed by everyone from moment to moment, mingling with the talk and bargaining and breath of life, with sunshine. If you try hard enough, even after many years, the chances are that you can reconstruct a good deal of everything that has happened. (I still remember, for instance, the look of my room in Milan that first night, and the smell of recent cement work.) But I cannot reconstruct anything from my first day in Verona but my own dazed feelings. I can recall my wanderings of that day as a kind of drunkenness, all this on perhaps one glass of wine at a lunch I cannot remember eating. I do know that under orders from my old Baedeker, I trudged to the outskirts of the town to see that (starred and not to be missed) Church of S. Zeno. I remember walking across the harsh stones of the old square before the church, with its bare upcurving sweep of romanesque façade tawny in the fall of the strong afternoon sun, and how I realized that anyone would have to feel its nobility. I saw then that what had been kept from me by a too strict Protestant upbringing was true—that art can express religious emotion more truly than any sermon. Much later I saw this very church in a beautiful English movie of *Romeo and Juliet*; if that story happened at all, it must have happened there.

Then Venice . . . Florence . . . Siena . . . Rome. . . . How to get it all down! It was all crammed, and not just with churches and palaces, galleries, piazzas, mosaics and frescoes, but also with people, a montage of remembered faces. Florence especially had (in addition to Michelangelo, Botticelli and all the rest) a free and lively feeling about it that year, an airiness that was all ease and rightness. In recent times I have been there, tourists seem about to carry it off, like trooping multitudes of ants methodically lifting whole the carcass of a wonderful beast. But not so in that early postwar year. Italians were glad to be alive in a life that was possible to live, and their gladness filled the air and reached out to all comers. All the dancing and romancing, the easy friendships and dates, meetings and partings, may seem frivolous to talk about—though there's not much wrong with frivolity, God knows—but it was more than that that one felt in France and Italy in those days. It had come up out of the inferno just endured; it was a resurrection. Maybe it never reached Germany at all. But it had taken up headquarters in Italy.

In Rome, a young Canadian who often ate at the same restaurant as I, asked me to the opera in the Baths of Caracalla. It was Berlioz's *The Damnation of Faust*. Every bit as ignorant as my friends in Germany believed, I loved the spectacle with little knowledge of what was going on. It was drama beneath the stars with attendant ruins and cypresses against a velvet Roman sky. We walked back along the Via Appia at midnight, holding hands.

Time to *go*! Oh, NO!!!

Back to a few days in Paris, retellings of everything, running into friends from the boat, evenings at the Deux Magots. Germany was almost forgotten except for the countryside, fairylike with some dark magic about it that seemed not to have heard of the war. The friendship on which I had based so much hope faded. But instead I had Italy, and the resolve to go back there when and how I could.

Four years later, with another novel published and the warm recognition of a Guggenheim Fellowship, I had my chance. I would spend a year there, I told myself, and finish a novel I had begun. But I met my husband in Rome and the year stretched out to two, then with marriage, to five in all. Even after we moved to Canada, I continued to visualize Italy, to see, as it were, by Italian light.

. . . Not everything, of course, that came after that magic summer of 1949 was good or even pleasant. Italy is a poor country where life is hard. Not all Italians are helpful and charming. Not everything is a delight. Illusion is, for one thing, that which comes before disillusion.

But Italy, not being an illusion, remains. It is itself the true measure of whatever is said or done or written about it. One can hope to rise up against that measure, but, failing that, at least to be seen by that light.

Montreal, Quebec
October 1985

THE WHITE AZALEA

Two letters had arrived for Miss Theresa Stubblefield: she put them in her bag. She would not stop to read them in American Express, as many were doing, sitting on benches or leaning against

the walls, but pushed her way out into the street. This was her first
day in Rome and it was June.

An enormous sky of the most delicate blue arched overhead. In
her mind's eye—her imagination responding fully, almost exhaust-
ingly, to these shores' peculiar powers of stimulation—she saw the
city as from above, telescoped on its great bare plains that the ruins
marked, aqueducts and tombs, here a cypress, there a pine, and all
round the low blue hills. Pictures in old Latin books returned to
her: the Appian Way Today, the Colosseum, the Arch of Constantine. She would see them, looking just as they had in the books, and
this would make up a part of her delight. Moreover, nursing
various Stubblefields—her aunt, then her mother, then her
father—through their lengthy illnesses (everybody could tell you
the Stubblefields were always sick), Theresa had had a chance to
read quite a lot. England, France, Germany, Switzerland, and Italy
had all been rendered for her time and again, and between the prescribed hours of pills and tonics, she had conceived a dreamy passion by lamplight, to see all these places with her own eyes. The
very night after her father's funeral she had thought, though never
admitted to a soul: *Now I can go. There's nothing to stop me now.*
So here it was, here was Italy, anyway, and terribly noisy.

In the street the traffic was really frightening. Cars, taxis, buses,
and motor scooters all went plunging at once down the narrow length
of it or swerving perilously around a fountain. Shoals of tourists went
by her in national groups—English schoolgirls in blue uniforms,
German boys with cameras attached, smartly dressed Americans
looking in shop windows. Glad to be alone, Theresa climbed the
splendid outdoor staircase that opened to her left. The Spanish Steps.

Something special was going on here just now—the annual display of azalea plants. She had heard about it the night before at her
hotel. It was not yet complete: workmen were unloading the potted
plants from a truck and placing them in banked rows on the steps
above. The azaleas were as large as shrubs, and their myriad
blooms, many still tight in the bud, ranged in color from purple
through fuchsia and rose to the palest pink, along with many white
ones too. Marvellous, thought Theresa, climbing in her portly,
well-bred way, for she was someone who had learned that if you

only move slowly enough you have time to notice everything. In
Rome, all over Europe, she intended to move very slowly indeed.

Halfway up the staircase she stopped and sat down. Other
people were doing it, too, sitting all along the wide banisters and
leaning over the parapets above, watching the azaleas mass, or just
enjoying the sun. Theresa sat with her letters in her lap, breathing
Mediterranean air. The sun warmed her, as it seemed to be warming
everything, perhaps even the underside of stones or the chill insides
of churches. She loosened her tweed jacket and smoked a cigarette.
Content . . . excited; how could you be both at once? Strange, but
she was. Presently, she picked up the first of the letters.

A few moments later her hands were trembling and her brow had
contracted with anxiety and dismay. *Of course, one of them would
have to go and do this! Poor Cousin Elec,* she thought, tears rising to
sting in the sun, *but why couldn't he have arranged to live through the
summer? And how on earth did I ever get this letter anyway?*

She had reason indeed to wonder how the letter had managed to
find her. Her Cousin Emma Carraway had written it, in her loose
high old lady's script—*t*'s carefully crossed, but *l*'s inclined to
wobble like an old car on the downward slope. Cousin Emma had
simply put Miss Theresa Stubblefield, Rome, Italy, on the envelope, had walked up to the post office in Tuxapoka, Alabama, and
mailed it with as much confidence as if it had been a birthday card
to her next-door neighbor. No return address whatsoever. Somebody had scrawled American Express, Piazza di Spagna? across
the envelope, and now Theresa had it, all as easily as if she had
been the President of the Republic or the Pope. Inside were all the
things they thought she ought to know concerning the last illness,
death, and burial of Cousin Alexander Carraway.

Cousin Emma and Cousin Elec, brother and sister—unmarried,
devoted, aging—had lived next door to the Stubblefields in
Tuxapoka from time immemorial until the Stubblefields had moved
to Montgomery fifteen years ago. Two days before he was taken
sick, Cousin Elec was out worrying about what too much rain might
do to his sweetpeas, and Cousin Elec had always preserved in the
top drawer of his secretary a mother-of-pearl paper knife which
Theresa had coveted as a child and which he had promised she

could have when he died. *I'm supposed to care as much now as then, as much here as there,* she realized, with a sigh. *This letter would have got to me if she hadn't even put Rome, Italy, on it.*

She refolded the letter, replaced it in its envelope, and turned with relief to one from her brother George.

But alack, George, when *he* had written, had only just returned from going to Tuxapoka to Cousin Elec's funeral. He was full of heavy family reminiscence. All the fine old stock was dying out, look at the world today. His own children had suffered from the weakening of those values which he and Theresa had always taken for granted, and as for his grandchildren (he had one so far, still in diapers), he shuddered to think that the true meaning of character might never dawn on them at all. A life of gentility and principle such as Cousin Elec had lived had to be known at first hand. . . .

Poor George! The only boy, the family darling. Together with her mother, both of them tense with worry lest things should somehow go wrong, Theresa had seen him through the right college, into the right fraternity, and though pursued by various girls and various mamas of girls, safely married to the right sort, however much in the early years of that match his wife, Anne, had not seemed to understand poor George. Could it just be, Theresa wondered, that Anne had understood only too well, and that George all along was extraordinary only in the degree to which he was dull?

As for Cousin Alexander Carraway, the only thing Theresa could remember at the moment about him (except his paper knife) was that he had had exceptionally long hands and feet and one night about one o'clock in the morning the whole Stubblefield family had been aroused to go next door at Cousin Emma's call— first Papa, then Mother, then Theresa and George. There they all did their uttermost to help Cousin Elec get a cramp out of his foot. He had hobbled downstairs into the parlor, in his agony, and was sitting, wrapped in his bathrobe, on a footstool. He held his long clenched foot in both hands, and this and his contorted face—he was trying heroically not to cry out—made him look like a large skinny old monkey. They all surrounded him, the family circle, Theresa and George as solemn as if they were watching the cat have kittens, and Cousin Emma running back and forth with a kettle of hot water which she poured steaming into a white enameled pan. "Can you think of anything to do?" she kept repeating. "I hate to call the doctor but if this keeps up I'll just have to! Can you think of anything to do?" "You might treat it like hiccups," said Papa. "Drop a cold key down his back." "I just hope this happens to you someday," said Cousin Elec, who was not at his best. "Poor Cousin Elec," George said. He was younger than Theresa: she remembered looking down and seeing his great round eyes, while at the same time she was dimly aware that her mother and father were not unamused. "Poor Cousin Elec."

Now, here they both were, still the same, George full of round-eyed woe, and Cousin Emma in despair. Theresa shifted to a new page.

"Of course [George's letter continued], there are practical problems to be considered. Cousin Emma is alone in that big old house and won't hear to parting from it. Robbie and Beryl tried their best to persuade her to come and stay with them, and Anne and I have told her she's more than welcome here, but I think she feels that she might be an imposition, especially as long as our Rosie is still in high school. The other possibility is to make arrangements for her to let out one or two of the rooms to some teacher of good family or one of those solitary old ladies that Tuxapoka is populated with—Miss Edna Whittaker, for example. But there is more in this than meets the eye. A new bathroom would certainly have to be put in. The wallpaper in the back bedroom is literally crumbling off. . . ." (Theresa skipped a page of details about the house.) "I hope if you have any ideas along these lines you will write me about them. I may settle on some makeshift arrangements for the summer and wait until you return in the fall so we can work out together the best . . ."

I really shouldn't have smoked a cigarette so early in the day, thought Theresa, it always makes me sick. I'll start sneezing in a minute, sitting on these cold steps. She got up, standing uncertainly for a moment, then moving aside to let go past her, talking, a group of young men. They wore shoes with pointed toes, odd to American eyes, and narrow trousers, and their hair looked unnaturally black and slick. Yet here they were obviously thought to be handsome, and felt themselves to be so. Just then a man approached her with a tray of cheap cameos, Parker fountain pens, rosaries, papal portraits. "No," said Theresa. "No, no!" she said. The man did not wish to leave. He knew how to spread himself against the borders of the space that had to separate them. Carrozza rides in the park, the Colosseum by moonlight, he specialized . . . Theresa turned away to escape, and climbed to a higher landing where the steps divided in two. There she walked to the far left and leaned on a vacant section of banister, while the vendor picked himself another well-dressed American lady, carrying a camera and a handsome alligator bag, ascending the steps alone. Was he ever successful, Theresa wondered. The lady with the alligator bag registered interest, doubt, then indignation; at last, alarm. She cast about as though looking for a policeman: this really shouldn't be allowed! Finally, she scurried away up the steps.

Theresa Stubblefield, still holding the family letters in one hand, realized that her whole trip to Europe was viewed in family circles as an interlude between Cousin Elec's death and "doing something" about Cousin Emma. They were even, Anne and George, probably thinking themselves very considerate in not hinting that she really should cut out "one or two countries" and come home in August to get Cousin Emma's house ready before the teachers came to Tuxapoka in September. Of course, it wasn't Anne and George's fault that one family crisis seemed to follow another, and weren't they always emphasizing that they really didn't know what they would do without Theresa? *The trouble is,* Theresa thought, *that while everything that happens there is supposed to matter supremely, nothing here is supposed even to exist. They would not care if all of Europe were to sink into the ocean tomorrow. It never registered with them that I had time to read all of Balzac, Dickens, and Stendhal while Papa was dying, not to mention everything in the city library after Mother's operation. It would have been exactly the same to them if I had read through all twenty-six volumes of Elsie Dinsmore.*

She arranged the letters carefully, one on top of the other. Then, with a motion so suddenly violent that she amazed herself, she tore them in two.

"Signora?"

She became aware that two Italian workmen, carrying a large

azalea pot, were standing before her and wanted her to move so
that they could begin arranging a new row of the display.

"Mi dispiace, signora, ma . . . insomma. . . ."

"Oh . . . put it there!" She indicated a spot a little distance away.
They did not understand. *"Ponere . . . la."* A little Latin, a little
French. How one got along! The workmen exchanged a glance, a
shrug. Then they obeyed her. *"Va bene, signora."* They laughed as
they returned down the steps in the sun.

Theresa was still holding the torn letters, half in either hand, and
the flush was fading slowly from her brow. What a strong feeling
had shaken her! She observed the irregular edges of paper, so
crudely wrenched apart, and began to feel guilty. The Stubblefields, it was true, were proud and prominent, but how thin, how
vulnerable was that pride it was so easy to prove, and how local was
that prominence there was really no need to tell even them. But
none could ever deny that the Stubblefields meant well; no one had
ever challenged that the Stubblefields were good. Now out of their
very letters, their sorrowful eyes, full of gentility and principle,
appeared to be regarding Theresa, one of their own who had
turned against them, and soft voices, so ready to forgive all, seemed
to be saying, "Oh, Theresa, how *could* you?"

Wasn't that exactly what they had said when, as a girl, she had
fallen in love with Charlie Wharton, whose father had unfortunately
been in the pen? Ever so softly, ever so distressed: "Oh, Theresa, how
could you?" Never mind. That was long ago, over and done with, and
right now something clearly had to be done about these letters.

Theresa moved forward, and leaning down she dropped the torn
sheets into the azalea pot which the workmen had just left. But the
matter was not so easily settled. What if the letters should blow
away? One could not bear the thought of that which was personal
to the Stubblefields chancing out on the steps where everyone
passed, or maybe even into the piazza below to be run over by a
motor scooter, walked over by the common herd, spit upon, picked
up and read, or—worst of all—returned to American Express by
some conscientious tourist, where tomorrow, filthy, crumpled,
bedraggled, but still legibly, faithfully relating Cousin Elec's death
and Cousin Emma's grief, they might be produced to confront her.

Theresa moved a little closer to the azalea pot and sat down beside it. She covered the letters deftly, smoothing the earth above them and making sure that no trace of paper showed above the ground. The corner of Cousin Emma's envelope caught on a root and had to be shoved under, a painful moment, as if a letter could feel anything—how absurd! Then Theresa realized, straightening up and rubbing dirt off her hand with a piece of Kleenex from her bag, that it was not the letters but the Stubblefields that she had torn apart and consigned to the earth. This was certainly the only explanation of why the whole curious sequence, now that it was complete, had made her feel so marvelously much better.

Well, I declare! Theresa thought, astonished at herself, and in that moment it was as though she stood before the statue of some heroic classical woman whose dagger dripped with stony blood. *My goodness!* she thought, drowning in those blank exalted eyeballs: *Me!*

So thrilled she could not, for a time, move on, she stood noting that this particular azalea was one of exceptional beauty. It was white, in outline as symmetrically developed as an oak tree, and blooming in every part with a ruffled, lacy purity. The azalea was, moreover, Theresa recalled, a Southern flower, one especially cultivated in Alabama. Why, the finest in the world were said to grow in Bellingrath Gardens near Mobile, though probably they had not heard about that in Rome.

Now Miss Theresa Stubblefield descended quickly, down, down, toward the swarming square, down toward the fountain and all the racket, into the Roman crowd. There she was lost at once in the swirl, nameless, anonymous, one more nice rich American tourist lady.

But she cast one last glance back to where the white azalea stood, blooming among all the others. By now the stone of the great staircase was all but covered over. A group of young priests in scarlet cassocks went past, mounting with rapid, forward energy, weaving their way vividly aloft among the massed flowers. At the top of the steps the twin towers of a church rose, standing clearly outlined on the blue air. Some large white clouds, charged with pearly light, were passing overhead at a slow imperial pace.

Well, it certainly is beyond a doubt the most beautiful family funeral of them all! thought Theresa. *And if they should ever object to what I did to them,* she thought, recalling the stone giantess with her dagger and the gouts of blood hanging thick and gravid upon it, *they've only to read a little and learn that there have been those in my position who haven't acted in half so considerate a way.*

~~

For the Literary Traveler

Rome stirs the memory, and memory may be the same thing as desire itself. The women in Edith Wharton's "Roman Fever" remember the erotic past; George Eliot's Dorothea desires what or whom she cannot name; Elizabeth Spencer's Theresa Stubblefield regrets and resolves. Where she is standing helps her to read the significance of her family against the background of her loveless past: viewed from the beautiful height of the SCALINATA or SPANISH STEPS, a life without passion looks in retrospect like the death she reads about in the letter from home. Theresa has walked a half block north from the American Express office and stops to read her letter on the Steps that connect the PIAZZA DI SPAGNA with the twin towers of the church of SANTA TRINITÀ DEI MONTI at the top. With the water flowing in Pietro (the elder) Bernini's barque-shaped fountain (FONTANA DELLA BARCACCIA), the people swarming in every direction, and the sun lighting the golden and pink salmon façades of the handsome palazzos behind a screen of palm trees, the piazza moves with an ecstasy of its own. Pots of azalea, that in the story promise resurrection, cover the Steps in spring. Eleanor Clark describes Piazza di Spagna and the Barcaccia in *Rome and a Villa*: "A sunken boat, ... co-image with the flowers on the steps a few feet away; water falls from various tongues and spigots in the boat...." Materiality in motion in the key of celebration defines Piazza di Spagna.

It's up to the reader whether Spencer means to suggest the life of the imagination as integral to a passionate life by setting the story at the center of the artistic and literary world of Rome. The HOUSE OF JOHN KEATS (no. 26 on the Piazza) is open to visitors; for centuries writers and artists lived and worked in this neighborhood—artists still do in the nearby VIA MARGUTTA off VIA DEL BABUINO at the northwest end of the Piazza.

THE SOUTH

It seems to me as if I had never before visited Italy—as if now, for the first time, the charm of the country was revealed to me. At every moment the senses, lapped in delight, whisper—this is Paradise. Here I find the secret of Italian poetry: not of Dante; he belonged to Etruria and Cisalpine Gaul: Tuscany and Lombardy are beautiful—they are an improved France, and abundant, sunshiny England—but here only do we find another earth and sky. Here the poets of Italy tasted the sweets of those enchanted gardens which they describe in their poems—and we wonder at their bright imaginations; but they drew only from reality—

—Mary Shelley, on her first trip
to the Mezzogiorno

Agrigento,* the ancient Akragas of Magna Graecia, is golden. The drive from Catania, through wheat-colored fields, then a series of rolling mountains, one behind another, like waves, with sudden outcroppings of rock, a landscape suited to dream. . . .

Flowers everywhere. Hibiscus outside our window, large, open, red. Geraniums growing like bushes, bougainvillaea like a weed, climbing up pine trees. Blue morning glory vines along the road. Clusters of petunias at the hotel, white with violet centers.

The magnificent temples on a rise overlooking the sea, a pure honey color, the main building material seemingly sandstone embedded with fossils, porous like a sponge and softly eroded. Illuminated by night, they seem to float in the darkness, like the low-hanging moon, the color of old gold. . . .

Interludes of lovemaking. At midday, the slanting light from the

*In Sicily.

shutters. Lying naked with wet linen over our bodies to reduce the heat. The slow, sweet spring of desire. The flesh that answers, the luxuriance and the sureness of touch. The open hand, the grateful heart. No knowledge, as we take and eat, as deep, as good, as this.

—Madelon Sprengnether, from *The House on Via Gombito*

NAPLES

Rose Macaulay

English novelist, travel writer, and critic, Dame Rose Macaulay (1881–1958) wrote twenty-three novels (the semi-autobiographical The Towers of Trebizond *[1956] is the best known), many of which address the theme of the reluctant exile. Her travel books are* Fabled Shore, *a description of her automobile tour of the coast of Spain in 1948, and* Pleasure of Ruins *(1953), an account of her journey through four continents in search of history's great ruins and her attempt to "trace the expression of the fascination with ruins in literature and art." Henry James's reference to his own "ruin-questing" as "a heartless pastime" and "a pleasure" that "shows a note of perversity" gave her the idea for her title. Praised by William Zinsser in* They Went: The Art and Craft of Travel Writing, Pleasure of Ruins, *in the words of novelist Anthony Powell, "combines travel, history, and bland, biting comment in an altogether enjoyable manner." This definitive work on what Rose Macaulay called* Ruinenlust *is the source of the following evocation of Posillipo on the Bay of Naples.*

FROM *PLEASURE OF RUINS*

Diocletian's is one of the few Roman imperial villas* now standing moderately intact; it is also the largest. But it lacks, with its huge formidable military-camp air, the delicious amenities of the palaces and villas that crowd the gulf of Naples, the Phlegraean fields so beloved of patrician Romans, poets, statesmen and emperors, the *optandosque sinus*, the *blandissima litora*, of *aestuantes Baiae*, the Sorrentine hills beloved of Bacchus, the shores where Roman *honos* and Greek *licentia* so happily mixed (*deversorium vitiorum*, growled Seneca), and where every one in Rome who was any one had his villa or his palace to retire to from the Roman

---

*Outside the Roman city of Salona, the capital of Dalmatia.

281

dog-days. We see their ruins now, or many of them; scattered down the mountains that run down to the sea, themselves too running into the sea, *villes englouties*, drowned as well as wrecked, for some who lacked enough room on the shore (so great was the competition for house-space) thrust out, as Horace jeered, into the sea, "and met there the freshness and salubrity of another element": but the cause of their drowning was that the sea of the bay, so often convulsed by volcanic commotions, rose twenty feet above its old level, so that, crossing the bay, "you will sail over ancient villas, you will discern deep under your boat, a branch of the Domitian way," wrote Joseph Forsyth a century and a half ago; and, as Lucretius wrote, nineteen centuries earlier,

> multae per mare pessum
> Subsedere, suis pariter cum civibus, urbes.

It is the case that the ruins of the villas have gradually or suddenly "tumbled over the rocks into the sea or else been submerged, and so if you take a boat beyond the Mergellina mole and look into the water in which the children are swimming like fishes, you can see the floors of Roman apartments in the seaweed twenty feet below."* Fynes Moryson, visiting the lovely bay in 1594, thought the ancient city of Baiae "most sweete":

> but all the houses neere to the shoare are drowned, except the Baths, and the houses on the mountains are all ruined, . . . yet these ruines show the pride and magnificence of that old time. . . . Here bee the foresaid ruines of Caligula his bridge. . . . Here we did see the stately ruines of two senators' houses, where the excellent pictures did yet remaine upon the highest roofe . . . all this Territorie, on both sides neere this Creeke or Bay of the Sea, are so full of ruined Palaces, Temples, and Sepulchres, as a man would say, they were not several villages, but one great Citie. . . .

as Pliny also remarked of the coast near Ostia where his Laurentum villa stood. One gathers that the whole Mediterranean coast of Italy

[*Bernard Wall, *Italian Life and Landscape* (1950).—Au,]

was crowded with resorts and fine villas; the bays of the Naples gulf being the smartest. Here were the palaces, and here, as John Evelyn said, "the sweet retirements of the most opulent and voluptuous Romans." George Sandys, visiting the elegant bay in 1610, mused pleasurably on the ruins, the opulence, and the vice.

"A declaration of the magnificency and riches of the Romans; but too much of their luxury; beautified with ample temples, multitudes of Bannios, Imperial Palaces, and the adjoining Mannorhouses of the principal Romans. . . . Egyptian Canopus was a school of virtue, compared to the voluptuous liberty of this City.

> The Inn (saith Seneca) and receptacle for vices: where luxury taketh the reins. . . . What a sight it is to see drunkards reeling along the shoar; the banquetings of such as are rowed on the water, the Lakes reckoning their continual canzonets and the like. . . . One winter only here enfeebled Hannibal, and the delights of Campania did what the snow and the Alps could not do; victorious in arms, yet by vices vanquished. . . .*

Harlots, he mused, sailed by in painted boats of diverse colours, the Lake was strewed over with roses, the night noises of singers would have displeased Cato. But see what happened to Baiae.

> *Baiae*, not much inferiour to *Rome* in magnificency, equal in beauty, and superiour in healthful situation, hath now scarce one stone left above another, demolished by War, and devoured by Water. For it would seem that the *Lombards* and *Saracens* in the destruction hereof had not only a hand, but that the extruded Sea hath again regained his usurped limits: made apparent by the paved streets and traces of foundations to be seen under water. The shore is all overgrown with bushes and myrtles, the vaults and thrown down walls inhabited by Serpents: and what is more, the air heretofore so salubrious is now become infectious and unhealthful.

Palaces, fishponds, lampreys, swimming-pools on the tops of houses, all were perished, leaving only their ruins under water or in

[*George Sandys, *Travels* (1636).—Au.]

caves. Here in these villas were held the house parties of the political and literary intellectuals; the gatherings and the topics discussed recall Falkland's house parties at Great Tew. Near Cumae
are the ruins of Cicero's villa, and that of his friend Catullus, and a
little way off was the house of Varro, which Cicero made the setting of the first Dialogue of his Academica; the second was held at
Hortensius's villa at Bauli, of which we see the ruins beneath the
sea; here Hortensius had his cisterns of lampreys, which, says Mar-
tial, came when called by name, and on which Antonia the wife of
Drusus (who, says the elder Pliny, was never known to spit) hung
golden ear rings. Here, too, wicked Nero planned the murder of
his mother by drowning (which she foiled on that occasion by
swimming too well), and here Cicero and Catullus and Lucullus,
seated in Hortensius's colonnade, discussed philosophy, logic and
what have you until it was time to sail for Naples and Pompeii
across the smooth evening bay before the breeze from the peach-
red west. The modern village of Bacoli is built among the vast scattered ruins of this villa. Those of Cicero's own villa are supposed to
lie between Pozzuoli and the Lucrine Lake. But the ruins scattered
all round the bay of Pozzuoli and Baiae down to the promontory of
Miseno are mostly indistinguishable, a huge jumble of the patrician
homes of the noblest Romans on holiday. The famed house of
Lucullus, which later passed to Tiberius, sprawled over the cape in
its huge and extravagant grandiosity, half of it under the sea.

"In the course of a few minutes," said Forsyth, "you sail past the
highest names of antiquity. You see Marius, Sylla, Pompey, Piso,
Tiberius, Nero, all crowding in for the most beautiful angles and
elbowing each other's villas. Yet where are those villas now? Alas!
nothing but masses of built tufo which you can hardly distinguish
from the tufo of the hill."*

Evelyn, who wisely accepted what he was told by guides,
had the pleasure of feeling sure which ruin had been which villa
or palace; he "rowed along towards a villa of the orator Cicero's,

[*Joseph Forsyth.—Au.]

where we were showed the ruins of his Academy, and at the foot of a rock, his Baths, the waters reciprocating their tides with the neighbouring sea;" he even believed that he saw the Elysian fields, "full of myrtles and sweet shrubs, and having a most delightful prospect towards the Tyrrhene Sea. Upon the verge of these remain the ruins of the Mercato di Saboto, formerly a Circus; over the arches stand divers urns, full of Roman ashes."*

But, though Virgil's traditional tomb on the cape of Posilipo has fallen into discredit, we can even to-day, climbing to the top of the promontory, see and accept without question Pausilypum, the great palace villa of Vedius Pollio, whose ruins cover the whole headland and drop down into the sea, jutting up from the water in huge fragments and blocks. It must have been the most palatial villa of all this palatial coast; it was bequeathed to Augustus. Vedius Pollio, despite his pleasure-palace, one cannot think of with pleasure, for he threw slaves into the lamprey stews to be devoured. Alas, there is always, or nearly always, something in the past of ruins which displeases, and probably one should not know too much of their late owners. Of the imperial palaces down this golden coast and on its islands, those of Nero, Caligula, Tiberius and the rest, there remain a few temples, great baths, cisterns, the fragments jutting from the sea, and the seaweed-green pavements dimly seen through clear blue water. You can still swim about among palace walls, though now you have to hire a cabin and swim from a crowded bathing beach or rocks brown with sprawling bodies. For more than ever crowds are drawn from the hot cities to the *blandissima litora* of *aestuantes Baiae*, where Boccaccio's Fiammetta was taken by him to be cheered when she was pining of love. He retailed to her its delights—

by ancient Cuma and Pozzuolo is the delightful Baiae above the sea shore, than which there is nothing more beautiful or more pleasing under the sky. There are beautiful hills covered with trees and vines . . . the oracles of the Cuman Sybil, the lake of Averno, the

[*John Evelyn, *Diary.*—Au.]

theatre of the ancient games, the baths, Monte Barbaro, and the vain works of the wicked Nero; which ancient things, new to modern minds, are no small cause of joy to see and wonder at.*

Fiammetta, foolish girl, pining of love, cared for none of these things. But, all down the ages, Italians and foreigners have rejoiced in them, agreeing with Evelyn that here is "doubtless one of the most divertissant and considerable vistas in the world" and full of the most stupendous rarities. To the ancient Roman and Italian enthusiasm for scenery, hills, woods, coast and sea, there has been added a pleasure they did not know, swimming among ruined palaces; for—*mira fides*—they did not go in much for bathing in the open sea, and the palaces were not yet in ruins. On the other hand, the coast was far more beautiful, being unspoilt by tram lines, industrial towns, and the sordid spread of Naples. Bishop Burnet's comment in 1685 is ironically interesting to-day.

> Though anciently [he wrote] this was all so well built, so peopled, and so beautifully laid out, yet no where doth one see more visibly what a change time brings upon all places. For Naples hath so entirely eat out this place, and drawn its inhabitants to it, that Puzzuolo itself is but a small village, and there is now no other in this Bay, which was anciently built almost all round; for there were seven big towns upon it.

The towns have returned, and Naples, instead of drawing the bay's inhabitants into itself, has spewed her own all round the bay. Yet one may still agree with Burnet that "it is certain, that a man can no where pass a day of his life both with so much pleasure, and with such advantage, as he finds in his journey to Puzzuolo, and all along the Bay."

[*Boccaccio, *Fiammetta*.—Au.]

🪶

For the Literary Traveler

The original Greek name for POSILLIPO, the promontory overlooking
the BAY OF NAPLES on the western edge of the city, was Pausilypon,
which means "the soothing of pain." On this hill, considered a paradise
almost three thousand years ago, was the site of the philosophical
school of the Epicureans, devoted to the pursuit of pleasure. Their
mentor, Syron, left his villa to his poetry student Virgil who loved
"Neapolis" on the bay and composed most of the *Aeneid* there. (The
tradition is that Virgil's Tomb, open daily, is there.) Rose Macaulay
sketches a few details of the carousing of the rich and famous in *Pleasure of Ruins*, concluding, "Nearly always, something in the past of
ruins ... displeases." "Probably," she remarks archly, "one should not
know too much of their late owners." (The favorite banquet fare of
the enormously wealthy Romans included moray eels fattened on
human flesh. Slaves—women, sold into slavery after their warrior husbands were defeated in the ongoing Mediterranean wars of the classical era; peasants, seized as the spoils of war; and the poor whose
ranks swelled under the burden of Roman war taxes—performed
sexual and other domestic services for their pleasure-loving hosts.)

To explore what remains of the paradise on the sea, take the C4
bus from the immense PIAZZA DEL PLEBISCITO in the city. (Its ROYAL
PALACE and church of SAN FRANCESCO DI PAOLA, modeled on the Pantheon in Rome, are the backdrops—along with leased-for-the-day
white Rolls-Royces—for families of First Communicants posing for
photographers on Sundays.)

The scenic bus route follows the coast road (Via Parthenope) along
the harbor, skirting the hill called PIZZOFALCONE (the divide between
the old and new quarters of Naples), and past the tiny island of CASTEL
DELL'OVO. This area was the site of PARTHENOPE, the original Greek city
settled by colonists from the island of Rhodes in the ninth century
B.C.E., and named after the siren Parthenope. (Here, according to
legend, Parthenope leaped to her death and was washed up to shore
after her spell was broken by Odysseus.) The bus route then winds
away from the bay and Riviera di Chiaia, through PIAZZA DEI MARTIRI,

and on over the hill, through a neighborhood of apartment buildings and small piazzas, until descending into MERGELLINA and the PIAZZA SAN-NAZZARO. Here are the foothills of Posillipo where the remains of the Roman settlement, designated as Parco Virgiliano, can be safely visited in daylight. The ascent on Via Petrarca (or on the *funicolare di Posillipo*) leads to a panoramic view of the Bay that Virgil loved.

Today Mergellina and the Posillipo cape are dense with old and new apartment complexes (the novel *The Bay of Noon*—see page 289—unfolds in one of them). But the ruins of the villa of Vedius Pollio, mentioned by Pliny in his *Natural History* and described by Rose Macaulay, remain. Exploring these sites and imagining the past they commemorate provoke questions about the progress of civilization. While watching the weekending crowds of Neapolitans enjoying the beach at Mergellina, the reader/traveler remembers the story of how Vedius Pollio used to amuse his guests at his "sooth-the-pain"/Posillipo vacation home: he used to throw his slaves into the waters where the lampreys swam, to be devoured.

Shirley Hazzard

Novelist Shirley Hazzard (Cliffs of Fall, The Evening of the Holiday, People in Glass Houses, The Bay of Noon—excerpted in these pages—and The Transit of Venus, which won the 1981 National Book Critics Circle Award) was born in Sydney, Australia, but has lived for many years in the United States and Southern Italy—the lower part of the peninsula, a region radiant beneath a seemingly perpetual noontime sun, which the Italians call the Mezzogiorno *(meaning literally "midday").*

In The Bay of Noon *(1970), a love story of post–World War II Italy, Shirley Hazzard imagines—and remembers—the setting with an intensity of feeling that makes place the novel's core: Naples is catalyst, history, the essential human character. Each of the lovers—Jenny, a lonely young exile from England (the narrating "I"); Gioconda, a beautiful Neapolitan writer;*

and Gianni, a flamboyant film director—discovers in this anarchic city of secrets their own hidden desires. Naples is tragic: in the ominous shadow of Mount Vesuvius, abiding reminder of mortality and the possibility of disaster, it yields no easy happy endings.

Shirley Hazzard's fiction has always received the highest praise: "near perfect" writing, "weaving an armchair traveler's dream landscape"; "the reader will enjoy a sense of place, drawn so perfectly it seems to breathe."

The epigraph of The Bay of Noon, *evoking the novel's affecting mood, is taken from W. H. Auden's poem, "Good-bye to the Mezzogiorno":*

> To bless this region, its vendages, and those
> Who call it home: though one cannot always
> Remember exactly why one has been happy,
> There is no forgetting that one was.

FROM *THE BAY OF NOON*

I

I possessed a single introduction to Naples—one letter provided by a London acquaintance who had encouraged me to present myself at the address on the envelope. "Somewhere in the thick of Naples," said this well-wisher, who had never himself been there. The address was that of a woman whose name had become known—and was by then becoming forgotten—in connection with one of the post-war films from Italy. There was *The Bicycle Thief*, you remember; there was *Shoeshine*, there was *Open City*. And then there was a film called *Del Tempo Felice* that was made from an obscure little book, a sort of prose poem; and it was the author of this book whose name was on my envelope.

I had never read it, her book. I had seen her film, but I was then very young and had remembered its darkly photographed interiors and flickering close-ups for two reasons—because it was the first time I had been to a film that used sub-titles; and the first time that I saw the lines of Dante from which the title was taken and which appeared, off-centre, on the screen along with the other credits, duly translated in sub-title but carrying, as sometimes happens, in their own, then unfamiliar language, the physical aspect of poetry that sends a shiver across the sight and skin.

And now that there was time to call myself to her attention, I could only think: a woman of this kind, with work, friends, admirers—a public, even—would hardly welcome a stranger with no better credentials than a note (a note which I had seen for myself began "Dear Signorina") from a remote acquaintance at Ealing Studios.

The name—her Christian name, that is—had struck me; also the address, for there was a street number, then simply "San Biagio dei Librai": Saint Biagio of the Booksellers. I had remarked on this address when the letter was handed to me. And the friend at Ealing—who had known the lady, it now came out, only outside Italy—said, "Let's hope I got it right. I rather gather this is the good old family palazzo. I hope she'll do you proud." All had, in fact, been in the realm of aspiration or surmise.

It occurred to me, as I walked back to the Hotel Vesuvio, that I might telephone this Signorina at once and see if she would have me. But the prospect of picking up the telephone and shattering her unsuspecting morning was more than I could face for her; and when I got up to my room I took out, instead of her address, a guidebook that had lain one month in the bureau drawer.

"The traveller who would know Naples"—so the guidebook dictated, open on the hotel counterpane—"must take himself to Spaccanápoli, the split of Naples, the street that traversed the city's nucleus in classical times, and is now called San Biagio dei Librai."

Nevertheless it took some time to make the call. First I got cut off, and in the wire a low voice asked, though not of me, *"Tu, come giudici?"* Then I heard the telephone ringing, ringing, and was about to hang up at the instant when the ringing exchanged itself for a voice. Tracing the hotel's stitched monogram with a nervous finger, I made myself known; and in English the voice cried, "Good. Good that you called. Yes, come, come. Come now. Come for lunch. Are you coming in a taxi?—my street is up, you can't enter, it's the drains. Tell him to let you out at the Gesù Nuovo, the church. Then ask the way, it's only a few minutes on foot from there."

Below the Gesù Nuovo there is a ramp of a street that rises to a corner where Degas once lived with his Neapolitan relatives. The ascent, oblique, suggests the piazza above by giving, as if through a door ajar on a high landing, a glimpse of the exorbitant, gem-cut façade of a church, with to the left a flash of red stucco, to the right an ornate obelisk, before it catapults you on to a scene that appears, from this method of approaching it, more bizarre than ever.

Had I been accompanied, I might have laughed out loud at the profligacy of imagination expended there; but solitude, which is held to be a cause of eccentricity, in fact imposes excessive normality, at least in public, and I cross the piazza with no outward sign of interest and placed myself against the faceted stones of the church. From there one looked, then, across at the bombed shell of Santa Chiara, half-reconstructed, and at a derelict campanile on the one hand and a massive palace on the other; and this I did for some moments, only showing it was new to me by enquiring, of the priest who came to close the church, the way to San Biagio dei Librai.

The day had deteriorated, it was winter again, and the piazza was abandoned for the siesta. One pre–war Fiat, as lonely, as historic as the single car on an antiquated postcard, had been parked in the middle of the square. And I, perhaps, walking away from the church door, would have something now of the same anonymous, arrested look—captured, as the saying goes, in the picture; serving to show, merely, by human contrast, the dimensions of buildings, to date the photograph unwittingly with my clothes and hair; somebody purloined from a crowd to act as an example. The light itself had dwindled to the joyless sepia of an old photograph.

The picture is re-animated—rather, it dissolves to life—and I enter a passageway of a street, the narrow channel that flows out from the farther side of the square. Past a hundred shops and stalls that sold, as they are selling still, song records, coloured nylon sponges, the gauze and sugar paraphernalia of christenings and first communions, plastic Bambis, bolts of print material, gold jewellery and silver representations of arms and legs to be offered up to departmental saints; past open sacks of coffee beans, stacks of books new and seventh-hand, and barrows piled with hand-tools—through this I came, that afternoon, into San Biagio dei Librai.

What could be closed was closing in a savage drum-roll of descending grilles; what could be wheeled was being trundled away. Over cobbled blocks—that were posted here and there with stone bollards intended to keep out the cars that expertly slid between them and rushed on to straddle a long trench of drainage repairs—I walked by palaces of stone and stucco, rusticated or red, white with grey facings, brown, orange, rose or ochre, no two alike, facing each other across the street's corridor as monumentally as if they had been rising, isolated, in some open place that did their proportions justice.

On to the flanks of those palaces, smaller buildings had been grafted in every age except our own—in any unlikely opening, on any precarious ledge, apparently with the sole provision that they bear no resemblance to one another. Forgotten or overlaid, antiquity had been buried in the walls, making its laconic signal—a sunken column, Greek, dark, smooth as silk, with acanthus capital; a Roman inscription, traces of a fortification, or crenellations that, centuries since, had been surmounted by a rooftop. In one vast courtyard was planted a colossal sculpture, Roman or Renaissance, of a horse's head; another ended in galleries of disintegrating frescoes.

It was a deep square of a building, hers; pale stucco, divided into a dozen apartments, or a hundred. The *portiere*, coming out from his lunch with his fork, spooled with pasta, in his hand, directed me to the piano nobile, taking me into the courtyard to point out, in a fold of that flaking parchment, the inner staircase I should take. There were several flights of deep stone steps, unlit, uncarpeted. Only on the last landing, in the spot where one paused to draw breath before ringing the bell, an oblong of shredding crimson had been placed before a pair of dark doors and carried dusty, tapering impressions of several days' shoes.

I rang the bell, heard nothing, rang again. The excitement of the street receded. Anticlimax brought back the sense of intrusion, as I stood there with the letter in my handbag like a warrant to search, to root out secrets.

From far off, as if it had been beyond the building, a woman's voice called, "Tosca!" There was silence, there was movement, and the same voice calling, "Tosca, Tosca." The voice approached the door, so full and musical that it might have been introducing an aria. A bolt was drawn, a handle rattled, and the dark door opened.

Gioconda's appearance has become merged now with knowledge of her, with moods and events and questions, so that in describing it I feel I am giving a false impression and introducing, even to myself, a woman I do not know. If one says that she was rather tall, dark-haired, dark-eyed, with in winter a pale colouring, paler than apricot, one has described nothing more than a woman who is in all probability good-looking. Even in giving these few facts I am getting off the track, for I myself would hardly recognise her from such a description: it is almost as if I were describing her skeleton, without the intercostal tissue that gave it life and singularity. Yet her physical beauty was as strong a part of her character as though she were personally accountable for the deep setting of the eyes or the long rise of the cheekbone. Its first and lasting impression was one of vitality and endurance. That is to say, of power: a power as self-contained, as unoppressive as that of a splendid tree. . . .

IV

Shortly after these meetings with Gioconda, I moved out of the hotel and took an apartment on the sea, along the foot of the Posillipo. In the sea, one might have said, since the apartment was in one of the villas that stand out in the bay all along the northern arc of Naples, and have a water life of their own. Beginning at Mergellina with a crumbling seventeenth-century colossus, they end at Gaiola with a Roman ruin; their names alone are an inventory of the eccentric. These buildings look on to the gulf of Naples, and are interspersed with grottoes and declivities of the pale gold stone of which that shore is composed, and even with shreds of a disappearing countryside and surviving groups of umbrella pines. Above them rises the headland of the Posillipo—already then encumbered with a ridge or two of the modern blocks that were to deface it completely over the next few years.

An open-air nightclub, wedged into the tufa near my building, lay in wait for its season; and a bedraggled restaurant or two commanded, from scruffy terraces, the incomparable, lake-like prospect of the bay.

In order to reach the apartment one entered quite a different building, that stood higher on the hillside, above and behind. From this one went down, in a tiny bathysphere of an elevator, through rock, and arrived at one end of a long corridor roughly tunnelled from solid stone, painted and tiled dark red. The corridor could be lit by a series of electric buttons whose sequence, timed for a loping run, provided a certain claustrophobic excitement. This deep crossing passed under Via Posillipo and through the tiny promontory of which my villa formed the prow. It ended in a flight of steep steps and a grilled door, beyond which were light, sky, and the sea. A glassed-in catwalk had been attached to the villa's side, leading past the doors of the many apartments into which the house had been divided.

Nothing could have been more canny, more uncanny, more Neapolitan, than this means of access. "Romantic," I wrote of it to Norah—and it did have something of the sinister that is an authentic element of romance.

There was another approach, by water, disembarking at a landing stage of stone steps glossy with moss, being admitted to the house through another green-grilled door. The building itself was red stucco, lifted clear of the water on foundations of grey stone; seen from a distance it floated forward in air like a rusty boat in the slips.

I had two big rooms there, and they were the most beautiful rooms, by far, that I had lived in. Like most missionaries, we lived better than those we had come to save; immunities and allowances broke our fall into this new ambience; we had cars to drive us and maids to keep us clean. My rooms gave on to a narrow terrace that, in turn, looked directly across the sea to the volcano: the rooms, the terrace, were like antechambers to the spectacle, their purpose was to disclose it. That view of the Bay of Naples has passed the point where it can ever find its master, its Guardi or its Canaletto; has become virtually a comic sight in art, its configurations too intimately known, even to those who have never seen them, now to be revealed. It gives an impression of indifference to the role humanly assigned to it—as if it will go on lending itself to posters, to chocolate boxes, without ever giving itself away; just as

Vesuvius goes on absorbing the tributes of those it clearly intends
to exterminate. . . .

VII

I had begun by then to treat the city with a show of familiarity; pretending, as people do with a celebrated acquaintance, to know it
better than I did, inserting myself into its landscape, another figure
in its vast *presepio*; acquiring habits of cafés and buses and hair-
dressers, uttering casual observations that sounded on my own ears
exotic as examples from a phrase-book: "There is snow on the
Apennines" or "Capri is always clearer in bad weather."

The assets of Naples are so secret, they give the impression of
having been deliberately concealed; lodged away, for the most part,
in malodorous side-streets, embedded in some squalid recess, they
partake of the city's poverty. Rarely do they give the sense, as do
the historic sights of other cities, of having died and been resur-
rected: from that illustrious after-life their own vitality, their
capacity for adaptation has excluded them; they are engulfed in
their own continuity.

It is the people, not the monuments, of Naples who are blatantly
featured, every face a subject for study—physiognomy evincing,
like architecture, here the Spanish influence, there the Arab or the
Greek. Civilisation has come upon them like one of their own cata-
clysms, flowing with ungovernable impetus down channels of its
own creation—in some respects total, all-permeating; in others
leaving inexplicable areas of innocence, of rusticity. For there
would occur, in that immensity of independent actions, incidents
that might have taken place in a village, or in some small town cut
off from any novelty or tide of history. I remember that one
evening I was looking in a shop window in Piazza dei Martiri—at
suede shoes of delicate colours, purses of indigo velvet, scarves of
satin flowers, Parisian stuff at odds with its southern setting—and
turned to find at my back a young couple, modestly though not
poorly dressed, the girl in grey, the man wearing a broad black
armband. Like a deputation they awaited me, timidly excusing
themselves before coming out with their question, "Are you Norwegian?" And, when I was not, excused themselves once more—

"Only we heard—you know—that Norwegian women were all fair, and with light eyes . . ."

It was inoffensive curiosity of the kind one might feel on finding a rare bird in one's garden—merely the desire to fix its identity before it disappeared forever. Yet it was, mysteriously, this same simplicity that grandly, gracefully expressed itself in the hairdresser's sturdy little shampoo girl when, sweeping my hair back into the washbasin with her plump arms, she praised its colour and abundance with the comment, *"Come la Maddalena"*—this "Like the Magdalen" as easily uttered as if it had been a flattering comparison with some film star.

The history and geography of calamity had so worked on these people that the excitement attending any public disaster was fundamentally devoid of surprise—if anything, there was an element of relief in the rupturing of an apparently continual suspense. Once, walking in a narrow street (it was Via Carlo Poerio, that has since blossomed into a rank of boutiques but then was strung with greengrocers and *salumerie*, dealers in wrought iron and kapok, and any number of minor junkies), I had crossed to look into an antique shop, when the ground was shaken by a tremendous crash, and I spun round to find that the entire façade of an old palazzo had collapsed into the street, flattening a parked car. From premonition, or from some preliminary sound, I had turned at the very moment of the impact, in time to see the shower of fragments sparking upward in a cloud of plaster-dust. No one was hurt. The car—so instantly and totally crushed that it now appeared to have been like this always—bore on its hollowed roof a heap of mortar, gesso, and masonry, topped by one of the stone garlands that had decorated an upper window and now lay on the summit of the pyre like a wreath on a tomb.

There was an interval of complete, cautious silence before the street's inhabitants came out to look. Far from causing indignation, the catastrophe produced any number of shrugs. *"Che buò?"* they enquired of one another, "What do you expect?" What might be expected, apparently, was just this—that the front of a building might fall off at one's feet. Somebody at last went off to telephone the fire brigade, children started to scale the eminence of masonry and car.

When interest had all but subsided, a placid-looking matron revived it by suddenly waving her arms and shrieking, "Danger, danger!"—the word *pericolo* uttered exactly as if it were spelt "breegolu."

It was this sense of catastrophe, impending and actual, that heightened the Neapolitan attachment to life and made an alleviation out of every small diversion or absurdity. The background of adversity, against which all else was to be posed, manifested itself involuntarily in attitude and gesture, in figures of speech, or in the mannerism, habitual as a tic, of warding off the evil eye; in the endless invoking of a patience with which they had been over-endowed in the first place, and which they pronounced almost as if it were the word for madness; in an old woman crying after a boy who had jostled her, "A fine consolation you are."

The city itself was marked by a volcanic extravagance. Its characteristics had not insinuated themselves but had arrived in inundations—in eruptions of taste and period, of churches and palaces, in a positive explosion of the baroque; in an outbreak of grotesque capitals, or double geometrical staircases; in a torrent of hanging gardens poured down over terraces and rooftops, spilt along ledges and doorsteps. The very streets were composed of blocks of lava, dark rivers that flowed through Naples and gave place, indoors, to a sea of ceramic tiles and marble intarsia: the word lava itself, in its volcanic sense, had originated at Naples. The Neapolitan painters had flashed through every considerable edifice of the town, leaving the place awash with Solimenas and Luca Giordanos and Lanfrancos, a flood-tide of decoration that rose over walls and across ceilings. Nothing in moderation might have been the motto of these people; who were yet, like their city, ultimately a secret.

Ordinariness, the affliction and backbone of other cities, was here non-existent. Phrases I had thought universal—the common people, the average family, the typical reaction, ordinary life—had no meaning where people were all uncommon and life extraordinary; where untraceable convulsions of human experience had yielded up such extremes of destitution, of civilisation.

Throughout the city there were inexhaustible sources of this or that—little fonts and geysers of commodity or personality: one street provided all the stringed instruments, another all the holy pictures, another all the funeral wreaths, or the coffins; the Hospital of the Pellegrini was the source of macabre jokes; the Albergo dei Poveri of the grimmest legends. And on New Year's Eve, in a revolting ritual, every window flung forth its annual accumulation of major garbage, burying the city under tons of broken utensils, plastic ornaments, cracked bottles and empty tins, from which, each January, it was slowly reexcavated by the street cleaners. . . .

🍌

For the Literary Traveler

With snatchable pocketbooks left behind in the hotel, safe from thieves on scooters and *scugnizzi* (street kids) who target tourists, the discovery of Naples's ancient historic center—the SPACCA-NAPOLI ("Split-Naples") of *The Bay of Noon*—can proceed in pleasure. To experience the place that the novel's protagonist Jenny comes to love—the city that Shirley Hazzard makes us see and hear—the reader/traveler needs a free, open mind.

Her travel essay "Naples: City of Secrets and Surprises" * sketches some historical background that helps with making sense of the old streets' ethnic and architectural jumble. Naples, the northernmost colony of *Magna Graecia*—Greater Greece—in Italy, has incorporated rather than lost its Greek past, as well as its Roman, Arabic, Moslem, Jewish, French, and Spanish influences, the legacies of twenty-six hundred years of Mediterranean trade, immigrations, and European conquests.

Jenny begins her love affair with Naples on the Saturday afternoon of her first visit to Gioconda, who lives in a palazzo on VIA SAN BIAGIO DEI LIBRAI, the street of the booksellers and of Saint Biagio, the patron saint of throats, and, therefore, of singers. (As her guidebook directs, "The traveller who would know Naples must take himself to Spacca-napoli, the split of Naples, the street that traversed the city's nucleus in classical times and is now called San Biagio dei Librai.")

* In a 1984 volume of *The New York Times Sophisticated Traveler* series entitled *Beloved Cities of Europe*.

She enters the street from its western end (approaching from Via Toledo/Via Roma) through the PIAZZA DEL GESÙ, struck silent by "the profligacy of imagination" expressed in the façade of the CHURCH OF GESÙ NUOVO (one of the landmarks of Naples) and "an ornate obelisk" (the GUGLIA DELLI IMMACOLATA, a pinnacle of wildly rococo decoration). From the piazza it is only a minute's walk to the fourteenth-century CHURCH OF SANTA CHIARA, which was devastated by Allied bombings, but is now restored. Jenny, however (the year is 1948), sees "the bombed shell of Santa Chiara, half-reconstructed."

Behind the church is the CLOISTER OF SANTA CHIARA, according to many visitors, the loveliest spot in Naples.

Reflecting Naples's Spanish heritage, the cloisters are decorated with majolica tiles painted with yellow, blue, and green floral designs and images. Arbors wound with vines of grapes and filled with flowering plants are surrounded by palm and orange trees. On low benches along the walls Franciscans visit quietly with friends; Neapolitan families and travelers rest. Barbara Grizzuti Harrison's idea of this enclosed sacred space—revered throughout her *Italian Days*—is to the point: "Cloisters are the architectural equivalent of a theological concept: perfect freedom within set boundaries." The lush atmosphere of the Cloister of Santa Chiara calls to mind the erotic and spiritual imagery of the biblical Song of Songs, which figures prominently in the writings and songs of many medieval women mystics:

> She is a garden enclosed,
> my sister, my promised bride;
> a garden enclosed,
> a sealed fountain.
> Your shoots from an orchard of pomegranate trees,
> bearing most exquisite fruit ...
> Fountain of the garden,
> well of living water,
> streams flowing down from Lebanon!

Jan Morris (see page 48) calls "the twin languages of earthiness and spirituality the vernaculars of Italy." In the Cloister of Santa Chiara the intimacy between interiority and the sensory embrace of life is palpable.

Walkers using a *Pianta Generale di Napoli* (the large street map of the city and environs) can easily follow the flow of the other streets of Spacca-Napoli. Via San Biagio dei Librai, Jenny's destination, is called Via Benedetto Croce as it passes Santa Chiara. Further along, the street passes another celebrated place of this ancient district, the PIAZZA and CHURCH OF SAN DOMENICO MAGGIORE. They belong to the ambiance of *The Bay of Noon*.

In the monastery next to the church, St. Thomas Aquinas lived and wrote part of his *Summa Theologica*; in the Dominican church of San Domenico Maggiore (1289), he preached his Lenten sermons in the vernacular and not the Latin of the educated classes. From 1515 to 1615, San Domenico Maggiore housed the law school and Greek department of the nearby University of Naples, founded by the legendary Hohenstaufen Emperor Frederick II (1194–1250), "Stupor Mundi" himself (see pages 353–54). Giordano Bruno also studied here in 1565 before he quit holy orders to study philosophy and wander through Europe. He was burned to death by the inquisition in the Campo dei Fiori in Rome where his larger-than-life sculptured image commemorates the tradition and penalties of intellectual freedom that Bruno's life represents. Today the Piazza San Domenico, with its Baroque pinnacle, is serene, with a pleasant outdoor cafe where students from the University of Naples sit beneath umbrellas reading, writing papers, and sipping lemon granità.

Moving on from the Piazza San Domenico, Jenny—and the literary traveler—enters Via San Biagio dei Librai, "a passageway of a street." In 1996, it seems not to have changed in any detail since Shirley Hazzard brought it to life in her novel. Cluttered with barrows of groceries, clothes, and junk for sale, it cuts narrowly through the heart of old Naples: past shops of small booksellers, violins, and proud *presepi*-makers (craftsmen of the Neapolitan Christmas mangers, also to be found in Via San Gregorio); under the shadows of towering palazzos and tenements, their bomb-blasted walls joined with clothes-lines thick with waving laundry. High above the street, on terraces, balconies, and rooftop gardens, down inside crumbling courtyards, and in the depths of twisting alleys, people live, work, sing, tend geraniums, and shout to their neighbors and children. Throughout this amazing labyrinthine mix of ancient, medieval, Renaissance, and Baroque architecture, some might focus on the poverty or the uncollected garbage. But Via San Biagio dei

Librai may also stir an awed respect for the resilience and improvisa-
tional genius of the human spirit in adversity. It may make you fall in love
with Naples. Jenny says simply to her new friend, Gioconda, with utter
sincerity, "Your street is marvellous." The narrow passageway of Via
Benedetto Croce/Via San Biagio dei Librai has been for the withdrawn
English girl a channel of deliverance to a new, more vibrant life. And
Gioconda, laughing about her neighborhood's squalor, confesses, "This
is Naples with a vengeance.... I couldn't live elsewhere."

A short time later, Jenny takes an apartment on the hill of POSILLIPO,
overlooking the BAY OF NAPLES (the focus of Rose Macaulay's pages
from *Pleasure of Ruins*—see page 281), and the setting of the culmination of the novel's love story. Jenny's prospect, appropriately, is full of
buried treasure from a past even older than Spacca-Napoli's. But
despite her remove to the outskirts of the city "along [its] northern
arc," her love for Naples deepens in the setting of its chaotic heart, in
Gioconda's neighborhood. The lovely street of VIA COSTANTINOPOLI
(where the antiques she looks at are still sold today) winds off to the
right, a bit uphill from its intersection with the Via Benedetto Croce
part of Spacca-Napoli, through PIAZZA BELLINI and past splendid vine-
covered specimens of palatial architecture in the courtyards of which
students gather, activists protest and declaim, and everyone listens to
street musicians.

Amidst the signs of catastrophe everywhere, Jenny understands "the
background of adversity" against which Neapolitans sustain a love of
life. The snobbery of northern Italians and many tourists toward "the
southern problem," highlighted by Naples, doesn't touch her. (Two
Edwardian visitors, Anne Buckland and Frances Power Cobbe, were
reminded here of the "squalor and degradation" of "the wretched
Irish" "a people always ready to give trouble to their rulers but never
likely to improve their own condition." Walking old Naples, the literary
traveler imagines how the city would have delighted James Joyce, who
loved "dear dirty Dublin." Giambattista Vico, whose philosophy of history and *Scienza Nuova*—the New Science—influenced the design of
Ulysses and *Finnegans Wake*, was born and lived in Spacca-Napoli.)

Shirley Hazzard's *The Bay of Noon* clearly belongs to the tradition of
Norman Lewis's *Naples '44*, the acclaimed memoir of wartime suffering and famine whose strongest theme is, in Lewis's words, "the

civilization and impressive humanity" of the people of Naples. Their courage in the face of the Nazi occupation—dramatized in the story of Gioconda and her family—is now legendary (and the subject of the film *Quattro Giornate a Napoli—Four Days in Naples*): the first city to liberate itself, their women and men, old and young, children, communists, ex-fascists, and prisoners fought four days of guerrilla warfare, forcing the Germans to abandon the city. Jenny observes, with admiration: "Nothing in moderation might have been the motto of these people; who were yet, like their city, ultimately a secret."

BASILICATA (LUCANIA)

Ann Cornelisen

Ann Cornelisen's books about Southern Italy make the reader see the lonely mountain villages in a region that many travelers (and travel guides) ignore, and she gives the people, especially the women, a voice. Reading her makes taking to heart what her subjects have lived and suffered feel like an existential necessity, as if their experience belonged to a region we know in our bones and must find. How she went from life in the American midwest and the study of archaeology to live and work for the Save The Children Fund in Southern Italy is the subject of her 1990 memoir, Where It All Began: Italy 1954. *(She mentions "the renunciation of rigidity," and academic study, theoretical life, as "an evasion.") Her other books include* Women of the Shadows *(1976),* Strangers and Pilgrims *(1980), and the comic novel* Any Four Women Could Rob the Bank of Italy *(1983)—set in Tuscany. Her masterpiece (and first book),* Torregreca *(1969), a portrait of a village in Basilicata (or Lucania), described as "an all-time classic" by Irish writer Sean O'Faolain and for which she received a special award from the National Institute of Arts and Letters in 1974, is represented in these pages. An outsider who came and stayed and made friends, Ann Cornelisen evokes with a novelist's art the harshness and terrible beauty of peasant lives. Rivaling the writings of Ignazio Silone and Carlo Levi, her narratives inspire astonishment at the heartiness of the human spirit. They make the reader want to see this place whose humanity, without her books, would be unvoiced.*

FROM *TORREGRECA: LIFE, DEATH, MIRACLES*

THE SETTING
*The town of Torregreca, in the region of Basilicata
in Southern Italy*

Basilicata. Region of Southern Italy, lying between Campagna, Puglia, the Ionian Sea, Calabria and the Tyrrhenian Sea: 9,988 square kilometers, 664,000 inhabitants (density 66 per square kilometer). *Provinces*: Potenza and Matera. Hilly in the east, the rest mountainous (Lucanian Apennines). Principal rivers (Bradano, Basento, Agri, Sinni) open into the Ionian Sea. *Economic resources*: the economy is essentially agricultural, but not highly productive; grain, olives, vegetables, vines. Cattle: cows and goats. Limited industry. Actually in process of development owing to discovery of natural gas. Small-scale weaving and food-processing enterprises. Limited communications (railroad Naples-Potenza-Taranto) complicated by the nature of the soil. *History*: in ancient times it was commonly known as Lucania; subjugated (272 B.C.) by the Romans; after fall of the Empire fought over by Greeks and Longobards; it passed then to the Normans (12th century) receiving from them its actual name. Subsequently its lot was that of the Kingdom of Sicily, then of Naples, and finally of the Two Sicilies.   —*Enciclopedia Garzanti* (1962)

It seems there never was a time I did not know all this and more about Torregreca, but there was—there must have been. My discovery of it must have been as gradual as the emergence of design in petit-point embroidery, a slow filling-in here and joining-up there, until it was no longer just an outline, but a dimensional picture of the "life, death and miracles" of Torregreca. I myself talk too much for it to have been, as I remember it, a discovery through monologues that I listened to on long winter evenings. But perhaps I will only know if I begin again, as I began so many years ago.

In 1954 I had come to Italy to study archaeology. Instead, without plan and almost against my will I became interested in a private British charitable agency that worked exclusively in the villages of Southern Italy. Their representative was a young Englishwoman who apparently saw something in me worth training—maybe nothing more than my passionate curiosity—and hired me on a semi-volunteer basis. For years I roamed the mountains of the Abruzzo, Lucania and Calabria learning the practical intricacies of nursery and infant-feeding center management. Our permanent demonstrations were used by Italian agencies for training teachers and social workers. We could not be theoretical. Everything had to work every day and on the simplest possible basis. Nor could we limit the work to the centers themselves. We were consultants to town councils; we visited institutions and collaborated on community development projects. We could not hope to feed, clothe and educate all the children of Southern Italy, but using simple, easily copied methods we tried to show how children could have the best care and food for the least money. I cannot honestly say special talents were needed. It was enough to know how to wash without water, how to de-louse children or dose them for worms, how to cope with fleas and eat gracefully whatever was offered—even pig's blood pudding mixed with chocolate and raisins. In time I became a specialist, one of the few who can fix a toilet float while confuting the Montessori System or expounding on the simplicities of Bowlby's theories of child development, and too I developed that all important quality—*serietà*. In Southern Italy even the simplest project involves a crochet of relationships and has no hope of success without that intangible aura of respectability. *Serietà* is more external than a moral code. It is proclaimed by a conservative, almost dowdy way of dressing, and a manner, slightly detached, very calm, that suggests incorruptibility. I worked on my *serietà* until men lounging in piazzas no longer considered me a loose woman even though I drove a car, smoked, and enjoyed a coffee or rum punch in a public bar. Indeed I doubt they considered me a woman at all.

Our centers were in villages where poverty was as naked as the children, and nurseries, if they existed, were nothing more than infant checkrooms. Methods that worked in such communities, however, were valid throughout the South. We traveled more and more until it seemed we were a flying advice squad for an ever-spreading network of children's centers. It was on one of those trips in September 1954 that I saw Torregreca for the first time. Much of the Appian Way was still unpaved and a woman driving a car was a novelty. I stopped for gas and all the unemployed men lurking in the Piazza came over to view the car and its driver. There was a delay while someone went for the pump attendant who never came but sent word there was no gas. I was not surprised. I already knew that in Southern Italy life is reversed; the simplest thing becomes the most complex.

Many of the trips I made through Lucania included a stop in Torregreca. I came to know the Mayor, several mayors in fact, the head of the hospital, and the nuns of San Fortunato. Most important of all, I came to know Luca Montefalcone, a nomad doctor famous all over Italy as *the* man who understands the South.

Luca Montefalcone has one passion, Torregreca, his native town, and wherever he goes, for whatever purpose, he talks about it, its peculiarities and its nightmares. I do not know that I can describe him. His hypnotic power over people depends on some inner tenderness beyond the reach of words. Is he handsome? I think not. As a young man he must have been a gaunt Arab; time has only softened what was angular. Now in his late forties, neither his height nor his hawk features are so startling as his wide brown eyes that glow with the compassion and wonder of a man who has accepted his own defeat as inevitable, but has never lost his faith in others. Those luminous deep-set eyes miss nothing. More than anything he says, they encourage the timid to speak, and he listens. A silent, lugubrious man, a pessimist by birth, he can beguile the most cynical when he chooses to talk. He is respected and, I think, envied by every man in Torregreca for his wealth, his outstanding career as an epidemiologist, his beautiful wife and his powerful friends. To the Torresi he is a success; to himself he is a failure because he can neither leave Torregreca nor stay there. If he lived there, he would be forced to change it; but to enrage his own people and destroy the only security he has ever known is more than he can face. So he has gone off—to Bari—just far enough to be away and still return to Torregreca when he can no longer rationalize his sense of defeat. He cannot leave it; he cannot reform it. Defeated he flees, bound forever to his failure by his love and his hatred. A shriveled kernel of optimism still remains . . . something *can* be done with the South . . . now, maybe if . . . Then someone tries his idea. The experiment leads to a law, and the South has changed a bit without noticing it. Luca meanwhile has gone on to something else.

Before we committed ourselves to training courses or new centers or experimental sections in institutions, we discussed them with him. His advice was always good, his help often invaluable. Everyone knew him and would support any project in which he believed. In 1958 our organization went to him with the idea of a new nursery training center to be built in one of the huge agricultural towns of Lucania or Puglia.

Why not Torregreca? he had asked.

Indeed, why not? It would fit in perfectly with a housing development—the *villaggio*—being finished on the ridge across from the town. It was he who convinced the town council to cede land to us, and then urged them to go one step further, to contribute to the running expenses of the nursery in exchange for our supervision of the housing nucleus.

He charmed the provincial authorities into thinking that Torregreca was the very place they themselves would have chosen. Quietly, unofficially, he buttonholed the members of the Communist-controlled provincial council to murmur that a modern, independent nursery would stimulate change in the hundreds of nurseries run by the nuns of San Fortunato. In fact he promised miracles—miracles I knew nothing about—and then, as the final touch, he said that I would live in Torregreca, not visit the town from time to time, but live there, and supervise the building of the nursery and its running. I was to carry out three of his pet experiments: teachers' training; resident supervision of housing; and reform of the nuns. Luca's optimism was a magic carpet that wafted us from one possibility to the next. From its giddy height obstacles were blurred into mere annoying details. A lay reformer, he assured us, would charm the nuns; truculent peasants would welcome a foreigner's interference in their lives. The town had waited centuries for just such a catalyst, he argued, and the more personal problems, such as finding a house for me to live in, would be a simple matter of my preference: I had only to choose. The nesting instinct is strong in women. I forgot the problems that should have worried me, and dreamed of fixing a two-room house in the Rabata. It is all unimportant now, for nothing worked out quite the way it was supposed to. First the delivery of my new car was delayed a month, and I had to take a train from Naples with all my possessions. It was June of 1959.

* *

In spite of its name the Naples-Taranto Express is a crosscountry trolley that meanders along the river bottoms of Lucania as though it were conscious of the futility of speed. When it arrives at the end of the line, it will have to trundle back, so it lingers at deserted station huts and waits patiently while herds of sheep graze on the right of way. To the peasants who ride a few stations up or down the line it is the symbol of the twentieth century with all the advantages and none of the disadvantages of a mule. They would never complain. But I was that exception—the long-distance traveler— and five hours to go one hundred miles seemed an unnecessarily cautious approach to the Middle Ages.

All around me women swayed and groaned in an ecstasy of fear. Beads clicked; reedy voices called on Mary, Jesus and Santa Rita. Down the way a beak-nosed woman in black had veiled her face with a black-bordered handkerchief. She groped in a voluminous plastic purse until she found a bottle of rose water which she dabbed on her temples, behind her ears, and under her nose. She sighed dramatically, reapppeared and folded her handkerchief neatly before returning to the school notebooks that were piled on the seat beside her. When another wave of nausea overtook her, she retired once more for the ritual exorcism. Her son, a spindly boy in very short pants and short elastic-topped socks, sat opposite her biting his nails.

Across the aisle a woman had wrapped her head in a fringed linen towel, making a burnoose from which she peered white-eyed and unseeing. Next to her a young woman spat up into a series of clean rags. Like human snails they shrank deeper into the shells of their bodies. They were waiting in cataleptic self-absorption for the dangerous journey to end.

At the front of the car men in sweaty corduroys and patched shirts hunched together in silence. Their faces sullen, their eyes wary, almost furtive under the visors of their caps, they bobbed and swayed with the train. They sought no contact with each other, even less with outsiders. They trusted no one, but preferred to brood, stringing and restringing the pearls of their discontent. A

hundred years ago such men were brigands. Today they are a cas-
trated menace; they resent, but they are afraid to act.

Except for a yellow-eyed hen who fixed me with a malevolent
gaze from her perch on an overhead luggage rack, no one paid any
attention to me until an irritable, red-faced man came to sit opposite me. He wore the corduroy suit of the peasant, but its very
neatness and the whiteness of his shirt established his superiority.
He had not bothered to take off his black fedora, but was settling
down to read his newspaper when something about me roused his
curiosity.

"Signora, are you a teacher?"

"No, I'm not."

"Studying to be one?"

"No, I'm not." I almost added, "I'm sorry."

"Too bad." His sigh emphasized the futility of the world. He
retired behind his newspaper and several stations later got off
the train without even a nod in my direction. I felt alone and
inadequate.

I turned away to watch the tufts of broom, their yellow flowers
twinkling as they swept the summer-white sky. There was no life on
the flats of checkered slag and still less on the ridges troughed by the
fingers of some malicious giant. At last the faintest shadow of pink
rimmed the barren hills and folded over the jagged furrows until
they softened to brown plush. It would be a desert sunset, I thought,
one shot with devils' tongues, and I would be in Torregreca.

I had arranged to stay at the Convent of San Fortunato until I
could find a house of my own, and had asked that they send
someone to meet me. They had. Stalking up and down the station
platform in front of a battered jeep was a gargantuan nun wearing a
rusty black coverall and a white veil so much askew that damp red
tendrils of hair curled out around its edges. A bent little man in
ragged clothes kippered in her wake. They were the welcoming
committee; my old friend Sister Clemente—whom I had got to
know well on my earlier visits to Torregreca—and her acolyte, the
half-demented Antonio who did the chores on the Convent farm.
She mopped her face in the crook of one arm, then the other,

achieving such a smear of sweat, dirt and freckles that she looked like a disgruntled child.

"*Oyee*, you got here! Thought you must have missed the train." Before I could say anything I was clutched to a jelly bosom that reeked of beer and pig stalls. "Get in the jeep. We'll take care of the bags. Anto', pick up anything you find loose. No, you ass, not the station master's trumpet . . . *Bags! Bags!* Over there! Go on." She watched him as he shambled away. "Have to watch him all the time. Last month he tried to rape me. Swear he did. Tore the clothes right off my back. We were down at the well on the old farm and all of a sudden he jumps me, throws me down and starts tearing at my smock. Not this one. *This* is my second-best. Before I could get the better of him, I was naked as a nursing mother. He's been mild as a baby ever since. The Mother Superior says we've got to get rid of him, but then she wants to change lots of things. . . ."

A NIGHT AT SAN FORTUNATO

The Mother Superior was a dumpy, moon-faced woman with piercing brown eyes and an unpleasantly lax, full mouth. She was not the imposing figure I had imagined from Sister Clemente's description, but she had that air of Olympian perseverance that is a Superior's most lethal weapon, and she was not afraid of silence. With her hands laced across her stomach she could wait indefinitely, never betraying irritation by the slightest movement. The fierce concentration of her waiting was disconcerting. Even the innocent felt driven to self-defense; absorbed in justification, they seldom noticed that when severely tried, she worried the knuckles of one hand with the fingers of the other. I think few have run the risk of telling her less than the truth.

She received me in a small, bare room behind the kitchen, known as the Mother General's dining room. I suspect she would have preferred a more formal reception without the domestic odors of sour tomato sauce or goat cheese, or the bustle of the novices cleaning great tubs of salad greens. It was time for supper, and chains on the derricks of the huge wood-burning range clanked as cauldrons were raised and lowered. The nuns of the kitchen crew bickered peevishly. Heavenly detachment was impossible with the business of housekeeping thundering on next door. The Mother General's dining room was the inner sanctum for guests who rated more than the ferns and Victorian settees of the front parlor, and though its round, plastic-covered table and hard chairs offered little comfort, it had two very important features: a fireplace, and an old-fashioned electric icebox. A fire, kept burning most of the year, was the only luxury the nuns allowed themselves. The icebox, which was useless in so large a household, had been the first such machine in Torregreca and was an honored status symbol. As we talked, I was reassured by its grumbling counterpoint.

Coffee is a ritual in Italy as tea is in China, a preamble to real business. I had not eaten since morning and did not want the thimble of black lye that was put before me, but courtesy required that I drink it, as courtesy required that the Mother Superior make polite conversation about the weather and my trip from Naples. Once the ceremony was over and the cup removed, her questions became entirely personal. She wanted information, felt she had every right to have it, and would probe until satisfied. No matter how much I resented her questions, no matter how personal or insinuating they might be, I had to answer them. In Southern Italy the facts of life are simple: without at least the tacit approval of the Church no outsider will last more than forty-eight hours.

The Mother Superior asked about my background, both at home in America and in Italy, my tastes, my hobbies, my politics, my nursery techniques, my theories of child psychology, my knowledge of dialects, my direct experience in Southern Italy and my motivations for the work I was doing. I listened to myself in the detached way sometimes possible when speaking a language not your own and thought I sounded very young and innocent . . . certainly too idealistic to be dangerous. When there seemed nothing more she could ask, she started again from the beginning. An hour and a half lengthened into two hours. I ruffled her composure by answering her specific questions and then waiting, as she waited, forcing her to ask me something else. We were picking a cadaver that had no more meat, and we might have pecked on into the night if Luca Montefalcone had not arrived and interrupted at a crucial point.

The Mother Superior had said, "I don't see what you expect to accomplish in Torregreca by setting up this nursery. The Torresi aren't interested in change, you know. In fact they use all their energy to fight improvements."

"Maybe they suspect the motives behind the improvements," had been my blunt answer.

She waited; I said nothing. There was a knock, then a shuffling of feet outside the door. Someone giggled. Finally the door opened a crack, revealing Luca's long, solemn face.

"Ah, so there you are! May I come in, Reverend Mother? You must protect me from Sister Gioiosa. She's lost her mind."

"I told him he couldn't. I *did* tell him, but he said . . . well . . . I won't repeat what he said." A fat, red-faced nun had come in behind Luca. It was the long-suffering Sister Joyful who was always cheerful and forgetful and plagued by faulty tear ducts that made her weep even in moments of happiness.

"That will be enough, Sister Gioiosa. Don Luca is always welcome here. Why don't you get him some coffee?"

"But, Sister," he said quickly, "don't poison me this time, please."

"Well, you don't have to drink it if . . ." Then she saw his gentle, mocking smile and stopped. "Oh, you're just teasing me." Sister Gioiosa blushed and wept at the same time and then bustled out of the room.

Luca laughed. Perhaps because his brother, Don Matteo, is a priest he has an easy manner with nuns, treating them as headstrong women who need jollying, but there is always a hint of challenge in what he says to them. All nuns are unnatural black crows to him. I think he sees each one as a woman who has rejected his masculinity, and his banter seems to say I'm a man and dammit you're still a woman. They play up to him and enjoy their brief flirtations with one of the few men in their lives who can never be suspect. After all, he *is* a doctor, and his brother *is* a priest. . . .

THE PROJECT REALIZED

Anyone who has children knows the clamor of the first days in a school or nursery. We had it all. The children who howled in terror, those who wanted to sit in a corner by themselves, others who found and clung to a doll in silence and the very few who stalked away from their mothers toward an enticing toy and never looked back. Many sat bewildered looking from the howlers to the players in an effort to decide which group they should join. We had them all: ragged and hungry and incredibly bright. If their manual skills and coordination were limited, so was their use of the spoken word. Speaking was saved for essentials—going to the toilet and food, at the sight of which they turned into vacuum cleaners. The afternoon nap on individual cots was never a struggle. They were sodden and sleepy with food, and the novelty of sleeping alone for the first time in their lives never wore off. They hit their beds like stones and had to be pried out two hours later. The teacher, a pretty Abruzzese girl, thought she would never understand what they said, but after the first week found she could untangle some of their tongue twisters and they, with the elastic ability of children, were rapidly learning Italian. The first strangeness was over for those *inside* the nursery, but not for those outside.

After the first day a rumor had flown through the town; the children were given *meat* for lunch. They had reported it . . . at length . . . when they went home, but no one could believe it. Each day at noon faces appeared at the windows to watch in wonder while the children, not in the least distracted, went about the serious business of filling their tummies with as much food as they could before it ran out. Chichella* in her new role of institutional cook made sure there was more than enough. She was the confidante of all the children who cried, or fought, or felt shy, and she appointed herself my spokesman with the mothers as well. How often I caught her whispering out the kitchen window, "And if

---

*The woman in whose house Cornelisen rented a room when she first came to Torregreca and with whom she made friends.

you don't clean him up, the Signora's going to send him home . . . and you know she'll do it too. That one does what she says."

She comforted the children and chided the mothers with equal ease; the nursery was hers because it was mine; and after eight years she still feels the same way. Every teacher and assistant who has worked there has had to subdue Chichella's sense of protective ownership. Few of them have ever had the last word. She has not been an easy person for them to deal with. Right is right and in her case right is "the way the Signora did it" . . . even now.

I had called a meeting of the mothers before the nursery opened and had discussed what we hoped to give the children, and what the mothers would be expected to give the nursery. For our part there would be hot milk in the morning, a full lunch—*pasta*, meat, cooked vegetable or salad and fresh fruit—and bread and milk before the children went home. Each morning they would change into play clothes and shoes supplied by us. They would be given vitamins and any special medicines the doctor suggested. They would *not* learn to read and write; they would not be divided by sex; they would *not* do anything in long snake lines; they would *not* be forced to sit all day repeating songs and poems; and they would *not* always look gloriously unruffled and clean. They were not little flowers. I promised food and rest, games that would increase their coordination and their ability to get along with children their own age. The families were not asked to pay anything; *however*, there were a few things I expected of them. The children did not have to come elegantly dressed, but I would not take them, nor would I allow a teacher to take them, if they were dirty. They would be sent home. Second, each child's play clothes, his bib, towel and his cot sheet would be sent home to be washed. Third, every Saturday afternoon two mothers would come and give the nursery a thorough cleaning. As they could figure out for themselves, each mother would have to come three times a year, which was not a large sacrifice. No one said a word; I was surprised. Luca, the Mayor, Don Matteo, the doctor, everyone had warned against my asking the mothers to clean. It made no difference what we normally did in other places—the mothers of Torregreca would rebel. They simply would not send their children. I argued that they would come, that they were too smart not to. They had nothing but time, and nowhere else in the town could they get such food for their children ... and without paying. The children would come and the mothers would do the cleaning—and not because we wanted to save the money of another salary. If the mothers came three times a year, we had three chances to teach them proper cleaning, three chances to woo them from the habit of sloshing dirty water around. It sounds an old saw, but it really does take less time to clean the right way—particularly if every bucket of water has to be hauled from a fountain—and unless the houses, toilets, plates and everything else were cleaner, there was no way to fight worms, impetigo, fleas and lice. There were no objections from the mothers. They divided up into two-women teams and picked their turns. The first Saturday one did not show up. Monday morning her child was turned back from the nursery (I walked home with him and gave the mother hell). The child would not be taken back unless she came the following Saturday. She sent the child every morning; every morning we sent him home. Saturday she came to clean. The try-on had not worked. She washed and starched curtains, or scrubbed toys with strong soapsuds along with the rest, and the problem vanished. It pops up once each year and is dealt with in the same way.

Hundreds of stories could be told of those children, sweet, funny, pathetic ones. They are the stories of all children. The first birthday party when the little boy sat looking at his candles in blushing joy while all the others howled their birthdays to make sure they would not be forgotten. The tears of the first little boy who came dirty and was walked back home. The little girl who woke up screaming from a bad dream and clung to me, saying, "He hit her again. He hit her." I did not ask who or what, but held her and murmured to her until she fell asleep again. The bandage on a skinned knee that was the envy of the others. The girls who retied their bows in front of the mirror in the bathroom before going home and the boys who scowled at themselves as they raked their hair with watery combs and slicked down their sideburns the way their fathers did before going out. The drawings of trains they had never seen, but that they imagined to be a series of carts strung together and attached to a belching dragon-tractor. Boats were another fascinating mystery. Every animal with four legs and two ears was a donkey, a dog, a sheep or a goat and they visualized cities as bigger Torregrecas with animal garages. The boys loved to play house; the girls wanted clay and paint . . . so many, many things they did over the years. A different person might remember different incidents, but there is one I can never forget.

The *villaggio* grew faster than the nursery which today has three sections for ninety-six children. One year we had to choose thirty-two children from some sixty families. The teacher and I visited every family, explaining that we would take the children who, for whatever reasons, seemed to need the nursery most. By then we knew our customers well and there was little chance of fooling us, but no one tried. One child I felt we had to take was Giovanna, a tall scrawny girl of five with fine delicate features and eyes as blue as the Mediterranean. She was next youngest of four children of the *villaggio* whore. In a sense her mother was a professional. She had never been willing to take a job, though priests and nuns were forever finding them for her. "I don't need to work, he'll feed me." *He* was whoever was living with her at the moment and more often than not he did feed her, but he was not interested in the children of other men. They wandered through the streets, abandoned, meek, dirty little things whose only sin in life was stealing food. The first morning Giovanna came to the nursery she was mute, but her eyes sparkled with curiosity and joy. She wanted to do everything, see everything, touch everything. When anyone came near her, she cringed away and hid her head, but she peeked from under her arm with those twinkling eyes. Never a word. We let her alone, tried to include her as normally as possible. I went to talk to her mother about cleaning her up. Her hair was long and matted, her clothes stank, but it was the mother's fault, not Giovanna's. Before I got in the house she was screaming at me.

"You can't send her home . . . you got to keep her now. Isn't my fault she wets her bed. You took her, you keep her." She was a screamer who yowled until the other person gave up in despair and went away. It was a well-planned system, but I tricked her into listening by keeping my voice so low she became curious. She stopped. I had my say and left. Giovanna was cleaned up some days, filthy others, but she played now and even talked a bit. For two or three days at a stretch she would not wet her bed, then she would. No one scolded her. I had worked long and hard on the teachers to make them understand the emotional causes. They were patient and sweet with her, but Giovanna developed a passion for me. If I came into the nursery a hand would sneak into mine and those eyes seemed to beg me to understand. I let her trail around with me. I talked to her, teased her, occasionally got a word out of her, but most of the time her conversation was tongue-clickings and jerks of the head. "No!" that meant. A month went by. She was cleaner, but her hair was a gummy, lice-ridden tangle. I knew that if I sent her home because she was dirty, her mother would turn her out in the road and forget about her. The others could be shamed, but not Giovanna's mother. She had threatened me with an axe when I told her either to cut and wash Giovanna's hair or I would. We had come to a draw, but not a permanent one.

One morning I took Giovanna in the kitchen with me and sat down to talk to her. She leaned against my knees peering into my eyes with such intensity I was afraid she did not understand what I was saying. Chichella came over to squat beside her.

"Did you hear what the Signora said? She's going to make you beautiful. Want to be beautiful, Giovà? Answer, or she'll go away. Who knows? Maybe you don't want to be beautiful . . ."

She nodded so violently her eyes bobbled and then threw her arms around Chichella's neck. They whispered happily; then Chichella stood up.

"Come on, then, if you're going to be beautiful like the Signora, we've got to get started." She winked at me and we three went off to the bathroom for our sesssion with DDT, scissors and soap. Giovanna radiated joy like the heat from an electric fire. She did not complain about the DDT that stung her scalp and got in her eyes. Combing the snarls was fun. Chichella and I made questioning faces behind her back. Something was very wrong . . . and then maybe we both realized at the same time . . . that little girl had never had so much attention, so much love spent on her in her life. We could have cut off her legs as long as we did something for and to her. When it was over and she was deloused, cut, washed, combed and more or less dry she said her first word.

"When do we wash it again?"

"But, *cara mia*, it's up to you to keep it clean now. You come show me a week from now if you've kept it this clean." She was smiling at herself in the mirror.

"I will, I will," and she threw her arms around my neck.

I have found her washing her hair at the fountain with yellow laundry soap and I have admired the scalloped cuts she gives herself; her hair has never been dirty or lousy again. It was a sapphire-eyed peacock who went back into the room with the other children that day; she knew she was special and especially loved, and I think that sense of being loved has stayed with her. She can see Chichella or me miles away. She waves and calls and runs to us with all the silent joy of that dirty little five-year-old.

The end of the story is that love is not enough. Her older brother raped her. The nuns at San Fortunato took her in, have kept her and have been as kind as they know how to be, but they chill my blood when they speak of her in her presence as "Our little Giovanna who was molested by her brother." She is twelve now, bright in school, beautiful with a strong, solemn beauty, and a few months ago I heard that an older couple wanted to take her into their home, which meant she would be their servant, but safe and perhaps loved. When the nuns told me about it, she was with me holding my hand timidly as she did so many years ago. This might be her chance, I thought, but just last week I heard she had been sent back to the Convent because she still wets her bed and the older couple lost patience with her. I know no answer except love and expert care, but Torregreca can offer neither to Giovanna, I am afraid.

People have asked me what one nursery, or for that matter ten such, accomplished. Little, perhaps. Better-adjusted, more curious children who were ready for school—that hardly seems enough. Health, yes. But less concrete things happened. The mothers reported that now no one in the family could go to the table without washing his hands. Tyranny of the five-year-old. *He* had to do it, so did everyone else. That helps with worms and so many other germy parasites. Clean clothes and occasional baths are

habit-forming; fleas and lice do not like them. If nothing else, wood
and potatoes cannot be stored in a tub that is used for baths. Curtains and everything else that is admired or found useful are
copied. I know that the hundreds of teachers who have spent time
in our nurseries—for courses or even short visits—have changed
their ideas of what a nursery can and should be. They have seen
that any local market can supply a wealth of inexpensive equipment, but that change in their nurseries depends entirely on their
willingness to work . . . and they have worked and changed. Those
thousands of children and their mothers have lost some of their traditional diffidence. A few have accepted that they can hope for fair
treatment. The children are not content only to learn by rote; they
want to know why. Is that enough? I cannot judge, but if even the
most tentative first wiggle toward true change has been made, we
have accomplished much. . . .

EPILOGUE

The mists and clouds of morning still burn off to be replaced by
the mists and clouds of evening, and there underneath is Torregreca but little changed in the years that have passed. I now read in
the authoritative newspapers of the world that Southern Italy has
been transformed. There is heavy industry, methane gas, work for
all. Strange that when I am there I feel none of this Utopian well-
being. We have water three hours a day now, peasant boys must go
through middle school where they wrestle with French . . . not that
they have learned Italian or a trade. There is a high school. Something called meat is for sale at prices higher than those of Rome or
New York. The tower is lighted every night at vast expense "to
attract tourists." Chichella has "new" second-hand furniture that is
very shiny and rather fragile, but at least made of real wood this
time. She cooks for the nursery, cleans for the utilities office,
washes for a neighbor . . . and is old at forty. Her brothers and all
their friends have come back from Turin and Germany. They came
six months ago. There is no more work there; there is none in Torregreca, but I learn from *The Economist* that the Southern Italian is
better off than ever before. No one seems to have noticed the

world has marched off and left them again. Recession has trimmed plans for Southern Industry. Some genius has proposed a huge vocational school ... a proposal our organization made twelve years ago and would have backed with money, but we were informed "the moment is not ripe." It may never be.

Luca tells me that these years of emigration and work have been years of "*disgregazione di una società*," the breaking up of a society, which had to happen so that the society could re-form in a modern structure. It has broken up and lost its cohesion. Now this new society must re-form ... on what basis ... hunger. That is not new in Southern Italy. . . .

It is a number of years now that I have not lived in Torregreca, though until recently I ran the nursery and spent ten days a month there. I built other nurseries, worked in other places, but always a part of me remains in Torregreca. I know now it always will. Every woman has one love affair that remains unfinished ... it is over, a closed book ... but still unfinished in that the mind plays with what might have been if passion and enchantment had been tempered by loving reason. I shall never be free of Torregreca; I have no desire to be. . . .

For the Literary Traveler

Ann Cornelisen traveled to her destination in Basilicata (Lucania) by train. She made her daily rounds for the Save The Children Fund by car, the most practical way for the traveler to see the world she presents in *Torregreca, Women of the Shadows,* and *Strangers and Pilgrims.*

The hazards of driving in Southern Italy are exaggerated. Renting a car in Naples and going south on the Autostrada (A3) and then east toward Potenza is an easy drive of about an hour and a half. To explore a small part of the landscape Cornelisen describes in *Torregreca*—"my mountain villages," in her words—leave the Autostrada at Potenza. Now the journey east proceeds along the APPIAN WAY. Renamed the S7, this secondary road winds along the track of the original ancient road across the eastern slopes and valleys of the southern Apennines. Long views of hills skirting riverbeds, distant towns—mounds of white chalk atop denuded mountains; ruins of Norman towers, medieval abbeys, abandoned farms, swaths of arid bleakness and sudden shadows, blinding sunlight, and color waves of wildflowers in spring—this desolate and heart-stopping region brings to mind another land of terrible beauty: the mountainous west of Ireland, which, like Southern Italy, lost its population to starvation and emigration.

The Appian Way, the road most traveled—from the Alban Hills on the outskirts of Rome, through Terracina, Capua, Benevento, and southeast across the Apennines to Taranto and Brindisi on the coast—represents centuries of history. Writers Dora Jane Hamblin and Mary Jane Grunsfeld, who hiked and drove more than 3,500 miles for two years to study the route, cast it as an ancient seductress in their book *The Appian Way, A Journey:*

> The most famous of all the world's roads was built by convicts, slaves and soldiers. It was named Queen by a poet.
>
> Publius Papinius Statius in the first century A.D. called it *lungarum regina viarum*—Queen of Long-Distance Roads. Strange, in the muscular military world of first-century Rome, that Statius should call this flinty triumph of engineers and impressed laborers a queen and not a king. Yet Statius was right.
>
> The Appia doesn't stamp and march its way from Rome to the Adriatic Sea. It seems almost to slide, sinuous and feminine. It flows softly between rows of cypresses and umbrella pines south of Rome, glides across the Pontine Marshes, slithers up the rocky slopes of the spine of the Apennine Mountains and down their valleys. It arches over rivers, rides viaducts up hills, goes on and on, quiet and enigmatic as a force of nature....
>
> There are older roads than the Appia. There are longer roads. There are topographically more dramatic roads. But no other highway on earth has seen so much of the traffic, the turbulence, the trade and triumph and bloodshed and glory which form the tapestry of Western civilization. No other road ever had so many poets....

Perched on a "giddy height," the village of TRICARICO, spectacular from a distance (about an hour or two past Potenza, depending on

the time you give to detours from the Appian Way/S7), is Ann
Cornelisen's *Torregreca*. The piazza, with its memorial to the war's
dead in the center, has the sleepy rhythm but wide-awake awareness
of the strangers that she describes. Built up the side and crowning the
summit of a mountain ridge, the top portion of the village is accessible
by climbing steps through narrow passageways that twist and turn and
are lined with small low-slung houses. The Franciscan nuns still occupy
their convent; a children's nursery Cornelisen started, identified with a
sign, is up a few steps immediately to the left as you pass beneath an
arch; alleys and small courtyards disclose cats, a child or two, motor-
bikes, hanging laundry, and glimpses of the hills and mountains beyond
Tricarico's heights. As stubborn as the circumstances and mentality of
the "Torresi" may have been—Cornelisen describes their resistance
to the possibility of improving things—the appearance of the village
today suggests change and progress. The people's small dwellings,
once dark mud caves, are now white-washed. Some are decorated
with flowerpots of geraniums; some have polished brass knockers.
Under the dazzling southern sun there is a sense of simple domestic
order.

So why the sense of mystery, of something sad or inexpressible
in Tricarico? Along the still passageways on the heights and below in
the streets and piazzas, there are few people to be seen. Through
the windows of the convent, a few old nuns can be seen ironing
and sewing. A few men stand around the piazza. A table of young
people sit outside a cafe on the main street that leads toward the
piazza. Two young male patrons in the only open restaurant, Pizzeria
Locomotiva, listen to American music (Bob Dylan) and claim to
know and admire New York. Two children play in a nicely furnished
park. Two women in black kerchiefs and black dresses, like characters in Cornelisen's *Women of the Shadows*, stand talking on a corner.
Along some streets, Tricarico seems deserted, evacuated. Statistics
show that unemployment here is very high. Tourists, obvious outsiders, are rarities. Yet, for all the stillness and apparent emptiness,
there is an undercurrent of consciousness. The traveler visits, walks,
chats briefly with merchants and waiters—everyone is pleasant, a
man giving directions has been to Brooklyn—climbs, watches bent
women in black carrying bundles and watching the visitors. Ann

Cornelisen's insight surfaces: "They are women of tremendous strengths, these women of the shadows. One of their strengths, and not the least, is their silence, which outsiders have understood as submission." But the silence also speaks of untold stories and suffering, of the vast unsifted layers of peasant history.

Further along the Appian Way, about two hours through winding, deserted hill country, is MATERA, another town well known to Ann Cornelisen as resident, worker, and archaeologist manqué in Southern Italy. (The National Museum in the convent church of St. Clare has archaeological collections of objects from the paleolithic and neolithic periods.) The capital of Basilicata (Lucania), it is dramatically situated on the sides and summit of an ancient hill overlooking the valley of the River Bradano.

Matera is drenched with light, signaling its nearness to the sea. The Adriatic and Ionian coasts—the end/beginning of the Appian Way—are only a short distance away. The morning sun is brilliant; the sunsets and the swooping seagulls over the *sassi*, the ancient cave dwellings carved out of the rock face of cliffs, are the stuff of poetry. The poetic voice, however, is tragic. The dwellings of monks escaping from Anatolia between the eighth and thirteenth centuries, the *sassi* became the homes of the poor: caves without light or water, where 15,000 children, adults, their donkeys and chickens, lived, starved, and died of disease together. The writer Carlo Levi, exiled to Basilicata for his opposition to Mussolini, describes the wretched conditions of the *sassi* and their resident poor in his brilliant political essay *Christ Stopped at Eboli*. In the post–World War II period, government housing projects provided alternative shelter. But the *sassi* and their stories remain. As exotic as they look today—German tourists explore them, and some of the caves, having been restored and reoccupied, look cozy, their honeycomb of lights glimmering at night toward viewers on the terrace of the *trattoria Il Terrazzino*—something haunting and eternal stirs the nighttime silence, perhaps the memory of history and the anonymous poor buried in the gorge below.

Minutes away from the *sassi*, water plays in the fountain, and the local people stroll arm in arm evenings in the radiant Piazza via Veneto, the heart of the city. History here, where children cavort and adults smile, seems a simpatico affair. Writing of this region, Ann Cornelisen concludes, "In the Torregrecas survival *is* life, all of it." Travelers to Southern Italy see that the springs of affection, profound and often silent, suffuse this process of survival, beside the flowing fountains in the centers of ancient moonlit piazzas.

SICILY

Barbara Grizzuti Harrison

Italian Days, *Barbara Grizzuti Harrison's first book about Italy—a master-piece of travel writing and spiritual autobiography—was praised by Eva Hoffman as "more than a sophisticated guide, . . . an account of a deepening encounter, of the way a sensibility enters into a culture and a culture acts upon the psyche and the mind. . . . As accommodating, tolerant, evocative and heterogeneous as the culture it describes." In* The Islands of Italy, *the source of the following pages about Palermo and environs, Harrison takes us to Sicily, Sardinia, and the Aeolian Islands. From the same autobiographical angle that makes* Italian Days *a provocative travel companion (and as absorbing as a good novel), she notices details of art, architecture, faces, history, clothes, colors, religion, and food, that, accompanied by glorious photographs, present Sicily as a feast for the imagination and the senses. Barbara Grizzuti Harrison was born and raised in Brooklyn in a family of immigrants from Southern Italy, the subject of her first memoir,* Visions of Glory: A History and a Memory of Jehovah's Witnesses.

FROM *THE ISLANDS OF ITALY*

SICILY

It is tempting to say that one visits the islands of Italy simply because they are beautiful and because they are there, which would of course be reason enough—except that no act has a single motive.

I went because of my love of water, which is mingled with and almost indistinguishable from a fear of water (I can float in a vertical position—I enter a fugue state—but I cannot bear to bury my face in water).

I went as a kind of memorial gift to my father, who, though he lived ten miles from the sea in Calabria, never saw the sea until he crossed it to come to America (over sixty years later, when he was dying, he made another crossing, almost as terrible as that first one: he crossed the bridge from Brooklyn to Manhattan to visit Mott Street and Hester Street and Mulberry Street, where he had grown up, but to which, in adulthood, for dark reasons that I can sometimes intuit—reasons having to do with love and betrayal and loss—he had never once returned).

I went, as a supplicant, to search once again for my mother and ask forgiveness of her spirit . . . which is to say, to try once again to comprehend the mystery of her life: water was one of the pleasures she banished, as she banished all earthly pleasure with fierce will, from her days. (I have never known why she was so dedicated to pain.)

I went for my Grandma DiNardo, fat and rosy and jolly in her long black wool bathing suit with remarkable décolletage, who played Ring Around the Rosie with me—just with me—at Coney Island, the froth of waves licking at our ankles. I cherish this image of play, and my gratitude to her was a driving force, too.

I went because the islands of Italy combine all the elements— fire, water, earth, and air—and that is irresistible.

I went to look for a dusty square that exists in my imagination: paths from the green countryside converge on a buttery yellow church and in this crossroad stands perpetually a woman dressed in black, a donkey, baskets of flowers . . . I almost thought to find this square in Corleone, but I did not. What I found instead in Sicily surprised and confounded me.

I went because water reconciles me to the hard world of stone . . .
And because the islands are so beautifully there.

Mountains, Mafia, marzipan, Solitary Greek temples, manic Spanish baroque, Moorish vermilion cupolas and golden Byzantine churches. Cloistered pleasure gardens, stern Norman forts. Market bazaars in which the North African and the Mediterranean, the savory and the seedy, mingle and mix: hot surprises in dark places. Seas of honey-colored wheat. Blood. Closed, secretive faces; chivalrous men; imperturbable courtesy. The world of the worldly rich and the world of the vanquished and lonely and poor. The elegant and the brutish.

The nourishing sea. The savage sun. . . .

PALERMO

On one side of the sea road from the airport to my hotel is the happy Mediterranean juxtaposition of date palms and pines, Christmas in July. Pink fleshy hibiscus and oleander which is deadly and prickly pears with elegant pale green flowers . . . what profligacy . . . But on the other side of the road are scrub and inhospitable hills—God is giving you a geography lesson: now you see me, now you don't; nature is profligate and varied, it is fickle too.

(So profligate that Goethe formed the fancy that he could discover here the "Primal Plant"—the plant from which all other plants were descended.)

Palermo is fabulous, intoxicating. And dangerous, too. Dangerous to the senses, upon which it places extravagant demands. And menacing—a city from which God often seems strangely absent: "God made the world," an unemployed Sicilian tells Danilo Dolci,* "and put it into the hands of men. Can He always give His mind to what's going on there? . . . God's in the church and has His own affairs to attend to."

Palermitani say their city is "degradato"—degraded, afflicted with corruption and decay, vile poverty and ugly suburbs into the building of which washed Mafia money has gone. Their love is darkened—and deepened—by grief.

Who would guess that the tiny whiteness of jasmine could release such an abundance of sweet perfume?

Severity, excess, absurdity, grandeur: in the center of Palermo, Spanish baroque and Moorish and Byzantine and Norman dazzlingly coexist; whoever conquered—Berber emir, Byzantine, Spanish viceroy—left his mark in stone.

Frothy, grimy, restless, at the intersection of two main streets are the Quattro Canti (the four corners), actually a monument in four

*The radical Christian writer and social activist who created a well-known center for community development in Partinico, about thirty minutes from Palermo.

elliptical parts, orchestral, silly, eventually rather lovable, that marks the division of the city into four parts; one fits into the four corners as snugly as Palermo fits between the mountains and the sea. Seventeenth-century architects had the same horror of a vacuum that later Victorians did; the monument, which D. H. Lawrence called "that decorative maelstrom and [with reference to the chaotic traffic at the four corners] death trap," is alive with statues of rulers and patron saints . . . including poor Saint Agatha, who sliced her breasts off to make her less desirable to men, and offered them to God . . . Lampedusa writes of "virgin's cakes shaped like breasts . . . Saint Agatha's sliced-off breasts, made at convents, devoured at dances." In my memory (memory being a form of desire) the four canted monuments make a perfect circle climbing almost to the sky, enclosing me in this voluptuous city.

In nearby Piazza Bellini are three churches so different one from the other that they might have been built to honor and house several gods radically different in purpose and in temperament.

Goethe said that the churches of Palermo "surpass even those of the Jesuits in splendour, but accidentally, not deliberately. It's as if an artisan, a carver of figures or foliage, a gilder, a varnisher or a worker in marble, without taste and without guidance, had wished to show what he could do in a given spot."

As the Spaniards—dark, passionate, mystical—differed so much from the Romans—earthy, pragmatic, exuberant—so do the Spanish baroque churches of Palermo differ from the baroque churches of Rome. In the overbearing richness of their decoration, in the redundancy of ornamentation, they are as irritable as the fires of the Inquisition (the Spanish brought as much energy to one as they did to the other); behind its sober doors, the church of Santa Caterina looks as if it will (like fire) of itself be consumed, as if it will fall of the weight of its own excrescences. The central dome of the nave, solidly encrusted, barnacled with meaningless gold, has spawned lesser domes in the transepts; saints dressed like cardinals frolic in skies of pale blue; lasciviously dimpled *putti*— marble cherubs indistinguishable from cupids—fly through pink sunsets trailing ribbons and garlands; marble—draped, folded, scalloped, serpentine—is heaped upon marble. Nothing is unelaborated upon; and the effect of all this is darkness and languor, not light.

In this perversely somber place a long-haired young girl wearing shorts makes her confession to a priest who inclines toward her sweetly in the open confessional (even the confessionals have domes), this transaction, anonymously public, is so friendly as to appear casual. A young man in dungarees and a checked red shirt reads the Liturgy of the Word, oblivious of gold . . .

The lovely church of La Martorana has walls of gold, too, but its Byzantine mosaics tell rapturous stories with dignity; La Martorana is intimate and mysterious, it is gorgeous, it is an Arabian nights cave, a child's dream of a cave, a womb of light . . .

One day we saw a fat sweaty bride at La Martorana. In the piazza a baby had convulsions and fell out of its cradle, and the bride was protected from knowledge of this. Next to the bride's car is a car on which a scribbled sign is posted: SINCE MAY PEOPLE HAVE BEEN SLEEPING IN THIS CAR CERVICAL CANCER EMBOLISM. . . . There is a baptism in La Martorana, several baptisms in the Greek rite, chatty and ambulatory. Boys in bow ties and short black pants and girls in white hold candles against the gold: light unto light. Baby boys and baby girls spectacularly dressed are undressed and immersed in a copper vessel, then toweled off and clasped to their parents' proud breasts. Light heals, water heals. St. Paul says that in Christ there are no males and no females; in the first step of their spiritual journey, the babies are equal in the sight of God and congregants . . . It was in this church that marzipan was first made, and sold.

Rectangular, linear, strong, severely Moorish, the chapel of San Cataldo shares a mossy little courtyard—it always smells of country rain—with Martorana. Three melon-colored domes reach into an impeccably blue sky. Lampedusa compared these domes to flattened breasts, empty of milk . . .

One day at lunch in the trattoria in Piazza Bellini I ate half a roast chicken flavored with marjoram, and a chardlike vegetable served cold with olive oil and lemon, and cold white wine—the antithesis of the baroque. Another day I eat a pizza with smoked salmon and tomato and thyme; the salmon matches, in the dry transparency of the air, the domes of San Cataldo.

On the doors of San Cataldo and Santa Caterina there is a poster of a poised and pretty little girl, smiling: RAPITA, the poster says—KIDNAPED.

Under the stunning sun the huge market of La Vucciria is draped with awnings, faded green, blue, orange; under the swaybacked awnings naked electric light bulbs burn all day long. One is never quite in sunlight, never quite in shadow; this is a contained city, both homely and exotic, of booths and tents, a *souk*.

The stall keepers vie with one another for inventiveness and volume and ribaldry: *My lettuce is as sweet as milk. My pears are tender as butter. Your breasts are like two pomegranates, here are pomegranates hard and delicious as your breasts.* Meat looks still sensate, and sacrificial—whole lambs with imploring milky eyes and blood-wet hair, their bellies split open to expose the health of iridescent, obscenely pale pink internal organs, the gash held tidily together with bamboo skewers. The vulnerability of flesh. Sartre—the thought of whom, his forced rationality, his reflexive dread, is ludicrous in this candid oriental bazaar—said that to love a human being one had to imagine his intestines and love them too. Ropes of goats' intestines, small intestines snowy white, large intestines ivory, are wrapped around wooden skewers. They are quite pretty, as an abstraction, a kind of rubbery, slidy, slippery organic macrame. It doesn't do to entertain them in the imagination too long. Fish: pink; coral; silver; sluglike; squishy; hard; palpable; russet; pearly; mottled; striped; openmouthed in arrested wonder, and intelligent-looking. Snails the size of thumbnails move in their baskets, a death dance. Livid *baccalà* surrounded by bright yellow tomatoes on improvised fountains made of pierced display tins—fountains among fountains in a city of extravagantly ugly fountains. Poor swordfish, futile great white eyes, futile, impotent beaks. *Hack!* goes the butcher, the fishmonger, on round sections of tree trunk supported on sturdy poles—no sanitized deception here. Smooth squashes, four feet long, of tender green culminating in decorative curlicues resting in nests of fuzzy green leaves. Four kinds and colors of eggplant. Music vaguely Arabian (perhaps this is my imagination) comes from the booths; and Madonna sings. A bakery with oven doors that resemble the façade of Santo Spirito in Florence: *panna brioche*, fat sandwiches filled with thick white cream.

In my immigrant family's southern Italian dialect, the word for squash, which I heard as *gugooz*, was used with a characteristic combination of affection and derision: Hey, *gugooz* . . . Hey, sweet nuisance, honeybunch-fool. Another word for squash, a word I heard as *zhoodrool*, signified only derision and contempt and was reserved for people outside the family. And the word for eggplant, which I heard as *mulinyam*, was applied to colored people. My family being Calabrese and Abruzzese, *Sicilians* were called *mulinyam*. They were thought, not without a shred of historical justification, to be Moors. . . .

On narrow streets, slippery with refuse, street urchins surround us. We are in the market of the Capo; it is poor. The children— brown and pretty girls with knobby knees and long dark hair— exchange coded signals with one another; their aggression is disguised as sauciness. Or perhaps it is the other way around. If we cannot understand what they want, it is probably because they have not decided what they want, or can reasonably expect to appropriate, from us. There are no boundaries between bodies; perhaps, poor, they sleep many to a bed, they are a tangle of children, and their prodding at our flesh seems natural, a primitive but absolutely reasonable exploration of their environment, which our presence has altered. We have come to find Art Nouveau mosaics on a bakery storefront. And we do (the children tire of their game . . . whatever it was, their game). Sun motes dance in narrow alleys. At the Panificio Morello, we find the object of our search: a brilliant mosaic, an angular stylized woman in gold and lapis lazuli and emerald green; plum-colored chiffon and milky skin in stone. It is aristocratic and denatured, I have a violent reaction to it in this dirty, swarming, yeasty place. It is self-referential art, it needs a context . . .

On the window of the storefront bakery is a poster of just such a pretty girl as those who have been following us: RAPITA, it says.

Men smoke and drink rapaciously and silently and without

apparent pleasure in dark, open storefronts, courting oblivion; it is worth a woman's life, to say nothing of her honor, to linger here. . . .

Five miles southeast of Palermo, in Monreale, is a twelfth-century cathedral combining Moorish and Norman styles. Sober and sumptuous, a discreet blaze of gold: mosaics glorify the walls. Every Bible story you're likely to have heard is depicted here in golden mosaics, amazingly plastic, articulated stone: a po-faced serpent climbs a lollipop tree (an odd thing: perfect Eve's breasts sag); Jesus cures a leper distinguished by his many many spots. Over the panoply of human, animal, and vegetable life broods a huge, majestic, calm, and sturdy Christ.

And underneath the cycle of Old and New Testament stories are abstract mosaics, they look like paper-doll cutouts or a child's drawings of Christmas trees.

The cathedral is close with the smell of hothouse lilies and of incense; its baroque *tesoro* (treasury) is close with the smell of human sweat.

In the cloister I do not know whether I am smelling the pale green formal smell of roses or my own perfume. Pigeons burble. Slender columns, no two alike: mosaic bands of black and emerald green and the red of dried blood, and aqua; incised serpents, rams, wise men, grapes, deer, apostles, doves. Within the cloister is a *chiostrina*, a smaller cloister, an enclosure that contains a slender fountain, the water a silken ribbon of light that caresses its shaft; the fountain anchors this corner, the *chiostrina* anchors the cloister, it is perfect psychological space, exciting and safe: a definition of joy? Nothing is single, everything is grouped: grouped in groups of twos.

Above the tiled roofs of the cloister, flowered sheets and men's underwear are hung out to dry.

What is the echo of a fragrance?

What is the color of shade?

In the piazza we have *spremuta d'arancia*, blood-red orange juice with coral foam.

Palermo's Cappella Palatina, in the immense Palazzo dei Normanni, is smaller than the cathedral at Monreale, exquisite. This gold is neither hot nor cold, it creates its own magic climate. I feel like a princess in a garment of gold in a cave of golden stalactites; I would like to be that princess and be married here. Indeed someone *is* being married here; she looks pregnant. If I were the princess of my fantasy I would have as my summer home the nearby deconsecrated church Immanuele, whitewashed, simple, its open door framed with jasmine and roses. From its cloisters I could see the church of San Giovanni degli Eremiti, four red domes on slender white stone pillars: Arabian nights.

For the Literary Traveler

Barbara Grizzuti Harrison's "Palermo" captures the mood swings that accompany walking through this city. Its fountains, winding streets, piazzas of palm trees, churches, grotesque sculptures, and crumbling palazzos communicate an urban tangle of historic grandeur, of grief and poverty. Palermo has a hypnotic sense of a beauty that breathes despair.

A route that follows a portion of Harrison's itinerary proceeds along VIA MAQUEDA (a main street paralleling Via Roma) north from the STAZIONE CENTRALE (Central Train Station) on Piazza Giulio Cesare. About ten to fifteen minutes along from the station, a turn to the left winds along Via Ponticello through an ancient, crowded neighborhood to the GESÙ (or the Baroque church of the CASA PROFESSA). The first Jesuit church in Sicily, the interior of the Gesù is an incredible, wild display of marble and sculptural decoration. (A wedding in progress on the early evening of our visit undercut the lavish setting: the bridal gown was simple and the guests' outfits of black, white, and gray, were conservative.) Harrison, understanding the dark side of exaggerated effects, captions her book's photograph of CASA PROFESSA with a quote from Lampedusa's *The Leopard* (translated in 1960):

> It was the religious houses which gave the city its grimness and its character, its sedateness and also the sense of death which not even

the vibrant Sicilian light could ever manage to disperse.... All Sicilian expression, even the most violent, is really wish fulfillment: our sensuality is a hankering for death; our laziness, our spiced and drugged sherbets, a hankering for voluptuous immobility, that is, for death again; our meditative air is that of a void wanting to scrutinize the enigmas of nirvana.

Yet in the streets around and behind Casa Professa, to the south and east—the QUARTIERE DELL'ALBERGHERIA, one of the poorest in the city—the produce stalls, the artisan workshops, and the university students hurrying back and forth to the nearby University communicate a taste for life and its flourishing, despite environs marred by a do-nothing, corrupt municipal government and the unrepaired war damage of fifty years ago. (Sicily suffered heavy Allied bombings in 1943.)

Back on the Via Maqueda, still walking north, on the right hand side in the PIAZZA PRETORIA, rises and gushes what the Palermitani call "the fountain of shame," a paradoxical sort of monument to pagan and Manichaean excess. The stone figures, in their reluctant sensuality, recall the tone of the passage from Lampedusa. Behind the piazza are the three churches in PIAZZA BELLINI visited and described in these pages by Barbara Grizzuti Harrison: SANTA CATERINA, LA MARTORANA, and SAN CATALDO.

Via Maqueda, just beyond Piazza Pretoria, intersects the CORSO at the renowned landmark QUATTRO CANTI, an operatic crossroads with four façades bearing fountains and statues of the four seasons, the four Spanish kings of Sicily, and the four patronesses of Palermo (Cristina, Ninfa, Oliva, and Agata, statues of whom also figure prominently in the high reaches of the nave of the Duomo). Turning left at the Quattro Canti, the walk west along the Corso (Palermo's main street) passes architecture and spaces of grandeur and devastation. These include the decrepit palazzos of PIAZZA BOLOGNI to the left and the crumbling façade of PALAZZO RISO-BELMONTE, on the right side of the Corso across from the piazza. Now an abandoned shell, the Palazzo Riso-Belmonte was once one of the most magnificent buildings in the city. Further along, on the right, is the golden-stoned Duomo.

Across the Corso, behind the public garden of palm trees on the corner, is the huge PALAZZO DEI NORMANNI, the palace of the Norman ruler Roger II (1130–1154), under whom Palermo became the center of trade between Europe and Asia, and later of the Hohenstaufen Frederick II (*Stupor Mundi*, who liked to weekend in Enna—see pages 353–54). At the rear of the Palazzo is the entrance to the CAPELLA PALATINA; its interior is considered by some the finest work of mosaic art in Italy, surpassing Ravenna, and celebrated in these pages by Barbara Grizzuti Harrison as she also contemplates the beauty of the nearby CHURCH OF SAN GIOVANNI DEGLI EREMITI (St. John of the Hermits) in Via dei Benedettini. Many travelers, like Harrison, find its cloister and garden beneath Arabic domes a sanctuary of imagination and light, one of the loveliest spots in Palermo.

Returning to the Corso and continuing west beneath the huge PORTA NUOVA leads to the PIAZZA INDIPENDENZA and, on the right alongside a few sidewalk produce stands, the stop for bus 389, which takes travelers without a car to Monreale.

The bus ride, 8 kilometers southwest of the city, ascends about 310 meters, providing exhilarating views of Palermo and the CONCA D'ORO (Golden Conch). In the city spread out below, against the crescent-shaped harbor and a headland of mountain, the point of her name becomes clear: The word "Palermo" derives from *Panormus*, a Greek word signifying "all harbor."

The CATHEDRAL at Monreale (iconographically Christocentric, though dedicated to the Assumption of Mary) and its adjoining spectacular cloisters (which are not always open when the guidebooks and the sign on the door say they are) are a repository of the world's most magnificent mosaic art. Together they show the cultural blend of Roman, Arabic, Oriental, Greek, Hebrew, and Norman influences that makes visiting Palermo and environs widen one's perspective about Italy and its diverse origins. The PIAZZA VITTORIO EMANUELE (across from the northside entrance to the Cathedral), framed by palms and busy with townspeople and tourists, is a good place to ponder the rich humanity of this multicultural island from Harrison's original angles.

Mary Taylor Simeti

*Born and raised in New York City, Mary Taylor Simeti traveled to Sicily in
1962 after graduating from college to work for a year in the Danilo Dolci
Center in Partinico. She never went home, or rather, with the man she married there—Tonino—and the children they had, she made a new home in
Sicily. In her memoir/travel book,* On Persephone's Island: A Sicilian
Journal, *she chronicles, in elegant prose, a year of life—farming, cooking,
history, politics, wine-making, religious ceremonies, family, and travel—in
the place she calls Persephone's Island, after the goddess who once made
Sicily her home and the mountain town of Enna the site of her temple. The
account, excerpted here, comes across as a woman's love affair with an island
and its culture that stirs the reader's desire to know the colors, tastes, fra-
grances, and mythology herself. To the seductive art of this autobiographical
travel writer, travel is the best response.*

FROM ON PERSEPHONE'S ISLAND: A SICILIAN JOURNAL

PROLOGUE—OCTOBER 1962

Like most young Americans traveling abroad in the early sixties, I
arrived in Sicily with an excessive number of suitcases, considerable ignorance, and a great many warnings. In college I had studied
the Sicilian Middle Ages, and over the summer I had read about
Sicilian poverty in the writings of Danilo Dolci, the social reformer
at whose center for community development I hoped to volunteer.
This kernel of fact, meager as it was, had been fleshed out by the
cautionary tales of friends and acquaintances, both at home and in
the north of Italy, who all considered me courageous, if not downright foolish, to set off by myself for an island of dazzling sun and

bright colors where bandits and mafiosi lurked in the shadows and where the rest of the population was proud and reserved, distrustful of foreigners, and sure to misinterpret the presence of a young girl alone.

But from the window of the train that was bearing me south to Palermo the only color to be seen was gray: gray storm clouds piled up against gray mountains, gray olive trees tossing up the silver undersides of their leaves to the wind, and a gray sea tossing up silver foam onto gray rocks and beaches as the train threaded its way through the necklace of tunnels and coves strung out along the coasts of Calabria and northern Sicily.

My mother was living in Florence at that time, and it was there that I boarded the train in the middle of the night. Living on my own in a Sicilian village was not what my mother had had in mind when she offered me a year in Italy to celebrate my graduation from Radcliffe, and as she saw me into my compartment she was obviously hard put to be both encouraging and liberal minded, and yet with the same breath remind me to be careful about the men, the Mafia, the drinking water, and all the other things that would no doubt come back to her as soon as the train pulled out of the station.

On her graduation trip in 1924 she and her college roommate had left the boat at Naples and taken a train across southern Italy to Bari. They were the only women on the train, and the soldiers who shared their compartment spent the whole trip comparing my mother's ankles to those of her friend by measuring them between thumb and forefinger. Yet I did not recognize in her story my own age, my own curiosity, my own train ride south, since I was still too young to believe that she might ever have had any experience relevant to mine. So I hushed her up and settled my suitcases as quickly as I could, anxious not to disturb my fellow travelers who were already sleeping in their bunks. The Florence stop was not a long one, and soon we were moving, my mother waving forlornly in the yellow light of the station platform as the darkness swallowed us up.

It was not a restful night. I was too excited to do more than doze, and two of my fellow travelers turned out to be under three and equally excited, so I was glad when the train pulled into

Naples in the uncertain light of a gray dawn, and I could abandon any pretense of sleep and introduce myself to the Sicilian family whose compartment I was sharing. My Italian was only just adequate and I was quite unaccustomed to the Sicilian accent, but I managed to understand that they had emigrated to Milan in search of work some years before and were returning to Palermo for a visit. I also managed to explain that I was traveling alone, via Palermo, to the town of Partinico, where I intended to live by myself and to work for the next year or two.

They were horrified. Throughout the morning, as we wove our way slowly down the Calabrian coast, they alternated between pressing me with large rolls and thick slices of salami from their shopping bag of provisions, and reiterating their surprise and indignation that a young American girl should choose—nay— should be allowed to wander off into the wilds of Sicily with no family to protect her. There was no censure, only commiseration. Surely my mother was out of her mind.

By the time the train had backed and filled itself, first on, then off the ferry that carried us across the Straits of Messina, it was early afternoon, but the heavy rain that shut out the landscape made it seem still later. Another passenger joined us at Messina, a man in his thirties who stared at me steadily from behind his dark glasses.

His gaze was, however, a minor discomfort. What I could not avoid was the fact that I had wired the Dolci Center asking to be met at the Palermo station at two-thirty, yet as the train rolled on it was becoming increasingly apparent that we couldn't possibly arrive anywhere near that hour. At last I broke the silence that had fallen upon the compartment since the man in dark glasses had joined us, and asked if we were far from Palermo. It turned out that we still had most of Sicily to cross, that the scheduled arrival time was two hours later than I had been told in Florence, and furthermore the man in dark glasses, who worked for the railroad, claimed that the train was already an hour behind schedule. As the afternoon wore on and the sky got darker and darker, it became clearer and clearer that there would be no one waiting for me at the Palermo station.

I was somewhat of an anachronism even for 1962: most of my traveling had been done with my family, and in almost the same style in which my mother had traveled in 1924 — not a step taken without the blessings of Wagon-Lits Cook. Confident of being met in Palermo, I had neglected to plan beyond my arrival there. I had no idea in which direction Partinico lay or how I could get there on my own. Neither, it turned out, did my fellow passengers, who were all true Palermitani and considered anything that lay beyond as unworthy of civilized interest. They supposed that there was a bus to Partinico, but when and from where it might depart, nobody knew.

The compartment took my plight to heart, discussing the pros and cons of the various possible solutions with what I was discovering to be a true Mediterranean love and enthusiasm for other people's problems. And, unfortunately for my already shattered peace of mind, with the true Mediterranean sense of melodrama: it seemed that wherever I might turn, a fate worse than death awaited me. I suggested a hotel. "A young girl alone?!" The couple insisted that I go with them to their parents' house, but with visions of sleeping six to a bed I assured them that that was quite impossible. The man in dark glasses then promised that the minute we arrived he would go off to find out about the bus, and it was on that note of dramatic suspense that the train finally emerged from the darkening rain into the relative cheer of the Palermo station.

Vast numbers of relatives were waiting to welcome home the young family, and, reluctantly accepting my last grateful but firm refusal of their offers of hospitality, they climbed down to be wrapped up and carried off in a cloud of tears, cries, and resounding kisses.

I had brought with me all and more than I needed for a year's stay and could not take a step without assistance. But the man in dark glasses helped me to assemble my luggage on the station platform and went off in search of a bus schedule. The astonishingly large crowd that had been waiting for the train had by this time captured and borne off its prey, and the platform was almost empty except for the railway workers. Perched on a large pile of suitcases, I watched the man in dark glasses disappear into the station. I felt sure that I would never see him again, and twenty-four hours of travel and admonitions had so flattened me that I never

SICILY

stopped to think how strange it was that this should upset me. But in a few minutes he was back.

"The last bus left an hour ago. There is nothing to be done. I must drive you to Partinico in my car."

My better judgment didn't stand a chance. It wasn't until my suitcases and I were piled into a little Fiat and parked by a bar where the man in dark glasses was telephoning to his mamma that he would be late for supper, that the voice of *my* mamma could be heard above my desperation. Who was this man who was driving me off into the night? I was still debating whether I had time to get out and make a note of the number on the license plate without being caught in what would have been an excruciatingly embarrassing position when he came back and we were off.

The lights of the city dropped rapidly behind and below us, as the road we were following climbed steadily upward. It was almost completely dark now, but the headlights reflecting off the wet tar gave enough light for me to see that we were curving back and forth along the side of a mountain, sheer rock on my side of the road, sheer drop on the other. It was interesting, he'd never driven this road before, said he as we skidded briskly around the bends. Very, said I, bracing myself for the crash.

It seemed an endless journey, but it can't have been more than half an hour before we were in Partinico, asking directions to the Center, and I was wondering how I could be sufficiently polite and grateful while discouraging any follow-up on our acquaintance. The Center was still open, and when I and all my luggage were safely unloaded, the man in dark glasses shook my hand, waved aside my thanks, and drove off. I never saw him again, or had another chance to express my gratitude for what he had done for me.

I owe him much more than just a ride. By his disinterested generosity toward a foreigner in difficulty, the man in dark glasses stripped me of the prejudices instilled by the warnings of well-meaning friends and delivered me to Partinico with my honor and belongings intact, my spirit cheered, and my mind free to discover Sicily for myself. Now, as twenty years later I attempt to draw a portrait of my destination, I can see that these two figures have stood sentinel throughout my journey: my mother, whose passionate curiosity for all that surrounded her was a legacy far more valuable to me than her warnings, and the nameless Sicilian whose chivalrous gesture was my introduction to the strong, impulsive soul of Sicily, a soul that reaches across and beyond all that is so distressing here and, like the island sun, warms and illumines even as it creates dark shadows. . . .

WINTER

Despite brief intervals of furious rainfall, Saint Martin's summer holds for the whole month: the morning crispness wilts in the sun, Francesco* bundles up only to return at noon in a T-shirt, his discarded sweaters stuffed into his book bag. On the farm the end of November brings a moment of respite, with nothing to be harvested, fermented, or cured, so I propose a different weekend to end the month: Saturday in Palermo for the pleasure of the kids, old enough now to prefer the company of their peers to the pastoral delights of Bosco, and on Sunday a trip to the city of Enna.

Tonino has often been to Enna for professional reasons, but the rest of us have seen it only from the *autostrada* to Catania, perched high on a mountain that marks the very center of the island, the "navel of Sicily." So strategic a location has naturally been a temptation to the many succeeding waves of conquerors that have swept over the island, and Enna has been besieged and stormed many times, yet surprisingly enough its thirteenth-century castle has managed to survive being such a bone of contention and remains one of the biggest and best-preserved fortresses in Sicily.

If it is the castle and the drive through the sweeping wheat fields of the interior, so different from the vineyards and orchards of the coastal plain around Bosco, that I use as bait for the family, for me this trip is something of a pilgrimage. Enna is the ancient seat of the cult of Demeter, the corn goddess, patroness of agriculture and the good harvest, bestower of fertility, the Mother. Together with her daughter Persephone she held all Sicily, the most fertile of the Mediterranean islands, in her protection, and her shrine stood on

*The writer's son.

the top of the mountain on Enna, overlooking the wheat fields and the flowering plain where Hades (or Dis) galloped his black horses as he bore off Persephone, known to the Romans as Proserpine, to be his queen in the Underworld.

> Near Enna walls there stands a Lake Pergusa is the name
> Cayster heareth not more songs of Swans than doth the same.
> A wood environs every side the water round about,
> And with his leaves as with a veil doth keep the Sun heat out.
> The boughs do yield a cool fresh Air: the moistness of the ground
> Yields sundry flowers: continual spring is all the year there found.
> While in this garden Proserpine was taking her pastime,
> In gathering either Violets blue, or Lillies white as Lime,
> And while of Maidenly desire she filled her Maund and Lap,
> Endeavoring to outgather her companions there. By hap
> Dis spied her: loved her: caught her up: and all at once well near:
> So hasty, hot, and swift a thing is Love, as may appear.
> The Lady with a wailing voice afright did often call
> Her Mother and her waiting Maids, but Mother most of all
> And as she from the upper part her garment would have rent,
> By chance she let her lap slip down, and out the flowers went.
> And such a silly simpleness her childish age yet bears,
> That even the very loss of them did move her more to tears.
>   —Ovid, *The Metamorphoses*

Of all my early schooling I best remember the many happy hours spent drawing scenes from the Greek myths as our teacher read them aloud to us, and I still visualize the gods as they appeared in the drawings pinned up on my classroom walls. Given this felicitous introduction to Greek civilization, it is odd that during my subsequent career as a history major I should have avoided any course in classical history. Indeed, I felt a distinct aversion to all things Greek, which only now I see might be related to the truly horrendous view that Olympian mythology takes of women. What was a young girl to make of such a bevy of first-class bitches? However expurgated a version we were given, there was little there to reconcile us to the role of wife and mother for which the 1950s were so assiduously preparing us. Aphrodite was a slut, Hera was a jealous shrew, and if Athena and Artemis, despite a rather nasty taste for revenge, came out middling well, the price to pay was eternal virginity. Last came Pandora, to heap all the world's ills on shoulders already bent under Eve's contribution. No wonder I developed a distaste for the Greeks.

One cannot, however, live twelve miles from the temple of Segesta and remain immune to the power of the Greek world. From finding passive pleasure in the contemplation of a classical landscape, I have slowly progressed to searching out the Greek sites and learning to listen to what they have to say to me. Sicily is studded with classical sites: the solitary perfection of the temple at Segesta; the overrestored and overcrowded temples at Agrigento strung out along a crest of land against the sea; the tumbled ruins of Selinunte; the giant altars and theaters of Syracuse. But I have most often found myself drawn to the lesser, more ancient sanctuaries that lie in the shadows of the magnificent monuments to Olympian deities, to the altars where the archaic cult of the Great Mother melded with the worship of the Olympian Demeter and her daughter, the Maiden, Kore, to become that of Persephone, Queen of the Dead, who holds in her hand the pomegranate as a promise of resurrection and rebirth. These underground, chthonic goddesses were worshiped in caves and at springs, at the Santuario Rupestre at Agrigento, where the fissures in the cliff behind the tiny temple gave up thousands of terracotta votive statues of Demeter and her daughter, and the floor of the temple precinct turns purple in April when tiny wild flags sprout between the stones, or in the lonely sanctuary of the Malaphorus, the Bearer of Fruits, across the river from the acropolis of Selinunte, where a cluster of poppies still dedicates the inner temple to the goddess.

At the same time, although I cannot point to any one initial moment of awareness, Persephone has begun to make herself felt in my life. Perhaps it was when I first read that she had been carried off from Sicily, or my pleasure in the old pomegranate tree that grows outside the gate at Bosco. Perhaps it was my growing interest in calendars: the story of Persephone's descent into the Underworld each winter and her return four months later with the spring was perhaps the earliest attempt to divide the year into seasons and to explain its rhythms.

At first I only joked about the seasonal pattern of my own life, Palermo the Hades from which I emerge each spring for a brief summer in the sun of Bosco; mythical affinities seemed more than slightly ridiculous in the prosaic context of my daily life. It was a chance encounter with the review of a children's book, a retelling of Greek myths with the intent of restoring to the Greek goddesses their archaic, pre-Hellenic dignity, that started me on a serious search for more and different information and led me to realize, as I hunted among the shelves of a feminist bookstore in New York last summer, that many American women are engaged in the same voyage of discovery on which I, independently, have embarked by mere geographical accident.

But I still have trouble taking myself seriously, especially when I look at the tall and graying forty-year-old in the mirror, of whom Junoesque is the very most I can say. Mindful of childhood drawings, of delicate nymphs in diaphanous garments, I am tempted to abandon the whole idea. At least it makes a good story, I tell myself, and, putting my tongue firmly in my cheek, I start off with the family for Enna to begin my search for Persephone.

The *autostrada* from Palermo to Catania runs east along the coast for about fifty miles before dipping south to cut through the center of the island. On this sunny Sunday morning we look out on a landscape remarkably different from our usual weekend fare on the western route to Bosco: the mountains are higher and more dramatic in their outlines, the transition from mountain to coastal plain is more abrupt, the river valleys cut more frequently and more deeply into the landscape. The soft mutations of green and yellow in the vineyards and olive orchards of the west here give way to the dark emerald of the lemon trees that blanket the plain, climb up and down the terraced valley walls, varying in hue only with the play of light and shade. The sun sparkles on the glossy lemon leaves just as it sparkles on the waves of a sea that is also darker here and more intense in color, while the roadsides are carpeted with deep-green acanthus plants. In the spring these will sprout tall spikes of pink-and-white flowers, similar to giant snapdragons, but now the spiky, curling leaves, as perfectly symmetrical on the plant as they are on a Corinthian capital, imitate only the green of the lemon trees.

The landscape changes abruptly as the highway turns south along the valley of the Hymera River and follows the base of the Madonie Mountains, which pose a formidable barrier between the wealthy coast and the barren interior. For a while yet the valley floor preserves the fertility of the coastal plain, its fields the soft blue-green of artichokes and cauliflower plants, but these soon give way to the wheat fields, the famous stands of grain that made Sicily the breadbasket of the Roman Empire. In an endless march they struggle up and down the hillsides, skirting the scarred troughs where erosion has raked away entire pieces of hill, skipping over the slopes too steep to plow, to the north climbing up to the cliffs of the Madonie, to the south disappearing over the crest and on to the next wave of hills. The concrete pillars of the highway viaduct striding along the rocky riverbed echo the infinite progression of the fields and are for long stretches the only sign, together with the careful contour plowing, of human passage. The arrows at the highway exits seem to point nowhere; only occasionally can one see a town crouched on a distant hilltop or a flock of sheep implying the presence of someone to herd and milk them.

In summertime the sun bleaches the stubble left after June's harvest to a blinding white-gold and grinds the earth to powder, but now this desolate landscape is softened by the rain and the plow, upholstered in a green velvet worn thin or even threadbare: the fallow fields are thick with grass; others, plowed early, are pale with the green tips of newly sprouted wheat; and in the most recently worked fields the fresh brown earth shows through completely. Here and there a tuft of orange or yellow where a tree begins to turn belies the green suggestion of spring.

Our destination, hovering high above the road, is entirely wrapped in cloud, and nothing is visible to indicate that we are nearing a large town. Enna is built on a narrow plateau that runs along the crest of a solitary mountain; the sides of the mountain drop away sharply, too steep for building, and the road that switchbacks up from the mountain runs through woods brilliant with autumn colors and carpeted with ferns, where only scattered rosemary bushes recall the Mediterranean.

The car enters the cloud, some walls appear, and we find

ourselves in the town. The change from the sunny warmth of
Palermo is hard to believe: a bitter wind shreds and agitates the
mist that appeared compact when seen from below, and it buffets
the car as we drive around the castle at the easternmost extremity
of Enna's mountain, to where the Rock of Demeter is poised like
an enormous boulder at the very edge of the cliff, over a drop of
more than twelve hundred feet down to the plain below.

A narrow footpath brings us up and out onto the flat surface of
the rock. This was the site of the shrine in which, according to
Cicero, stood giant statues of Demeter and of Triptolemus, son of
the king of Eleusis and only witness to Persephone's rape. Grateful
for his revealing what had happened to her daughter, Demeter "supplied Triptolemus with seed-corn, a wooden plow, and a chariot
drawn by serpents and sent him all over the world to teach mankind
the art of agriculture." No sign of the temple remains, but the mist
that blots out all evidence of later centuries, save the iron railings to
which we cling, re-creates its numinous bulk, repopulates the fields
below with white-draped figures, and suggests the tangible and welcome presence of the great goddess, surveying the crops from on
high and bringing them to a safe harvest.

Only a few yards but more than a millennium away, the arched
portal of the castle awaits us. It is an enormous structure, the outer
walls of which were once girded by twenty towers. We pass
through two vast courtyards, each large enough to camp an army,
before gaining the smaller inner courtyard of the citadel, which
gives access to the only remaining tower, the Torre Pisano.

The walls of this square tower, made of the same gray stone as
the rest of the castle, rise up in sharp, clean lines for about three
stories before ending in very simple crenellations. The austerity of
the outline is softened by the ivy growing up the walls, as elsewhere
in the courtyard the occasional shrub or rosebush suggests what
medieval gardens once flourished here. The tower is fully restored,
and we are able (and, in obedience to the law of ascending motion
that governs travel with children, required) to climb up the narrow
inner staircase and stand on the top for as long as we can resist the
bite of the wind, staring out from between the crenellations and
waiting for the wind to blow holes in the curtain of mist that hangs

all around us. Occasionally the folds draw back and we can look down for a moment to the sunlit plain below, see Lake Pergusa sparkling in the distance, glimpse Etna, the great volcano that dominates eastern Sicily.

Perhaps it is the overly thorough restoration that has obliterated the character of this building, suitable for toy soldiers or for someone who has only read about castles. Whatever charm it may retain for us cannot compete with the discomfort inflicted by the wind, and although we are in better shape after a dish of pasta and a couple of glasses of wine, there is still no question of doing any leisurely exploration on foot, so we make our way toward Enna's southern gate, driving slowly through piazzas deserted during the Sunday siesta and peering down curving streets and ancient alleyways that would be inviting on a summer day.

As we drive down the southwestern flank of the mountain, the clouds lift and the island is spread out before us, wave on wave of hills flowing through the mists toward the sun, already low in the sky, a troubled sea of gold and lavender that stretches out to the horizon where the real sea, invisible, begins.

Lake Pergusa proves to be a bitter disappointment, a brilliant example of the Sicilians' best efforts to ruin their landscape. As is true of all the island's interior, the wooded hills and flowering meadows that once attracted Persephone have long since been sacrificed to Sicily's need to produce more and more grain, but here the subsequent erosion has given way to a more contemporary blight. The lake itself, hardly more than a large and stagnant pond with neither inlet nor outlet, lies in a gentle and recently reforested valley, which has been invaded by myriad summer villas in the same hideous architectural style—modern misallied to Mediterranean and generating flights of fancy—that desecrates the Sicilian coasts. All around the marshy shore runs a fancy track for car racing. It is a landscape neither Greek nor Sicilian, totally without character, and although we feel obliged, having come all this way, to make the drive around the lake, we are glad to be done with it.

The road leading back to the highway skirts the eastern end of the mountain. Demeter's rock hangs over us, golden against the finally blue sky, and to the east broods the dark purple cone of Etna, rising high above the intervening mountains and smoking leisurely in the setting sun. This is a moment such as I had hoped for, when the spine-tingling echo of the goddess's footsteps rings softly across the centuries.

The children doze as we drive back toward Palermo, and Tonino's thoughts have returned to his work. I am content to sit in silence, watching the changes that the waning light works on the countryside, at present pink, lavender, and russet where the morning showed green and yellow and brown. Sifting through the day now ending, I feel slightly cheated: for all that I had put tongue in cheek, I expected something more from this pilgrimage, some greater indulgence than a brief lifting of the clouds at the end of the day. I had imagined myself standing on Demeter's rock and looking down onto the shores of the lake, watching Persephone, sharing Demeter's moment of distraction and the horrible clutching of her bowels as she turns her gaze back and Persephone is no longer there.

That was not how it happened. There was no moment of distraction. Lake Pergusa is too far away for Demeter to have watched Persephone from her rock in any mortal fashion. Although the goddess does not seem overly generous of herself today, perhaps this fact of geography conveys a first message. Perhaps a mother *cannot* be present at her child's rite of passage, or offer her own wisdom and experience to ease the journey, and it is useless to resent one's own mother or to expect to succeed where she had failed.

And perhaps the weather that has so blighted the day is a reprimand. The cold winds and rain of Demeter's grief will darken Sicily as long as her daughter dwells below the earth. Go back to Palermo, then, attend to winter business, seek Persephone in the spring, when, attended by rites of propitiation and welcome, she returns to the land.

It is dark by the time we reach Palermo, and the city lights, man's most felicitous addition to the natural landscape, string a web between the high mountains to the south and the startling black forms of Monte Pellegrino and Aspra, the two promontories that rise straight from the sea to guard the port. The lights catch us and draw us back into the city.

🦃

For the Literary Traveler

Enna, the destination of Mary Taylor Simeti's family excursion described in these pages, is worth the trouble of getting there. For travelers without a car, the train from Palermo to Catania (from the central railway station in Piazza Galleria Cesare) stops at Enna, in about two hours. The route follows the northern coast east for fifty miles and then turns inland, heading south. The topography of the ride is enchanting: walls of mountains give way to honey-colored fields of grain (Sicily was the breadbasket of the Roman Empire, as Simeti reminds us); in June, goats and sheep graze and people farm steep hillsides colored with poppies, purple wildflowers, and orange and lemon trees. Though Sicily is only the size of Vermont, wide rolls and dips of river valleys swept by clouds and a dazzling sun suggest great distances beyond the mountains. ("A melting light embracing memory, distance, indefinable tenderness," writes the Sicilian writer Leonardo Sciascia in *The Wine-Dark Sea* [1973]).

At Enna's train station, five kilometers from the city center, buses (eleven a day)—or friendly Ennans sharing taxis—transport passengers up to the top of *Belvedere della Sicilia*, Enna's nickname for its glorious position on the side of a steep hill with spectacular views of the medieval hill town of Calascibetta, the Madonie Mountain Range, and Mount Etna.

The civility and peacefulness of Enna (after some harrowing moments in Palermo) are palpable. One explanation is that the mountaintop city is the only provincial capital not controlled by the Mafia. Whatever the reason, walking (or ascending) the Via Roma—the main street—en route to ROCCA DI CERERE (Rock of Ceres) at the top of the road, the legendary site of the TEMPLE OF DEMETER, is a relaxing stroll past interesting preserves of Enna's ancient history. Mary Taylor Simeti, visiting in cold November, drove this route. In June, friendly, bright-eyed elementary schoolchildren, exhibiting their end-term history/art projects in the Municipio, the Municipal Gallery in Piazza Umberto I, turned out to be good resources. They gave precise directions and shared their enthusiasm for the Hohenstaufen Emperor Frederick II, who loved Enna and thought of himself as a Sicilian.

The DUOMO, the Cathedral of Our Lady of the Visitation, on the left-hand side of Via Roma facing Piazza Mazzini, was founded by Eleanora of Aragon, wife of Emperor Frederick II (1194–1250); he was known as *Stupor Mundi* ("The Amazement of the World"), probably for the magnificence of his court in Palermo, famous in Europe for its learning which included Greek, Jewish, Islamic, and Christian cultures. (Barbara Grizzuti Harrison's *An Accidental Autobiography* [1996] includes an adoring profile of *Stupor Mundi*.) The Duomo is filled with fantastic spiraling carvings and capitals, altar screens and altarpieces (some in the process of restoration in 1996). The imagery is so different from the usual iconography of a Christian temple that it's easy to believe the theory that the cathedral stands on the site of the temple of Demeter's daughter, Persephone. (Spirals are prehistoric symbols of the mother goddess.) The interior has a sense of older and more mixed traditions than mere Christianity.

Since its recorded beginnings in the seventh century B.C.E., Enna has been a Sicilian stronghold; a Greek colony; a Roman colony; a Saracen (Moslem) outpost; and after 1087, a Norman conquest. (Paul Hofmann notes that until 1927, when Mussolini restored the town's ancient name of Enna—from *Henna*—it had been called Castrogiovanni, a corruption of its Arab name, Kasr Janni, or Janna, conferred in 859 by the Saracens, who took it from the Romans by crawling in through a sewer.) Enna (and Sicily) as a mixed cultural breed is utterly clear within the Duomo's exotic interior. Mary, Mother of Jesus and Queen of Heaven, is the dominant iconic presence, but the spatial memory predates her.

Further along the Via Roma, on the right, is a bronze memorial to the slave EUNO who led the first revolt against the occupying Roman Empire in 135 B.C.E. The huge slave population of Sicily was made up of prisoners of war captured by the Romans in their wars in the east. Partly because of the impregnability of Enna, the Roman army did not defeat the slave rebels for two years. The plaque attached to the Euno memorial quotes Abraham Lincoln who, referring to the history of slavery, invoked the name of the heroic Euno.

Beyond the CASTELLO LOMBARDO (a more idyllic place in spring than in November, lush with wildflowers and fragrant pines), explored by

Mary Taylor Simeti and her family, is the ROCK OF DEMETER, "poised like an enormous boulder at the very edge of the cliff." At the high point of "the navel of Sicily," Enna's nickname for its location at the exact center of the island, the Rock has a beautiful prospect overlooking the sprawling fertile earth of Sicily lit by moving currents of Mediterranean light under a cover of cosmic silence.

The themes of motherhood and loss implicit in the myth of Demeter and Persephone receive a different interpretation in the literature of goddess-centered spirituality than in Simeti's meditations. In her essay "Why Women Need the Goddess," feminist theologian Carol Christ writes:

> Almost the only story of mothers and daughters that has been transmitted in Western culture is the myth of Demeter and Persephone that was the basis of religious rites celebrated by women only, the Thesmophoria.... What is important for women in this story is that a mother fights for her daughter and for her relation to her daughter. This is completely different from the mother's relation to her daughter in patriarchy. The "mood" created by the story of Demeter and Persephone is one of celebration of the mother-daughter bond, and the "motivation" is for mothers and daughters to affirm the heritage passed on from mother to daughter and to reject the patriarchal pattern where the primary loyalties of mother and daughter must be to men.... The symbol of Goddess has much to offer women who are struggling to be rid of the...devaluation of female power.... As women struggle to create a new culture in which women's power, bodies, will, and bonds are celebrated, it seems natural that the Goddess would reemerge as symbol of the newfound beauty, strength, and power of women.

Letting go or hanging tough: the mother—Mary Taylor Simeti—and the scholar—Carol Christ—take different and complementary messages from Enna's ancient Rock. Simeti's memoir, though conscious of contemporary issues of gender politics, is relaxed and finely nuanced about her role as a woman and mother in Sicily.

If, on returning to the town center, you stop again in the Duomo—now on the right side of Via Roma—dedicated to the Visitation, the occasion of an unmarried pregnant Mary dropping in on her old cousin

Elizabeth, also strangely pregnant, you will see what is clear in many of the churches of Italy: that the Goddess also figures prominently in the post-classical religious world. According to feminist theologian Elisabeth Schüssler Fiorenza in her book *In Memory of Her*, "The traditions about the Goddess and those of the New Testament are conflated in the Catholic community's cult of Mary.... [O]n an *emotional, imaginative, experiential* level the Catholic child experiences the love of God in the figure of a woman.... the 'human face' of God is almost solely experienced in the image of a woman."

Besides fertility, the divine Mother Goddess, in both classical and Judeo-Christian traditions, was also associated with wisdom. As religion scholar Elaine Pagels explains in *The Origin of Satan*, the Greek feminine word for wisdom, *sophia*, like the word for spirit, *ruah*, translates a Hebrew feminine word, *hokhmah*.

Sicily abounds in ruins of Greek temples that preserve the memory of the fierce, wise goddesses Athena, Juno, Hera, and Demeter. In her book, Simeti writes about AGRIGENTO, SYRACUSE, TAORMINA, and SEGESTA. Though their environs also feature ugly modern temples of industry and tourism, many sites, especially Segesta, are as intact as the temples of Greece. Though, like the town of Enna, they are accessible by public transportation, to see them all in a limited amount of time, requires a car.

Visiting the Greek temples and Catholic churches of Sicily, scholar Lucia Chiavola Birnbaum, of Sicilian parents and an American midwestern upbringing and author of *Liberazione della Donna: Feminism in Italy*, asserts that from their subterranean religious beliefs—a cultural memory of a universal Mediterranean earth mother/Goddess—Sicilian peasant women have developed a clearly unorthodox theology that contradicts church doctrine. It shows up in the legends they tell their children in which

The mother of Jesus was central, universal grace embraced all humanity, morality was grounded on realism. One legend recounted the reluctance of Jesus to extend universal grace to all—until his mother delivered an ultimatum. Either Jesus would allow all souls to enter heaven or she would leave paradise and, as queen of heaven, take her entire dowry with her: all the angels, patriarchs, apostles, martyrs, and saints. Whereupon Jesus, paling before this depopulation of heaven, conceded universal grace.

What comes to mind again and again while visiting and reading about southern Italy is Ann Cornelisen's (see page 305) point in *Women of the Shadows* that Italy, in its peasant villages, despite the patriarchal façades of institutions, is matriarchal, "a *de facto* system, felt by everyone."

For Further Reading

PRIMARY SOURCES

Jane Addams, *Twenty Years at Hull House.* New York, 1910.

Francesca Alexander, *Roadside Songs of Tuscany.* New York and London, 1885.

Elizabeth Bowen, *A Time in Rome.* New York, 1959.

Elizabeth Barrett Browning, *Casa Guidi Windows.* London, 1851.

Eleanor Clark, *Rome and a Villa.* New York, 1952.

Ann Cornelisen, *Torregreca.* Boston, 1969.

George Eliot, *Romola.* New York, 1863.

———*Middlemarch.* New York, 1873.

Margaret Fuller, *At Home and Abroad or Things and Thoughts in America and Europe.* Ed., Arthur B. Fuller. Boston, 1874.

Patricia Hampl, "Umbrian Spring," from "Italian Two Part Invention" in *The House on Via Gombito.* Eds., Madelon Sprengnether and C. W. Truesdale. Minneapolis, 1991.

Barbara Grizzuti Harrison, *The Islands of Italy.* New York, 1991.

Marcella Hazan, *The Classic Italian Cookbook.* New York, 1973.

Shirley Hazzard, *The Bay of Noon.* Boston, 1970.

Erica Jong, "My Italy." In *Travel and Leisure.* September, 1996.

Flora Lewis, *Europe: A Tapestry of Nations.* New York, 1987.

Rose Macaulay. *Pleasures of Ruins.* New York, 1953.

Mary McCarthy, *The Stones of Florence.* New York, 1959.

Lady Mary Wortley Montagu, *Embassy to Constantinople.* London, 1763.

Jan Morris, *The World of Venice.* Published by James Morris. New York, 1960.

Florence Nightingale, *Florence Nightingale in Rome: Letters.* Ed., Mary Keele. Philadelphia, 1981.

Iris Origo, *Images and Shadows.* New York, 1970.

———*War in Val d'Orcia: An Italian War Diary 1943–1944.* London, 1947.

Francine Prose, "Cauliflower Heads" in *The Peaceable Kingdom.* New York, 1993.

Claudia Roden, *The Food of Italy*. London, 1989.

Mary Wollstonecraft Shelley, *Rambles in Germany and Italy*. 2 vols. London, 1844.

Mary Taylor Simeti, *On Persephone's Island: A Sicilian Journal*. New York, 1986.

Kate Simon, *Italy: The Places in Between*. New York, 1970.

Muriel Spark, "Venice in Fall and Winter" in *The Sophisticated Traveler: Winter, Love It or Leave It*. New York, 1984.

———*Territorial Rights*. New York, 1979.

Elizabeth Spencer, Introduction, *The Light in the Piazza*. New York, 1986.

———"The White Azalea," in *The Collected Stories of Elizabeth Spencer*. New York, 1961.

Elizabeth von Arnim, *The Enchanted April*. London, 1932.

Vita Sackville-West, *Vita and Harold: The Letters of Vita Sackville-West and Harold Nicolson*. Ed., Nigel Nicolson. New York, 1992.

Edith Wharton, "Roman Fever," in *Roman Fever and Other Stories*. New York, 1934.

———"Picturesque Milan," in *Italian Villas and Their Gardens*. New York, 1904.

Virginia Woolf, "Siena" from *A Writer's Diary*. New York, 1968.

SECONDARY SOURCES

Lucia Chiavola Birnbaum, *Liberazione della donna: Feminism in Italy*. Middletown, CT, 1986.

Blue Guides: to *Florence*, 6th ed., New York, 1995; to *Northern Italy*, 9th ed., New York, 1991; to *Rome*, 4th ed., New York, 1989; to *Sicily*, 4th ed., New York, 1993.

Carol Brightman, *Writing Dangerously: Mary McCarthy and Her World*. New York, 1992.

Cadogan Guides: Tuscany, Umbria & The Marches. 2nd ed., Chester, CT, 1990.

Carol P. Christ, "Why Women Need the Goddess," in *Womanspirit Rising*. San Francisco, 1992.

Ann Cornelisen, *Women of the Shadows*. Boston, 1976.

Robert Craft, "Women Musicians of Venice and the Red Priest," in *The New York Review of Books*. Nov. 2, 1995.

Joseph Jay Deiss, *The Roman Years of Margaret Fuller*. New York, 1969.

Norman Douglas, *Naples '44*. New York, 1994.

———*Effie in Venice: Unpublished Letters of Mrs. John Ruskin Written from Venice between 1849–1852*. Ed., Mary Luytens. London, 1965.

Joan Mowat Erikson, *St. Francis and His Four Ladies*. New York, 1970.